THE LAST OF THE FATHERS

James Madison in 1833. Portrait by Asher Durand. (Courtesy of the New-York Historical Society, New York City).

THE LAST
OF THE FATHERS

*James Madison
and the Republican Legacy*

✳

DREW R. McCOY

Harvard University

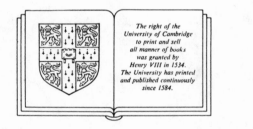

The right of the
University of Cambridge
to print and sell
all manner of books
was granted by
Henry VIII in 1534.
The University has printed
and published continuously
since 1584.

CAMBRIDGE UNIVERSITY PRESS
Cambridge

New York   Port Chester

Melbourne   Sydney

Published by the Press Syndicate of the University of Cambridge
The Pitt Building, Trumpington Street, Cambridge CB2 1RP
32 East 57th Street, New York, NY 10022, USA
10 Stamford Road, Oakleigh, Melbourne 3166, Australia

First published 1989
Reprinted 1989

Printed in the United States of America

Library of Congress Cataloging-in-Publication Data
McCoy, Drew R.
The last of the fathers : James Madison and the republican legacy
/ Drew R. McCoy.
p. cm.
ISBN 0-521-36407-8 (U.S.)
1. Madison, James, 1751–1836.   2. Presidents – United States –
Biography.   3. United States – Politics and government – 1815–1861.
I. Title.
E342.M33   1989
973.5'1'0924 – dc 19
[B]   88-20375
British Library Cataloguing in Publication applied for.

FOR BETSY

Contents

Illustrations

Preface

"MY SENSATIONS for many months past have intimated to me not to expect a long or healthy life." These were grim words from a privileged young man who might have anticipated, notwithstanding some evidence of poor health, the best that his society could offer. In this case, however, the best may not have been enough. Writing in the early 1770s to another recent graduate of the College of New Jersey, James Madison was troubled by more than his fragile constitution and a recent bout of mysterious nervous seizures. His morbid premonitions were also aroused by confusion about what he should do with his life and perhaps by some doubt that he would find anything worth doing. Proclaiming himself "too dull and infirm now to look out for any extraordinary things in this world," the twenty-one-year-old Virginian seemed to despair of finding a vocation worthy of his idealism.[1]

Within a few years, however, the young man discovered a Revolutionary cause that inspired a career that was anything but ordinary. And another sixty years later, he had no choice but to marvel at his unanticipated longevity. Writing to the historian Jared Sparks in the summer of 1831, the octogenarian Madison, now a hero revered by new generations of young men, admitted that he was wandering alone into another age. Indeed, among the members of several of the most important groups from America's Revolutionary past, including the delegates to the Constitutional Convention of 1787, only he survived. "Having outlived so many of my cotemporaries," he quipped to Sparks, "I ought not to forget that I may be thought to have outlived myself."[2]

In fact, Madison had another five years to ponder the phenome-

---

1 Madison to William Bradford, Nov. 9, 1772, in William T. Hutchinson et al., eds., *The Papers of James Madison* (Chicago, Charlottesville, 1962–), I, 75.
2 Madison to Jared Sparks, June 1, 1831, in Gaillard Hunt, ed., *The Writings of James Madison* (New York and London, 1900–1910), IX, 460.

non. Save for Aaron Burr, whom he had known at college (and whose career followed a rather different trajectory into well-deserved ignominy), Madison survived longer than any other member of the most remarkable generation of public leaders in American history, one that his descendants now vaguely revere as the "Founding Fathers." Even for that generation his career was exceptional in both its sweep and its significance, for it intersected every major phase of the history of the American Revolution, the adoption of the Constitution, and the early republic. Three years after announcing his premature demise, the "dull and infirm" youth first entered public life as a member of his local Revolutionary committee, which he later represented at the Virginia Convention of 1776 – the constituent body, the elderly Madison reminded Sparks, that had drafted the commonwealth's first republican constitution. Within a few years the young Revolutionary's career carried him to the federal Congress, where he served with distinction during the final phase of the war for independence and then under the Articles of Confederation. And later in the same decade, of course, he earned his enduring reputation as the "Father of the Constitution" for his pivotal role in drafting and defending, most notably in *The Federalist* papers, the system of government that replaced that Congress – and that still remains in place two hundred years later.

Enough for any lifetime, perhaps; but Madison's work as Revolutionary and as Founder proved far from done. By the early 1790s he was busy organizing the Democratic–Republican movement that, as he interpreted the challenge, rescued both the Revolution and the Constitution from a renewed threat of monarchy in a second revolution, this time at the ballot box, which became known as the "Revolution of 1800." And then, as he entered his fifties and the young republic entered the nineteenth century, Madison rounded out his career with eight years as secretary of state and another eight as president. He even led the aged survivors of the first Revolution and their sons and daughters through a second war for independence against England. No wonder the octogenarian, surrounded by what his friend Thomas Jefferson had earlier called "a new generation whom we know not, and who know not us," seemed bemused by the thought that he was still alive.[3]

3 Jefferson as quoted in Gordon S. Wood, "The Disappointments of Jefferson," *New York Review of Books* 28 (Aug. 13, 1981), 8.

Given his immense contributions both to political theory and to the founding of the American republic, Madison has not suffered from lack of scholarly attention, and the historians, biographers, and political scientists who have taken his measure have generally concentrated their attention – with good reason – on his active years in public life. In this book, I focus instead on a relatively neglected phase of Madison's republican odyssey, the period between his retirement from public office in March 1817 and his death on June 28, 1836. I hope to convey the resonant significance of this final chapter in the life of a Revolutionary patriarch, and my basic premise is straightforward: Madison's survival well into the fourth decade of the nineteenth century presents a unique opportunity to enrich our understanding of some critical themes in American history between the Revolution and the Civil War. His two decades of retirement were fascinating and important years, both for him and for the republic whose history seemed inseparable from his own.

Madison was sixty-six years old when he completed his second term as president and returned to Montpelier, his gracious estate abutting the foothills of the Blue Ridge Mountains in Orange County, Virginia. All evidence – from his voluminous correspondence to the accounts of those who visited him – suggests the extraordinary immunity of his intellect, if not his body, to the ravages of age. Sparks, who spent several days at Montpelier in 1830, spoke for all such pilgrims when he confided to his journal that "the intellect and memory of Mr. Madison appear to retain all their pristine vigor."[4] Indeed, only a few days before the patriarch's death, another visitor, observing a wasted body that encased a mind "still as bright and sun-like as ever," commented appropriately: "Never have I seen *so much mind in so little matter!*"[5] Madison sustained his familiar habit of reading voraciously; he kept abreast of contemporary developments to a greater extent than did most Americans, young or old; and he avidly deepened his lifelong intellectual pursuits. This was no period of dotage. If nothing else, Madison's retirement offers inspiring commentary on the possibilities of old age. But his later years are significant for more than the tenacity of his singular intellect.

4 "CC" Proctor, ed., "After-Dinner Anecdotes of James Madison: Excerpt from Jared Sparks' Journal for 1829–1831," *Virginia Magazine of History and Biography* 60 (1952), 264.
5 Reported in *Richmond Enquirer*, July 1, 1836.

We can begin to appreciate the symbolic interest of Madison's longevity simply by recalling that he was born in the middle of the eighteenth century, almost a decade before the accession of George III, and lived long enough to correspond with Princess Victoria, which he did in 1834.[6] A boy who had once been a subject of George II died a citizen of Andrew Jackson's republic. Historians tell us that this was a transitional period of especially intense and disruptive change in Anglo-American culture and society. Madison's character, as well as his republican vision, took form in the enlightened, neoclassical age of the American Revolution, and his reflections during the retirement years reveal his persistent effort to comprehend — and to influence — the fate of that Revolutionary vision as he encountered both its failures and the shocks of a new era. To that extent, Madison is notable for projecting a distinctively eighteenth-century vision of government and society into an explosive, rapidly fragmenting America that even he, ever mindful of the future, had only dimly anticipated. Indeed, compared to his close friend and political ally Jefferson, who died a decade earlier in 1826, Madison was privileged to observe more of the developments that dramatize what the historian George Dangerfield has aptly described as "the agonized passing of the Jeffersonian world."[7] In addition to the appearance of railroads, the emergence of militant abolitionists who demanded an immediate emancipation of all black Americans, and the eruption of a major slave rebellion close at hand in Virginia — none of which Jefferson lived to see — these developments included matters of such profound importance to "the Father of the Constitution" as a revolution in American political culture (that became dramatically apparent in the presidential election of 1828) and a constitutional crisis that pushed the republic to the brink of disunion.

Throughout these years Madison had to straddle, sometimes quite awkwardly, two different worlds — and eras — of political and cultural experience. As "Publius" in the late 1780s he had sought a cure for the dangerous disorder and injustice that traditionally afflicted

6 See Madison to Princess Victoria, Feb. 1, 1834, in [William C. Rives and Philip R. Fendall, eds.], *Letters and Other Writings of James Madison* (Philadelphia, 1865), IV, 568–569.

7 George Dangerfield, *The Awakening of American Nationalism, 1815–1828* (New York, 1965), 300.

(and discredited) popular government; in that respect as in others, his republican character and career were unmistakably cut from a neoclassical mold. But if Madison was at home in an enlightened world in which reason was enjoined to discipline the unsettling effects of passion, he grew old in a more modern world of romantic democracy in which passionate individualism threatened to overwhelm all restraints of custom, tradition, and history. His struggle to accommodate the conflicting values and demands of these two cultures, and to convey to a new generation the meaning of a Revolutionary past that was fast receding from memory, informs the central theme of the narrative that follows.

I might add that I also hope to serve another, quite different set of purposes in writing this book. Madison's achievements as political theorist and republican statesman have been duly acknowledged, and I am but one of many scholars who continue to be drawn to the task of enriching our understanding of his thought and statecraft. If the power of Madison's intellect has not diminished through the years, however, something important has been lost. That Madison has been unjustly consigned to the shadow of his ostensibly more brilliant and captivating colleague Jefferson is only part of the problem. The best efforts of Madison's intimates and admirers notwithstanding, very little sense of his personal qualities – his personality, character, and temperament – has survived. This is a significant loss, and not simply because he was a far more appealing figure than is commonly realized. Madison's personal character reflected the triumph of values that had resonant public, as well as private, significance. I believe that many of his contemporaries understood this. If, in subsequent years, this image of Madison has faded, and been replaced by a less flattering sense of him as deficient in some of the necessary qualities of character and leadership that make for true greatness, perhaps the problem is as much ours as his.

I make no effort in the following pages to disguise my admiration of Madison, at the risk, I suppose, of alienating the more skeptical reader. Although the book ultimately points clearly to Madison's shortcomings, both as a thinker and a leader, readers should understand that my emphasis, from the outset, is on presenting Madison through the eyes both of those who knew him well and of other contemporaries who came to admire him. In doing so, I seek to develop fresh perspectives that place conventional images of

Madison in better balance. And I hope to suggest, above all, the numerous, quite different, and sometimes tragic ways in which his character and the circumstances of his private life merged almost imperceptibly with the larger public issues that preoccupied him during his retirement.

I should add that my choice of this biographical approach to what is, in effect, intellectual and political history extends beyond Madison to include a small group of much younger, less prominent Virginians who plausibly considered themselves his legatees and who survived long enough to witness the Civil War and the early years of Reconstruction. Readers will note that I place particular emphasis on a conspicuous trio of young disciples – Edward Coles, Nicholas P. Trist, and William Cabell Rives – whose close association with Madison during his later years shaped their distinctive concerns and careers in quite different but revealing ways. As the story unfolds, I hope that my methodological point will become clear: without the biographical approach, it is simply impossible to appreciate the emotional urgency that attended Madison's commitment to a republican dream that, for him, defined the meaning of his own life. And that dream, embedded in the powerful force of his example, in turn inspired the impassioned but flawed endeavors of his legatees. As members of a generation old enough to have vivid memories of Madison but still young enough to see Madisonianism put to its supreme test in the holocaust of civil war, Coles, Trist, and Rives could not escape their own urgent choices. In that sense they represent variant resolutions of the tensions and issues that had once been united in Madison; in their careers we can discern the bending and distorting of ideas that their mentor had struggled, not always successfully, to keep in some workable balance. For both Madison and his heirs, in short, I hope to dramatize the actual working out in human lives of critical cultural and political issues.

Finally, a brief word about the book's structure may be helpful to the reader. The following chapters are organized topically and do not follow a strict chronological line through Madison's later years. They are meant, however, to form something more than a collection of separate essays on particular aspects of the larger subject. Since each succeeding chapter depends for its full thematic texture and development on its predecessors, and since the whole comprises more than a sum of the parts, the chapters should be read in order. And the reader will discover, too, that while the book is focused on Madison's retirement, it frequently looks back, as he did, to the past. To that extent, *The Last of the Fathers* is concerned with more than just the final two decades of its subject's life. It seeks to offer fresh insight into the character of a republican commitment that, stretching across two centuries and several generations, defined a career that the morbid young man of the early 1770s could scarcely have imagined.

Besides, the life of a good and great man, when fairly delineated and committed to history, will survive when the pyramids of Egypt shall have passed away: it will stand forever a lofty beacon amid the vicissitudes and the wastes of time. Athens and Rome, the master states of antiquity, where liberty once delighted to dwell, for two thousand years have been doomed to ignorance, to superstition, and to worse than Egyptian bondage; yet the lives of their great worthies, shining with an undiminished lustre, after this long and fearful eclipse, warmed the bosoms of modern patriots, by whose efforts has been regained the jewel of inestimable value, so long lost to the world.

And if, in fulfillment of that stern decree which denounces decay and death on all human things – a decree before which Babylon and Jerusalem, Athens and Rome, and all that was illustrious in antiquity, have crumbled into dust – if it be irreversible to all, and America be doomed to travel through ages of bondage, let us indulge the consolatory hope that the life of Madison, triumphing over the injuries of time, may become a pillar of light by which some future patriot may reconduct his countrymen to their lost inheritance.

James Barbour, *Eulogium on the Life and Character of James Madison*

Montpelier in the early nineteenth century. Engraving by J. F. E. Prud'homme, after John G. Chapman, in James B. Longacre and James Herring, *The National Portrait Gallery of Distinguished Americans*, vol. III (Philadelphia, 1836). A visitor from New England in 1834 observed that "the estate of Montpelier is situated in the centre of an amphitheatre of mountains, and is one of the most romantic spots I ever beheld; just such a one as a philosopher might choose, there to close his earthly career." (Courtesy of the Library of Congress, Prints and Photographs Division)

Prologue

AT SIX O'CLOCK in the morning of the eighteenth of February 1835 a small party of weary travelers arrived at Orange Court House, Virginia. After a brief rest and break-fast at noon, two of the group boarded the carriage that would take them across five miles of very poor road to their destination. It was a beautiful day, with hints of an early spring everywhere; the patches of snow left under the fences and on high ground were melting quickly. Although the travelers would soon discover that the people at the inn in Orange had cheated them and ignored the wishes of their host that a messenger be sent immediately for his own carriage, they later made light of the incident. Harriet Martineau proudly recalled that "this was the only occasion but one, in our journey of ten thousand miles in the United States, that we were overcharged," adding that "the undercharges, where any literary reputation is in the case," had been "more numerous than can be reckoned."

After a wintry month in the capital city of Washington, the young Englishwoman's first glimpses of Montpelier were exhilarat-ing. The road was "one continued slough up to the very portico of the house," but the dwelling stood on "a gentle eminence, and is neat and even handsome in its exterior." Stretching behind the house were a lawn and woods that must have been pleasant in summer. From the front there was "a noble object on the horizon" that could be admired at any season. "The shifting lights upon these blue mountains," Martineau recalled, "were a delightful refreshment to the eye after so many weeks of city life as we had passed."

She found her host confined to a single room of the mansion. He had suffered so grievously from rheumatism the previous winter that he dared not venture far from the easy chair in which he sat until ten o'clock each night. Although he appeared "perfectly well" during her visit, Madison complained to Martineau that he was deaf in one

I

ear and that his sight, which had never been acute, now prevented him from reading as much as he would like. Her initial view of the invalid found him in his chair, with a pillow behind him; his "little person" was "wrapped in a black silk gown," with "a warm gray and white cap upon his head" and "gray worsted gloves" on his hands. His voice, though, was "clear and strong, and his manner of speaking particularly lively, often playful." Martineau had no difficulty recognizing him from the engraving she had seen. His face was smaller, and of course older, but he seemed not to have lost any teeth, and "the form of the face was therefore preserved, without any striking marks of age." It was, she remarked, "an uncommonly pleasant countenance."

At thirty-two, Martineau was more than a half-century younger than her host. She had physical handicaps of her own. Severely hard of hearing, she had to be spoken to through the ear trumpet that vanity had prevented her from using until just recently. She was a woman of great physical as well as intellectual vigor, however. During her two years in the United States she stoically endured the most daunting hardships of travel – by stage, by canal barge, by Mississippi riverboat, by railway, and on horseback – across the vast and often primitive landscape of Jacksonian America. Her energetic presence impressed many, including the Madisons. She was "so interesting," Dolley Madison wrote to a friend a month after she left them, "that we hastened to procure her books and are now reading her Political Economy so handsomely Illustrated." Martineau's *Illustrations of Political Economy*, published not long before she had embarked for America, had caused a sensation among English readers. After three days of spirited conversation with the author, Madison apparently wanted a look for himself.

Martineau's impressions of Madison, in turn, only enhanced her prior admiration. She worried, at first, that she was imposing on the old man and would tire him out. "In perpetual fear of his being exhausted," she made polite efforts to afford him the rest he would obviously need: at the end of every few hours of conversation she left her seat by the arm of his chair and went to the sofa by Mrs. Madison on the other side of the room. "But he was sure to follow," she reported, "and sit down between us; so that, when I found the only effect of my moving was to deprive him of the comfort of his chair, I

James Madison as Harriet Martineau saw him. Engraving by T. B. Welch, from a drawing by J. B. Longacre taken from life at Montpelier, July 1833. (Courtesy of the Library of Congress, Prints and Photographs Division)

returned to my station, and never left it but for food and sleep, glad enough to make the most of my means of intercourse with one whose political philosophy I deeply venerated." "There is no need," she insisted, "to add another to the many eulogies of Madison."

By Martineau's own account she was overwhelmed by the

seemingly inexhaustible energy of her host, whose "relish for conversation could never have been keener." On the morning of the second day of her visit, she wryly noted, "the active old man, who declared himself crippled with rheumatism, had breakfasted, risen, and was dressed before we sat down to breakfast." He talked for several hours about past American presidents and living politicians. When his letters and newspapers were brought in, "he gayly threw them aside, saying he could read the newspapers every day, and must make the most of his time with us." Often Madison's talk was stimulated by current issues and crises. Martineau listened eagerly to "his luminous history of the nullification struggle" and "his exposition, simple and full, of the intricate questions involved in the anomalous institution of the American Senate." Glancing at the newspapers, which were "full of the subject of the quarrel with France, the great topic of the day," Madison gave a thorough account of the relations between the United States and that country. The present quarrel was absurd, he admitted, but he was apprehensive that it might issue in a war. "He said it would be an afflicting sight if the two representative governments which are in the van of the world should go to war; it would squint towards a confirmation of what is said of the restlessness of popular governments." After all, "if the people, who pay for war, are eager for it, it is quite a different thing from potentates being so who are at no cost."

The conversation was by no means restricted to politics and current events. Madison spoke eagerly on a subject that had long intrigued him: the size of Roman farms. He analyzed the population theories of T. R. Malthus and William Godwin. He spoke his mind on the subject of education, recounting a discussion he had once had with Robert Owen about the role of women in the British reformer's experimental communities. He mused "about what would eventually become of all existing languages and their literature; declaring that he had little hope of the stability of languages when terms of even classical derivation are perpetually changing their meanings with time." He discussed his taste in poetry. During all their conversations, Martineau observed, "one or another slave was perpetually coming to Mrs. Madison for the great bunch of keys; two or three more lounged about in the room, leaning against the doorposts

4

or the corner of the sofa; and the attendance of others was no less indefatigable in my own apartment."

The finest of Madison's characteristics, Martineau believed, was "his inexhaustible faith" that "a well-founded commonweath" might be immortal, "not only because the people, its constituency, never die, but because the principles of justice in which such a commonwealth originates never die out of the people's heart and mind." This faith "shone brightly" through the whole of his conversation, except on the subject about which he talked most. "With regard to slavery," she noted, "he owned himself almost to be in despair." Martineau recorded in some detail her host's reflections on this topic, one on which she had quite emphatic opinions of her own. She reported that Madison acknowledged "without limitation or hesitation" all the evils with which slavery had ever been charged; he remarked, for instance, that "the whole Bible is against Negro slavery; but that the clergy do not preach this, and the people do not see it." Martineau was obviously impressed by the sincerity of Madison's antislavery convictions and by the depth of feeling that his remarks conveyed. No doubt his descriptions of the suffering and injustice, drawn largely from personal observation, were vivid and concrete.

But the young Englishwoman was utterly at a loss to understand why Madison advocated the solution to the problem of slavery that he did, and why he refused to acknowledge its impracticality. What mitigated his despair was the American Colonization Society, an organization committed to removing free blacks from the United States and colonizing them in Africa. Much to Martineau's consternation, Madison believed that colonization offered a gradual, long-term, but potentially feasible means of eradicating slavery in the American republic. Martineau said that he gave no reason why the blacks could not remain where they were, once they ceased to be slaves. She was unable to fathom the logic behind his assumption that "the negroes must go somewhere" and that Africa was "their only refuge." Clearly, Martineau objected to colonization on both moral and practical grounds. The facts were there for everyone, including Madison, to see. As he admitted when speaking of his own slaves, there was a prevalent "horror" among the blacks of going

5

to the new colony of Liberia, which appeared to her "decisive as to the unnaturalness of the scheme." Moreover, in eighteen years the Colonization Society had removed fewer than three thousand persons from the United States, while the annual increase of the slave population was more than sixty thousand. "How such a mind as his could derive any alleviation to its anxiety from that source," Martineau could not discern. In the end she could attribute Madison's incongruous naiveté and poor judgment only to "his overflowing faith."

Martineau's description of her encounter with Madison was brimming with undisguised reverence. Here was a man inspired by what she described as "the true religion of statemanship, faith in men, and in the principles on which they combine in an agreement to do as they would be done by." After observing her venerable host, she offered the thought that this "political religion" was indeed a form of personal piety, for it had the effect "of sustaining the spirit through difficulty and change, and leaving no cause for repentance, or even solicitude, when, at the close of life, all things reveal their values to the meditative sage." Crippled with rheumatism, confined to a single room, often deeply troubled by what he read in the newspapers and confronted in his everyday experience as a slaveholder, the Sage of Montpelier "reposed cheerfully, gayly, to the last, on his faith in the people's power of wise self-government."[1]

In the spring of the year following Martineau's visit, Madison's health grew worse. Unable to walk, he spent much of his time recumbent; he had to be carried from his bed to the sofa to receive

---

[1] This extended description of Harriet Martineau's visit to Montpelier and her impressions of Madison is based on the chapter entitled "Madison" in Martineau's *Retrospect of Western Travel* (London and New York, 1838), I, 189–198. My portrait of Martineau is derived principally from two biographical works: R. K. Webb, *Harriet Martineau: A Radical Victorian* (New York and London, 1960) and especially Valerie Kossew Pichanick, *Harriet Martineau: The Woman and Her Work, 1802–1876* (Ann Arbor, Mich., 1980). The quotation from Dolley Madison is from her letter to Ann Maury, March 31, 1835, in the Manuscripts Division of the Alderman Library at the University of Virginia.

Harriet Martineau, c. 1835. (Courtesy of the Library of Congress, Prints and Photographs Division)

company. Paul Jennings, the Montpelier slave who was Madison's body servant, recalled nevertheless that "his mind was bright, and with his numerous visitors he talked with as much animation and strength of voice as I ever heard him in his best days." By June, however, matters had taken an ominous turn. The mere dictation of a letter became a vexing and painful ordeal. Jennings had shaved Madison every other day for sixteen years, and was present at his bedside on the morning of June 28. Another slave, Sukey, brought him his breakfast as usual. When he seemed unable to swallow, his favorite niece, Mrs. Willis, asked: "What is the matter, Uncle James?" Jennings recalled his master's response: "Nothing more than a change of *mind*, my dear." With that, Jennings added, "his head instantly dropped, and he ceased breathing as quietly as the snuff of a candle goes out."[2]

2 Jennings's recollections of Madison's final months and the death scene are record-ed in Paul Jennings, *A Colored Man's Reminiscences of James Madison* (Brooklyn, 1865), 18–19. It should be noted that the document was edited by "J. B. R.," who acknowledged in the preface that he recorded Jennings's recollections "in almost his own language." I have corrected a typographical error in the original. Additional information about Madison's last days has been drawn from an extract from a letter written by his brother-in-law, John Payne, on June 20, 1836, printed in the *National Intelligencer* on July 2, 1836.

1. The Character of the Good Statesman

IN THE SPRING of 1817, when James Madison quit public office for the last time, he behaved as if he were beginning rather than ending a career. Making the first leg of his journey home from Washington by steamboat, a novel means of approaching Montpelier, he was accompanied by a young writer from New York with an endearing blend of wit and patriotism. During their brief voyage down the Potomac River, James Kirke Paulding recalled, the elder statesman was "as playful as a child"; talking and jesting with everyone on board, he resembled "a school Boy on a long vacation."[1] Perhaps Madison savored memories of his first journey along the Potomac, on horseback, almost fifty years before, when an eighteen-year-old youth bound for college in Princeton, New Jersey, had confronted poor roads and seemingly countless ferries. What proved to be Madison's final passage through this area was a telling measure of the changes he had witnessed in his lifetime, and no doubt the convenience and excitement of traveling by steamboat buoyed the old man's spirits. But his good cheer also surely reflected the happy condition of his country after a crisis-ridden term as chief executive that had nearly issued in disaster. As Henry Adams observed three-quarters of a century later, with a characteristic touch of irony, "few Presidents ever quitted office under circumstances so agreeable as those which surrounded Madison."[2]

Most of Madison's countrymen in 1817 would probably have shared Adams's judgment but missed the irony. An old friend and neighbor, Francis Corbin, welcomed Madison home in words that

---

1 Ralph L. Ketcham, ed., "An Unpublished Sketch of James Madison by James K. Paulding," *Virginia Magazine of History and Biography* 67 (1959), 435.
2 Henry Adams, *History of the United States During the Administrations of Jefferson and Madison* (New York, 1889–1891), IX, 103.

appear to have caught the sentiments of a wider citizenry: "Long may you enjoy, in health and happiness, the well earned and truly legitimate plaudits of a grateful Country, and that sweetest of all consolations, an approving conscience." Corbin had served with Madison in the Virginia House of Delegates during the pivotal and trying years just after the Revolution. At the Richmond convention of 1788 they had joined hands to win the difficult struggle to secure the commonwealth's ratification of the Constitution. Now, in April 1817, Corbin assured Madison that his recent tenure as President was the glorious capstone to an illustrious career. "The End," he exclaimed, "has indeed crowned the Work!"[3]

Few historians today would take seriously, much less share, Corbin's flattering assessment of his friend's eight years in the White House. Scholars generally agree that Madison achieved greatness much earlier in his career, especially in the late 1780s and early 1790s when he did more than any other individual to create and secure a republic that would, with amendments and a rather momentous interregnum in the 1860s, endure for the next two centuries. From there, convention has it, his career went into decline. Riddled with diplomatic blunders and other grievous errors of judgment, Madison's presidency was characterized by something close to colossal ineptitude in leadership, constituting a profound embarrassment to him and to the government he administered during the War of 1812. The British invasion and burning of Washington, D.C., in August 1814 and the near collapse of that government marked the appropriate nadir of a failed administration. Writing in 1938, for instance, Edward M. Burns leveled a withering blast. As chief executive, Madison "added nothing to his reputation"; in fact, his record was one "of treason to his own ideals, of humiliation and failure."[4]

Some of Madison's biographers have tried to soften this harsh view, but with little success. Certainly Madison's popularity after the war – what Ralph Ketcham has described as "the adulation

3 Corbin to Madison, Apr. 29, 1817, James Madison Papers, Library of Congress, series one (microfilm).
4 Edward McNall Burns, *James Madison: Philosopher of the Constitution* (New Brunswick, N.J., 1938), 19.

surrounding him during his last two years as President and his twenty years in retirement" – has counted for little.[5] No one is surprised, after all, that when his contemporaries celebrated the happy conclusion of "Mr. Madison's War," some of the goodwill rubbed off on their commander in chief, no matter how hapless his leadership had been. Indeed, historians have generally portrayed this postwar euphoria among the American people as naive and short-sighted, blithely unmindful of the military and political catastrophe that had barely been averted; and Madison as president has thus been denied, for the most part, the credit and even the glory that his countrymen lavishly bestowed on him.[6] When Madison's present-day admirers are not apologizing for his presidency, they feel compelled, at the least, to unravel the puzzle of "how such a brilliant man could become a less effective statesman as he grew older and more experienced."[7]

This unfavorable image of Madison's presidency has obscured the depth and precise nature of his postwar popularity. When Corbin referred to the sweet comfort of "an approving conscience," he doubtless echoed the sentiments of a committee of citizens from

5 Ralph Ketcham, *James Madison: A Biography* (New York and London, 1971), 605.

6 For a recent portrait of both Madison's inept leadership and the inadequacy of the federal government he had been so instrumental in creating twenty-five years earlier, see J. C. A. Stagg, *Mr. Madison's War: Politics, Diplomacy, and Warfare in the Early American Republic, 1783–1830* (Princeton, N.J., 1983). Along with Irving Brant, Madison's most thorough biographer, Ralph Ketcham has made a creditable case for viewing Madison's presidential leadership less harshly. See especially "James Madison: The Unimperial President," *Virginia Quarterly Review* 54 (1978), 116–136; "Party and Leadership in Madison's Conception of the Presidency," *Quarterly Journal of the Library of Congress* 37 (1980), 242–258; and *Presidents Above Party: The First American Presidency, 1789–1829* (Chapel Hill, N.C., 1984), 113–123. Perhaps the most balanced and judicious assessment of Madison's leadership during the war is Marcus Cunliffe, "Madison (1812–1815)," in Ernest R. May, ed., *The Ultimate Decision: The President as Commander in Chief* (New York, 1960), 21–54. For an interesting discussion of Madison's leadership during his first presidential administration, see Abbot Smith, "Mr. Madison's War: An Unsuccessful Experiment in the Conduct of National Policy," *Political Science Quarterly* 57 (1942), 229–246.

7 Robert A. Rutland, in a review of Ralph Ketcham's 1971 biography, in the *William and Mary Quarterly*, 3d ser., 29 (1972), 171.

Washington who addressed Madison on the day he left office. After elaborating the salutary consequences of the recent war, the committee's spokesman paid homage to Madison's principled leadership: "Power and national glory, Sir, have often before, been acquired by the sword; but rarely without the sacrifice of civil or political liberty." It was with reference to his use of "the sword," indeed, that Madison's presidency deserved special commendation. He had earned the profound gratitude of his fellow citizens, the committee declared, for "the vigilance" with which he had "restrained [that sword] within its proper limits," for "the energy" with which he had "directed it to its proper objects," and for "the safety" with which he had "wielded an armed force of fifty thousand men, aided by an annual disbursement of many millions, without infringing a political, civil, or religious right."[8] Madison had led his nation through a difficult, but ultimately successful, second war for independence – and he had done so without violating its republican soul. Writing from Paris in the summer of 1817, his Republican colleague Albert Gallatin echoed Corbin's and the committee's emphasis when he observed that "few indeed have the good fortune, after such a career as yours, to carry in their retirement the entire approbation of their fellow citizens with that of their own conscience."[9]

Such praise reminds us of the extraordinary restraint that Madison had exercised as a wartime leader. Although few Presidents have been subjected to so much personal invective and abuse, he never hinted at measures abridging freedom of speech or press, even in the face of rampant obstruction of his government's policies and countless cases of outright treason in the "eastern states" of New England. His administration pursued nothing akin to the repressive Alien and Sedition Acts of 1798 – the distasteful badge of the high Federalism that, merely anticipating war, had outlawed virtually any show of opposition to the federal government and that Madison, earlier in his career, had vigorously assailed. Less than two years after the end

8 James Blake, chairman on behalf of a committee of Washington, D.C., citizens, to James Madison, March 4, 1817, Madison Papers, Library of Congress, series one (microfilm).

9 Gallatin to Madison, July 17, 1817, Madison Papers, Library of Congress, series two (microfilm).

James Madison in 1817. Portrait by Joseph Wood. Madison sat for this portrait in Washington as he prepared to leave public life. When an acquaintance first saw it, she exclaimed that "the likeness . . . almost breathes, and expresses much of the serenity of his feelings at the moment it was taken. In short, it is, *himself*." (Courtesy of the Virginia Historical Society, Richmond)

of "Mr. Madison's War," one of his admirers proudly noted that not only a powerful foreign enemy, but violent domestic opposition as well, had been "withstood without one trial for treason, or even one prosecution for libel."[10] As the historian Harry L. Coles has noted, this absence of repressive legislation "enabled the country quickly to unite after the war with a minimum of bitterness and resentment."[11] And there is ample evidence that appreciation of Madison's behavior outlived the surge of postwar euphoria. Among the editors and orators who eulogized him in 1836, we find what one biographer has called "grateful memory of his unswerving protection of civil liberties" at a time when "provocations" had been "greatest for their restraint."[12]

Just as important to his countrymen, Madison had not used the occasion of war to expand executive power or to create a vast patronage machine. "Of all the enemies to public liberty," Madison himself had written in 1795, "war is, perhaps, the most to be dreaded, because it comprises and develops the germ of every other." As "the parent of armies," of course, war encouraged "debts and taxes," which republicans recognized as "the known instruments for bringing the many under the domination of the few." But as Madison so powerfully argued, the danger was especially acute in relation to a particular branch of the government. "In war, too," he added, "the discretionary power of the Executive is extended; its influence in dealing out offices, honors, and emoluments is multiplied; and all the means of seducing the minds, are added to those of subduing the force, of the people."[13] War always nourished the potential for corruption; in a young and experimental republic like the United States, the danger of executive usurpation was particularly ominous.

Two decades later, in quite different circumstances, Madison's

---

10 Benjamin Lincoln Lear quoted in Irving Brant, *James Madison: Commander in Chief, 1812–1836* (Indianapolis and New York, 1961), 407.

11 See the judicious assessment in Coles, *The War of 1812* (Chicago and London, 1965), 257.

12 Brant, *Madison: Commander in Chief,* 523.

13 Madison, *Political Observations,* April 20, 1795, in William T. Hutchinson et al., eds., *The Papers of James Madison* (Chicago, Charlottesville, 1962–), XV, 518.

adversaries could wax eloquent in describing this very danger in his own administration. In March 1814, for instance, a Federalist congressman from Massachusetts, Artemas Ward, vehemently opposed increasing the size of the federal army, imputing to Madison's regime nothing less than an intention "to change the form of Government." Lest his fellow legislators dismiss his words as "the vagaries or wanderings of a jealous, perhaps, distempered mind," Ward played upon the central themes of a republican melody that Americans had been humming for the better part of four decades. "All the Republics which have gone before us have lost their liberties," he reminded his fellow legislators, imploring them "to consider what has taken place in our time, and what they have read in the history of other times." They had seen "the Legislature of France turned out of the Hall of Liberty by a military force which it had nurtured and established." History told them "that the same was done in England in the days of Cromwell." And "however secure gentlemen may feel in their seats," they should not ignore the possibility that "they may witness the reaction of the same scenes here"; the military force they now voted to raise might indeed "ere long put an end to their existence as legislators." Above all, Ward cautioned the members of Congress, "Executive patronage and Executive influence are truly alarming."[14]

Within a year, however, any such suspicions of Madison were exposed as unfounded, even absurd. To be sure, given Madison's modest bearing and his utter lack of military experience or ambition, the thought of him becoming a dictator on horseback is ludicrous; but we might also note that he prevented anyone else from assuming that role in the midst of an unprecedented political and military crisis. And in an age dominated by the specter of Napoleon, and in a republican political culture still very much tied to classical referents, including the danger of "Caesarism," President Madison's executive restraint confirmed his principled resistance to all temptations of power and thus drew effusive retrospective praise from his

14 Joseph Gales, comp., *Debates and Proceedings in the Congress of the United States, 1789–1824* (Washington, D.C., 1834–1856), 13th Cong., 2d sess., II, 1826, 1827.

15

constituents, including many Federalists.[15] An orator at a Fourth of July celebration in 1816 boldly predicted that Madison's name would "descend to posterity with that of our illustrious Washington," since "one achieved our independence, and the other sustained it."[16] He was wrong about Madison's image in history, of course, but the linking of Madison to Washington, quite common in the postwar years and almost inconceivable today, points again to the source as well as to the extent of the adulation that surrounded him.[17]

Although Madison's republican restraint as president and commander in chief contributed, ironically, to his later reputation as indecisive and incompetent, it earned substantial dividends in his own time. Writing from Braintree shortly after the presidential election of 1816, John Adams told Madison (who had not stood for reelection) that "such is the State of Minds here, that had Mr. Madison been candidate, he would probably have had the votes of Massachusetts and consequently of all New England."[18] Adams was generally not one to flatter rivals for public esteem. But even if we allow for some measure of polite hyperbole in his estimation of his correspondent's popularity in the vicinity of Boston – only recently the center of intense opposition to the war against England – his statement to Jefferson a few months later confirms his sincerity. "Notwithstand[ing] a thousand Faults and blunders," Adams

15 For an interesting discussion of related themes for a later period, see Edwin A. Miles, "The Whig Party and the Menace of Caesar," *Tennessee Historical Quarterly* 27 (1968), 361–379.
16 Quoted in Brant, *Madison: Commander in Chief*, 407.
17 For greater insight into this unlikely link between Washington and Madison – who were, in fact, as alike as they were different in representing a new, republicanized conception of heroic leadership – see the brilliant analysis in Barry Schwartz, *George Washington: The Making of an American Symbol* (New York and London, 1987), esp. chaps. 4–6. As I will suggest below, so many of the character traits ascribed to the decidedly uncharismatic Washington by his adoring contemporaries – diffidence, modesty, self-restraint, patience, steadiness, and perseverance, for instance – were also especially applicable to Madison's character and behavior, and were therefore central to his countrymen's veneration of him.
18 Adams to Madison, Dec. 6, 1816, in Washburn Papers, Massachusetts Historical Society, IX, 12.

mused, Madison's administration had "acquired more glory, and established more Union, than all his three Predecessors, Washington Adams and Jefferson, put together."[19] The mood captured in Adams's penetrating judgment was not always evanescent, either. Some of Madison's countrymen remembered the last two years of his presidency as the pinnacle of republican triumph, as nothing less than a golden age in which "a balmy peace" had overtaken the profound crisis of national confidence that had accompanied the tumultuous passions of war and regional partisanship. Moreover, they could attribute this happy situation, to a remarkable extent, to the diffusive influence of Madison's personal character. Writing in 1844, the Whig John Pendleton Kennedy attempted to evoke the spirit of this luminous postwar world, in which "the calm and philosophic temper of Mr. Madison, the purity of his character, the sincerity of his patriotism, and the sagacity of his intellect" had inspired "universal trust."[20]

Kennedy's allusion to Madison's sage intellect jibes nicely with our image of him as a profound thinker. But his references to Madison's "calm and philosophic temper" and to "the purity of his character" were probably more vital to the nostalgic reverence that many Americans of the antebellum era, especially Whigs, came to feel for him and his presidency. In 1845 Charles Jared Ingersoll (a Democrat) published a multivolume "historical sketch" of the War of 1812 that assessed both Madison's leadership and his reputation. Compared to Jefferson and Washington, Ingersoll acknowledged, Madison must be judged deficient in genius and command. Yet "no mind has stamped more of its impressions on American institutions than Madison's," and his presidency was especially revealing of both his limitations and his peculiar virtues. Assuming the position of chief magistrate "bequeathed to him by his more salient predecessor with a complication of difficulties," Madison, Ingersoll averred, "went through the war meekly, as adversaries alleged shrinkingly,

19 Adams to Jefferson, Feb. 2, 1817, in Lester J. Cappon, ed., *The Adams–Jefferson Letters* (New York, 1971 [orig. publ. 1959]), 508.
20 [John Pendleton Kennedy], *Defence of the Whigs, by a Member of the Twenty-Seventh Congress* (New York, 1844), reprinted in Daniel Walker Howe, ed., *The American Whigs: An Anthology* (New York, 1973), 87.

no doubt with anxious longing for the restoration of peace, but without ever yielding a principle to his enemies or a point to his adversaries; leaving the United States, which he found embarrassed and discredited, successful, prosperous, glorious and content." Ingersoll went on:

A constitution which its opponents pronounced incapable of hostilities, under his administration triumphantly bore their severest brunt. Checkered by the inevitable vicissitudes of war, its trials never disturbed the composure of the commander-in-chief, always calm, consistent and conscientious, never much elated by victory or depressed by defeat, never once by the utmost emergencies of war, betrayed into a breach of the constitution. Exposed to that licentious abuse which leading men in free countries with an unshackled press cannot escape, his patience was never exhausted; nor his forbearance deprived of dignity by complaint, retort, or self-defence, but in the quiet serenity of rectitude, he waited on events with uninterrupted confidence.[21]

American readers, of course, could hardly fail to see the appropriate analogy. Madison may not have been the equal of General Washington; no one was. But in his stoical perseverance in the face of countless setbacks, not to mention his steady adherence to principle amid alarming confusion and disorder, Madison, as a civilian commander in chief during this second war for independence, offered a display of bravery and self-command reminiscent of the heroic example set on the battlefields of the Revolution. As Ingersoll suggested, everything that went into his quiet but firm leadership – his unflappable dignity; his unwillingness to despair; his unyielding confidence in American institutions and the character of the people; and his dogged persistence – somehow overcame all of his specific failures and misjudgments. This kind of leadership may, in fact, have literally saved the republic. Modern historians remind us that a different, less happy outcome was far from inconceivable. "That government should have survived in Washington at all after August 1814 [following the successful British invasion] was itself no mean achievement," the historian J. C. A. Stagg has recently noted, "and

---

21 Charles J. Ingersoll, *Historical Sketch of the Second War Between the United States of America and Great Britain* . . . (Philadelphia, 1845), I, 260, 262–263.

for this Madison was largely responsible. By persisting in his duty and refusing to admit defeat, even under the most difficult circumstances, he ensured that his administration could survive the war and enjoy the benefits of peace when it came."[22]

Ingersoll's survey of Madison's career (and his two decades of retirement, when he provided "a model for American statesmen"), culminated in the question he expected his readers in 1845 to have: "What then is the shading of this seeming strain of panegyric?" "No one has been more abused than Madison," he admitted, "but not only did it all die away, but died before he died." Although "a remnant of inveterate, respectable federalists" still denied his merits, "the great body of his countrymen" were now "unanimous in awarding him immortality." Much more than Jefferson, Madison enjoyed "undivided favour." And Ingersoll knew why: "He was no hero, not a man of genius, not remarkable for the talent of personal ascendency. But his patriotic services are parcel of the most fundamental civil, and the most renowned military grandeur of this republic, and his private life without stain or reproach."[23]

Those who had known Madison well, especially during the War of 1812, seconded Ingersoll's contention that Madison's public conduct was best understood as the projection of an exemplary character and temperament. No better example of this common insight can be found than the testimony of Edward Coles, who was the president's private secretary for six years and hence a member of the White House family. Madison's "persevering and indefatigable efforts to prevent the war" as well as his "manner of carrying it on," Coles remarked in the 1850s, "were in perfect keeping with the character of the man, of whom it may be said that no one ever had to a greater extent, firmness, mildness, and self-possession, so happily blended in his character."[24] A fellow Virginian by birth and a cousin of Madison's wife, Dolley, Coles's acquaintance with the Madisons went back to the 1790s, when as a child he had helped his family welcome the middle-aged congressman and his young bride for a

22 Stagg, *Mr. Madison's War*, 436.
23 Ingersoll, *Historical Sketch*, I, 263, 265.
24 Edward Coles to William Cabell Rives, Jan. 21, 1856, printed in *William and Mary Quarterly*, 2d ser., 7 (1927), 164.

postnuptial visit. From 1809 to 1815, Coles, now in his mid-twenties, became Madison's regular companion. Much later, when he wished to convey to his countrymen an accurate sense of his mentor's greatness, Coles made an intriguing observation – one wholly at odds with Madison's modern historical reputation – that casts fresh light on Madison and on the reverence his presence, and later his memory, frequently evoked.[25]

Writing in 1854 to the Virginia historian Hugh Blair Grigsby, who had solicited his recollections, Coles drew extensive parallels between Madison and Washington. He noted of Madison, in this connection, that "if History do him justice, posterity will give him credit, more for the goodness of his heart, than for the strength and acquirements of his mind."[26] Coles acknowledged Madison's intellectual brilliance, but he insisted that his impressive mind (and the fascinating conversation it produced, for which he was justly renowned) were "but decorations to set off to advantage his pure and incorruptible virtue and integrity." At first glance Coles's observation smacks of republican ritual in its celebration of Madison's disinterested commitment to the public good, long a sine qua non of the virtuous statesman; yet clearly he meant something more specific than that. A just history, he said, would show Madison to have been "the most virtuous, calm, and amiable, of men, possessed of one of the purest hearts, and best tempers with which man was ever blessed." It was Madison's peculiar temperament and the character it shaped, more than the depth of his mind or even his specific achievements, Coles believed, that entitled him to sit by Washington's side in the pantheon of classical heroes that had graced the American scene in the days of the Founding.[27]

25 Coles is discussed at some length in the chapters that follow. There are several perfunctory accounts of his life but no full-scale biography. Probably the best single source of information on him remains Elihu Benjamin Washburne, "Sketch of Edward Coles, Second Governor of Illinois, and of the Slavery Struggle of 1823–4" (Chicago, 1882), reprinted in Clarence W. Alvord, ed., *Governor Edward Coles* (Springfield, Ill., 1920).
26 The relevant extract from this Coles-to-Grigsby letter of Dec. 23, 1854 may be found in Coles's hand in the William Cabell Rives Papers, Library of Congress, box 85.
27 *Ibid.*

As his secretary, Coles had observed Madison's conduct under the kind of "trying circumstances" that indeed put character to the test. As Charles Francis Adams noted in 1841, "foreign war and domestic discord came together upon him in a manner that would have tried the nerves of the strongest man."[28] But "amidst all the troubles and excitement attendant on a foreign war, and provoking feuds at home," Coles recalled, he had never once heard the president "utter one petulant expression, or give way for one moment to passion or despondency." It seemed that "nothing could excite or ruffle him"; no matter how vexing the provocation, he had remained "collected" and "self-possessed." Coles asserted that this rigorous self-control – a calm, deliberate steadiness of mind and behavior (again, so reminiscent of Washington) – had shaped Madison's leadership in entirely admirable ways. Without a single lapse, he told Grigsby, Madison had succeeded in abiding by his own "maxim" that "public functionaries should never display, much less act, under the influence of passion." Moreover, he had been "ever mindful of what was due from him to others, and cautious not to wound the feelings of any one." Indeed, at times during the war Coles had found the president's patience with his many critics exasperating. Besieged by deputations of citizens with advice and instructions, Madison's habit was to listen with the utmost attention, despite the tax on his valuable time and patience. Once, when Coles had pleaded with him to ignore an importunate group of delegates soliciting an interview, Madison had told his secretary, in no uncertain terms, that since these citizens had come a long distance to advise him, surely their president owed them his attention for an hour or two.[29]

Coles's portrait of Madison's temperament and its influence on his public conduct was confirmed by other intimates. James Barbour, a major figure in both Virginia and national politics in the early nineteenth century, was also Madison's Orange County neighbor. In 1836 he eulogized his friend in terms that Coles must have appreci-

---

28 [Charles Francis Adams], "The Madison Papers," in *North American Review* 53 (1841), 75.

29 Coles to Grigsby, Dec. 23, 1854, in Rives Papers, Library of Congress, box 85. Reference to the specific instance cited may be found in Mary Cutts's memoir of the Madisons, in the Cutts–Madison collection (microfilm), Library of Congress.

ated, praising Madison's "private virtues, equal to, if not beyond, his public worth" and paying great attention to "the force of his character" on public life. Above all, Barbour said, Madison was distinguished "for a serenity of temper, which, under no circumstances, in public or private, did I ever see disturbed." This serene temperament was not the demeanor of a bland or dull man, however, as Barbour emphasized Madison's gentle charm and benevolence. Cheerful by nature, he frequently indulged in "a playful Attic wit," but "always without a sting" – it was, Barbour said, "the rose without the thorn." Scrupulously attentive to the needs and feelings of others, Madison had an uncanny ability to make acquaintances and visitors comfortable. "With the less intelligent of these," Barbour observed, "he seemed anxious to veil his superiority, and, by kindness and affability, to elevate them to a feeling of equality with himself"; quick to discern "the bent of their minds," he was always able to give to the conversation "a congenial direction." But what Barbour saw as most remarkable about Madison was his ability either to control or to vanquish altogether the darker side of his passionate nature, which in other men nourished the selfish motives of revenge and spite. In testimony that other acquaintances often corroborated in a similar tone of disbelief, Barbour declared that he had never heard Madison "speak ill of any one." And such extraordinary "magnanimity of character" saved him, as a public leader, "from the degradation of prostituting his high trust to the gratification of private malice," of which, indeed, he simply had "none to gratify."[30]

Madison's sensitive respect for the opinions, motives, and feelings of others was so much a part of the man that few who knew him – no matter in what capacity – failed to comment on it. Paul Jennings, the slave who witnessed his death, proclaimed him "one of the best

30 James Barbour, *Eulogium upon the Life and Character of James Madison* (Washington, D.C., 1836), passim (the quotations are, in sequence, from pages 6, 25, 28, 27, 28, and 21). On Barbour and his ties to Madison see Charles D. Lowery, *James Barbour, A Jeffersonian Republican* (University, Ala., 1984), passim. When Charles Jared Ingersoll visited Montpelier shortly before Madison's death, he was struck by Madison's extraordinarily balanced temperament, noting that he never once spoke disparagingly, in personal terms, of anyone, even his political adversaries, throughout the visit. See "Visit to Mr. Madison," *Richmond Enquirer* (from the Washington *Globe*), August 19, 1836.

men that ever lived." Like Coles and Barbour, Jennings recalled that he had never seen his master "in a passion," which from his perspective manifested its significance in Madison's treatment of his chattels. Jennings had never known him to have struck a slave or allowed an overseer to strike one. And whenever any of Madison's servants had been charged with theft or misbehavior, "he would send for them and admonish them privately, and never mortify them by doing it before others."[31]

Unlike Jennings, the historian Grigsby – Coles's correspondent in 1854 – had no intimate knowledge of Madison. At the tender age of twenty-three, however, he had met and observed the seventy-eight-year-old patriarch for several months when they served as fellow delegates to the Virginia Constitutional Convention of 1829–30. Grigsby later wrote historical sketches of both this convention and an earlier one that Madison had attended before Grigsby had been born – the Virginia Ratifying Convention of 1788. The historian drew his evocative portrait of Madison at both gatherings from a variety of sources, including information provided by intimates like Coles and the collective memories of earlier generations that now comprised a form of Virginia folklore. But Grigsby's personal memories of the elderly Madison, still vivid many years later, apparently did more than simply confirm the composite portrait that emerged from these other sources. They helped him understand why Madison had been so influential in the founding of the American republic – indeed, why his distinctive temperament, his mild reserve and modest detachment, had in fact enhanced rather than diminished his public influence, especially at the 1788 ratifying convention that Grigsby later chronicled.

Weighed down by the infirmities of age and by an aversion, Grigsby suspected, to "mingling too closely in the bitter strifes of a new generation," Madison had taken little part in the formal proceedings of the 1829 convention in Richmond. It was in private conversation that he had made "the strongest impression on the hearts" of young people like Grigsby. "The accuracy and freshness of his literary and political reminiscences astonished the admiring listener," the historian recalled. Amid a swirl of youthful vigor, the

31 Jennings, *A Colored Man's Reminiscences of James Madison* (Brooklyn, N.Y., 1865), 15.

23

old man had somehow managed to be "the delight of the social circle." After listening to Madison, moreover, Grigsby had concluded that he was simply "incapable of imputing a harsh motive to any human being." He had watched, for instance, as Madison spoke warmly to a young friend, "fresh from a New England College," of "Quincy, Otis, Daggett, Dexter, and the younger Sherman." Here the former president recalled men who had opposed his administration and the War of 1812 "with a zeal that brought them to the verge of disunion." Much to Grigsby's surprise, Madison spoke of them "with as deliberate an appreciation of their merits as if they had held a far different course."[32]

Grigsby clearly revered the patriarch he met in Richmond in 1829, but as an historian he admired Madison more for his character than for his political judgment. In fact, Grigsby was a fervent latter-day Antifederalist. He introduced his history of the 1788 convention by patronizing the Madison-led Federalists, whom he charged with having misjudged Virginia's need for the protection of a more powerful federal government. Grigsby contended, on the contrary, that the commonwealth had been in the midst of a prosperous era of free trade when the convention met; not understanding – with "disastrous results" – the great truths of the science of political economy, "our fathers" had hastily adopted an unnecessary Constitution that forced Virginia to relinquish control over her commerce. Despite Grigsby's outspoken reverence for the Articles of Confederation (a government that he modestly judged "the most perfect model of a confederation which the world has ever seen"), he respected Madison's achievement in overthrowing that government and, most important, attributed his success to the public influence of an exemplary character and temperament.[33]

One of Madison's most admirable qualities, Grigsby suggested, was "the courtesy and the respect with which he regarded the mo-

32 Hugh B. Grigsby, *The Virginia Convention of 1829–30: A Discourse Delivered Before the Virginia Historical Society* (Richmond, 1854), 9, 11, 12. Obviously Madison's admirers, including Grigsby, exaggerated his benevolent temper. Earlier in his career, especially, he had been most capable of imputing harsh motives to others and of indulging his own measure of partisan passion.
33 Hugh Blair Grigsby, *The History of the Virginia Federal Convention of 1788 . . .*, reprinted in *Collections of the Virginia Historical Society*, new series, IX, 11–13, 18, 21.

tives and treated the arguments of the humblest as well as the ablest of his opponents." Viewing an argument in debate "not in respect of the worth or want of worth of him who urged it," but solely "in respect of its own intrinsic worth," Madison's oratory, as Grigsby revealingly put it, was "in unison with his general character." This "philosophical cast of mind" not only kept him "free from the personalities of debate"; it was a key to understanding the outcome of the 1788 convention.[34] According to Grigsby, Madison's calm, judicious, and high-minded commentary on his opponents' taunts and tirades – including emotional outbursts from the Antifederalist leaders Patrick Henry and George Mason – exercised tremendous, ultimately decisive, influence on many of his fellow delegates. This wise posture offered a striking contrast to that of his friend Edmund Randolph who, lacking Madison's control, "could not repress a spirit of sarcasm and defiance in answering the purely political interrogatories of Henry." And according to Grigsby, Madison's exemplary behavior at this 1788 convention established a reputation for him that, "diffused throughout the State," became "the groundwork of his subsequent popularity."[35] What the young historian had seen in the elderly Madison whom he met in Richmond in 1829, in sum, was winning evidence of the distinctive character and temperament that had made Madison, four decades earlier, Virginia's premier statesman and "the Father of the Constitution."

❊

By Edward Coles's standards, history has failed to do Madison justice. The dominant image that has come down through the years is not the appealing portrait sketched by Coles, Barbour, and Grigsby,

---

34 *Ibid.*, 97–98; Grigsby, *Virginia Convention of 1829–30*, 10–11. Senator Thomas Hart Benton, in his recollections of Madison, made a similar point when he referred to Madison's speeches and writings "as illustrations of the amenity with which the most earnest debate, and the most critical correspondence, can be conducted by good sense, good taste, and good temper." See *Thirty Years' View; or, A History of the Working of the American Government for Thirty Years, from 1820 to 1850* (New York, 1854), I, 679. I am indebted to Elaine Swift for bringing this material to my attention.

35 Grigsby, *History of Convention of 1788*, 97–98.

but rather one of a diminutive scholar characteristically clothed in black – a reclusive, soft-spoken, colorless figure, intelligent and learned perhaps, but lacking both the warmth and the vigorous presence of his charismatic colleague Jefferson. Those who knew better – which is to say, those who knew Madison well – would be peeved, but probably not surprised, to learn what history has made of him. Margaret Bayard Smith, a sensitive observer of the Washington scene and an especially astute judge of both character and ideas, always found Madison captivating. After spending a long evening at Montpelier in 1828, she reported to a correspondent that her host's conversation – "a stream of history . . . so rich in sentiments and facts, so enlivened by anecdotes and epigramatic remarks, so frank and confidential as to opinions on men and measures" – had an overwhelming "interest and charm" that the conversation of few living men could. She then added sadly, however, that "this entertaining, interesting and communicative personage, had a single stranger or indifferent person been present, would have been mute, cold and repulsive."[36]

Smith's comment reminds us of the conspicuous qualities of modesty, reserve, and detachment that generated what was in fact a common impression among "strangers": that Madison was cold, gloomy, and unsociable. His reluctance to assert his presence – and to impose himself and his views on others, whether in the drawing room or in the public arena – helped form the familiar image of him as the shy, sober, withdrawn intellectual who was simply too timid to inspire, much less command, his fellow citizens. But those qualities have been too easily exaggerated and misconstrued, in Madison's time and our own, and we must be especially wary of inadvertently conflating Madison's diminutive stature, his mild temperament, and the Federalist caricatures of his ineptitude as president[37] and mistaking the result for the prevalent image of him in his own time, especially during his retirement. When one of

---

36 Gaillard Hunt, ed., *The First Forty Years of Washington Society* . . . (New York, 1906), 235.

37 For a discussion of how the Federalists created "a Madison mythology" that has (regrettably) dominated the writing of history, see Irving Brant, "Madison and the War of 1812," *Virginia Magazine of History and Biography* 74 (1966), 51–67.

Madison's twentieth-century biographers observes of his public demeanor, for instance, that "as always throughout his life, he was regarded as a learned and agreeable person, but not as an inspiring leader," we can see better how modern judgments of "leadership" (as well as the Federalist caricature) can shade imperceptibly into assessments of how Madison's contemporaries must have viewed him.[38] And we can learn even more about Madison and the cultural significance of his character by viewing him through the eyes of a few acute observers who juxtaposed him with his most famous associate.

Most but not all of Madison's admirers also admired Jefferson. The tradition of comparing the two men began while they were alive, especially after 1817 when it was common for American and foreign travelers alike to call upon the two retired presidents who lived only thirty miles apart. Some visitors recorded their impressions and, without necessarily drawing invidious distinctions, tended to judge each in the light of the other. George Ticknor, a young professor at Harvard College who had met and befriended Jefferson ten years earlier, visited both Montpelier and Monticello in December 1824. Now in his mid-seventies, Madison struck Ticknor as "certainly the gayest person of that age" he had ever known. Declining to talk about "passing political events" for fear of becoming embroiled in partisan controversy, he nonetheless sparkled in conversation. Ticknor, who taught languages and belles lettres at Harvard, judged Madison's "power over the English language" as "quite remarkable"; he had seldom encountered anyone "whose common conversation was marked with such a richness, variety & felicity of expression." Yet Ticknor also noticed that Madison tended to confine this conversation within "narrow boundaries" and that his range of subjects was "somewhat limited." As Ticknor described Madison, there was indeed a marked quality of restraint about the man. He declined to discuss matters he considered inappropriate or about which he judged himself uninformed or ignorant. Although Ticknor did not present Madison's discretionary caution and apparent intellectual timidity as serious deficiencies, his tone suggested disappointment.

Jefferson, by contrast, was far less inhibited in Ticknor's pres-

38 Abbot Emerson Smith, *James Madison: Builder* (New York, 1937), 329–330.

Thomas Jefferson in 1821. Replica of a portrait painted from life by Thomas Sully at Monticello. (Courtesy of the Library of Congress, Prints and Photographs Division)

ence. He talked about anything and everything, which impressed the professor from Cambridge. Here was a man who, at eighty-one, still studied Greek and Anglo-Saxon and kept abreast of the "progress of knowledge" far better than did most of Ticknor's students.

If Madison had declined to comment on the current political scene, moreover, Jefferson expressed himself on this subject as freely as on any other, vigorously conveying, for instance, his distaste for the presidential candidacy of Andrew Jackson. Yet Ticknor also noticed something else that appears to have disturbed him: despite his voluble candor, Jefferson was in fact "singularly ignorant & insensible on the subjects of passing politics." He received only one newspaper and failed to maintain "a strict intercourse with the post office." Indeed, though Jefferson expressed strong views on the presidential contest, he was badly misinformed, believing, for example, that Connecticut had cast its votes for Jackson. "In all this," Ticknor wrote, "he differs very signally from Mr. Madison, who receives multitudes of newspapers, keeps a servant always in waiting for the arrival of the Post – and takes anxious note of all passing events."[39]

Ticknor was not the only professor drawn to comparative observation. George Tucker, who taught moral philosophy at Jefferson's University of Virginia, had even greater opportunity to contemplate the two retired statesmen whom he so much admired. In 1835 he published a highly complimentary biography of Jefferson which he dedicated to Madison. Over twenty years later, when Tucker began to sketch a history of his own life, he included recollections of the two legendary patriarchs that quietly juxtaposed their characters and personalities. He confided to his journal that Madison had been "an especial favorite with me ever since I had known him, for independent of his profound and far-reaching views in the science of government and legislation, he had unwonted gentleness and suavity of manner, which joined to a large fund of anecdote which he told very well, made him one of the most companionable men in existence." Tucker found this "habitual cheerfulness" all the more remarkable after learning from Madison's physician that he had suffered from three diseases during his retirement, "any one of which might at any moment have carried him off." Tucker was moved to add, moreover, that "Mr. Jefferson too had most winning manners when he chose to exert them, but he was occasionally somewhat

39 George Ticknor to George Bancroft, Dec. 26, 1824, Bancroft Papers, Massachusetts Historical Society.

29

dictatorial and impatient of contradiction, which Mr. Madison never appeared to be."[40]

Tucker adverted here to a significant contrast in temperament that had not been lost upon others. In 1807 Sir Augustus John Foster, a young British diplomat, included both Montpelier and Monticello on his itinerary when he journeyed south from Washington. Foster was not enamored of either the young republic or its leading lights, but before this journey he had apparently viewed Jefferson as "more of a statesman and man of the world" than his secretary of state, the pedantic Madison, whom Foster thought "rather too much the disputatious pleader." Foster discovered, however, that Madison was not only "better informed" but "a social, jovial and good-humoured companion full of anecdote and sometimes matter of a loose description relating to old times, but oftener of a political and historical interest." The Englishman noticed, indeed, that Madison differed from his more famous compatriot in subtle but telling ways. According to Foster, Jefferson was notorious "for his holding to any opinion that he had taken up, no matter whose, with great obstinacy." Apparently the English diplomat saw nothing at Monticello to call into question the gist of an anecdote that had been related to him in Washington by Daniel Clark, the elected delegate to Congress from the New Orleans Territory. Having been invited one evening by President Jefferson to discuss the Territory, Clark remained at the White House for three hours. During their interview Clark discovered that the president had been "falsely informed" on several points. When the congressman attempted to correct him, however, Jefferson continually recurred "to his own sentiment founded on such false reports." The exasperated Clark concluded that Jefferson's aim was to try to get him to commit himself, "by hook or crook," to the president's own theory, "getting at the real fact appearing with him to be quite of inferior importance."[41]

40 "Autobiography of George Tucker," *The Bermuda Historical Quarterly* 18 (1961), 141–142.
41 Richard Beale Davis, ed., *Jeffersonian America: Notes on the United States of America Collected in the Years 1805–6–7 and 11–12 by Sir Augustus John Foster, Bart.* (San Marino, Calif., 1954), 154–155.

Foster's preference for the less imperious and self-absorbed Madison was shared by a later European visitor, who also recorded his impressions of the two men. In the late spring of 1825, Carlo Vidua, a widely traveled and well educated forty-year-old Italian count, undertook the American presidential tour. After visiting John Adams in Massachusetts, he turned south to Virginia. Stopping first at Montpelier on the morning of May 11, Vidua sketched a vivid portrait of Madison for a correspondent in Italy:

My visit lasted until the next day because he invited me to dinner, then did not let me leave that night, and would have liked me to remain there some days longer. He is a small, thin old man, but of a kindly and pleasant face; his bearing is very aristocratic, and without assuming the air of importance and dignity befitting one of his station, he displays an indescribable gentleness and charm, which I thought impossible to find in an American. I have heard very few people speak with such precision and, above all, with such fairness.[42]

Two days later Vidua was at Monticello. Suffering from the arrival of hot weather, the eighty-two-year-old Jefferson was barely well enough to receive the visitor, who hoped to use a letter he carried from the renowned German traveler and scholar Alexander von Humboldt to gain his host's attention. Vidua was finally able to ask Jefferson the same list of questions that he had posed to Madison and Adams, ranging over such topics as the recent revolutions in Spanish America, the prospects for the abolition of slavery in the United States, and the potential effects of extending the American system of government to Europe. Both Jefferson and Madison, Vidua wrote, gave "complete and detailed answers" to his queries. He hinted, with a touch of irony perhaps, that Madison – who had never been to Europe – displayed a much more sensitive understanding of the complex issues involved in the last subject than did the more cosmopolitan Jefferson. And on the whole, Vidua concluded, Madison's reflections struck him as "the most profound" and "the most weighty," denoting both "a great mind and a good heart."[43]

42 Elizabeth Cometti and Valeria Gennaro-Lerda, "The Presidential Tour of Carlo Vidua with Letters on Virginia," *Virginia Magazine of History and Biography* 77 (1969), 396.
43 *Ibid.*, 399–400.

The Italian confessed, however, that his comparative judgments may have been affected by Madison's exceptional kindness. Vidua apparently had serious difficulties with English. "It may be that I feel myself transported with gratitude," he mused, because although all of his presidential hosts "indicated that they enjoyed my conversation," only "Mr. Madison was kind enough to speak slowly and clearly in order to allow me to understand, and to pay careful attention to comprehending my English so full of gallicisms." According to Vidua, the American people generally celebrated Jefferson as "the first man" of the republic and, in keeping with their practice of boasting, "the first of the whole world." Only "a few persons" shared his own preference for Madison – but "the kind of men these few are," he added, "consoles me for not adhering to the common people's view."[44]

John Quincy Adams believed he had taken fair measure of both men in the years after 1800. In his eulogy of Madison in 1836, the former secretary of state and president made no secret of his dislike of Jefferson and his reverence of the less celebrated colleague. Madison's relationship with Jefferson, Adams concluded, was "the friendship of a mind not inferior in capacity and tempered with a calmer sensibility and a cooler judgment."[45] Six years later, another New Englander who had embraced Jeffersonianism during Jefferson's presidency, Supreme Court justice and Harvard law professor Joseph Story, echoed Adams's judgment. Story privately shared his admiration of Madison with Ezekiel Bacon – who also had been a Jeffersonian in the early years of the century. "I entirely concur with you," he told Bacon, "in your estimate of Mr. Madison – his private virtues, his extraordinary talents, his comprehensive and statesman-

44 *Ibid.*, 400.
45 John Quincy Adams, *Eulogy on James Madison* (Boston, 1836), 54. As Merrill D. Peterson has wryly noted, Adams's funeral eulogy was "a remarkable performance," nothing less, indeed, than "an apology for Madison's Jeffersonianism." See Peterson, *The Jefferson Image in the American Mind* (New York, 1960), 136. Even more explicit and specific indications of Adams's strong feelings about the two men can be found in his letter to Edward Everett of October 10, 1836, in the Edward Everett Papers, Massachusetts Historical Society.

like views. . . . in wisdom I have long been accustomed to place him before Jefferson."[46]

No doubt Story and Bacon recalled their days together as Jeffersonian members of Congress during the final months of the great embargo of 1807–1809. No doubt, too, they knew that an enraged Jefferson had never forgiven them for their role in persuading Congress to repeal his administration's system of commercial legislation. What they did not know was that when President Madison had been desperately searching for a nominee to the Supreme Court in 1810, he had floated Story's name past Jefferson. The sage of Monticello had dismissed the candidacy of the thirty-one-year-old Massachusetts lawyer, whom he called "a pseudorepublican." Jefferson reminded Madison, indeed, that the loathsome Story was a "tory" who had "deserted us." Madison appointed Story to the Court.[47] Speaking of the two leaders of their old party, Story observed to Bacon in 1842 that "you and I know something more of each of them in trying times, than the common politicians of our day can possibly arrive at. I wish some one who was perfectly fitted for the task, would write a full and accurate biography of Madison. I fear that it can hardly be done now; for the men who best appreciated his excellences have nearly all passed away. What shadows we are!"[48]

❈

To use Charles Ingersoll's phrase: what, then, is the shading of this seeming strain of panegyric? Viewed through the eyes of Story and the many others who admired him, Madison approached and pro-

---

46 Joseph Story to Ezekiel Bacon, Apr. 30, 1842, in William W. Story, ed., *Life and Letters of Joseph Story* (Boston, 1851), II, 420.

47 Jefferson to Henry Dearborn, July 16, 1810, and Jefferson to Madison, Oct. 15, 1810, in Paul Leicester Ford, ed., *The Works of Thomas Jefferson* (New York, 1905), XI, 143, 151–152. See also James McClellan, *Joseph Story and the American Constitution: A Study in Political and Legal Thought* (Norman, Okla., 1971), chap. 1, and R. Kent Newmyer, *Supreme Court Justice Joseph Story: Statesman of the Old Republic* (Chapel Hill, N.C., 1985), 70–72.

48 Story to Bacon, Apr. 30, 1842, in Story, *Life and Letters*, II, 420.

jected the eighteenth-century ideal of a republican statesman as much as any member of his renowned generation – and in Jefferson's case, even more. He embodied in ways that intimates and casual acquaintances alike never forgot the classical principles of self-control and benevolence. The inner dynamics of how Madison had achieved what Coles and others portrayed as a remarkably healthy and well-integrated personality will always remain obscure; but the vital interplay of private and public in Madison's character was readily apparent to his contemporaries and, through them, to at least some in later generations. In Madison they found a classical hero worthy of America's neoclassical age. Writing about him in the 1850s, Senator Thomas Hart Benton of Missouri spoke admiringly of "the qualities of head and heart" that "so nobly went into the formation of national character while constituting his own." Old enough to have personal memories of the Revolutionary patriarch, the senator recalled that "purity, modesty, decorum – a moderation, temperance, and virtue in every thing – were the characteristics of Mr. Madison's life and manners," adding that "it is grateful to look back upon such elevation and beauty of personal character in the illustrious and venerated founders of our Republic."[49]

Above all, Madison's admirers agreed that he had sought and achieved the banishment of selfish, disruptive passion from his temperament for his own and his country's good. Modesty and self-restraint, if not self-effacement, were political virtues in a leader who pursued the noble quest of transcending partisan self-absorption. Compared to Jefferson, especially, Madison was neither impulsive nor judgmental. Because he respected the opinions and, when necessary, tolerated with equanimity what he regarded as the errors of his fellows, he was not haunted by the demons of spite and retribution, which made utterly alien to his character any fixation on "enemies" or the lust for personal vindication that such a fixation might breed. Most notably during the debate over the Constitution in the late 1780s, and then again during the War of 1812, he had risen above bitter partisan passions and separated all petty considerations of personal pride or vanity from his dispassionate concern for the public good. Knowing that unrestrained passion was destructive

49 Benton, *Thirty Years' View*, I, 678–679.

of moral order within individuals as well as in society, he had placed the appropriate premium on balance and stability – in his own character and in the republic that he regarded as an extension of himself. And that emphasis beautifully caught the animating spirit of the enlightened, neoclassical world that had shaped his sense of purpose.

It is in this sense that Madison's joyful withdrawal from the national scene in early 1817 was, in truth, laced with irony, because he ventured on his retirement just when America was about to explode in new paroxysms of private and public passion that would define what one historian has appropriately called "an age of boundlessness."[50] From his retreat at Montpelier Madison would soon ponder a new phase in the history of American republicanism, one sufficiently unstable and disruptive to unsettle this most self-controlled of men who had, after all, withstood the most spectacular revolutions of the eighteenth century. His young English friend Harriet Martineau, for one, caught telling glimpses of both worlds in the short space of a month.

Three weeks before she visited Madison in the winter of 1835, Martineau attended a state funeral for a member of Congress in Washington.[51] As she described the scene in the Capitol, the solemnity of the occasion brought together in close and peaceful proximity some of "the fiercest political foes in the country." After prayers there was a sermon, "in which warning of death was brought home to all, and particularly to the aged; and the vanity of all disturbances of human passion when in view of the grave was dwelt upon." Martineau glanced around the room and noticed Andrew Jackson.

50 The reference is derived from John Higham's seminal essay, *From Boundlessness to Consolidation: The Transformation of American Culture, 1848–1860* (Ann Arbor, Mich., 1969). The themes of a momentous shift in American culture and society – and of late eighteenth-century America and early nineteenth-century America constituting two very different worlds of experience – are brilliantly developed in Robert H. Wiebe, *The Opening of American Society: From the Adoption of the Constitution to the Eve of Disunion* (New York, 1984).

51 The following account and quotations are drawn from Harriet Martineau, *Retrospect of Western Travel* (London and New York, 1838), I, 161–164.

The "gray-headed old president" looked drawn and tired, scarcely able to go through the ceremonial. "I saw him apparently listening to the discourse; I saw him rise when it was over, and follow the coffin in his turn, somewhat feebly; I saw him disappear in the doorway." Moments later Martineau was met by a member of Congress, pale and trembling, who informed her that the president had been waylaid in the portico of the Capitol and twice fired at with a pistol. Fortunately, both shots had missed fire. Then suddenly the would-be assassin appeared, pursued and surrounded by a crowd. Martineau saw his hands and half-bare arms struggling, above the heads of the crowd, to resist the handcuffs. Soon he was overpowered, dragged to a carriage, and whisked before a magistrate. Calm, however, had not been fully restored. The abortive attack had thrown President Jackson into "a tremendous passion," and Martineau found his behavior regrettable. "He fears nothing," she noted, "but his temper is not equal to his courage. Instead of his putting the event calmly aside, and proceeding with the business of the hour, it was found necessary to put him into his carriage and take him home." Bystanders had been forced to restrain the president, who repeatedly attempted to beat his assailant with a walking stick.

Martineau's regret turned quickly to disgust. Although it was abundantly clear that the aspiring assassin was mad – "a poor maniac" – within two hours she had heard the name of almost every eminent politician implicated in the attack. "The president's misconduct on the occasion," she recalled, "was the most virulent and protracted." Jackson, it seemed, had been feuding for some time with Senator George Poindexter of Mississippi, and lately the "deadly enmity" subsisting between them had become so aggravated that few doubted the inevitability of a duel once the expiration of Jackson's term permitted the issuance of the proper challenge. Now Martineau discovered, much to her dismay, that Jackson saw fit to accuse Poindexter of masterminding the abortive assassination. He repeated the charge frequently in casual conversation, then went further. After obtaining affidavits from "weak and vile persons whose evidence utterly failed," the president went to the trouble of conducting personal interviews with "these creatures," openly displaying a disposition "to hunt his foe to destruction at all hazards."

Martineau had made plans to visit the White House the day after

The attempted assassination of President Andrew Jackson, January 30, 1835. Drawn from a sketch by an eyewitness. (Courtesy of the Library of Congress, Prints and Photographs Division)

the funeral, but she heard so much of Jackson's determination "to consider the attack a political affair" that she stayed away as long as she could, doubtless hoping that the "old soldier" would calm down. Before finally going, Martineau received assurances from one of the physicians who had examined the president's assailant that he was indeed insane; one of his complaints, it seemed, was that Jackson had denied him the British crown, to which he was heir. At the White House, however, when Martineau politely adverted to the "insane attempt" on Jackson's life, her choice of words provoked an unseemly outburst from the chief executive. "He protested, in the presence of many strangers, that there was no insanity in the case. I was silent, of course. He protested that there was a plot, and that the man was a tool, and at length quoted the attorney-general as his authority." Martineau found it painful, indeed, to hear "a chief ruler publicly trying to persuade a foreigner that any of his constituents hated him to the death." She took the liberty of changing the subject as quickly as she could.

37

2. The Character of the Good Republic:
Justice, Stability, and the Constitution

SOMETIME during his retirement Madison began to relive the 1780s. He came more than ever to regard an understanding of this period as essential to comprehending the republican experience itself. The years just after the war for independence assumed great significance in his eyes not simply because they had culminated in the adoption of the Constitution; in a far larger sense, they had dramatized for a generation that had fought a revolution in the name of republicanism the salient, inescapable dilemmas that arose from investing sovereign authority in the people. Madison's vivid memories of this era were aroused, and indeed energized, by more than personal nostalgia. They were stimulated by what he observed from Montpelier and read about in the newspapers he so avidly procured – which is to say, Madison saw remarkable parallels between the events and trends of the 1820s and 1830s and the prior experience of the confederation period. And at times his characteristic equanimity was more than ruffled by a new generation's reckless disregard, even contempt, for the sobering lessons in their fathers' experience.

Madison's principled commitment to popular government had taken clear shape even before the Revolution, but during the last phase of the war and the years that followed he had also encountered the profound dangers in that system. For ages republican government had been severely criticized, and generally dismissed, for its vulnerability to the tumultuous whims of popular passion and thus for its inherent instability. Even in the eighteenth century it was commonly assumed that formal mechanisms of monarchical or at least aristocratic authority were the necessary sources of public order and civilized justice. If the American dream was to silence, through practical demonstration, what Madison described as late as 1823 as the "long triumphant argument for hereditary power drawn from an

39

anarchical tendency imputed to Governments founded on popular suffrage," the experience of the United States in the 1780s had challenged the faith of many devout republicans — including the young Virginian who, joining penetrating observation of his own society to systematic study of the past, sought fresh solutions to the age-old problem of reconciling popular government and stability.[1]

During the years leading to the Philadelphia convention, Madison's attention was directed more to the problems of the individual state governments than to the weakness of the federal Congress. He lamented the failure of the states to honor their constitutional responsibilities to the Confederation, most notably in providing the Congress with the revenue that was necessary to service the Revolutionary debt and to gain the respect of foreign governments. Even more important, he saw in the general activities of the state legislatures the horrifying specter of what one scholar has appropriately called "democratic despotism."[2] As a member of the Virginia General Assembly on four separate occasions between 1784 and 1787, Madison saw abundant, distressing evidence that a republican revolution had indeed gone awry. Scrutinizing his fellow legislators, he found many obscure men who, with seemingly modest qualifications to govern, appeared primarily concerned with furthering their own immediate and partial interests. Since these representatives were also acutely responsive to the needs and wishes of their local constituents (who often shared the same interests), the will of popular majorities in Virginia could be promptly translated into public policy. Madison knew that a similar situation obtained in most of the other states. Viewed superficially, nothing might appear more republican, more fulfilling of the spirit of the Revolution. But Madison regretted this majoritarian expression of republican politics in the individual states on several principled grounds.

First, he decried the abundance and inconsistency of the laws which, by shifting as rapidly as public opinion and the unstable

1 Madison to Richard Rush, July 22, 1823, in [William C. Rives and Philip R. Fendall, eds.], *Letters and Other Writings of James Madison* (Philadelphia, 1865), III, 332.
2 Gordon S. Wood, *The Creation of the American Republic, 1776–1787* (Chapel Hill, N.C., 1969), part four, esp. 409–413.

coalitions of interests in the legislatures, tended to sow discord and confusion among the people. This unsteadiness in the laws often reflected, moreover, the narrow, illiberal, even ignorant views of inexperienced legislators who seemed alarmingly oblivious both to private rights and to any broader notion of the public good. Madison vehemently condemned the injustice of much of this popular legislation, especially in the wake of a commercial depression that overtook much of the country in the mid-1780s. Paper money laws, so-called "stay" laws that offered relief to debtors, laws that impugned the sanctity of contracts; all may have expressed the immediate will of a people suffering the consequences of economic hard times, but they just as clearly violated the rights of both individuals and minorities. And in Madison's judgment, he and other critics of this debtor legislation were defending much more than the specific interest of creditors or any other particular group. By wantonly disregarding the rules of property and justice that raised men from savagery to civilized order, these laws threatened to bring republican government in America into profound disrepute. Amid this legislative unsteadiness and injustice, Madison feared, even more than faith in popular government was at risk. The "unstable and unjust career of the States" during these critical years, he later observed, "forfeited the respect and confidence essential to order and good Government, involving a general decay of confidence and credit between man and man" that threatened, he despaired, to unravel the very fabric of civilized society.[3]

Madison believed, above all, in a permanent public good and immutable standards of justice, both of which were linked to the rules of property that stabilized social relationships and that together defined the proper ends of republican government. He further believed that these ends were not always promoted by – and certainly ought never to be automatically equated with – the appar-

3 Preface to Debates in the Convention of 1787, in Max Farrand, ed., *The Records of the Federal Convention of 1787*, rev. ed., 4 vols. (New Haven, Conn., 1937), III, 548. For contemporary evidence of the point see, for example, "Notes for Speech Opposing Paper Money" [Nov. 1, 1786], and Madison in Virginia ratifying convention, June 14, 1788, in William T. Hutchinson et al., eds., *The Papers of James Madison* (Chicago, Charlottesville, 1962–), IX, 158–159, XI, 143.

ent will of "the people" as reflected in these momentary legislative majorities. The Scottish thinker David Hume, whose apparent influence on Madison has caught the fancy of more than one modern scholar, nicely sketched the essence of the problem that confronted the Virginian in the 1780s. Hume defined justice as an artificial virtue, consisting largely of a respect for the property rights of others; it followed that the rules that defined just behavior were human conventions essential to the well-being of any civilized society.[4] According to Hume, all men were generally "sensible of the necessity of justice to maintain peace and order" and, in turn, of "the necessity of peace and order for the maintenance of society." Nevertheless, such was "the frailty or perverseness" of human nature that it proved impossible "to keep men faithfully and unerringly in the paths of justice." Sometimes a man found his interests to be "more promoted by fraud and rapine, than hurt by the breach which his injustice makes in the social union"; just as often, he could be "seduced from his great and important, but distant interests, by the allurement of present, though often very frivolous temptations." And this calamitous inversion of the proper hierarchy between the immediate and the remote – between temporary, selfish advantage and the "real and permanent interests" of the community – was especially likely, Hume suggested, in popular regimes.[5]

In the 1780s Madison saw far too many of his countrymen who fell into each of Hume's categories and who, to make matters worse, did not have to resort to devious or extralegal means of advancing their specious interests; they could do so through the conventional and legitimizing forms of republican government and the principle of majority rule. Pondering the legislative chaos of these postwar years, Madison may indeed have appreciated the Scot's wisdom in defining the fundamental purposes of government in terms of administering justice and preserving moral order. If so, Hume had another relevant message for the young political scientist in North

4 For a lucid and succinct discussion of this matter, see David Miller, *Philosophy and Ideology in Hume's Political Thought* (Oxford, 1981), chap. 3 ("Justice As An Artificial Virtue"), 60–77.
5 Hume, "Of the Origin of Government," in *Essays Moral, Political and Literary* (Oxford, 1963 [orig. publ. 1741, 1742]), 35–36.

America: the "great weakness" that caused men to ignore what they knew were the proper standards of justice was "incurable in human nature." Statesmen could only "endeavour to palliate," therefore, what they could never hope to remove altogether.[6] In this connection, Madison's signal intellectual achievement in the late 1780s — this time, perhaps, with the direct guidance of Hume — was to discern in the new Constitution a potential "Republican remedy" for what he so memorably described in *Federalist* number ten as "the diseases most incident to Republican Government."[7] Those diseases, of course, were faction, injustice, and instability; and the remedy devised by the Philadelphia convention was to extend the sphere of republican government from the state level, where it was working so poorly, to the federal level, where majority factions were less likely to form and be oppressive and where a "filtration of talent" would likely empower those wise and able statesmen who were the "proper guardians of the public weal." And this remedy,

6 *Ibid.*, 36.
7 Jacob E. Cooke, ed., *The Federalist* (Middletown, Conn., 1961 [orig. publ. 1788]), 65. Hume's influence on Madison now appears indisputable, though clearly subject to exaggeration and misconstruction. Douglass Adair's famous essay, "'That Politics May Be Reduced to A Science': David Hume, James Madison, and the Tenth Federalist," *Huntington Library Quarterly* 20 (1957), 343–360, is the necessary point of departure. The essay is conveniently reprinted in Trevor Colbourn, ed., *Fame and the Founding Fathers: Essays by Douglass Adair* (New York, 1974), 93–106. Adair pointed to several of Hume's essays – "Of the Independency of Parliament," "Of the First Principles of Government," "Of Parties in General," "Of the Parties of Great Britain," and "Idea of a Perfect Commonwealth" – for evidence of Madison's almost literal borrowing of ideas and even language. More recently, Garry Wills has pushed the thesis harder, in different, often dubious directions, lengthening the list of influential Hume essays and focusing on other Madison writings than *Federalist* ten. Wills's emphasis on what he calls "the Humean sources" (p. 33) of *Federalist* forty-nine, for instance, is immensely suggestive, but his reading of that essay, which essentially presents Madison as an antidemocratic authoritarian, is grossly distorted and misleading. See *Explaining America: The Federalist* (New York, 1981), esp. chap. 3. Two recent articles place the Hume/Madison connection in a more cautious and sensible light; see Theodore Draper, "Hume and Madison: The Secrets of Federalist Paper No. 10," in *Encounter* 58 (1982), 34–47, and Edmund S. Morgan, "Safety in Numbers: Madison, Hume, and the Tenth *Federalist*," in *Huntington Library Quarterly* 49 (1986), 95–112.

Madison could boast, was suitably republican precisely because it neither violated nor compromised the Revolutionary commitment to the sovereignty of the people.[8]

Thirty years later, the venerable "Father of the Constitution" could still bask in the glow of that remarkable achievement. From the vantage point of his retirement, Madison doubtless believed that, notwithstanding many disappointments and unexpected developments, this ingenious, peculiarly American experiment of "extending the sphere" of republican government had on the whole been vindicated. But another legacy of these postwar years – Madison's fear of popular passion and public disorder – proved deepseated and tenacious. Indeed, his republicanism contained a serious tension that surfaced often during his retirement, and the roots of that tension can be found in the confederation period, when he first sought to accommodate his unshakeable commitment to popular government, with all of its manifest dangers, to his principled concern for preserving order, upon which he placed all hope of furthering justice and the public good. What arose from this creative tension was a republican commitment that differed in significant ways from the republicanism of even his closest political ally, Thomas Jefferson.

The conventional view of the Jefferson–Madison partnership as, in Adrienne Koch's words, "the great collaboration," tends to obscure the significance of their genuine theoretical differences. Madison's sensitivity to the dangers of passionate disorder shaped a fundamentally conservative vision of popular government, the origins and character of which can best be discerned by juxtaposing his and Jefferson's views on fundamental matters at two very different, but thematically linked, stages of their careers – during the late 1780s and, much later, during their final years in retirement.[9] As

8 Madison, *Federalist* ten, in Cooke, ed., *The Federalist*, 62; the phrase "filtration of talent" is taken from Wood, *Creation of the American Republic*, 506–518. For elaboration of the issues hastily summarized here, see Wood, passim, esp. 471–615.

9 For extended analysis of the Jefferson–Madison relationship and of their comparative views, see Adrienne Koch, *Jefferson and Madison: The Great Collaboration* (New York, 1950). As her title suggests, Koch emphasizes the complementary and mutually enriching nature of her subjects' political ideas – a sensible and

such an examination confirms, Madison's principled emphasis on justice and stability was the enduring legacy of his troubled journey through the 1780s. And that legacy defined his understanding of the Constitution in ways that continued not only to inform the central concerns of his retirement years, but to distinguish those concerns, in important ways, from Jefferson's.

I

When Madison departed the Philadelphia convention in the late summer of 1787, he had not seen or spoken to Jefferson for over three years. Their separation during the latter's tenure as minister to France proved no obstacle to a budding intimacy, however, so long as they could sustain a regular correspondence. Madison would later write that during the fifty years of their acquaintance, there had never been "an interruption or diminution of mutual confidence and cordial friendship, for a single moment in a single instance."[10] This was a moving tribute both to the memory of Jefferson and to the most influential collaboration in American political history. But Madison's surge of emotion for his lost friend should not blind us to what was easily overlooked in 1826: for a brief time just after the Constitutional Convention, their relationship appears to have been in no little jeopardy.

Since he had been away from the United States for several years, Jefferson lacked his fellow Virginian's intimate knowledge of both the convention and American affairs in general. Their contrasting perspectives on the Constitution clearly reflected the influence of their different surroundings. If Madison was overwhelmed by the evidence of potential chaos emerging from popular licentiousness in the various American states, Jefferson — from a vantage point in ancien régime France that magnified the evils of monarchical despotism — seemed far more concerned with the traditional danger of

---

effective approach that minimizes, however, the substantially different philosophical casts of their republicanism.

10 Madison to N. P. Trist, July 6, 1826, in Gaillard Hunt, ed., *The Writings of James Madison* (New York and London, 1900–1910), IX, 248.

concentrated power in government. In their rich and frank correspondence during late 1787 and early 1788, the two men did more than exchange thoughts on the proposed Constitution and discover that they differed on certain specific issues; they also doubtless sensed how different in thrust and emphasis their republican perspectives, broadly conceived, actually were. Accordingly, perhaps for the only time in their long friendship, the intercourse between them became conspicuously awkward, even strained.[11]

Jefferson's initial failure to endorse the Constitution that had emerged from the convention greatly distressed Madison. In their letters they were able to air their differences with amicable candor — at least to a point. Jefferson bluntly conveyed his uneasiness with certain aspects of the document. He had not liked the convention's decision to impose secrecy on its proceedings, and in the final product he detected further evidence of an imprudent, if not suspicious, lack of respect for popular rights and opinions. Under the Constitution, the president was to be eligible for indefinite reelection, and Jefferson considered this failure to limit the tenure of the executive an open invitation to tyranny. Above all, he decried the absence of a bill of rights that protected liberty and the essential rights of men from the predatory sweep of government power. Jefferson was sufficiently disturbed by these flaws in the Constitution to suggest, indeed, that perhaps it would be best for four states to withhold their consent to ratification until the necessary modifications were in place. Characteristically expressing such views without reserve to many of his American correspondents, Jefferson unwittingly placed Madison in a difficult and uncomfortable position: during the ratification struggle, Madison heard his best friend quoted, and that friend's considerable authority invoked, in apparent support of the Antifederalists' opposition to prompt acceptance of the Constitution.[12]

Moreover, for reasons that resist easy explanation, Madison chose

---

11 For a general discussion of this troubled phase of their relationship, see Koch, *Great Collaboration*, 33–61.

12 *Ibid.* See also Robert Allen Rutland, *The Ordeal of the Constitution: The Antifederalists and the Ratification Struggle of 1787–88* (Norman, Okla., 1966), esp. 89–90, 188–189, 272–278.

not to inform Jefferson of his coauthorship of the *Federalist* papers until almost a year after his work on that project had begun – after, indeed, the completed essays had been published together in two volumes and Jefferson had learned of Madison's role from other sources. This curious silence may reflect, in part, Madison's reluctance to tell his friend that he was collaborating with the two New Yorkers, Alexander Hamilton and John Jay, whose republican credentials might strike Jefferson as dubious. Perhaps Madison's curious silence was tied as well to the substance of his contribution to the *Federalist*. Under the veil of anonymity provided by "Publius," Madison had explicitly criticized at least one of Jefferson's ideas presented in the latter's *Notes on the State of Virginia*. Indeed, Madison's decision in the forty-ninth *Federalist* to challenge Jefferson's call for frequent popular conventions to resolve constitutional disputes is immensely revealing – not, as it turned out, of an impending breach in their personal relationship, but of fundamental differences in outlook which, though often obscured by the subsequent political partnership, persisted for the remainder of their lives. [13]

The essay in question was part of a series in which Madison analyzed and defended the separation of power in the different departments of the proposed national government. In the previous number of the *Federalist*, he had quoted approvingly from Jefferson's *Notes* in order to substantiate the danger of concentrating power in the legislative branch. But in number forty-nine, Madison politely turned on his friend, dismissing what he chose to interpret as one of

13 Marvin Meyers has drawn the attention of scholars to the significance of *Federalist* forty-nine in the larger sweep of Madison's understanding of the founding process. See the brilliant analysis in "Founding and Revolution: A Commentary on Publius-Madison," in Stanley Elkins and Eric McKittrick, eds., *The Hofstadter Aegis: A Memorial* (New York, 1974), 3–35, esp. 15-17; "Revolution and Founding: On Publius-Madison and the American Genesis," *Quarterly Journal of the Library of Congress* 37 (1980), 192–200; and "Reflection and Choice: Beyond the Sum of the Differences – An Introduction," in *The Mind of the Founder: Sources of the Political Thought of James Madison*, revised edition (Hanover, N. H. and London, 1981), xi-xlvii. See also the relevant discussion in Harry V. Jaffa, *Crisis of the House Divided: An Interpretation of the Issues in the Lincoln–Douglas Debates* (Chicago, 1982 [orig. publ. 1959]), 230–232, 236–238.

Jefferson's specific proposals for maintaining the requisite balance between the executive, the legislature, and the judiciary. In his draft of a revised constitution for Virginia, Jefferson had written that "whenever any two of the three branches of government" concurred, by a two-thirds vote of each, that either amendments or correction of "breaches" in the Constitution were necessary, "a convention shall be called for the purpose."[14]

Madison readily acknowledged the "great force" in Jefferson's reasoning. After all, since "the people" were "the only legitimate fountain of power" from which fundamental law was derived, it was "strictly consonant to the republican theory" to recur to that "same original authority" in order to fix the precise meaning of any written constitution. Prudence, however, dictated that any such "reference of constitutional questions" to "the decision of the whole society" be strictly confined to "certain great and extraordinary occasions." On the one hand, Madison worried that popular adjudication of such disputes would simply "not answer the purpose of maintaining the constitutional equilibrium of the government." After all, who doubted that "the people" would normally side with the branch of government closest to them, thereby heightening the familiar "tendency of republican governments" toward "an aggrandizement of the legislative, at the expence of the other departments?" But Jefferson's scheme was unsatisfactory – indeed, profoundly dangerous – for even more fundamental reasons. By mandating regular and probably frequent recurrences to the people, it promised to erode confidence in the government and to unleash the perilous juggernaut of popular passion.[15]

Madison feared, first of all, that Jefferson's frequent recourse to the people would jeopardize popular faith in the Constitution. This extraordinary inference was not as paradoxical as it might appear, because every appeal, by carrying "an implication of some defect in the government," would serve to deprive it of what Madison called "that veneration, which time bestows on every thing, and without which perhaps the wisest and freest governments would not possess the requisite stability." Paraphrasing Hume, Madison suggested

14 Cooke, ed., *The Federalist*, 339.   15 *Ibid.*, 339–341.

48

that the stability of any government ultimately rested on opinion and that the strength and practical influence of an individual's opinion depended largely on his sense of the numbers who shared, or who had shared, his view. "The reason of man, like man himself," Madison observed, "is timid and cautious, when left alone," acquiring "firmness and confidence in proportion to the number with which it is associated. When the examples which fortify opinion are *antient* as well as *numerous*, they are known to have a double effect." Applying this insight to the probable effects of Jefferson's scheme, Madison drew the inescapable inference: the Constitution might easily become a mutable plaything in the hands of a whimsical public, under which condition the requisite "veneration" would vanish. The American governments were unavoidably "young"; but despite – indeed because of – that circumstance, Madison appeared anxious to invest them with as much "antiquity" as he could. Here, then, was the crux of the issue: Jefferson's regular reliance on popular conventions, by insidiously undermining what Madison called "the prejudices of the community" in favor of the standing order, threatened to dissolve a useful, indeed essential, pillar of stability in all regimes, including the "wisest and freest" that Americans might hope to establish. [16]

Madison's analysis of the psychological foundations of political allegiance in *Federalist* forty-nine parallels, often in striking ways, the insights of Hume, who pointedly denied that reason was a sufficient basis for obedience to government and hence for stability. Habit, custom, and precedent – not purely rational consent – explained why most men submitted to the authority of a given regime, Hume argued, and apparently Madison found lessons in Hume's teaching that applied even to American governments that were ostensibly founded on reason. Hume had begun his essay "Idea of a Perfect Commonwealth," to which Madison was particularly attentive, with his customary warning against frequent and reckless changes in the form of government. "An established government has an infinite advantage, by that very circumstance, of its being established," he noted, "the bulk of mankind being governed by authori-

16 *Ibid.*, 340.

ty, not reason, and never attributing authority to any thing that has not the recommendation of antiquity."[17] Since men were normally guided by history and custom, their "prejudices" – what Hume in another essay referred to as "the most endearing sentiments of the heart, and all the most useful biases and instincts which can govern a human creature" – were an essential part of political science.[18] Not even the wisest statesman in the most liberal republic, Hume implied, could afford to disregard their necessary and salutary influence. Madison, if not Jefferson, clearly agreed.

In *Federalist* forty-nine, Madison acknowledged that, in theory, a republican regime should not have to depend on anything but "the voice of an enlightened reason" to evoke the requisite loyalty and reverence for its laws. But the United States, he insisted, was not and never would be "a nation of philosophers." Plato had fantasized about a philosophical race of kings; now some Americans, republicanizing this heady vision, just as naively dreamed of a philosophical race of citizens whose judgment could regularly be invoked to define and revise the Constitution.[19] As a sincere republican, of course, Madison happily acknowledged and honored the ultimate sovereignty of the people. But he also wanted to protect republican government as much as possible from the disruptive and unsettling effects of immediate popular influence – precisely because in America, as elsewhere, the large body of the people were not always or even ordinarily guided by enlightened reason. If Jefferson's frequent appeals to the people at large, assembled in conventions, became the rule, Madison never doubted that "the passions" rather than "the reason" of the public would usually "sit in judgment." This inverted the proper relationship between reason and passion, and between a

17 Hume, *Essays*, 499. For Madison's interest in this particular essay, see Adair, "That Politics May Be Reduced to a Science," in Colbourn, ed., *Fame and Founding Fathers*, 98–100. A relevant and lucid account of Hume's political thinking can be found in Miller, *Philosophy and Ideology in Hume's Political Thought*. See also, among other secondary sources, Frederick G. Whelan, *Order and Artifice in Hume's Political Philosophy* (Princeton, N.J., 1985), and James Moore, "Hume's Political Science and the Classical Republican Tradition," *Canadian Journal of Political Science* 10 (1977), 809–839.
18 Hume, "Of Moral Prejudices," in *Essays*, 573–574.
19 Cooke, ed., *The Federalist*, 340.

republican government and the people: according to Madison, "the reason of the public alone" should "controul and regulate the government," which in turn must control and regulate those passions.[20]

Indeed, Madison's rejection of Jefferson's proposal reflected how deeply he feared the prospect of "disturbing the public tranquillity by interesting too strongly the public passions." Referring in *Federalist* forty-nine to the flurry of constitution-writing in the American states during the Revolution, Madison applauded his countrymen's achievement, which certainly did "much honor" to their "virtue and intelligence." But it was obvious to him that such "experiments" were "of too ticklish a nature to be unnecessarily multiplied." Madison urged his readers not to forget that the state constitutions had been formed under extraordinary circumstances, amid both "a danger which repressed the passions most unfriendly to order and concord" and "an enthusiastic confidence of the people in their patriotic leaders." During the flush years of the Revolution, in other words, Americans had responded to an extreme threat and acted in unison with their venerated leaders, "whilst no spirit of party, connected with the changes to be made, or the abuses to be reformed, could mingle its leaven in the operation." Such was the spirit of classical republicanism – and the stuff, indeed, of a revolutionary moment. But under ordinary and expected future circumstances, Madison cautioned, there would be no "equivalent security" against the predictable dangers of party excitement and popular turmoil.[21] It went without saying that the present unrest and instability both in the state legislatures and among the people – Shays' Rebellion, an armed insurgency of debtor farmers in Massachusetts, was fresh in Madison's memory – offered telling evidence of the point. Unlike Jefferson, therefore, Madison thought it unwise to entrust constitutional interpretation and hence the stability of government, even in a republic, to the routine judgment and immediate will of the people.

Madison's critique of his friend's draft of a revised constitution for Virginia was not confined to *Federalist* forty-nine. Not long after he belatedly informed Jefferson of his authorship of the *Federalist*, Madison extended that critique in his private correspondence. Writ-

20 *Ibid.*, 343. 21 *Ibid.*, 340–341.

ing to friends in Kentucky who had solicited his advice on a constitution for their prospective state, he systematically exposed the deficiencies in the specific plan Jefferson had publicized in an appendix to his *Notes on Virginia*. The editors of the modern edition of Madison's papers are correct to observe that there was "scarcely a section" of Jefferson's proposed constitution that Madison "did not find fault with."[22] And the larger thrust of that detailed critique is quite clear. Madison criticized Jefferson, for instance, for failing to distinguish sharply enough the upper and lower houses of the legislature, especially through suffrage qualifications; he also chided his friend for placing too much power in the legislature, the branch of government closest to the people, and too little in the executive and the judiciary. In both cases, Madison wanted better guarantees of stability and better protection for the rights of minorities against the rampaging force of the immediate, unrestrained, and unrefined will of the people.[23] And perhaps it bears emphasis that Madison did not construe his conservative quest for stability, or for justice for minorities, as in any sense unrepublican or inimical to the spirit of the American Revolution. As he viewed the crisis of the 1780s, indeed, securing public order against the threat of popular unrest and legislative mischief, on the one hand, and vindicating the very capacity of man for self-government, on the other, were interlocking dimensions of the same great challenge.

In retrospect, of course, the extraordinary friendship of Jefferson and Madison survived the bumps and bruises of the late 1780s with remarkable ease. His initial and emphatic reservations notwithstanding, Jefferson was reconciled to Madison's federal Constitution soon enough. And within a few more years, their mutual opposition to Alexander Hamilton's objectionable system of political economy (and to all that it entailed) reinforced the personal bond that anchored their stable, long-term partnership in American national politics.[24] But shortly after the inception of the new general govern-

---

22 Madison, "Observations on Jefferson's Draft of a Constitution for Virginia," ca. Oct. 15, 1788, in Hutchinson et al., eds., *Madison Papers*, XI, 281–295 (editors' quote from 282).

23 *Ibid.*

24 For my own analysis of some relevant issues, see Drew R. McCoy, *The Elusive*

ment – just as the two men were about to become formal political allies – they articulated more clearly than ever, in a private exchange of ideas, the very different philosophical shadings of their respective republican faiths. Although their broad visions and specific programs were politically compatible, especially in facing the grave threat of the northern-based Federalist party that emerged in the 1790s, some of their most fundamental assumptions about man and government in fact sharply diverged. Before leaving France, Jefferson had drafted a letter to his friend on a subject of immense speculative and practical significance, which, together with Madison's response in a letter of February 4, 1790, extended and clarified the terms of their "debate" in *Federalist* forty-nine and in Madison's correspondence with his Kentucky friends.

"I sit down to write to you without knowing by what occasion I shall send my letter," Jefferson had opened his remarkable missive; the subject he wished to attend to could not, indeed, be developed "in the hurry of the moment of making up general dispatches." As he proceeded to explore the full and resonant meaning of the bold notion that "the earth belongs always to the living generation," Jefferson categorically denied the right of any generation to encroach on the sovereignty of its successors. "Between society and society, or generation and generation," he reminded Madison, "there is no municipal obligation, no umpire but the law of nature." He then added, in ringing words that may well have unnerved his correspondent, that "we seem not to have perceived that, by the law of nature, one generation is to another as one independant nation to another."[25]

Jefferson had taken up this idea of generational autonomy and bent all of his genius to it, it would seem, at the urging of an eccentric English physician, Dr. Richard Gem, who had infused his

---

Republic: Political Economy in Jeffersonian America (Chapel Hill, N.C., 1980) and "James Madison and Visions of American Nationality in the Confederation Period: A Regional Perspective," in Richard Beeman et al., eds., *Beyond Confederation: Origins of the Constitution and American National Identity* (Chapel Hill, N.C., 1987), 226–258.

25 Jefferson to Madison, Sept. 6, 1789, in Julian P. Boyd et al., eds., *The Papers of Thomas Jefferson* (Princeton, N.J., 1950–), XV, 392, 396, 395.

ministrations to Jefferson in Paris with a healthy dose of radical politics.[26] The American was simply swept off his feet by this notion of the sovereignty of the living generation, and he proceeded to suggest to Madison, in searching detail, the full range of its practical applications. Although Jefferson's attention was directed primarily to monarchical France, now in the throes of social upheaval and the exciting promise of political regeneration, he suggested that even a comparatively pure republic like the United States could profit from adhering to the full implications of this great political truth. On the basis of some ingenious but dubious mathematical reckoning tied to mortality tables, Jefferson calculated the duration of a political generation as the length of time necessary for a majority of the adult population to die – approximately nineteen years. Hence, he deduced, no nation could rightly incur more public debt than could be retired in that interval; to spend more was to expropriate the resources of the next generation and unjustly infringe on its sovereignty. Above all, Jefferson hoped that observing this sacred principle might restrain reckless governments from pursuing expensive and corrupting wars, that traditional and horrific bane of Old World monarchies. But he did not stop there. "On similar ground," he informed Madison, "it may be proved that no society can make a perpetual constitution, or even a perpetual law." In fact, since every constitution and every law "naturally expires at the end of 19 years," Jefferson asserted that continued enforcement beyond that period had to be considered "an act of force, and not of right."[27]

If Madison was uncomfortable with Jefferson's relatively modest suggestion that popular conventions be called to resolve constitutional controversies, it is hardly surprising that he tossed a healthy dose of cold water on this breathtaking assault on institutional continuity and the vestigial authority of the past. His reply to Jefferson, while couched in modest and respectful language, was also firm and unequivocal. Ever polite, Madison tried to frame his dissent in terms of Jefferson's idea being "a great one" that, carried to the extent he suggested, would prove in many respects incompatible

26 See editorial note, *ibid.*, 384–392.   27 *Ibid.*, 395–396.

"with the course of human affairs."[28] But one hardly has to read between the lines to see that Madison objected as much to the substance of the broad theory as to any practical difficulties in implementing it. Echoing his thoughts in *Federalist* forty-nine, Madison promptly raised the issue that Jefferson appeared utterly unconcerned with: how to ensure stability — which meant wisdom and steadiness in the laws, among other things — in a government that, while properly dependent on the will of the people, was also vulnerable to the vagaries of popular opinion and to the vicissitudes occasioned by partisan turmoil.

Imagining Jefferson's system in practice, Madison posed a question that vividly echoed one of David Hume's principal concerns: "Would not a Government so often revised," he chided, "become too mutable to retain those prejudices in its favor which antiquity inspires, and which are perhaps a salutary aid to the most rational Government in the most enlightened age?" Even more ominous, "would not such a periodical revision engender pernicious factions that might not otherwise come into existence" and therefore encourage unnecessary and dangerous divisions in society? Madison was especially troubled by the probable effects of Jefferson's principle on property rights and, by extension, on the very character of society. If the laws governing property were widely known to expire after a fixed interval, property values would surely depreciate, and most of "the rights of property" become "absolutely defunct" while "the most violent struggles" between "those interested in reviving and those interested in new-modelling the former State of property" ensued. Obviously all confidence and credit among the members of such a society would erode; but the moral fallout would hardly end there. This "frequent return of periods superseding all the obligations depending on antecedent laws and usages," Madison told Jefferson, would severely weaken "the reverence for those obligations" and give further impetus to "motives to licentiousness already too powerful." Specifically, it would "discourage the steady exertions of industry produced by permanent laws," while giving "a disproportionate advantage to the more, over the less, sagacious and

28 Madison to Jefferson, Feb. 4, 1790, in Hutchinson et al., eds., *Madison Papers*, XIII, 18–19.

James Madison, c. 1792. Replica of a portrait by Charles Willson Peale. (Courtesy of the Library of Congress, Prints and Photographs Division)

interprizing part of the Society." And the only relief from this catastrophic scenario, according to Madison, was what he called the "received doctrine" of "tacit assent" – an assent necessarily inferred from the absence of "positive dissent" – to all "established Constitutions and laws."[29]

29 *Ibid.*, 19–20.

Thomas Jefferson in 1791. Replica of a portrait by Charles Willson Peale.
(Courtesy of the Library of Congress, Prints and Photographs Division)

As inspiring as its spirit surely was, in sum, Jefferson's formula
for generational autonomy promised to foster popular disaffection
and public unrest in any popular regime that adhered to it. It also
blithely ignored, in Madison's judgment, the sternest challenge in
the science of republicanism: how to protect the integrity of free
institutions from the threat of their most dangerous enemy, the
disorder that arose from passionate contention among the people

57

themselves. As Madison had noted in the Virginia ratifying convention of 1788, "if we review the history of all republics, we are justified by the supposition, that if the bands of the government be relaxed, confusion will ensue." And such confusion, accelerated by loss of confidence in a regime whose forms were regularly changing, would insidiously undermine republicanism itself, because the ultimate danger Madison always foresaw, anarchy, "ever has, and I fear ever will, produce despotism."[30]

One point bears emphasis: Madison found serious fault with the underlying logic of Jefferson's theory of generational relationships. Contrary to his friend, he believed that generations were unavoidably linked in largely salutary, indeed "natural" ways. When one generation improved the earth, for instance, its descendants automatically inherited the advantages. As Madison shrewdly implied, Jefferson, perhaps overwhelmed by the horrors of European despotism, unwittingly assumed that "the dead" showered only burdens, never blessings, on "the living." As for public debts, Madison reflected that some – such as the Revolutionary War debt in the United States – were contracted in the service of causes, such as freedom from political slavery, that benefitted posterity even more than the living generation that incurred them. "There seems then to be a foundation in the nature of things, in the relation which one generation bears to another, for the *descent* of obligations from one to another," he concluded. "Equity requires it," and "mutual good is promoted by it."[31]

In this fundamental sense, Madison's republicanism was infused with a philosophical conservatism, largely absent from Jefferson's

30 Madison in Virginia ratifying convention, June 14, 1788, *ibid.*, XI, 143.
31 Madison to Jefferson, Feb. 4, 1790, *ibid.*, XIII, 19–20. Toward the end of his letter, Madison reassured Jefferson that his observations were not meant "to impeach" what he called "the utility of the principle" in relation to the "particular issues" Jefferson had in view – namely, public debts and war. Madison also affirmed his own fervent wish that living generations be restrained from imposing "unjust or unnecessary burdens" on their successors; *ibid.*, 21. And two years later, in a partisan essay inspired by their mutual fear of Hamilton and his cohorts, Madison publicly invoked Jefferson's principle in connection with precisely this issue of public debts and unnecessary wars. See "Universal Peace," printed in the *National Gazette* on Jan. 31, 1792, *ibid.*, XIV, 206–208.

formal thought, in which the dead and the living – as well as the past, the present, and the future – were inextricably and on the whole happily bound together. In his essay "Of the Original Contract," Hume had anticipated Madison's objections to Jefferson's generational philosophizing with typically vivid imagery. "Did one generation of men go off the stage at once, and another succeed, as is the case with silk-worms and butterflies," Hume admitted, "the new race might voluntarily, and by general consent, establish their own form of civil polity, without any regard to the laws or precedents which prevailed among their ancestors." But men were not silkworms or butterflies; "as human society is in perpetual flux, one man every hour going out of the world, another coming into it, it is necessary, in order to preserve stability in government, that the new brood should conform themselves to the established constitution, and nearly follow the path which their fathers, treading in the footsteps of theirs, had marked out for them."[32] Madison's conservatism was hardly identical to Hume's, of course, since the American was an ardent defender of a revolutionary regime, based on principles of natural right, that was anything but conventional. But the analogy to Hume, which is by no means strained, is not the only one that comes to mind.[33]

Although Madison would surely have been uncomfortable with the comparison, there is a striking affinity between his ideas and the spirit of Edmund Burke's famous definition of society, offered a year later, as "a partnership not only between those who are living, but between those who are living, those who are dead, and those who are to be born." Like Hume and Madison, Burke spoke approvingly of what he called "wise prejudice," of the popular "reverence" for constituted authority that by inhibiting frequent or extensive revisions of government promoted a necessary and beneficial measure of stability. In words strikingly reminiscent of Madison's rejection of Jefferson's generational theory, Burke condemned the specter of "the living" posing as "the entire masters" of a commonwealth by tinker-

32 Hume, *Essays*, 463.
33 For an interesting and relevant comparison of Hume, Adam Smith, and Edmund Burke as "conservatives," see Miller, *Philosophy and Ideology in Hume's Political Thought*, 187–205.

ing, at their pleasure, with its inherited fabric and institutions. "By this unprincipled facility of changing the state as often, and as much, and in as many ways as there are floating fancies or fashions," he warned, "the whole chain and continuity of the commonwealth would be broken. No one generation could link with the other. Men would become little better than the flies of summer."[34] Again, of course, merely the context of Burke's remarks – his broad condemnation of the first stirrings of revolution in France and his specific defense of a state religious establishment – dramatically underscores the profound limits of the analogy. But we might say that Madison's conservatism represented a republicanized expression of a Burkean spirit that celebrated, in a fashion inimical to Jefferson's doctrinaire attachment to "the law of nature," generational bonding. Even Madison's qualified emphasis on tradition and on reverence for the past clashed sharply with Jefferson's strict reliance on "nature," rather than institutions, as the repository of meaning and purpose in human affairs.[35]

We should note as well Madison's emphasis on the importance of popular deference to those who were superior in wisdom, experience, and reputation. As a confirmed republican, he invested far more confidence in the virtue and integrity of the common citizen than did Burke. Yet he also shared with the British conservative, especially in the late 1780s, an emphatically hierarchical under-

---

34 Conor Cruise O'Brien, ed., *Reflections on the Revolution in France . . .* by Edmund Burke (London, 1968 [orig. publ. 1790]), 194–195, 192–193.
35 For a brilliant discussion of the Jeffersonian emphasis on nature rather than institutions, see Daniel Boorstin, *The Lost World of Thomas Jefferson* (Chicago, 1948). It is interesting – and altogether appropriate – that Boorstin does not include Madison in the "circle" of thinkers from whom he deduces fundamental Jeffersonian assumptions. For a recent attempt to describe and emphasize the differences between Jefferson and Madison, see Richard K. Matthews, *The Radical Politics of Thomas Jefferson: A Revisionist View* (Lawrence, Kansas, 1984). Matthews may carry the point too far – and I do not share what is clearly his relative assessment of the two men as political thinkers – but he is quite right to draw the lines of distinction that he does. For an excellent analysis of the fundamental, lifelong differences in Jefferson's and Madison's understandings of representation, for instance, see J. R. Pole, *Political Representation in England and the Origins of the American Republic* (Berkeley, Calif., 1966), part 3, esp. 296–300.

standing of how ordinary people must function in a well-ordered commonwealth. At the Virginia ratifying convention, for instance, Madison admitted that if his countrymen were completely lacking in virtue, as some pessimists claimed, the republican cause was surely lost; "to suppose that any form of government will secure liberty or happiness without any virtue in the people," he asserted, "is a chimerical idea." Yet Madison candidly defined his faith in "the people" in unabashedly elitist terms: he went on to affirm his hope that ordinary citizens in America had, in effect, sufficient "virtue and intelligence" to elect to office wiser and more distinguished men than themselves.[36] As the historian Gordon Wood has persuasively argued, Madison believed with many of his fellow Federalists in the late 1780s that "the people" in America generally had the right – as well as sufficient virtue – to vote responsibly in free elections. But he also questioned whether most of them had the requisite wisdom, character, and vision to perform well the duties of the statesman and exercise responsible leadership themselves.[37] Indeed, during the great debate over the Constitution, Madison was openly skeptical that many, perhaps most, Americans could even think responsibly about the most important and complex issues that faced them, including the matter at hand. As he noted in passing to Jefferson in December 1787, this "new and intricate" question of whether to accept the work of the Philadelphia convention was one that "certainly surpasses the judgment of the greater part" of what he casually referred to as "the mass of the people."[38]

Writing to Edmund Randolph a month later, Madison elaborated the implications of his understanding of popular competence, which

36 Madison in Virginia ratifying convention, June 20, 1788, in Hutchinson et al., eds., *Madison Papers*, XI, 163.
37 Wood, *Creation of the American Republic*, esp. 471–518.
38 Madison to Jefferson, Dec. 9, 1787, in Hutchinson et al., eds., *Madison Papers*, X, 313. Madison was initially excited by the apparent fact that many of Virginia's common folk were in fact contravening the stated views of some of the commonwealth's most popular leaders. This exceptional situation proved, he said, that "the body of sober & steady people, even of the lower order, are tired of the vicissitudes, injustice and follies which have so much characterized public measures, and are impatient for some change which promises stability and repose" (*ibid.*).

had a decidedly different tone and emphasis from Jefferson's more relaxed confidence in "the people." If we can imagine the possible effect on Jefferson of Madison's brief observation – which may well have grated on him as much as his own later statements about the autonomy of generations would on Madison – then it may have been fortunate for the future of their partnership that Randolph, and not Jefferson, heard what Madison had to say on January 10, 1788. Madison explained to Randolph, who was vacillating in his support for ratification, why the idea of a second convention to amend the work of the Philadelphia gathering (an idea that appears to have held some appeal for Jefferson, too) was profoundly dangerous. "Whatever respect may be due to the rights of private judgment, and no man feels more of it than I do," Madison wrote, "there can be no doubt that there are subjects to which the capacities of the bulk of mankind are unequal, and on which they must and will be governed by those with whom they happen to have acquaintance and confidence."[39] (Perhaps it would not be going too far to recall here Burke's belief in the political incapacity of ordinary men, of whom he once noted that "God and nature never made them to think or act without guidance and direction.")[40] Since the proposed Constitution, as Madison had indicated to Jefferson, clearly fell into this category, "the great body of those who are both for & against it, must follow the judgment of others not their own." The "mass of the people" were necessarily responding, Madison insisted, not to the application of their own reason to the substance of the document but rather to the positions taken by their social betters whose reputations they knew and could therefore judge.

To illustrate his point, Madison observed that if the same Constitution – identical in every word and clause – had been drawn up by "an obscure individual, instead of a body possessing public respect & confidence," it would have little support and no chance of public approval. On the other hand, if the respected members of the Virginia elite who were now announcing their opposition – men like George Mason, Patrick Henry, and Richard Henry Lee – instead

39 Madison to Edmund Randolph, Jan. 10, 1788, *ibid.*, 355.
40 Burke quoted in Leo Strauss and Joseph Cropsey, eds., *History of Political Philosophy*, 2d ed. (Chicago and London, 1972), 671.

agreed with Madison and George Washington, not a murmur of dissent against the Constitution would be heard from the people at large. The inference Madison drew was simple: if the significant reform of the American polity that was urgently needed were to occur, it would have to proceed "from a fortunate coincidence of leading opinions, and a general confidence of the people in those who may recommend it."[41]

It was from this context that Madison's vehement opposition to a second convention drew such force. Obviously the very attempt to convene a new convention would strike at "the confidence" of the people in the original convention and its work, seriously jeopardizing the chances of ratification. And the actual existence of a second convention, "by opposing influence to influence, would in a manner destroy an effectual confidence in either, and give a loose [rein] to human opinions; which must be as various and irreconcileable concerning theories of Government, as doctrines of Religion." Knowing how difficult it had been to arrive at a consensus that accommodated the differing views of the delegates to the Philadelphia convention, who had been shielded from public scrutiny and debate while performing their delicate task, Madison shuddered to think of reopening fundamental issues in such a highly charged political atmosphere as now existed. Just as important, the ensuing confusion would arouse the worst passions of ambitious politicians and "give opportunities to designing men which it might be impossible to counteract." And under these kinds of circumstances, the movement to effect meaningful reform, and thereby save the republic, would surely abort in a passionate maelstrom of conflicting opinions and rival ambitions.[42]

We see here the roots of Madison's belief, expressed so often toward the end of his life, that the adoption of the Constitution had been nothing short of a miracle. For a brief moment in the late 1780s, he believed, the convergence of a severe crisis and an exemplary spirit of accommodation and broad purpose among the nation's elite had overcome what was endemic to any free and just society: a

41 Madison to Randolph, Jan. 10, 1788, in Hutchinson et al., eds., *Madison Papers*, X, 355.
42 *Ibid.*, 356.

tendency toward passionate conflict among men, ideas, and interests that endangered a necessary measure of stability. Not only had the American republic been forged in the midst of such rare and propitious circumstances, in effect snatching order from the jaws of chaos; Madison also doubted that such conditions were likely to recur, especially as he witnessed what the Revolution had wrought in the United States by the 1820s and 1830s.[43] We should not be surprised, therefore, that Madison would insist throughout his retirement that the Constitution be elevated to a separate plane of discourse and debate, as far removed from the frenzied excitement of partisan furor and popular controversy as republican principle allowed.

II

If Madison entered retirement in early 1817 amid the reassuring glow of postwar confidence and the promise of continued calm, it was not long before his conservative instincts were pricked into action. Writing to John Adams two months after leaving the presidency, he gave notice of his enduring concern with the issues — and with the underlying dichotomy of passion and reason — that had preoccupied him in the 1780s. Adams had sent Madison his thoughts on the political writings of the French philosopher Condorcet, and the Virginian was quick to endorse Adams's critique of the idea of a government "in one centre." It was revealing indeed, Madison said, that in each of the American states that had "approached nearest" to the theory of legislative supremacy, changes had soon been made "assimilating their constitutions to the examples of the other States, which had placed the powers of Government in different depositories, as means of controling the impulse and sympathy of the passions, and affording to reason better opportunities of asserting its prerogatives." Now the great question to be decided in the United States — one, he added, "in which humanity is more deeply interested than in any political experiment yet made" —

43 See, for example, "Outline," Sept. 1829, in [Rives and Fendall, eds.], *Letters and Other Writings*, IV, 20.

was whether "checks and balances sufficient for the purposes of order, justice, and the general good" might be created by dividing and distributing power among "different bodies, differently constituted, but all deriving their existence from the elective principle, and bound by a responsible tenure of their trusts." On the national level, he added, the American experiment was favored by "the extent of our Country," which above all "prevents the contagion of evil passions." Invoking his familiar notion of "prejudice," he concluded that much was "to be hoped from the force of opinion and habit, as these ally themselves with our political institutions."[44]

As the familiar world of the founding generation steadily receded from view and the experimental republic encountered a host of daunting problems, some familiar and some not, Madison's emphasis on stability, as well as his regard for habits of popular deference in a fragile polity, assumed renewed relevance. As he clearly understood, of course, the process of change that ineluctably led to the kind of leadership offered by Andrew Jackson – and to a political culture that celebrated what he appeared to represent – had firm roots in both the spirit and the consequences of the Revolution that Madison had himself joined as a young man. Nevertheless, as his memories of the 1780s made so vividly clear, the gravest danger to both national union and republicanism in America remained the instability that arose from popular licentiousness. Balance, restraint, and the discipline of personal and public passion were Madisonian – which is to say, enlightened, eighteenth-century – imperatives that appeared ever more incongruous, hence all the more necessary, in the new, nineteenth-century world that a younger generation of Americans now busied itself in making. As Madison looked on from Montpelier, indeed, those familiar values became ever more vulnerable, not only to the disruptive force of unprecedented geographical and economic expansion, but to the fulsome appeal of the democratic expectations that these changes, fueled by Revolutionary ideology, abundantly nourished.[45]

---

44 Madison to John Adams, May 22, 1817, *ibid.*, III, 41–42.
45 An excellent discussion of many of these broad issues can be found in George Dangerfield, *The Awakening of American Nationalism, 1815-1828* (New York, 1965).

In 1819, the brief interval of exhilarating prosperity and feverish land speculation that had surrounded Madison's retirement ground to a sudden halt in the throes of an economic panic that heralded, in turn, a lingering depression. The repercussions of this Panic of 1819 proved decisive in setting political agendas on both the state and federal levels. They also affected popular images of an eighteenth-century Revolution that now lay beyond the reach of memory for all but a few aged survivors. In Kentucky, for instance, the economic hard times of the early 1820s created an atmosphere almost eerily reminiscent of the 1780s. And some who remembered the confederation period were quick to complain that the vital and necessary links with the past were either ignored or grossly distorted. In the summer of 1825, a seventy-seven-year-old native of Virginia wrote eloquently of his vanishing hopes for the Revolutionary dream. Although his adopted home of Kentucky was a fine country, George Thomson opined to his old friend Madison that it was being ruined by an unscrupulous race of debtor politicians. When the speculative bubble of the late teens had burst, he explained, it had spawned a vast web of debt as well as importunate cries for relief that had not gone unheeded. The Kentucky legislature wantonly interfered between debtors and creditors, Thomson complained; first there had been a sixty-day stay law, then one of twelve months, and finally, as if in parody of the 1780s, paper money issued through a bank. "Dreadful have been the effects of this Course," Thomson told Madison, among which he named "loss of confidence between man and man, paralysis of industry, Demagoguery in its most disgusting forms, depression or retirement of honest public men, [and] the elevation of worthless time servers and Bankrupts."[46]

The ultimate horror, moreover, was that these laws were put forth under a popular banner of "majority rule" that allegedly conferred historical legitimacy on what was patently unjust. According to

---

46 George Thomson to Madison, June 3, 1825, James Madison Papers, Library of Congress, series one (microfilm). For insight into why the apparent restrictions in Article I, Section 10, of the Constitution failed to prevent such legislation after 1789, see Steven R. Boyd, "The Contract Clause and the Evolution of American Federalism, 1789–1815," *William and Mary Quarterly*, 3d ser., 44 (1987), 529–548.

Thomson, the debtor politicians stopped at nothing in their shameful misrepresentation of the legacy of the American Revolution. Their antics included, for instance, an assault on the state's judiciary that, invoking the essential distinction between the fundamental law contained in a state constitution and the momentary interest of legislative majorities, was vainly attempting to restrain "the people" from perpetrating such egregious injustice. In the imaginary world of false and contrived tradition that now held sway, Thomson wrote, inanity was often laced with the cruelest irony. He bitterly reported that the vaunted ideal of an omnipotent legislature – deemed just, of course, because it represented the pure and unfettered will of the people – was now being sold to the people of Kentucky in the name of the Revolutionary fathers, including Madison. Actually, this rewriting of history produced some curious, often outrageous, twists and turns that could apparently affect Madison's public standing and reputation in rather different ways. Any man in Kentucky "who dares to say any thing against unlimited legislative power," Thomson told his friend, was promptly "denounced as an Aristocrat, a Federalist, a Tory, an Enemy to the People." What better way to forget the lessons of the 1780s than to dismiss the *Federalist*? Much to Thomson's mortification, this shallow and partisan cast of mind engendered contempt for the most profound wisdom of the Revolutionary past: "the letters of Publius (formerly our Textbook) must not be read or quoted (even yours) because Hamilton was a Federalist!" "My Dear Sir," Thomson wailed, "has it all been an idle dream about the safety and importance of having a Written Constitution?"[47]

While Madison found his friend's "sad picture of the condition of Kentucky" duly sobering, he characteristically fought off, as best he could, Thomson's urgent despair. The Kentuckian hoped to enlist Madison's open support against the debtor miscreants, but the Virginian resisted being drawn into partisan controversy in a neighboring state. He was anxious to reaffirm privately, nonetheless, that "no doctrine can be sound that releases a Legislature from the controul of a Constitution." In a republic, he insisted, a constitution

---

47 Thomson to Madison, June 3, 1825, Madison Papers, Library of Congress, series one (microfilm).

was as much a law to a legislature as the acts of the latter were to individuals. A properly republican constitution was "always liable to be altered by the people who formed it" – but not by the mere authority of legislators chosen by the people to carry that constitution into effect. For Madison, there was indeed a profound difference between the popular will expressed in inherently unstable legislative majorities, such as the one that had temporarily gained the upper hand in Kentucky, and a more durable public will expressed through carefully stipulated procedures for establishing and revising fundamental law. Madison believed this distinction to be "so vital a principle" – one "so justly the pride of our popular Governments" – that a denial of it among Americans could hardly "last long, or spread far." If some men of the republican faith had been knocked off balance by the unsettling repercussions of economic distress and "surprised into such an error" as Thomson described, surely "time and reflection," he calmly reassured his friend, would "rescue them" from their folly.[48]

As his correspondence with Thomson suggests, Madison never proposed to withhold from the people the essence of their right to self-government by denying their ultimate authority to determine what was constitutional. But as he had argued at some length in the 1780s, and reiterated now during his retirement, frequent and direct appeals to the people for the resolution of constitutional disputes were simply inimical to a stable and well-ordered republic – which is to say, a republic that would enjoy the confidence of the people and also be capable of furthering justice and the public good. Indeed, Madison's debate with Jefferson on this broad matter at the time of the Founding was resumed, albeit in a different context, in the early 1820s, when both men responded to a series of controversial decisions of the Supreme Court under the leadership of Chief Justice John Marshall.[49]

Marshall's activities prompted Jefferson and Madison to ponder anew a fundamental question about the meaning of the federal Con-

48 Madison to Thomson, June 30, 1825, in [Rives and Fendall, eds.], *Letters and Other Writings*, III, 491.
49 For context and elaboration, see esp. Dumas Malone, *The Sage of Monticello* (Boston, 1981), 351–361.

stitution. Obviously that document had drawn a line between the legitimate spheres of federal and state authority. But amid continuing disagreement about whether particular powers properly belonged to the federal or to the state governments, who was empowered to resolve the dispute? Who, in other words, was the "ultimate arbiter" of the constitutionality of controversial federal laws? Profoundly alarmed by the Court's assertion both of federal power and of its own specific jurisdiction over this matter, Jefferson warned of a crypto-Federalist plot to promote a system of national "consolidation" that would, in effect, draw the necessary line between the spheres of federal and state authority almost entirely in favor of the former. For Jefferson, this marked a vicious betrayal of the spirit and principles both of the Revolution of 1776 and of the "Revolution of 1800," which had rescued the Constitution from an earlier, similar threat. Indeed, by vanquishing "the monarchists" in free and open elections, the Jeffersonians had swept the Federalists from power in both Congress and the presidency. But now, Jefferson cried, a small remnant of die-hard Federalists was manipulating its tenacious hold on the judiciary – the only branch of the federal government protected from the will of this Jeffersonian majority – to further its evil designs. First in the pages of the *Richmond Enquirer*, and then in a series of letters to William Johnson, a fellow justice of Marshall's whom he had appointed to the Court, Jefferson vigorously denied the Court's constitutional right to serve as the ultimate arbiter of constitutional disputes between the federal and state governments. In his contemptuous dismissal of Marshall's assertion of that power, he conceded that there must be an "ultimate arbiter" somewhere. But he found it in neither party to the dispute – not in the federal or the state governments, in other words – but rather in "the people of the Union, assembled by their deputies in convention, at the call of Congress, or of two-thirds of the States." Whenever uncertainty or controversy arose about the meaning of the Constitution, Jefferson insisted, the people must "decide to which they mean to give an authority claimed by two of their organs."[50] In

---

50 Jefferson to William Johnson, June 12, 1823, in Paul Leicester Ford, ed., *The Writings of Thomas Jefferson* (New York and London, 1899), X, 232. For a good discussion of the correspondence between Jefferson and Johnson, see Donald G.

Article V, which described the requisite procedures for amending the Constitution to which he adverted, Jefferson discovered the happy alternative to investing this necessary power in an unelected judicial body that was, by its very nature, utterly unresponsive to the will of the people.

Madison politely informed Jefferson that his understanding of the Constitution was wrong, both historically and in principle. To be sure, Madison objected to several of Marshall's specific rulings for reasons quite similar to Jefferson's. The Court, he agreed, had manifested a disturbing tendency to enlarge the power of the "general" government "in derogation of the local" and to "amplify its own jurisdiction" to an extent that had "justly incurred the public censure." Nevertheless, Madison declared that the federal judiciary was unquestionably the proper "Constitutional resort for determining the line between the federal and State jurisdictions." "The abuse of a trust," he lectured his friend, "does not disprove its existence." The members of the Philadelphia convention had clearly intended to invest this authority somewhere in the general government; and after rejecting Madison's schemes for both a federal negative on state laws and a "council of revision," they had placed that authority in the federal judiciary. Such had been, more generally, "the prevailing view of the subject when the Constitution was adopted and put into execution" – at least as Madison now preferred to remember it. And he reminded Jefferson that evidence of his early support for this idea could be found in *Federalist* thirty-nine.[51]

Madison admitted that judicial review was fraught with the danger of abuse and that such a danger was amply demonstrated by the recent maneuverings of the Court. But it was, in addition to being the stipulated intent of the Founders, clearly superior to any alternative yet proposed, including Jefferson's. "To refer every new point of disagreement" between the general and state governments "to the people in Conventions," Madison argued, would be "a process too tardy, too troublesome, and too expensive." In words reminiscent of

Morgan, *Justice William Johnson, The First Dissenter: The Career and Constitutional Philosophy of a Jeffersonian Judge* (Columbia, S.C., 1954), chap. 9.
51 Madison to Jefferson, June 27, 1823, in [Rives and Fendall, eds.], *Letters and Other Writings*, III, 326–327.

of his commentary of the late 1780s, moreover, he reminded Jefferson that no friend of stable government could overlook "its tendency to lessen a salutary veneration for an Instrument so often calling for such explanatory interpositions." If the Court's abuse of its proper constitutional trust became unbearable, Madison acknowledged, then "a resort to the nation for an amendment of the tribunal itself" would be in order. What he could not endorse, in theory or in practice, was Jefferson's imprudent call for "continual appeals" to what Madison certainly agreed was, in principle, the "ultimate arbiter" of constitutionality – the sovereign people assembled in popular conventions.[52]

Madison's larger understanding of the amendment process is immensely revealing precisely because it helped define a salutary mean between two undesirable extremes: an unjust government that derived its constitutional authority from a source other than the governed, and an unstable government that responded directly to the immediate, unfiltered urges of popular majorities. Part of the unexampled genius of the Constitution, Madison believed, was providing for its own amendment, especially in a way that encouraged innovation only when experience and sober reflection had clearly demonstrated the wisdom of change. If the awesome promise of the United States was to vindicate man's capacity not simply for self-government, but for stable and responsible self-government, this power of amendment was indeed the key to any prospects for long-term success. We might say that it represented for Madison the best means of honoring the republican spirit of Jefferson's notion of the sovereignty of the living generation while also acknowledging what his friend either denied altogether or ignored: the wholesome benefits of stability and of a necessary continuity across generations.

Thus while Madison put great stock in the Constitution's amending power, he did not see it as something that should be resorted to frequently or regularly; it was not to be, in short, what Jefferson's proposal hinted it might be, a mechanism for making constitutional whatever "the people" happened to will at a given moment. It was instead "the final resort within the purview of the Constitution" against the threat of "usurpations and abuses" on the part of the

52 *Ibid.*, 325, 327.

federal government, including the Supreme Court, as well as the means whereby new generations might make necessary and prudent adjustments to changed circumstances.[53] The constitutional guidelines for amendment – requiring two-thirds of Congress or of the states to initiate the process and three-quarters of the states to ratify – purposely discouraged what Madison regarded as a reckless indulgence of popular sovereignty. And he insisted, above all, that amendment of the Constitution – indeed, resolution of any constitutional issue – occur only after calm, principled, and prolonged deliberation, when "the paroxysms of party and popular excitements" had subsided and reason had overcome the madness of unrestrained passion.[54] As Hume had written, and Madison would have emphatically concurred, "some innovations must necessarily have place in every human institution; and it is happy where the enlightened genius of the age give these a direction to the side of reason, liberty, and justice."[55]

In 1827, therefore, Madison characteristically discouraged attempts "to amend the phraseology of the Constitution on a point essentially affecting its operative character" until "the state of the political atmosphere," which was then quite turbulent and unsettled, had substantially improved.[56] Hasty, indiscriminate use of the amending process, especially in times of great passion and partisan ambition, would only jeopardize the essential stability of the republic – and hence its momentous promise. "The attempts of party zeal, when pursuing its favorite object, to break into the domain of the Constitution," Madison solemnly warned, "cannot be too much

---

53 Madison to Edward Everett, Aug. 1830, *ibid.*, IV, 101. In this important letter, which Madison intended for the public as well as Everett, he reiterated other familiar concerns rooted in the 1780s. "To have referred every clashing decision" between the general and state governments "for a final decision to the States as parties to the Constitution," he noted, "would be attended with delays, with inconveniences, and with expenses amounting to a prohibition of the expedient, not to mention its tendency to impair the salutary veneration for a system requiring such frequent interpositions" (97–98).

54 Madison to John M. Patton (Confidential), Mar. 24, 1834, *ibid.*, 343.

55 Hume, "Of the Original Contract," *Essays*, 463.

56 Madison to Martin Van Buren, Mar. 13, 1827, in [Rives and Fendall, eds.], *Letters and Other Writings*, III, 569.

deplored." Indeed, ten years into retirement, the voice from Montpelier registered increasing concern "that constitutional questions" should, with so many Americans, "be merged in passions having inferior objects."[57]

III

As the last of the fathers, Madison was widely revered for his prominent role in the founding of the American republic. Well known for his leadership at the Philadelphia convention, his coauthorship of the *Federalist*, and his magnificent triumph over Patrick Henry at the Virginia ratifying convention, he appeared to many Americans to deserve the title of "Father of the Constitution," which Charles Jared Ingersoll first publicly bestowed on him in 1825.[58] Although Madison took little pleasure in (and certainly did nothing to encourage) such encomiums, it is hardly surprising that he was showered with requests for assistance in interpreting the Constitution or that he was generally happy to comply. Certainly no one was more eager than he to keep the past alive. "The infant periods of most nations are buried in silence, or veiled in fable," he reflected in 1819, "and perhaps the world may have lost but little which it need regret." But "the origin and outset of the American Republic contain lessons of which posterity ought not to be deprived."[59] He placed such emphasis on the past, especially on this critical period, because history offered more than wisdom; it constituted, he believed, a unique and indispensable source of stability in a sprawling and increasingly turbulent republic.

In the early 1820s, Madison undertook the onerous task of organizing and preparing for eventual publication his voluminous cache of papers, including his comprehensive records of the debates at the

---

57 Madison to C. J. Ingersoll, Nov. 17, 1827, *ibid.*, 601, and the deleted paragraph in Madison to Andrew Stevenson, May 2, 1827, Madison Papers, Library of Congress, series one (microfilm).

58 Irving Brant, *James Madison: Commander in Chief, 1812–1836* (Indianapolis and New York, 1961), 471.

59 Madison to Dr. William Eustis, July 6, 1819, in [Rives and Fendall, eds.], *Letters and Other Writings*, III, 140.

1787 convention. He also preserved his correspondence during these years more carefully than he had during earlier periods of his life. Many of his letters – especially those that considered constitutional issues and the nature of the Union – were addressed as much to posterity as to the nominal recipient. We might say, indeed, that Madison's self-conscious effort to preserve an eighteenth-century legacy became the burden of his retirement, which was in effect no retirement from public life at all. Claiming no monopoly on knowing the meaning of the Constitution, he nevertheless had wisdom to impart to a new generation that, in its better moments, sought his advice on how it might properly honor the legacy of the fathers.

Eventually, despite his resolve to stand aloof from all partisan squabbles, Madison publicized and defended his position on several divisive issues. He consistently shunned involvement in public debate over particular candidates; even his intimates found him, in the words of one, "habitually reserved on questions involving the relative merits or rival pretensions of public men, however unreserved in the expression of his opinions on principles only."[60] But when contests of principle, rather than personality, threatened the Constitution itself, Madison overcame his scruples and plunged into the public arena – and predictably became a figure of controversy rather than the venerable pundit he would have preferred to be. What Madison wished most to convey to Americans of the 1820s and 1830s was not so much the orthodox view of this or that constitutional issue – although he had firm, even insistent, views on many such matters – but rather a sound sense of how they should approach the general task of interpreting the Constitution. Once they understood the proper guidelines, appreciated what was required of them, and honored the spirit of their obligation, they could approach specific issues intelligently and responsibly on their own. Madison did not want to dictate orthodoxy of any kind to a free people. But he did want them to understand – and to accept – the wisdom and necessity of consulting the past, including the authority of the founding generation, for guidance.

Madison believed that the Constitution had derived its legitimacy

60 William Cabell Rives to George Bancroft, Nov. 22, 1836, William Cabell Rives Papers, Library of Congress, box 54.

– and thus its precise meaning – from the process of its adoption. Hence the only true guide to its interpretation in the 1820s and 1830s was history. Emphasizing "the propriety of resorting to the sense in which the Constitution was accepted and ratified by the nation" because "in that sense alone it is the legitimate Constitution," Madison insisted that without a proper grasp of how the document had been understood by the nation at the time of its ratification, accurate and just construction of its meaning forty years later was impossible.[61] This meant that modern interpreters had to reach beyond the text of the document to the historical facts that informed the text, which included understanding the evils that the new government had been meant to cure and the benefits it had been designed to realize. Thus the 1780s – the decade that had shaped Madison's own understanding of republicanism – assumed momentous importance for posterity as well. Given his participation in the events that culminated in the adoption of the Constitution, Madison was not likely to separate text and historical background. But now he conferred on a new generation, lacking his memories and experience, the solemn burden of historical research.

Madison consistently pointed this post-Revolutionary generation of Americans to the state ratifying conventions as the most important source of relevant information. For guidance in fixing the precise meaning of the Constitution, he wanted them to revert to the debates at these conventions and to the amendments that had been formally proposed by several of them – thirty-three by New York, twenty-six by North Carolina, twenty by Virginia, and smaller numbers by others.[62] Madison's position was straightforward: as the expression of popular sovereignty and consent, these conventions had given the Constitution whatever "validity and authority" it had, and it was therefore appropriate to interpret the document in their revealing light.[63] Indeed, Madison believed that the ratifying conventions were a better standard by which to judge original intent

61 Madison to H. Lee, June 25, 1824, in [Rives and Fendall, eds.], *Letters and Other Writings*, III, 442.

62 See Edward McNall Burns, *James Madison: Philosopher of the Constitution* (New Brunswick, N.J., 1938), 111–113.

63 Madison to N. P. Trist, Dec. 1831, in Hunt, ed., *Writings of Madison*, IX, 477.

than even the Philadelphia convention in which he had figured so prominently (and whose debates he had risked his fragile health to record). This scale of priority was, in fact, an old idea of his, one that he had clearly expressed in Congress in 1796. "Whatever veneration might be entertained for the body of men who formed our Constitution," he had then humbly declared, "the sense of that body could never be regarded as the oracular guide in expounding the Constitution. As the instrument came from them it was nothing more than the draft of a plan, nothing but a dead letter, until life and validity were breathed into it by the voice of the people, speaking through the several State Conventions." If Americans were searching for "the meaning of the instrument" beyond what Madison referred to as its "face," therefore, they would find the best clues to that meaning "not in the General Convention, which proposed, but in the State Conventions, which accepted and ratified the Constitution."[64] Twenty-five years later, when pressed to release his notes of the Philadelphia debates, the elder statesman reiterated the point in virtually identical language. If "a key" to the "legitimate meaning of the Instrument" were to be sought anywhere beyond the text itself, it would be found "not in the opinions or intentions of the body which planned and proposed the Constitution, but in the sense attached to it by the people in their respective State Conventions, where it received all the authority which it possesses."[65]

As the historian Donald O. Dewey has correctly observed, Madison's approach here may have made nice theoretical sense, but as a precise guide to interpretation it was riddled with practical difficulties. Where, for example, were Americans to find reliable transcripts of the debates at the state conventions, especially before Jonathan Elliot began in 1827 to compile and publish in convenient form the fragments that had survived? More important, how were they to determine from a morass of conflicting views and statements from so many different conventions what "the sense" of the ratifiers had actually been? And what precise meaning were they to attach to

64 Joseph Gales, comp., *Debates and Proceedings in the Congress of the United States, 1789–1824* (Washington, D.C., 1834–1856), 4th Cong., lst sess., 776.
65 Madison to Thomas Ritchie, Sept. 15, 1821, in [Rives and Fendall, eds.], *Letters and Other Writings*, III, 228.

the recommendatory amendments, especially those that never became part of the Constitution?[66] These were formidable questions.
Nevertheless, one important example can suggest not only the sense
in Madison's perspective but also its practicality, despite such
problems.

Madison loathed what is familiarly known as the "general welfare"
clause of the Constitution. Appearing near the beginning of Section
8 of Article I, preceding the delegation of specific powers to Congress, this clause states that "the Congress shall have Power To lay
and collect Taxes, Duties, Imposts and Excises, to pay the Debts
and provide for the common Defence and general Welfare of the
United States." By 1830, this clause was being construed as a substantive grant of power by many Americans who were eager to
enhance the authority of the federal government. By authorizing
Congress to collect funds for the "general welfare," they inferred,
these words in effect gave that body the broader power to legislate
for the public good. Madison objected so vehemently to this construction of the Constitution that he was, for once, actually eager to
publicize his views.[67]

He believed, of course, that such an interpretation effectively
transformed what everyone in the late 1780s had understood the
Constitution to create – a government of limited and specified
powers – into something quite different. And he relied on history to
buttress his position. The terms "common defence and general welfare," he contended, had simply not meant to the Founders what
many of their sons and grandsons now chose to read into them.
Copied from the Articles of Confederation – where obviously they
had not represented a substantive grant of power – they had been

66 Donald Odell Dewey, "The Sage of Montpelier: James Madison's Constitutional
   and Political Thought, 1817-1836," Ph.D. diss., University of Chicago, 1960.
   Dewey's excellent dissertation is the only thorough study of Madison's thought
   during the retirement years. Unfortunately, it is limited to his views of constitutional matters and neglects at least one important issue – slavery in the
   territories – within that area. Dewey published a brief but superb summary of
   his understanding of Madison's approach to constitutional interpretation; see
   "James Madison Helps Clio Interpret the Constitution," *American Journal of
   Legal History* 15 (1971), 38–55.
67 See Dewey, "Sage of Montpelier," 147–151.

"regarded in the new as in the old instrument, merely as general terms, explained and limited by the subjoined specifications, and therefore requiring no critical attention or studied precaution."[68] Had they been understood otherwise, Madison reasoned, surely they would have drawn the unrelenting fire of Antifederalists. But re-collection or perusal of the ratification debates would reveal that the clause had gone largely unnoticed by both defenders and opponents of the Constitution, and that when objections to it had been raised, the Federalists had been quick to dismiss them as fatuous. Indeed, in *Federalist* forty-one Madison had himself answered objections to this clause in precisely the same terms as he did now, over forty years later. Moreover, the elderly Madison provided a specific example of how second- and third-generation interpreters should use the recom-mendatory amendments of the ratifying conventions to fix the meaning of the Constitution: among the many proposed amend-ments that had been clearly designed to protect the states from federal power, none had mentioned the general welfare clause. This conspicuous lack of concern, Madison concluded, was empirical proof, if further proof were needed, that the terms in question had never been construed "to convey the comprehensive power which, taken literally, they express."[69]

As this debate over the general welfare clause suggested, there were other ways than relying on history and the explicit or inferred sense of the Founders to approach the challenge of constitutional interpretation. One likely alternative was for later generations to rely solely on textual exegesis, or simple analysis of the meaning of the language of the Constitution. This approach Madison em-phatically rejected as profoundly dangerous. He believed that histo-ry must take priority over the arguments of present-day theoreti-cians who scrutinized text alone, because history provided, in addition to legitimacy, the only viable basis for stable government under the Constitution. If the past were not the guide to interpret-ing the Constitution, he argued in 1824, "there can be no security for a consistent and stable, more than for a faithful, exercise of its

68 Madison to Andrew Stevenson, Nov. 27, 1830, in [Rives and Fendall, eds.], *Letters and Other Writings*, IV, 126, 121-139.
69 *Ibid.*, 122.

powers."[70] Madison had watched the meaning of words, even those of classical derivation, change so much and so quickly during his lifetime that, as he later commented to Harriet Martineau, he held out little hope for the stability of languages, all of which were liable to innovations from causes "inseparable from the nature of man and the progress of society."[71] Indeed, if the meaning of the Constitution's text were "sought in the changeable meaning of the words composing it," it was evident to Madison that "the shape and attributes of the government" would be profoundly altered. By analogy, he exclaimed, "what a metamorphosis would be produced in the code of law if all its ancient phraseology were to be taken in the modern sense!" Linguistic changes were proceeding so rapidly, in fact, that a scant thirty-five years after its adoption, the Constitution was already "undergoing interpretations unknown to its founders." Without the "unbiased" inquiries into "the history of its origin and adoption" that Madison demanded, its meaning would therefore become as mutable, and the government itself as unstable, as the language in which the document had been couched.[72]

Madison's fundamental concern for stability shaped other aspects of his approach to interpreting the Constitution as well. He put great stock in the force of precedent, for example. Given his broadly historical approach, it is not surprising that he valued the actions of the first few Congresses – which contained many members who had been delegates to the ratifying conventions – as a reliable expression of the Founders' intent. But Madison also made a strong case for honoring precedents that had been established during succeeding

70 Madison to H. Lee, June 25, 1824, *ibid.*, III, 442.
71 The quotation is from Madison to Converse Sherman, Mar. 10, 1826, *ibid.*, 519. For the reference to Martineau, see the prologue to this volume.
72 Madison to H. Lee, June 25, 1824, *ibid.*, 442. See also, for example, Madison to Andrew Stevenson, Mar. 25, 1826, *ibid.*, 520–522, and Madison to James Robertson, Apr. 20, 1831, *ibid.*, IV, 171-172. For a recent discussion of some of these issues in the context of the controversy in the 1980s over so-called "original intent," see H. Jefferson Powell, "The Original Understanding of Original Intent," *Harvard Law Review* 98 (1985), 885–948. For a more brief and less technical, but far superior, analysis of Madison on this matter, see Jack N. Rakove, "Mr. Meese, Meet Mr. Madison," *The Atlantic* 258 (Dec. 1986), 77–86.

years, especially by Congress with the acquiescence of the other branches of the government. Indeed, one of his cardinal rules of interpretation was to respect the authority of "early, deliberate and continued practice under the Constitution."[73] For Madison, a single act did not establish a binding precedent, especially if it were what he called a spurious "midnight" precedent — part of the customary flurry of legislation that came at the close of a congressional session, when laws were too often rushed to passage without careful and reasoned deliberation. "In resorting to legal precedents as sanctions to power," he observed in 1819, "the distinctions should ever be strictly attended to between such as take place under transitory impressions, or without full examination and deliberation, and such as pass with solemnities and repetitions sufficient to imply a concurrence of the judgment and the will of those who, having granted the power, have the ultimate right to explain the grant."[74] In other words, when measures reflecting a particular understanding of the Constitution were uniformly sustained by successive legislatures, and their constitutionality openly debated and acceded to, especially by other divisions and levels of government, such legislation constituted binding precedent for subsequent generations and governments. If, on the contrary, new legislatures and presidents were allowed to ignore such precedents and merely determine for themselves what was constitutional, the likely outcome would be confusion, uncertainty, and disorder. Here as elsewhere in his political theory, Madison feared above all the onset of that insidious spiral of popular disillusionment and instability, in both the laws and the regime, that had haunted him since the 1780s.

Madison's respect for constitutional precedent is best revealed in his consideration of a national bank, because here precedent obliged him to change his own public position. When Alexander Hamilton had first proposed a Bank of the United States in 1791, Congressman Madison had vigorously disputed its constitutionality. During his retirement he doubtless continued to believe, as an abstract

---

73 Madison to Martin L. Hurlbert, May 1830, in Hunt, ed., *Writings of Madison*, IX, 372.

74 Madison to Spencer Roane, May 6, 1821, in [Rives and Fendall, eds.], *Letters and Other Writings*, III, 221.

proposition, that the framers and ratifiers had never intended to confer such a power on Congress. But this belief had been superseded, in effect overruled, by the force of events. Madison understood that the Bank had been scrutinized by Congress in the early 1790s before it was established, with its constitutionality openly debated; that it had operated for the subsequent twenty years with annual recognition of its existence by Congress; that it had even been extended into new states; and above all that it had received during its operation "the entire acquiescence of all the local authorities."[75] As president, therefore, he acknowledged what had indisputably been, by any meaningful standard, "early, deliberate, and continued practice under the Constitution." When he vetoed a bill to recharter a national bank in 1815, he did so explicitly on expedient, not constitutional, grounds, informing Congress that he waived the question of constitutionality "as being precluded . . . by repeated recognitions under varied circumstances of the validity of such an institution in acts of the legislative, executive, and judicial branches of the Government, accompanied by indications, in different modes, of a concurrence of the general will of the nation."[76] And a year later he happily signed into law what he thought was a better bill, which created the Second Bank of the United States.

During his retirement the Bank suddenly became enmeshed once again in constitutional controversy, and Madison had to remind his countrymen — some of whom chided him for his apparent inconsistency — that precedents must always overrule personal opinion, even that of a president. To declare a national bank unconstitutional in the 1830s, he said, was "a defiance of all the obligations derived from a course of precedents amounting to the requisite evidence of the national judgment and intention." Even before Andrew Jackson's veto on constitutional grounds, as congressional debate heated up, Madison framed the issue in resonant terms that recall his most salient and deep-seated concerns. "Let it, then, be left to the decision of every intelligent and candid judge," he declared in 1831, "which, on the whole, is most to be relied on for the true and safe

---

75 Madison to Charles J. Ingersoll, June 25, 1831, *ibid.*, IV, 183–187.
76 See "Veto Message," Jan. 30, 1815, in Hunt, ed., *Writings of Madison*, VIII, 327.

construction of a constitution; that which has the uniform sanction of successive legislative bodies, through a period of years and under the varied ascendancy of parties; or that which depends upon the opinions of every new Legislature, heated as it may be by the spirit of party, eager in the pursuit of some favourite object, or led astray by the eloquence and address of popular statesmen, themselves, perhaps, under the influence of the same misleading causes."[77] Just as he generally relied on the authority of history as an essential source of constitutional stability, so too did Madison depend on the binding force of cumulative precedent.

✳

When he made history and precedent the touchstones of constitutional interpretation, Madison reasserted the wise necessity of the generational continuity that he had defended in his correspondence with Jefferson at the time of the founding. He sought, furthermore, to anchor an evolving – perhaps drifting – republic to his own generation's heroic accomplishment. The Founding Fathers had been inspired by unborn generations in their quest for glory; they had viewed posterity as their audience, as well as their beneficiaries.[78] Now posterity must not lose sight of them. Without deference to the Constitution as it had been understood by those who had created it, Madison wondered, what would prevent the government from becoming whatever happened to serve, from one moment to the next, the people's sense of their own immediate convenience? As history amply revealed (and as David Hume, especially, had warned), reason and principle were generally no match for expedience and interest, for faction and intrigue. And if the government became as mutable as popular opinion – and vulnerable, as well, to the demagogic influence of ambitious partisans – who could honestly say that the battle of the 1780s had been won?

77 Madison to Charles J. Ingersoll, June 25, 1831, in [Rives and Fendall, eds.], Letters and Other Writings, IV, 186. See also Madison to Charles E. Haynes, Feb. 25, 1831, ibid., 164–165.
78 See Adair, in Colbourn, ed., Fame and Founding Fathers, 3–26.

Honoring Madison's prescription for a stable republic placed an onerous burden on a self-governing people who worshipped the founders but jealously guarded their own sovereignty. His way required humility and self-restraint – above all, a voluntary deference to the authority of ancestral intent – in a culture that appeared now to celebrate the autonomy of the passionate, untutored individual, liberated from the burdens of institutional restraint, and the sovereign authority of Jefferson's living generation, free from the tyranny of the past.[79] Madison's constitutional approach demanded patient, even painstaking historical research, rather than impulsive and self-serving polemics. And he clearly hoped to keep a vital past alive, at least in part, through the force of his personal influence. Much to his disappointment, if not surprise, he found ample cause to doubt his countrymen's respect for the integrity of the past – and for him.

79 For a perceptive portrayal of this dimension of American culture during the Jacksonian era, see, especially, John William Ward, *Andrew Jackson: Symbol for an Age* (New York, 1955).

3. Retrospect and Prospect:
Congress and the Perils of Popular Government

IN THE SUMMER of 1821, Madison's recollections of the founding of the republic and of his own career assumed new significance with the publication of Robert Yates's notes of the debates in the Constitutional Convention. Yates, who had ascended by the time of his death in 1801 to the position of chief justice of the New York state judicial system, had been a fierce Antifederalist. As a delegate to the convention, he had attended for less than seven of the sixteen weeks before departing in disgust, never to return. But his incomplete notes were the first "record" of the Philadelphia gathering beyond its formal proceedings to reach the public. Deeply disturbed by interpretations of the Constitution that had surfaced during the recent crisis over admitting Missouri to the Union, Madison had already begun the arduous task of organizing his own papers. The unexpected appearance of Yates's notes prompted him to redouble his efforts. Friendly correspondents pressed Madison for his opinion of the new publication and for a disclosure of his intentions regarding the voluminous, extremely valuable papers he was rumored to possess.

In reply, Madison attributed the "egregious errors" that he found in Yates's notes to the unavoidable effects of the New Yorker's well-known partisan "prejudices" against strengthening the federal government.[1] Acutely suspicious of the motives and purposes of his fellow delegates, Yates had naturally construed their utterances in the light of those prejudices.[2] Although Madison did not question

---

1 Madison to John G. Jackson, Dec. 27, 1821, in [William C. Rives and Philip R. Fendall, eds.], *Letters and Other Writings of James Madison* (Philadelphia, 1865), III, 244.
2 See, for instance, Madison's observations to "Mr. Gales" on August 26, 1821: "Besides misapprehensions of the ear, therefore, the attention of the note-taker

Yates's integrity – he had doubtless attempted in good faith, Madison said, to record what he had heard – the Virginian categorically dismissed the value of his colleague's fragmentary, "erroneous," and "mutilated" transcriptions of the speeches of the delegates. Modern scholars now know more than Madison did at the time: prior to publication, Yates's manuscript notes had been heavily edited, in fact distorted, by none other than Edmund ("Citizen") Genêt for the express purpose of embarrassing Madison.[3] But despite the unreliability of Yates's fragmentary report, Madison also warned his correspondents in 1821 not to expect prompt publication of his fuller, more reliable notes. Their arrangement would take some time, and he believed for a variety of reasons that their publication should probably be posthumous.[4]

Madison would stick to this position, despite the prodding of his friends. Some clearly believed that Yates's "mutilated" renderings of Madison's own speeches were a potential source of considerable embarrassment, because they suggested, to put it mildly, that the Virginian had been a far more thorough and fervent nationalist in 1787 than in subsequent phases of his career. Indeed, within a decade, extreme advocates of state rights were using Yates's notes to ridicule Madison for his inconsistency and to discredit him as a reliable authority on the meaning of the Constitution.[5] Madison saw no need in 1821 to publicly explain or defend his posture at the convention (or, for that matter, the consistency of his long career), but he was moved to address, at least privately, the misleading inferences that might be drawn from Yates's notes. When his brother-in-law, John G. Jackson, urged him to answer Yates by presenting his own notes to the public (now desperately in need of their

---

would materially be warped, as far, at least, as an upright mind could be warped, to an unfavorable understanding of what was said in opposition to the prejudices felt." *Ibid.*, 227.

3 See James H. Hutson, "Robert Yates's Notes on the Constitutional Convention of 1787: Citizen Genêt's Edition," *Quarterly Journal of the Library of Congress* 35 (1978), 173–182.

4 Madison to Thomas Ritchie, Sept. 15, 1821, in [Rives and Fendall, eds.], *Letters and Other Writings*, III, 228–229. Madison's use of the terms "erroneous" and "mutilated" to describe Yates's transcriptions occurs in this letter.

5 See, for example, "Mutius" in the *Richmond Enquirer*, Aug. 20, 1833.

light and guidance, Jackson said), Madison responded with an immensely revealing retrospective commentary on both the history of the republic and his understanding of the Constitution.

Jackson clumsily tried to reassure Madison that he should not feel embarrassed if Yates's notes were essentially correct in portraying his desire, as a framer, "to infuse more vigor, & strength into the national government" than it later possessed. After all, recent experience had fully convinced Jackson – who had served in Congress during the War of 1812 – that the Madison of 1787 had been right; in other words, that "the Union has more to fear from inadequacy of power in the head, & anarchy in the members; than from every other danger combined."[6] Madison did not need his brother-in-law's comforting words. Indeed, he felt no urge to apologize for the strongly nationalistic views that he and many other delegates had brought to Philadelphia in 1787. He deemed it essential, however, to place those views firmly in the context of the times and also to relate them to subsequent events.

Most of the delegates, Madison explained to Jackson, had developed "a profound impression" of "the necessity of binding the States together by a strong Constitution." This impression came from several sources: the experience of ancient and modern confederacies (including their own), the shock of Shays' armed insurrection in Massachusetts, and above all from "the gross and disreputable inequalities which had been prominent in the internal administrations of most of the States." This alarming "aspect of things" had appeared to constitute a crisis that would determine nothing less than the fate of the American Revolution, or, as Madison revealingly put it, "whether the American experiment was to be a blessing to the world, or to blast forever the hopes which the republican cause had inspired." Many delegates even feared – not without cause, Madison argued – that crypto-monarchists in "some quarters" of America hoped to prolong the confusion and disorder in order to ensure the demise of popular government. It had been this urgent sense of crisis, Madison explained to Jackson, that had aroused among so many delegates the disposition, fairly if imperfectly captured in

6 Jackson to Madison, Dec. 9, 1821, James Madison Papers, Library of Congress, series two (microfilm).

87

Yates's notes, "to give to a new system all the vigour consistent with Republican principles."[7]

Speaking for himself, Madison insisted that "from the first moment of maturing a political opinion down to the present" he had "never ceased to be a votary of the principle of self-government." In fact, he had been so anxious to rescue those principles from the abundant dangers confronting them in 1787 that he had been especially eager upon arrival in Philadelphia "to give to a Government resting on that foundation as much energy as would insure the requisite stability and efficacy." It was possible, he conceded, "that in some instances this consideration may have been allowed a weight greater than subsequent reflection within the Convention, or the actual operation of the Government, would sanction." This was a telling admission. Because he had learned both from his fellow delegates and from later experience, Madison's perspective had not necessarily remained what it had been at the opening of the convention.[8] And even more important, he had been obligated, as had all the framers, to accommodate his original views to the sovereign will of the people as that will had been manifested in the ratifying conventions. "Whatever might have been the opinions entertained in forming the Constitution," he reminded Jackson in 1821, it immediately became "the duty of all to support it in its true meaning, as understood *by the nation* at the time of its ratification."[9]

Madison was by no means suggesting that his own views had undergone wholesale revision, or that he and the other delegates had been compelled to abandon their fundamental principles. Rather, he averred that he had honored the spirit of his commitment to popular government by deferring when necessary to the sovereign authority

7 Madison to Jackson, Dec. 27, 1821, in [Rives and Fendall, eds.], *Letters and Other Writings*, III, 244.

8 *Ibid.*, 244–245. For a telling analysis of the evolution of Madison's views during and just after the convention, see especially Lance Banning, "The Practicable Sphere of a Republic: James Madison, the Constitutional Convention, and the Emergence of Revolutionary Federalism," in Richard Beeman et al., eds., *Beyond Confederation: Origins of the Constitution and American National Identity* (Chapel Hill, N.C., 1987), 162–187.

9 Madison to Jackson, Dec. 27, 1821, in [Rives and Fendall, eds.], *Letters and Other Writings*, III, 245. The emphasis is Madison's.

of those who, in debating and ultimately accepting the work of the convention, had clarified and in fact established the meaning of the new regime. "No one felt this obligation more than I have done," he added, "and there are few, perhaps, whose ultimate and deliberate opinions on the merits of the Constitution accord in a greater degree with that obligation." If Madison's critics drew the ironic inference from Yates's notes that his career reflected the inconsistency and instability he so much feared, they simply missed the point. As Madison declared to Jackson, his career had to be understood in the light of the founding of the republic: the "true and fair construction" of the Constitution had been fixed during the ratification process, and departures from that construction "have always given me pain, and always experienced my opposition when called for."[10]

And the need for such opposition, Madison told Jackson, had surfaced almost immediately. At the outset of the new government, he had introduced amendments in Congress which, by addressing the concerns of Antifederalists who had decried the absence of a federal bill of rights, were "in conformity to the known desires of the body of the people." These amendments were especially significant in Madison's eyes precisely because they fulfilled "the pledges of many, particularly myself, when vindicating and recommending the Constitution" during the struggle for ratification. He never forgot his daunting experience at the 1788 convention in Richmond; the Federalists' razor-thin margin of victory there had reflected the strength, among many delegates whom Madison greatly respected, of the fear that excessive power would accrue to the general government. During his campaign for election to the new government, moreover, he had deferred to the obvious desire of his prospective constituents for the addition of a bill of rights. Madison therefore regarded efforts in the first Congress to defeat his proposed amendments – which he described as "safe, if not necessary" and "politic, if not obligatory" – as "an occurrence not a little ominous."

And indeed, there soon followed "indications of political tenets" and "the abandonment of all rules" in interpreting the Constitution that threatened to transform the new government "into something very different from its legitimate character as the offspring of the

10 *Ibid.*

national will."[11] Thus Madison's stint as an opposition leader in the 1790s was hardly an unprincipled or expedient reversal of his nationalist perspective as a framer; as he clearly suggested to Jackson, it was instead a measure of his principled commitment to the founding of the new regime as an expression of popular sovereignty. Contrary to his stipulation, some public leaders – led by his former ally, the indomitable Alexander Hamilton – had boldly construed the Constitution according to their own private views and preferences rather than in the light of the public will. We might say that Madison had never embraced Hamilton's particular strain of nationalism anyway, since it was attached to a system of political economy that he had always found objectionable.[12] But more important, Madison had not doubted in the early 1790s – nor did he doubt in 1821 – that the people had ratified a very different regime from the one that the secretary of the treasury and his "loose construction" allies soon began to tease from the text of the Constitution. Less than two years before his death, when pressed by Nicholas Trist to explain why he had deserted his *Federalist* ally in the early 1790s, Madison turned the question on its head. "Colonel Hamilton deserted me," he reflected, "from his wishing to . . . administer the Government . . . into what he thought it ought to be."[13]

Jumping from the past to the present in his comments to Jackson in 1821, Madison lamented that such "constructive innovations" in the meaning of the Constitution had not "altogether ceased." It remained to be seen, however, where the greatest threat to the delicate balance established in the late 1780s lay. "Whether the Constitution, as it has divided the powers of Government between the States in their separate and in their united capacities, tends to an

---

11 *Ibid.*
12 See especially two articles by Lance Banning: "James Madison and the Nationalists, 1780–1783," *William and Mary Quarterly*, 3d ser., 40 (1983), 227–255, and "The Hamiltonian Madison: A Reconsideration," *Virginia Magazine of History and Biography* 92 (1984), 3–28. Banning argues, on the whole persuasively, that Madison's misgivings about Hamilton's and Robert Morris's "Court" approach to political economy were expressed as early as 1783.
13 From "Memoranda" by N. P. Trist, Sept. 27, 1834, in Max Farrand, ed., *The Records of the Federal Convention of 1787*, rev. ed., (New Haven, Conn., 1937), III, 534.

oppressive aggrandizement of the General Government, or to an anarchical independence of the State Governments," he mused to Jackson, "is a problem which time alone can absolutely determine." Madison would have ample time during the remainder of his retirement to ponder this matter, parry threats from both directions, and arrive at an unequivocal answer to his question. In 1821 he could only observe that there had been "epochs when the General Government was evidently drawing a disproportion of power into its vortex" – an obvious reference to the 1790s – as well as others "when States threatened to do the same," adding that "at the present moment" it seemed that "both are aiming at encroachments, each on the other."[14]

He told Jackson, however, that "one thing" seemed "certain" to him: although the danger of the balance tilting too far in favor of the federal government had not disappeared, it had changed fundamentally in character since the crisis of the 1790s. "In the present condition and temper of the community," he observed, "the General Government cannot long succeed in encroachments contravening the will of a majority of the States and of the people." The democratization of both politics and political culture in the United States, accelerated if not caused by the Jeffersonian insurgency of the 1790s, had made the general government so responsive to those majorities that the threat of minority usurpation at the national level had effectively disappeared. As the "Revolution of 1800" had proved, relief from the impositions of a power-hungry minority faction was promptly secured through the republican principle of mobilizing popular opinion through the electoral system. But this acute sensitivity of the general government to the will of the people had generated its own danger, and added a new twist to the familiar problem of an undue concentration of national power. If "the powers of the General Government" were now to be "carried to unconstitutional lengths," Madison declared, this evil would be "the result of a majority of the States and of the people, actuated by some impetuous feeling, or some real or supposed interest, overruling the minority" – a very different situation from the 1790s, when the uncon-

14 Madison to Jackson, Dec. 27, 1821, in [Rives and Fendall, eds.], *Letters and Other Writings*, III, 245–246.

stitutional extension of federal power had resulted temporarily from "successful attempts by the General Government to overpower" both state and popular majorities.[15] Indeed, Madison's longstanding fear of "impetuous feelings" and unrestrained popular majorities, rooted in the 1780s as so many of his republican concerns were, had been extended by the early 1820s from the state to the federal level – and above all, to the United States Congress itself.

I

On March 2, 1817, two days before President Madison's second term expired, a group of Republican congressmen called on the chief executive to tender their congratulations and official farewell. But what had promised to be a pleasant formality on a quiet Sunday in Washington took an unexpected turn. John C. Calhoun had taken leave of the president and started for the door when he was abruptly called back. Madison took him aside and broke the news privately: as one of his last acts in office he intended to veto, on constitutional grounds, a bill currently before him that the South Carolinian had patiently shepherded through the House of Representatives. Calhoun averred that he was taken entirely by surprise, since he had assumed the administration's support of the so-called Bonus Bill. This bill proposed to set aside the one-and-a-half-million-dollar bonus paid to the federal government by the newly chartered Second Bank of the United States, as well as all future dividends from the government's stock in the Bank, as a fund for constructing roads and canals. The young congressman from South Carolina was not the only person in Washington to be stunned by the president's decision, which was officially conveyed to Congress the following day. Speaker of the House Henry Clay later claimed that "no circumstance, not even an earthquake that should have swallowed up half this city, could have excited more surprise."[16]

15 *Ibid.*, 246.
16 This account is derived from Charles M. Wiltse, *John C. Calhoun: Nationalist, 1782–1828* (Indianapolis and New York, 1944), 137, and Norman K. Risjord, *The Old Republicans: Southern Conservatism in the Age of Jefferson* (New York

This famous veto was not a sudden decision and, from Madison's perspective at least, should not have occasioned surprise at all. He assumed that he had made his position on internal improvements abundantly clear in several of his annual messages to Congress, including the one three months earlier that had spurred Calhoun into action.[17] He had repeatedly urged Congress to attend to "the great importance of establishing throughout our country the roads and canals which can best be executed under the national authority." Indeed, in 1815 Madison had offered nothing less than a glowing paean to roads and canals in his first postwar message. "No objects within the circle of political economy so richly repay the expense bestowed on them; there are none the utility of which is more universally ascertained and acknowledged; none that do more honor to the governments whose wise and enlarged patriotism duly appreciates them." Nor was there any country, he added, in more need of such improvements than the United States. He especially noted, in this connection, their salutary "political effect" in "bringing and binding more closely together the various parts of our extended confederacy." Although individual states had already begun "with a laudable enterprise and emulation" to undertake such projects, Madison urged Congress to recognize the importance of "similar undertakings, requiring a national jurisdiction and national means," which alone could systematically complete "so inestimable a work."[18] That the president enthusiastically supported the idea of a federal system of improvements in transportation and communication, in short, was hardly in doubt.[19]

But apparently Calhoun and many others failed to appreciate the

and London, 1965), 168–174, from the latter of which the Clay quote is taken (p. 173).

17 Madison's Eighth Annual Message, Dec. 3, 1816, in James D. Richardson, ed., *A Compilation of the Messages and Papers of the Presidents, 1789–1897* (Washington, D.C., 1899), I, 576.

18 Madison's Seventh Annual Message, Dec. 5, 1815, *ibid.*, 567–568.

19 Madison's support of such improvements, promoted at both the state and federal levels, would continue unabated for the next twenty years. For typical statements of his enthusiasm in the 1820s, see Madison to Joshua Gilpin, Mar. 11, 1822, and Madison to Mathew Carey, May 12, 1825, in [Rives and Fendall, eds.], *Letters and Other Writings*, III, 262, 489–490.

significance of the constitutional caveats that Madison invariably appended to his encomiums on internal improvements. In the 1815 message he had concluded his discussion in genial but somewhat cryptic words, with the "happy reflection" that "any defect of constitutional authority which may be encountered can be supplied in a mode which the Constitution itself has providently pointed out."[20] A year later he muddied the waters a bit more by inviting the legislators to attend to "the expediency of exercising their existing powers, and, where necessary, of resorting to the prescribed mode of enlarging them, in order to effectuate a comprehensive system of roads and canals."[21] In both cases he believed that he had adverted specifically to the need for a constitutional amendment. Such an amendment was the proper means of supplementing Congress's existing powers – including its power to establish post roads, as well as its "uncontested authority" over the federal territories, under which rubric some improvements, perhaps including the Cumberland Road that Congress had provided for beginning in 1796, might fall – to encompass the kind of comprehensive system that the president now advocated. Madison later argued that his language in these messages had not been "more carefully guarded against" false inferences because he relied "on a presumed notoriety of my opinion on the subject."[22]

Nevertheless, it is not difficult to sympathize with Calhoun's surprise. The tone of Madison's messages, not to mention his enthusiastic support of a national bank and a higher tariff, understandably conveyed the impression that Hamilton's old adversary had accommodated his earlier views to the lessons of experience, as well as to the exigencies of unprecedented geographical and economic expansion. The president articulated an expansive spirit of postwar nationalism, premised in large measure on the need to rectify the conditions that had made the republic woefully unprepared for war

20 Seventh Annual Message, Dec. 5, 1815, in Richardson, ed., *Messages and Papers*, I, 568.
21 Eighth Annual Message, Dec. 3, 1816, *ibid.*, 576.
22 See, for instance, Madison's explanation in his letter to Edward Livingston, Apr. 17, 1824, in [Rives and Fendall, eds.], *Letters and Other Writings*, III, 436–437.

in 1812 and subsequently hard pressed to meet the war's demands. Indeed, Madison's first postwar message had been sufficiently bold and forceful to alarm a small group of conservative Republicans, who feared that it squinted toward national "consolidation." Everyone knew that the president had waived the question of the Bank's constitutionality as resolved by precedent, and during the debates over a protective tariff in 1816 constitutionality was not even an issue. Why was there reason to think that he would suddenly choke on a bill that reflected the same broad vision and concerns? Even if nationalistic Republicans like Calhoun were aware of Madison's constitutional reservations about internal improvements, they doubtless hoped that the force of congressional opinion would override his personal reservations and change his mind – or push him, perhaps, to accede to the manifest will of the people as it was expressed through their representatives.[23]

If such were their hopes, however, they were not only wrong, they inadvertently dramatized the essence of Madison's rejection of the bill. His veto reflected two different but closely connected levels of concern. First, unlike its supporters, Madison saw important distinctions between this bill and the Bank and tariff legislation that he had recently approved. The constitutionality of the tariff, as Madison would strenuously argue during the second decade of his retirement (and as I shall discuss in depth in the next chapter), was as indisputable thirty years after the adoption of the Constitution as it had been in 1789; and as we have seen, he maintained that open debate and cumulative precedent had resolved any ambiguity about a national bank. But there was no comparable means of establishing the constitutionality of internal improvements that Madison could accept. If the Constitution were properly construed – that is, as it had been understood by the nation at the time of its adoption – all doubt and uncertainty vanished. None of the clauses that the bill's proponents pointed to as justification – from "the power to regulate commerce among the several States" to the alleged (but spurious) power to provide for the "common defense and general welfare" –

23 For sound analysis of these and related issues, see David John Russo, "The Southern Republicans and American Political Nationalism, 1815-1825," unpublished Ph.D. dissertation, Yale University, 1966, chap. 1.

had been understood in the late 1780s to confer upon Congress the authority to create a national system of roads and canals. Madison recalled that even Hamilton, in his 1790 report on the Bank, had conceded that canals "were beyond the sphere of Federal legislation." He also remembered that such a power had been "more than once proposed" in the Philadelphia convention (and, he might have added, supported by him) but "rejected from an apprehension, chiefly, that it might prove an obstacle to the adoption of the Constitution" – or, as Madison put it on another occasion, "negatived, either as improper to be vested in Congress, or as a power not likely to be yielded by the States." Surely the delegates had been right; had "the construction which brings canals within the scope of commercial regulations" been "advanced or admitted by the advocates of the Constitution in the State conventions," Madison declared, it would have been "impossible" to secure ratification.[24] Moreover, for a variety of reasons that he found persuasive, Madison emphatically denied that, in this case, constitutionality had been established by precedent, as it had with the Bank.[25] No doubt his determination not to provide another spurious "midnight" precedent on this issue buttressed his decision to veto the bill that Congress now placed before him during the end-of-the-session rush.

To this extent, then, Madison's veto reflected his principled commitment to the historically based standards of constitutional interpretation that he would defend throughout his retirement. Appropriately, he was as disturbed by the broad approach of the bill's supporters as he was by their specific arguments. Ten months after he left office, he received a letter from a young Virginia congressman, Henry St. George Tucker, who was preparing a formal committee report that would deny the need for Madison's proposed amendment. Tucker was suitably deferential to the venerable patriarch – after all, he told Madison, he was indebted to him "for every principle of Constitutional law which in early life was im-

---

24 Madison to Reynolds Chapman, Jan. 6, 1831, in [Rives and Fendall, eds.], *Letters and Other Writings*, IV, 148, 149, and Madison to Livingston, Apr. 17, 1824, *ibid.*, III, 435.
25 For an elaboration of Madison's rejection of the precedents argument, see, above all, Madison to President Monroe, Dec. 27, 1817, *ibid.*, 54–57.

pressed upon my mind." But if Tucker was anxious to dispel the impression of disrespect in his overt deviation "from the lessons of my preceptor," Madison's correspondingly polite response was not without the hint of a hard edge.[26] Their difference of opinion, of course, did not diminish his esteem for Tucker's talents or his confidence in the younger man's motives. Madison also said that he had too much respect for "the right and the duty of the Representatives of the people to examine for themselves the merits of all questions before them" to expect – or to want – Tucker's blind deference to his personal authority. But the irony in Madison's acknowledgment of his own peculiar "bias" in interpreting the Constitution – a bias that a younger generation clearly did not share – was not especially subtle. If Madison respected Tucker's right to think for himself, he did not respect the careless abandonment of principle in his approach to determining constitutionality. As he wrote, "I am not unaware that my belief, not to say knowledge, of the views of those who proposed the Constitution, and, what is of more importance, my deep impressions as to the views of those who bestowed on it the stamp of authority, may influence my interpretation of the Instrument. On the other hand," he was quick to add, "it is not impossible that those who consult the instrument without a danger of that bias, may be exposed to an equal one in their anxiety to find in its text an authority for a particular measure of great apparent utility."[27]

Madison's thinly veiled reference to Tucker's opportunistic confounding of utility and constitutionality points to the second, broader, and more urgent level of his concern in vetoing the Bonus Bill. This dimension of his response has been lost on virtually all modern scholars.[28] He perceived nothing less than a threat to constitutional government itself. Several weeks before the veto, when the president first heard of the bill, his incredulity conveyed the

26 Tucker to Madison, Dec. 18, 1817, James Madison Papers, Library of Congress, series one (microfilm).
27 Madison to Tucker, Dec. 23, 1817, in [Rives and Fendall, eds.], *Letters and Other Writings*, III, 53–54.
28 For the most recent example, see John Lauritz Larson, "'Bind the Republic Together': The National Union and the Struggle for a System of Internal Improvements," in *Journal of American History* 74 (1987), 377–385.

97

intensity of his concern. "Another Bill has gone to the Senate which I have not seen," he remarked to Jefferson, "and of a very extraordinary character, if it has been rightly stated to me. The object of it, is to compass by law only an authority over roads and Canals."[29] For Madison, indeed, this was the crux of the matter. Congress was not simply making a poor or faulty judgment about the constitutionality of a single issue; it was experimenting with a new approach to establishing constitutionality and perforce threatening to transform the character of America's republican system.

The most blatant manifestation of the threat, of course, arose from the tendency of some congressmen, including Calhoun, to invoke the "common defense and general welfare" clause and to claim for Congress the right to legislate on all matters, including internal improvements, that it deemed relevant to the promotion of these lofty national ends. Since these broad terms embraced "every object and act within the purview of a legislative trust," Madison argued in his veto message that such a view of the Constitution gave to Congress "a general power of legislation" instead of the "defined and limited one" clearly intended by those who had drafted and ratified the document. Obviously this approach represented a dangerous encroachment of the federal government on the legitimate powers of the states. But even more important, perhaps, it allowed Congress to judge the constitutionality of its own acts by making mere "policy and expediency" the relevant standard of judgment. If Congress could decide which measures were necessary to promote the common defense and general welfare, and if this judgment became the accepted basis of constitutionality, then obviously Congress could, in effect, declare constitutional whatever it pleased. The laws of Congress would thereby be placed not only above the laws of the states, but also above the rulings of the Supreme Court and indeed above the Constitution itself. "Inasmuch as questions relating to the general welfare, being questions of policy and expediency, are unsusceptible of judicial cognizance and decision," Madison concluded, there would be no effective judicial checks or limits on

29 Madison to Jefferson, Feb. 15, 1817, in [Rives and Fendall, eds.], *Letters and Other Writings*, III, 35.

congressional power.[30] If Congress succeeded in establishing the dangerous precedent contained in the Bonus Bill, Americans might be left with something that could be considered a republican form of government; but it would be something very different from what Madison believed his generation had established in response to the crisis of the confederation period. Indeed, Madison's analysis ultimately pointed to the same problem that his friend George Thomson would bemoan when contemplating the antics of the Kentucky legislature in the early 1820s: the failure of a new generation of republicans to respect, or perhaps even to understand, the essential distinction between fundamental law, as expressed in a constitution, and derivative law, as made by legislatures in pursuance of that fundamental law.[31]

Madison's concern intensified a few years later when even the Supreme Court appeared to him to endorse this dangerous, innovative approach to establishing constitutionality. The Marshall Court's decision in the landmark case of *McCulloch vs. Maryland* in 1819 – in which it upheld the right of Congress to incorporate a national bank, even though such a right was not explicitly stated in the Constitution – disturbed Madison for any number of reasons. He agreed, of course, with the Court's conclusion that the Second Bank of the United States (which he himself had signed into law) was constitutional; but he did not think the case had warranted the statement of a "general and abstract doctrine," and he would have preferred seriatim opinions, rather than a single statement from the Chief Justice, on a ruling that was obviously intended to serve as an important precedent. Along with a growing phalanx of angry Virginians headed by Spencer Roane and Thomas Jefferson, moreover, he strongly objected to the Court's aggressive efforts to enlarge federal

---

30 See Madison's veto message of March 3, 1817, which must be read quite carefully; Richardson, ed., *Messages and Papers*, I, 584–585. For a perceptive discussion of the relevant issues see Russo, "Southern Republicans and Political Nationalism," esp. 140–143.

31 For the reference to Thomson, see Chapter 2 of this volume. For elaboration, see Paul Eidelberg, *The Philosophy of the American Constitution: A Reinterpretation of the Intentions of the Founding Fathers* (New York and London, 1968), chap. 10.

power at the expense of the states. But there was an added dimension to Madison's reaction that distinguishes it in important ways from Jefferson's and Roane's. Unlike them, he blasted the Court not for usurping, but rather for relinquishing, power. The primary source of Madison's concern was not the federal judiciary – which aroused Jefferson's wrath in large part because it was impervious to the will of the people – but Congress, which worried Madison precisely because it had become so responsive to popular opinion. What he feared most, indeed, was that the Court had effectively unleashed the most dangerous branch of the federal government.[32]

Rather than the dreaded "general welfare" clause, Chief Justice Marshall had seized upon the "necessary and proper" clause of Article I, Section 8. This clause, appended to the list of specific powers conferred on Congress, empowered that body to "make all Laws which shall be necessary and proper for carrying into Execution the foregoing Powers." Marshall thus proclaimed the Court's bold position: "Let the end be legitimate, let it be within the scope of the Constitution, and all means which are appropriate, which are plainly adapted to that end, which are not prohibited, but consist with the letter and spirit of the Constitution, are constitutional."[33] Madison was shocked by this revival of Hamiltonian construction. He decried "the high sanction" given by the Court "to a latitude in expounding the Constitution" that effectively erased the enumeration of Congress's specific and limited powers, substituting "for a definite connection between means and ends, a legislative discretion as to the former, to which no practical limit can be assigned." In the "great system of political economy" for securing the national welfare, Madison argued, "everything is related immediately or remotely to every other thing," and therefore "a power over any one thing, if not limited by some obvious and precise affinity, may amount to a power over every other." Thus the problem with Marshall's approach, he concluded, was that "ends and means" might

32 See esp. Madison to Roane, Sept. 2, 1819, in [Rives and Fendall, eds.], *Letters and Other Writings*, III, 143.
33 As reprinted in John P. Roche, ed., *John Marshall: Major Opinions and Other Writings* (Indianapolis and New York, 1967), 181.

now "shift their character at the will and according to the ingenuity of the legislative body."[34]

Madison's reference to the will and ingenuity of "the legislative body" bears emphasis. Although he worried, on one level, that the Court's position threatened the necessary division of powers between the general and state governments – a fear that he shared with Roane and Jefferson – he worried even more that the Court's new ends-and-means doctrine conferred unprecedented and frightening power upon a particular branch of the federal government, the Congress, through which the immediate voice of the people was most powerfully expressed. Above all, Madison indicted the Court for a pernicious train of thinking that undercut its own responsibility for judicial review of "the legislative exercise of unconstitutional powers." According to the Court's understanding of means and ends, Madison argued, expediency and constitutionality were made "convertible terms," and most ominous, Congress was openly admitted to be the proper "judges of the expediency." Indeed it was the only possible judge; in words almost identical to those in his 1817 veto message, Madison added that "the court certainly cannot be so; a question, the moment it assumes the character of mere expediency or policy, being evidently beyond the reach of judicial cognizance." It was true, he admitted, that Marshall had served notice to Congress that the Court always reserved the right to strike down any law the legislature might pass "for the accomplishment of objects not intrusted to the government." But Madison put no stock in this feeble caveat. Congress could simply misrepresent its unconstitutional laws as a means to a legitimate end, he argued, and the Court, hoist on its own petard, would be helpless.[35]

This direct link between Madison's veto of the Bonus Bill and his reaction to *McCulloch vs. Maryland* – a link that reveals far more than a nervous defense of state rights – clarifies the essential thrust of his constitutional concerns during the early years of his retirement. As he came to see, the Bonus Bill had portended not simply the expan-

34 Madison to Roane, Sept. 2, 1819, in [Rives and Fendall, eds.], *Letters and Other Writings*, III, 143–144.
35 *Ibid.*, 144.

sion of federal power, but even more ominous, a prevalent urge to resolve complex constitutional issues through the mere legislative expression of public opinion. Reflecting on the internal improvements issue ten months after his veto, he noted to his successor that perhaps the gravest danger to be apprehended was "the influence" that "the usefulness and popularity of measures" invariably had "on questions of their constitutionality." Nothing short of that influence, he told James Monroe, could possibly have overcome the many objections to the noxious bill that both houses of Congress had carelessly approved at the end of his term.[36] In Madison's view, the underlying dilemma was clear enough: turnpikes, canals, and even harbor improvements were so useful, both to local communities and to the nation, that popular support for their construction by the federal government was fast becoming public demand – a demand that found powerful expression in the national legislature, where solemn constitutional obligations were cavalierly ignored or sacrificed to convenience. "The great temptation of 'Utility,' brought home to local feelings," Madison later told Jefferson, was in truth "the most dangerous snare for Constitutional orthodoxy." He concluded, therefore, that "the Judiciary branch of the Government" – which was, after all, deliberately protected from the impulsive pressures of popular opinion – was perhaps "a safer expositor of the power of Congress" than congressmen would be "when backed, and even pushed on, by their Constituents."[37]

Madison had completed his presidency and launched his retirement, in sum, with a principled defense of what he understood to be the true meaning of both the Revolution and the adoption of the Constitution. If the Bonus Bill reflected popular enthusiasm for roads and canals in an expansive commercial republic, such public support should not automatically make the legislation constitutional, even in a republic premised on the sovereign will of the people – not, at least, without recourse to the amendment process that Madison had insisted on from the beginning. No matter what the Marshall Court might inadvertently suggest, there was a necessary

36 Madison to Monroe, Dec. 27, 1817, *ibid.*, 56.
37 Madison to Jefferson, Feb. 17, 1825, *ibid.*, 483. See also the relevant discussion in Madison to Roane, May 6, 1821, *ibid.*, 218–219.

difference between convenience or utility – mere "expediency" as determined by the people's representatives in Congress – and constitutionality. And until an appropriate amendment had been ratified, the Constitution should be interpreted as it had been understood at the time of its adoption, not in ways that would doubtless have made its adoption impossible. As Madison explained to Roane in 1819, "it has been the misfortune, if not the reproach, of other nations, that their governments have not been freely and deliberately established by themselves." The United States, however, was the enviable exception: "It is the boast of ours that such has been its source, and that it can be altered by the same authority only which established it. It is a further boast, that a regular mode of making proper alterations has been providently inserted in the Constitution itself." For these reasons, Madison was anxious that "no innovations" take place "in other modes," especially through "a constructive assumption of powers never meant to be granted." Instead, he defended the need to reaffirm, through the solemn act of amending the Constitution, the essential distinction between fundamental law and normal legislative authority: in America at least, "if the powers be deficient, the legitimate source of additional ones is always open, and ought to be resorted to."[38]

II

Madison's resonant fear that congressionally mandated constitutionality would supplant the authority of historically derived fundamental law rapidly became the central concern of his early retirement. This concern surfaced in connection with issues other than internal improvements. In 1820, for example, Congress quietly passed a law that limited the tenure of certain executive appointments to four years. The offices in question were not particularly consequential – district attorneys, customs collectors, naval officers, apothecaries, and the like – but Madison greatly feared the precedent of what he judged a dangerous and unconstitutional act. Except where the Constitution stipulated otherwise (as in the case of the Senate having an explicit veto over certain appointments, for in-

38 Madison to Roane, Sept. 2, 1819, *ibid.*, 145.

stance), Madison believed that the appointment and especially the removal of officers were strictly executive functions. He therefore proclaimed the so-called Tenure Act of 1820 "pregnant with mischiefs" and a blatant "encroachment on the Constitutional attributes of the Executive." The law was especially ominous, he argued, in that it quietly overturned all valid precedents on this matter — precedents that had been established beginning in the First Congress when, he might have added, he had personally made the decisive case for executive autonomy.[39] Since Madison had long supported an independent executive as one way of defending minority interests against rampaging legislative majorities, he was clearly worried in this instance about preserving the proper separation of powers in the federal government. But he worried, too, about the same larger danger that he had perceived in the Bonus Bill. If each new Congress could so easily defy the clear intent of the Constitution, in this case to serve its own immediate interest, the legislature could effectively alter or amend the Constitution at will.

First aroused by Congress's activity in 1820, Madison's fear of legislative encroachment on executive authority (and hence on the Constitution itself) lingered into the 1830s, when he privately blasted the efforts of President Jackson's Whig enemies in the Senate to interfere with executive removals from office. Such a fundamental matter as appointments and removals, he insisted, had to be "fixed by the Constitution." If it was instead "alterable by the Legislature" and therefore vulnerable to the pressures of popular opinion and partisan maneuvering, the proper relationship between Congress and the Constitution was inverted: the government, Madison appropriately warned in 1835, became "the creator of the Constitution," rather than its "creature."[40] And as he sternly admonished Edward Coles, whose hatred of Jackson bordered on fanaticism, partisans who manipulated the Constitution in this fashion were utterly irre-

39 For Madison's harsh reaction to this law, see esp. Madison to Jefferson, Dec. 10, 1820, *ibid.*, 196, and Madison to Monroe, Dec. 28, 1820, *ibid.*, 200. For general elaboration of Madison's support of an independent executive, see Ralph Ketcham, *Presidents Above Party: The First American Presidency, 1789–1829* (Chapel Hill, N.C., 1984), esp. 114–117.
40 Madison to Charles Francis Adams, Oct. 12, 1835, in Gaillard Hunt, ed., *The Writings of James Madison* (New York and London, 1900–1910), IX, 562–563.

sponsible. Indeed, to the extent that their shenanigans contributed to the instability that was the bane of all popular governments, they ignored the single greatest lesson of their fathers' experience.[41]

But it was yet another issue – one that Madison began as early as 1821 to tie directly to internal improvements and hence to the Bonus Bill – that was destined to be far more explosive than either this uncertainty about appointments and removals or the controversy over roads and canals. Madison clearly recognized that mere personal preferences, as well as narrowly partisan passions, could threaten to override the necessary commitment to fundamental law, interpreted historically, that he now desperately sought to uphold. So too, however, could urgent moral imperatives, imperatives that were derived, ironically, from the visionary legacy of his own generation. Thirty-five years after Madison's death, this explosive issue, more than any other, brought the marvelous edifice constructed in the late 1780s crashing to the ground in ruins.

In late 1819 Madison received from an unlikely source what appeared to be a humble, even obsequious, plea for assistance in interpreting the Constitution. Robert Walsh, Jr., a writer and editor then residing in Philadelphia, was well known to the retired statesman. They had first met in Washington in 1809, when the twenty-five-year-old Walsh had conveyed to the president a diplomatic message from William Pinkney in London. When Walsh subsequently pursued a career as an editor, he became notorious, and in Jeffersonian quarters was reviled, for his unabashedly anglophilic Federalism. Walsh had earlier studied law in his native Baltimore under the implacable Federalist Robert Goodloe Harper, an influence that surely informed the young journalist's frequent and vituperative attacks on the Madison administration. As John Quincy Adams recalled, Walsh "came out originally as a political fanatic against Bonaparte and subsequently as a federalist of the highest color. In this character he wrote and published himself completely

41 Madison to Edward Coles, Oct. 15, 1834, in [Rives and Fendall, eds.], *Letters and Other Writings*, IV, 366–371.

down in this country."[42] After the War of 1812 and the demise of any realistic hope of a Federalist restoration, however, Walsh abruptly changed his tune. He suddenly developed a desire to join the Jeffersonian government, telling Henry Clay only five days after Madison left office that he had reason to hope that President Monroe would do what his predecessor, whom Walsh had attacked so often and so stridently, never could: appoint him to public office. Walsh's change of political heart may have reflected more than rank opportunism. He had visited Monticello with the Abbé Correa in 1817 and apparently been quite taken with Jefferson. But his hopes of political appointment were absurdly naive, and he was soon resigned to the "speculative life" of a faltering literary career in which Jefferson, at least, took some sympathetic interest.[43]

Sometime during the winter of 1818-19 Walsh found a convenient and profitable outlet for his energetic ambition. For some time the British press had been littered with attacks on American institutions and social conditions, but now, in the face of the burgeoning unrest and popular upheaval in England that made the North American specter of republicanism ever more alarming, unprecedented torrents of abuse poured from the pages of such periodicals as *Blackwood's*, the *Edinburgh Review*, and the *Quarterly Review*. Walsh decided to vindicate his country against this flood of criticism and did so in a book appropriately titled *An Appeal From the Judgements of Great Britain Respecting the United States of America*.[44] In preparing this rebuttal to foreign calumny, he solicited relevant information and assistance from, among others, Madison and Jefferson, telling the former that he wished "to make amends for the encouragment which my early writings gave to the foreign slanders."[45] Madison responded positively to Walsh's contrite overtures and supplied both data and analysis, pertaining largely to Virginia and slavery, that

42 For a sketch of Walsh's life and career, and for the Adams quote (p. 86), see Sr. M. Frederick Lochemes, *Robert Walsh: His Story* (New York, 1941).
43 *Ibid.*, 84–85 and passim.
44 *Ibid.*, 89–101.
45 Walsh to Madison, Feb. 15, 1819, James Madison Papers, Library of Congress, series two (microfilm).

the young editor incorporated almost verbatim into his *Appeal*.[46] In November 1819 Walsh wrote to thank him for his help as well as for his kind words about the book, which, he happily reported, had just gone into a second edition. Walsh was so pleased, in fact, that he wanted to draw further on Madison's wisdom and advice. "I am occupied in considering what is called *the Missouri-Slave* question," he explained, "and am anxious to be fixed in my private opinion, concerning the constitutional powers of Congress in this matter."[47]

Earlier in the year Congress had erupted in acrimonious debate when Missouri had applied for admission to the Union as a slave state. Congressman James Tallmadge of New York had precipitated the controversy by unexpectedly introducing an amendment to the enabling bill that prohibited the further introduction of slaves to the region and gradually freed the prospective children of slaves already there. More was at stake than the simple question of whether Missouri would become a free state; at issue was a series of larger questions that had surfaced at least occasionally before. Did the Constitution confer upon Congress the power to restrict slavery in the territories or, more broadly, to regulate the movement of slaves within the United States? Did Congress have the power to attach conditions to the admission of a new state that would deny it, once admitted, the equal rank, station, and rights possessed by the other states? Clearly the resolution of the Missouri controversy would establish at least tentative answers to these and other constitutional questions, and Walsh threw himself into the fray with great vigor. "You are the one to whose judgment in this case, I would, of course, attach most weight," he assured Madison, since "no one can know as well as you do, what were the views & intentions of the framers of the Constitution in regard to the extension or rather the restriction of negro-slavery." In particular, he queried Madison about the intended meaning of Article I, Section 9, which presently elicited a wide range of conflicting interpretations; and more broadly, Walsh

46 For further discussion of the view of slavery in Virginia that Madison forwarded to Walsh, see Chapter 6 of this volume.
47 Walsh to Madison, Nov. 11, 1819, James Madison Papers, Library of Congress, series two (microfilm).

wondered whether the founders had intended to extend the three-fifths clause to new states — whether, indeed, they "could have looked to the existence of slavery at all in such states."[48]

Perhaps Madison should have inferred from the tone of Walsh's letter that the brash young editor already had his answers and was merely looking for a convenient and imposing authority to "fix" his opinions. Whether or not Madison understood the biased character of Walsh's request, his response was far more thorough and detailed than his correspondent expected, and it said all the wrong things. On the question of whether the framers had anticipated the existence of slavery in new states, Madison suggested that "the great object of the convention seemed to be to prohibit the increase by the *importation* of slaves. A power to emancipate slaves was disclaimed; nor is anything recollected that denoted a view to control the distribution of those within the country."[49] Above all, Madison was especially eager to clarify the intended meaning of the unexpectedly controversial "slave trade" clause that Walsh had explicitly inquired about. During the early stages of the recent Missouri debates, some congressmen had maintained that Article I, Section 9 — which stipulated that "the migration or importation of such persons as any of the States now existing shall think proper to admit, shall not be prohibited by the Congress prior to the year one thousand eight hundred and eight" — empowered Congress to prevent the transportation of slaves from one state to another (and to the territories) after 1808. Supporters of this interpretation — an argument, Madison would soon learn, to which the elderly John Jay was now lending public support — denied that "migration" and "importation" were merely synonymous terms that referred exclusively to the movement of people to the United States from foreign countries.[50] Instead, they argued that the term "migration" referred specifically to the

48 *Ibid.* On the Missouri controversy, see Glover Moore, *The Missouri Controversy, 1819–1821* (Lexington, Ky., 1953), or more briefly, George Dangerfield, *The Awakening of American Nationalism, 1815–1828* (New York, 1965), chap. 4.

49 Madison to Walsh, Nov. 27, 1819, in [Rives and Fendall, eds.], *Letters and Other Writings*, III, 154–155.

50 Moore, *Missouri Controversy*, 44–45. See John Jay to Elias Boudinot, Nov. 17, 1819, in Henry P. Johnston, ed., *The Correspondence and Public Papers of John Jay* (New York and London, 1893), IV, 430–431.

movement of people *within* the boundaries of the United States; the slave trade clause thus covered *both* the foreign ("importation") and domestic ("migration") transportation of slaves.

Madison found this interpretation astonishing, even incomprehensible.[51] He offered Walsh a thorough account of the circumstances that had shaped this section of the Constitution, including a specific explanation of the troublesome phrase "migration or importation of such persons." Some of the states represented in the Philadelphia convention, he told Walsh, had not wanted to admit the term "slaves" into the document; the purpose of the phrase was thus to allow those who were "scrupulous of acknowledging expressly a property in human beings to view *imported* persons as a species of emigrants" – while others, he added, "might apply the term to foreign malefactors sent or coming into the country." He also mentioned the possibility that some members might have "had an eye to the case of freed blacks as well as malefactors," but he frankly confessed the inadequacy of his memory on this point. On the salient issue at hand, however, Madison felt not a scintilla of doubt: whatever ambiguity there might have been in the precise application of the terms "migration" or "persons," it was absolutely certain that

51 Madison to Walsh, Nov. 27, 1819, in [Rives and Fendall, eds.], *Letters and Other Writings*, III, 149–157, and Madison to Monroe, Feb. 10, 1820, *ibid.*, 164–166. The twentieth-century legal scholar Walter F. Berns launched a savage assault on both Madison's interpretation of Article I, Section 9, and his integrity in denying at the time of the Missouri crisis its applicability to the domestic slave trade; see "The Constitution and the Migration of Slaves," *Yale Law Journal* 78 (1968), 198–228. For a convincing critical assessment of both Berns's argument and the larger issue, see David Brion Davis, *The Problem of Slavery in the Age of Revolution, 1770–1823* (Ithaca, N.Y., and London, 1975), 119–131, esp. 128n–129n. The exceedingly complex and convoluted issue of what powers the Constitution conferred on Congress in relation to the expansion of slavery has bedeviled scholars almost as much as it did antebellum Americans. For instance, Duncan MacLeod, in his excellent monograph *Slavery, Race, and the American Revolution* (London and New York, 1974), develops an analytical perspective that in effect suggests that Madison was correct in his larger understanding of what, broadly conceived, the founders intended; see esp. 47–61. On the other hand, Don E. Fehrenbacher's approach in *The Dred Scott Case: Its Significance in American Law and Politics* (New York, 1978), suggests a perspective on Madison's views circa 1819 that appears much closer to Berns's; see esp. chap. 4.

"they referred exclusively to a migration or importation from other countries into the United States, and not to a removal, voluntary or involuntary, of slaves or freemen from one to another part of the United States." Indeed, he assured Walsh, "nothing appears or is recollected that warrants this latter intention."[52]

As usual, Madison relied on more than personal memories of the Philadelphia convention to sustain the constitutional point. Applying the relevant historical standards of interpretation, he reminded Walsh that "nothing in the proceedings of the State Conventions" indicated a comprehension of the expanded construction that some now claimed. Had the slave trade clause been understood to refer to more than importation from foreign parts, indeed, "it is easy to imagine the figure it would have made in many of the States, among the objections to the Constitution, and among the numerous amendments to it proposed by the State Conventions." In fact, "not one" of those amendments "refers to the clause in question."[53] Madison later expressed the same sentiments to Monroe, who had staunchly opposed the Constitution at the Virginia convention of 1788. "No one can decide better than yourself," Madison reminded the former Antifederalist turned president, what would have occurred if the advocates of the Constitution had openly avowed this elastic meaning of the slave trade clause. Ratification under these circumstances would have been impossible, especially (but not only) in the states that had so jealously protected their right to import slaves for another twenty years; and even the "suspicion" of such a construction "would at least have made a conspicuous figure among the amendments proposed to the Instrument."[54] Who could doubt, in sum, that the American people had ratified in the late 1780s a very different Constitution from the one that some interpreters now contended for? From Madison's perspective, indeed, no measure of good intentions and wishful thinking, not even the most ingenious and sophisticated textual analysis, could override that simple historical fact.

52 Madison to Walsh, Nov. 27, 1819, in [Rives and Fendall, eds.], *Letters and Other Writings*, III, 150.
53 *Ibid.*, 150–151.
54 Madison to Monroe, Feb. 10, 1820, *ibid.*, 165.

Walsh clearly thought otherwise. When Madison's letter arrived, he had already "committed to the press" part of a combative pamphlet on the Missouri question. He decided to finish it before acknowledging Madison's "very interesting and instructive" missive.[55] Walsh's anonymous pamphlet – *Free Remarks on the Spirit of the Federal Constitution* – was a stunning and brilliant piece of forensic prose. In contending that "importation" and "migration" were not synonymous terms and that the framers had therefore intended in the slave trade clause to confer upon Congress the power to prevent the spread of slavery beyond the original slave states, Walsh drew upon a larger argument: the Founding Fathers had in fact been fervent abolitionists who had designed a Constitution that would aggressively promote the demise of slavery. Indeed, when Walsh quoted liberally from the debates at the Virginia Ratifying Convention, he did so not in the way Madison found appropriate to judging a constitutional issue, but rather to confirm the antislavery views of a Revolutionary generation of southern Americans – and to contrast these noble heroes with their morally and intellectually deficient descendants, who now advanced preposterous arguments that violated the intended spirit and purposes of their fathers' ingenious creation.[56]

Shortly after the publication of the pamphlet, Walsh sent Madison a copy and finally acknowledged the former president's letter. It was an awkward moment, and while Walsh struggled to be diplomatic he also made it clear that he would not recant his views; the pamphlet would stand. He confessed freely that he remained unconvinced by Madison's letter, though he felt "the weight of its contents" and "an almost unbounded deference" for the older man's authority. In a refreshing and quite revealing burst of candor, moreover, Walsh frankly disclosed that his constitutional views were impervious to the kind of argument that Madison deemed relevant but that Walsh, in effect, subsumed under more urgent moral imperatives: "I did not, in fact, wish to be convinced, as to the con-

---

55 Walsh to Madison, Jan. 2, 1819 [1820], in James Madison Papers, Library of Congress, series one (microfilm).

56 [Robert Walsh, Jr.], *Free Remarks on the Spirit of the Federal Constitution* . . . (Philadelphia, 1819), 18–25, 85, and passim.

Robert Walsh, Jr. Lithograph by Albert Newsam, after Thomas Sully, c. 1830. (Courtesy of the National Portrait Gallery, Smithsonian Institution, Washington, D.C.)

stitutional point, so deep were my impressions of the inexpediency and even criminality of the establishment of the institution of slavery beyond the Mississippi." He had therefore laid his honest impressions before the public, "and I trust," he implored Madison, "you will give me credit for good intentions."[57]

Madison did. He thanked Walsh for the pamphlet, politely acknowledging their continuing disagreement. "Those who cannot assent to your conclusions as to the powers of Congress," he conceded, "must still be sensible of the lustre which ingenuity and eloquence have bestowed on some of your premises. And there cannot be many whose feelings will not accord with your pictures of the

57 Walsh to Madison, Jan. 2, 1819 [1820], in James Madison Papers, Library of Congress, series one (microfilm).

evils inherent in slavery itself."[58] Madison was doubtless not surprised that his restatement of some of his reservations in this second letter failed to deter the passionate abolitionist. Indeed, Walsh organized mass meetings and petition drives in Philadelphia, vigorously condemning the eventual congressional compromise that admitted Missouri as a slave state and left the western territories below latitude 36° 30' open to slavery. With the support of Roberts Vaux, a Quaker activist, Walsh soon established an antislavery newspaper that he would edit for the next sixteen years. "Mr. Walsh," a disgusted observer informed Jefferson, "has begun a malignant and wicked career."[59]

Like Walsh, Madison was not entirely comfortable with the eventual Missouri compromise, though for rather different reasons. He accepted it, however, with far greater equanimity than many other prominent Virginians, young and old, who mounted the barricades in defense of state rights and the honor of the Old Dominion.[60] In drawing the 36° 30' line Congress had unequivocally asserted its constitutional right to prohibit the extension of slavery into the federal territories. Madison knew that Congress could not possibly derive that power from the slave trade clause, as Walsh and others so foolishly contended, but he acknowledged the existence of other possible sources, the most likely being the clause that gave Congress power "to make all needful rules and regulations respecting the territory or other property belonging to the United States." Actually, Madison — influenced, as he admitted, by his customary "habit of a guarded construction of Constitutional powers" — leaned heavily toward the belief that the restriction of slavery even under this clause was not "within the true scope of the Constitution."[61] The territorial power, he believed, could not "well be extended beyond a

58 Madison to Walsh, Jan. 11, 1820, in [Rives and Fendall, eds.], *Letters and Other Writings*, III, 163.
59 Moore, *Missouri Controversy*, 131–169; the letter to Jefferson, from Thomas Cooper, is quoted in Lochemes, *Robert Walsh*, 114.
60 See esp. Moore, *Missouri Controversy*, 232–242.
61 Madison to Monroe, Feb. 23, 1820, in [Rives and Fendall, eds.], *Letters and Other Writings*, III, 168–169.

power over the territory, as property, and a power to make the provisions really needful or necessary" – the exclusion of slavery clearly not being "necessary" in this sense – "for the government of settlers until ripe for admission as States into the Union."[62] Nevertheless, he conceded that the power in question was "of a ductile nature," leaving ample "room for difference of opinion" and indeed "legislative discretion." For this reason he was unwilling to charge Congress, as some of his fellow Virginians were, with an egregious usurpation of power.[63]

More important, notwithstanding his own private reservations, Madison conceded that the position now taken by Congress on this intrinsically ambiguous issue reflected the opinion of a clear majority of both houses of the federal legislature. Senator James Barbour told him so in early February when the compromise was brewing, and Madison readily acceded to the wisdom of accommodating this majority sentiment.[64] Although the support of a majority of both the states (in the Senate) and the people (in the House of Representatives) did not in itself make this or any other particular interpretation of the Constitution correct or just by Madison's standards, such support prompted him to link the Missouri and internal improvements controversies in quite interesting and revealing ways. And it greatly affected, above all, his understanding of how dissenters, on both issues, should interpret and therefore respond to Congress's controversial actions.

Madison first linked the two issues when responding to Roane's complaints about the alleged usurpations of the Marshall Court in May 1821. In making the case that "the impulses" given to Congress "by a majority of the states, seduced by expected advantages" actually made the legislature a far more dangerous threat than the Court to "the reserved sovereignty of the States," Madison assured Roane that neither the Court, nor even the Court and an ambitious Congress detached from the will of its constituents acting together, would likely succeed in what he called "*durable* violations of the

---

62 Madison to Walsh, Nov. 27, 1819, *ibid.*, 152.
63 *Ibid.*; Madison to Monroe, Feb. 23, 1820, *ibid.*, 168.
64 Barbour to Madison, Feb. 10, 1820, and Madison to Barbour, Feb. 14, 1820, in James Madison Papers, Library of Congress, series one (microfilm).

rights and authorities of the States." Just such an effort had been made, of course, with the Alien and Sedition Acts of the late 1790s, when "the usurping experiment was crushed at once, notwithstanding the co-operation of the federal judges with the federal laws." Madison remained confident, in other words, that the American system of representative government was sufficiently responsible to its constituent body of the people and the states to defeat all such schemes of minority usurpation. "But what," he asked Roane, "is to control Congress when backed, and even pushed on, by a majority of their constituents, as was the case in the late contest relative to Missouri, and as may again happen in the constructive power relating to roads and canals?" Obviously the Supreme Court under Marshall's leadership could not be expected to exercise meaningful restraint; indeed, in view of "the latitude of power which it has assigned to the national legislature" in cases like *McCulloch vs. Maryland*, one might say that it had exacerbated the danger of popular usurpation. Madison was thus prompted to answer his own question: "Nothing within the pale of the Constitution, but sound arguments and conciliatory expostulations addressed both to Congress and to their constituents."[65]

During the next several years, especially after John Quincy Adams became president, Madison had ample occasion to chastise embittered Virginians for losing sight of this "essential distinction, too little heeded, between assumptions of power by the General Government, in opposition to the will of the constituent body, and assumptions by the constituent body through the Government as the organ of its will." In incidents of the first case — what better example, again, than the Federalists' reign of political terror in the late 1790s? — a remedy was secured "through the forms of the Constitution" merely by rousing the attention of the people. But when militant Virginians led by Thomas Ritchie and the venerable patriarch Jefferson objected to the "consolidating" tendencies of the federal government in the mid-1820s, they were responding to something quite different: incidences of the second kind, perfectly illustrated "by the apparent call of a majority of the States and of the

65 Madison to Roane, May 6, 1821, in [Rives and Fendall, eds.], *Letters and Other Writings*, III, 218–219.

people for national roads and canals." Here there was no simple remedy for alleged usurpations, Madison said, because the problem arose directly from the popular character of the American system. "The appeal can only be made," he concluded, "to the recollections, the reason, and the conciliatory spirit of the majority of the people against their own errors, with a persevering hope of success, and an eventual acquiescence in disappointment, unless, indeed, oppression should reach an extremity overruling all other considerations."[66]

Madison's earlier letters to Tucker and Walsh, reminding them of the relevant historical standards for interpreting the Constitution, not to mention his dramatic veto of the Bonus Bill, had indeed been appeals of just this kind. But on both internal improvements and the restriction of slavery in the territories, Madison had failed to persuade, despite his perseverance, and now he was prepared to acquiesce, even without the formal amendment he continued to prefer, in what appeared to be the firm and final decision of a majority of both the states and the people.[67] The alternative, after all, was unthinkable. Disgruntled and genuinely aggrieved minorities might continue to appeal to "the recollections" and "the reason" of the people – above all, to the guiding authority that could be found in the experience of the founding of the Constitution – in the hope of tempering the will of the majority. But in words that paraphrased his most memorable contribution to *The Federalist*, Madison explained clearly during the first year of the Adams administration why disgruntled Virginians must eventually accede to the workings of a system that, however far from perfect, was emphatically less prone to abuse than any other. "All power in human hands," he reminded Ritchie, "is liable to be abused":

In Governments independent of the people, the rights and interests of the whole may be sacrificed to the views of the Government. In Republics, where the people govern themselves, and where, of course, the majority govern, a danger to the minority arises from opportunities tempting a sacrifice of their rights to the interests, real or supposed, of the majority.

66 Madison to Thomas Ritchie, Dec. 18, 1825, *ibid.*, 506–507.
67 As Madison wrote to Jefferson on February 17, 1825, "I consider the question as to canals, &c., as decided, therefore, because sanctioned by the nation under the permanent influence of benefit to the major part of it." *Ibid.*, 483.

No form of government, therefore, can be a perfect guard against the abuse of power. The recommendation of the republican form is, that the danger of abuse is less than in any other; and the superior recommendation of the federo-republican system is, that while it provides more effectually against external danger, it involves a greater security to the minority against the hasty formation of oppressive majorities.[68]

Madison obviously sensed – and was palpably disturbed by – the increasingly militant tone of the disaffected Virginians who now opposed President Adams. Even Jefferson, while proclaiming a rupture of the Union "as among the greatest calamities" that might befall the people of his state, added that it was "not the greatest," since "submission to a government of unlimited powers" would be far worse.[69] Madison would not have objected to this statement in principle; but unlike his dear friend, he perceived not the trace of such a threat in the condemned activities of the federal government. Madison, in fact, accepted calmly what now prompted his impulsive and disillusioned colleague to speak of dire oppression and the revolutionary recourse to disunion. As Madison had noted to Jefferson earlier in the same year when discussing the internal improvements controversy, "the will of the nation being omnipotent for right, is so for wrong also; and the will of the nation being in the majority, the minority must submit to that danger of oppression as an evil infinitely less than the danger to the whole nation from a will independent of it."[70]

Madison's longstanding fear of majority abuse, in sum, remained as resonant in 1825, after the problem had surfaced on the national level, as it had been in the 1780s, when the states had been the focus of his concern. In neither period, however, did that fear take precedence over his broader commitment to republicanism as the least imperfect form of government, or to the belief that "extending the

68 Madison to Ritchie, Dec. 18, 1825, *ibid.*, 507.
69 Jefferson's draft of "The solemn Declaration and Protest of the commonwealth of Virginia on the principles of the constitution of the US. of America & on the violations of them," enclosed with Jefferson to Madison, Dec. 24, 1825, in Paul Leicester Ford, ed., *The Writings of Thomas Jefferson* (New York and London, 1899) X, 351, 348–354.
70 Madison to Jefferson, Feb. 17, 1825, in [Rives and Fendall, eds.], *Letters and Other Writings*, III, 483.

sphere" of the representative system was the essential means of vindicating America's Revolutionary promise. Shortly after Jefferson's death in the summer of 1826, indeed, Madison's defense of the Founding became as impassioned as the cries of the Virginia dissidents he endeavored to restrain, when he confronted what would become the greatest trial of his retirement: the nullification crisis of the early Jacksonian era.

4. Memory and Meaning:
Nullification and the Lost World of the Founding

THE TURN of the new year in 1829 brought days of great promise for a young congressman from Albemarle County, Virginia. William Cabell Rives had more than enough reason to rejoice at the political complexion of his country. As an ardent supporter of Andrew Jackson, he could bask in the glow of his hero's smashing defeat of the incumbent president, John Quincy Adams, in the presidential election of 1828. No doubt the ambitious Rives also had some inkling of the prominent role he might play in the new administration. Within the next few months, in fact, he would be named minister to France – an appropriate assignment, he must have thought, for it placed him in the diplomatic shoes of his former tutor in law, Thomas Jefferson. But in several anxious letters to William M. Rives, a relative who sat in the Virginia House of Delegates, the thirty-five-year-old Jacksonian zealot appeared more disturbed than pleased. On January 8, 1829, he reported that Thomas Ritchie, one of Jackson's most influential supporters and the powerful editor of the *Richmond Enquirer*, had "made up a *formal* issue with Mr. Madison on the constitutionality of the Tariff." For the past several issues, indeed, editor Ritchie had been "constantly *pecking*" at Madison "with his argumentations," and what was worse, with "illiberal insinuations and remarks" on his conduct. Considering Madison as much as Jefferson his personal and political mentor, Rives was "utterly astonished at the madness and temerity" of Ritchie's course. [1]

---

1 William Cabell Rives to William M. Rives, Jan. 8, 1829, in William Cabell Rives Papers, Library of Congress, box 45. There are two other relevant letters, in the same box, dated Jan. 1, 1829, and Jan. 2, 1828 (incorrectly dated). The only biographical treatment of Rives is Raymond C. Dingledine, Jr., "The Political Career of William Cabell Rives," unpublished Ph.D. dissertation, University of Virginia, 1947.

119

Controversy over federal tariffs — laws that regulated commerce for the purpose of encouraging domestic manufactures — had recently exploded into a political storm in the Old Dominion. Two years earlier, at the urging of Governor William Branch Giles, the general assembly had abruptly proclaimed the tariff unconstitutional. Now the governor was asking the legislature to endorse the even more emphatic statements of protest from South Carolina and Georgia against the latest, most egregious evidence of federal injustice, the so-called "tariff of abominations" that Congress had enacted in 1828. Madison had studiously remained silent — at least officially and publicly — during the Missouri crisis and other earlier constitutional disputes, but on this issue he formally reentered the public arena by publishing in the newspapers two long letters to his friend Joseph Cabell in which he defended the constitutionality, if not the expediency, of protective legislation. It was Ritchie's editorial criticism of those public letters that Rives decried.

"Is it possible," Rives wondered, that Ritchie was so arrogant as to suppose "that his opinion on a question of constitutional law, even backed by the whole Richmond party and the southsiders to boot, will weigh a feather with the great body of the people, when put in the scale against Mr. Madison's?" Obviously the editor had taken leave of his senses, since he appeared oblivious to "the weight of Mr. Madison's character and authority." "Be assured," Rives reminded his namesake in Richmond, "that we can never get along, either at home or abroad, upon any great question of constitutionality or policy, with Mr. Madison against us." After all, Virginia was nothing "without her great men," which made it "all-important to keep with Mr. Madison, whose name, in times like these, when the passions have subsided, and judgment has resumed her empire, will be a host in itself." Rives's letter was brimming with veneration of the "sober, sage, calculating statesman" whose recent counsel, he admitted, had shielded his own judgment from the untoward effects of the tornado of passion now sweeping the state. He therefore forwarded to his friends in Richmond a manuscript, intended for the newspapers, formally defending his mentor against Ritchie's assault.[2]

2 Rives to Rives, Jan. 8, 1829, Rives Papers, Library of Congress, box 45. For Madison's tutoring of Rives on the tariff, see especially Rives to Madison (draft),

Rives was hardly alone in his appreciation of Madison's guidance and in his deference to the patriarch's wisdom. Richard Rush, who had served as attorney general during the War of 1812, described Madison's letters as "the Voice of reason, suddenly interposed to still jarring elements"; they had made, he told his former boss, "a powerful impression upon the public." The young Pennsylvanian was especially grateful for the history lesson contained in Madison's reflections. By recalling the experience of the 1780s, the retired statesman's letters placed him "in the light of a witness bearing testimony; useful, solemn testimony." "Most of us now on the stage," Rush admitted to Madison, "were too young to retain a recollection of the day when we had no general government; and those who have only read of the train of political and commercial evils that marked that day, seem to have forgotten them. We needed to be reminded of them, as you have reminded us."[3]

Thanking Rush for his kind words, Madison expressed hope that the pernicious influence of the antitariff movement would quickly abate. "Opinions whose only root is in the passions," he reflected, "must wither as the subsiding of these withdraws the necessary pabulum."[4] It soon became clear, however, that Madison was unduly optimistic about the waning of public passion and that both Rives and Rush had overestimated the weight of his "character and authority," especially among the people of Virginia. Ritchie's initial attacks on Madison's tariff letters, which had incensed Rives, had at least been marginally respectful, even polite. Regretting his disagreement with the venerable sage, Ritchie had told his readers that "the day of prophets and oracles has passed; and tho' we humbly feel our inferiority, yet we are free citizens of a free country, and must think for ourselves."[5] The patronizing tone of such comments was

Dec. 17, 1828, ibid., box 44; Madison to Rives, Dec. 20, 1828, in [William C. Rives and Philip R. Fendall, eds.], Letters and Other Writings of James Madison (Philadelphia, 1865), III, 663–664; Rives to Madison, Dec. 31, 1828, in Rives Papers, Library of Congress, Box 46; and Madison to Rives, Jan. 10, 1829, in [Rives and Fendall, eds.], Letters and Other Writings, IV, 3–4.

3 Rush to Madison, Jan. 10, 1829, in Rush Papers, Historical Society of Pennsylvania.

4 Madison to Rush, Jan. 17, 1829, in [Rives and Fendall, eds.], Letters and Other Writings, IV, 5–6.

5 Richond Enquirer, Jan. 3, 1829.

unmistakable, to be sure, but cannot compare with the criticism —
indeed, abuse — of Madison that followed in the weeks to come.

One writer in the *Enquirer*, advising Virginians to ignore the
political somersaults of a pitiful old man, echoed Ritchie's declaration of independence when he exhorted: "Reader, in all your reasonings, banish great names, consult your own understanding."[6] This
acid-tongued critic became increasingly mocking and contemptuous, even when answering the charge that his commentaries showed
an unbecoming lack of respect for the Father of the Constitution.
After all, the doddering old man from Montpelier had invited the
embarrassment and ridicule he now suffered. Rather than enjoy his
geriatric repose, he had impulsively thrust himself onto the public
stage, "backed by a course of reasoning too far-fetched, ambiguous,
irrelevant, and unsatisfactory . . . to produce conviction on the
mind of one intelligent human being." That Madison's reasoning
was "in direct hostility," moreover, to "the whole course of his
reasoning for 40 preceding years" made his fumbling performance
nothing short of farcical.[7]

These were harsh and mean-spirited words in the throes of a
dangerous controversy. They aptly reflected the defiant spirit of self-
reliance that inspired a passionate generation of republicans who,
while professing deference to the wisdom and authority of patriarchs
from another age, claimed the right not only to think for themselves
but to instruct their elders, when necessary, on the meaning of the
past. The jabs and pricks from the pages of the *Enquirer* that disturbed Rives were only a mild indication of what was to come.
Before long, Madison's critics would routinely claim the right to
interpret for him the meaning of his own past words and deeds. If,
in the midst of the Jacksonian celebration of early 1829, Rives
caught a fleeting glimpse of an insidious chain of events that might
bring the Union to the brink of collapse — and his mentor to the
verge of utter (and utterly uncharacteristic) despair — his concern
proved prescient. And with the Constitution obscured in a haze of
partisan passion and ignorance, Madison's hopes for the future rested
precariously in the hands of the few legatees who, like Rives, would

6 *Ibid.*, Feb. 24, 1829.   7 *Ibid.*, Mar. 13, 1829.

heed his admonition to resurrect and honor the lost world of the Founding.

I

Had Madison been told during his journey home to Montpelier in early 1817 that he would live to see a serious constitutional crisis, he would never have guessed that the tariff would be its occasion. Beginning with the first session in 1789, Congress had regularly approved protective duties, which had been raised to their highest levels without any great fuss or controversy only the year before Madison retired. At the height of the Missouri crisis a few years later, the apprehensive former president took comfort in the thought that although the tariff question promised to exacerbate tensions in Congress, "its issue" could not be "very serious," in part because "no great constitutional question" was involved.[8] That, indeed, was the point. Madison was not surprised that the tariff proved controversial, but he expected debate to focus merely on its expediency – was it wise? was it just? what specific levels were appropriate? – rather than on its constitutionality, which was indisputable.

The novel idea that the tariff was unconstitutional – in other words, that it represented the assumption, on the part of the federal government, of a power that had never been delegated to it – gradually emerged after 1819 among that vocal coterie of state rights Virginians whom Madison knew so well. By the mid-1820s their initial attacks on the "consolidation" doctrines of the Marshall Court had been extended to include the legislative proposals of neo-Jeffersonians like Henry Clay, whose "American System" – a program of economic nationalism that included a high tariff as well as a federal system of internal improvements – constituted for them nothing less than a monstrous revival of Hamiltonian heresies. During the great congressional debate on the tariff in 1824, representative Philip P. Barbour of Orange County, Virginia, made what appears to have been the first systematic case against protective

8 Madison to Richard Rush, Dec. 4, 1820, in [Rives and Fendall, eds.], *Letters and Other Writings*, III, 195. See also Madison to George Joy, Nov. 25, 1820, in Madison Papers, Library of Congress, series two (microfilm).

duties on constitutional grounds.[9] And when President Adams's ringing endorsement of the American System appeared to lend even greater force to the threat of consolidation, some Virginians, including Jefferson, verged on panic. Madison's efforts to restrain his old friend and others of a similar bent, including Ritchie, were generally effective – at least for a time.[10] It was not until Jefferson was gone, in early 1827, that Madison's political ally from the early 1790s, Governor Giles, armed with a recent letter from the Sage of Monticello that might be construed to support his action, took the Virginia legislature with him in explicitly denying the constitutionality of federal tariff laws.[11]

Madison ventured to hope during the legislature's deliberations that it would act judiciously, but he also registered his fear – one that he would harbor for the rest of his life – that "the political atmosphere is too turbid every where for distinct views of any subject of a political complexion."[12] A month later Madison was certain not only that Virginia had taken an indefensible position, but that she would stand alone. He found the constitutional assault on the tariff so absurd, so much an outburst of unreflecting passion, that he may, at first, have underestimated its popular appeal. Even as he limited his criticism of the legislature to private conversations and correspondence, Madison's concern about the "turbid" state of the political atmosphere in Virginia steadily deepened. In October 1827 he found it necessary to publicly repudiate a newspaper in Lynchburg that had erroneously quoted him referring to Governor Giles as "that dog in the manger."[13] By the end of the year, Madison had even more reason to stiffen his resolve "to keep aloof from the political agitations of the period."[14] The presidential election may

---

9 Merrill D. Peterson, *Olive Branch and Sword – The Compromise of 1833* (Baton Rouge, La., 1982), 13–14.

10 See Chapter 3 of this volume.

11 For elaboration see Dice Robbins Anderson, *William Branch Giles: A Study in the Politics of Virginia and the Nation from 1790 to 1830* (Menasha, Wis., 1914).

12 Madison to Nicholas P. Trist, Feb. 7, 1827, in [Rives and Fendall, eds.], *Letters and Other Writings*, III, 551.

13 See Madison to editor of "Lynchburg Virginian," Oct. 10, 1827, *ibid.*, 590–592.

14 Madison to Monroe, Dec. 18, 1827, *ibid.*, 602.

have been a year away, but aggressive campaigning was not, and poor Madison found the partisan beast pounding at his door. First there was an attempt to involve his name in a dispute concerning orders he had given to General Jackson during the War of 1812; then he was appalled to discover that Adams men in his own state had cynically put his name on their list of presidential electors not only without his sanction, but "on sufficient presumptions" that it would be withdrawn.[15] When two of his most respected political friends, Joseph Cabell and James Barbour, begged him in early 1828 to take a public stand against Jackson in order to save the republic, Madison realized the full extent to which partisan furor had seized the public mind.[16] As he explained to Lafayette a month later, "the extravagances produced by the Presidential contest," having found their way into Congress and the state legislatures, had assumed "forms that cannot be too much deplored"; the tariff and internal improvements issues, divisive enough on their own, "are blended with and greatly increase the flame kindled by the electioneering zeal."[17]

Madison was, of course, no stranger to partisan zeal, having served as a principal catalyst in the political conflagration of the 1790s. And he had not forgotten that part of his past. Writing in the midst of the tariff controversy to Henry Gilpin, who was pursuing research on the early republic, Madison offered a polite apology for "the tincture of party spirit" that was so visible in his own writings from the early years of the government. He sent Gilpin a copy of "a small evanescent pamphlet," whose partisan hue, he said, "will be explained, if not excused, by the origin and the epoch of the publication."[18] Perhaps Madison's recollection of his own vul-

---

15 See Madison to Monroe, Nov. 16, 1827, *ibid.*, 600, and especially Madison to Lafayette, Feb. 20, 1828, *ibid.*, 620.
16 See letters from the two men to Madison in January 1828, in Madison Papers, Library of Congress, series one (microfilm).
17 Madison to Lafayette, Feb. 20, 1828, in [Rives and Fendall, eds.], *Letters and Other Writings*, III, 619.
18 Madison to Henry D. Gilpin, Oct. 25, 1827, *ibid.*, 595. See also Madison to Jacob Gideon, Feb. 20, 1818, *ibid.*, 60. For additional evidence of Madison's awareness of partisan excess in his own career, see Madison to Edward Everett, June 23, 1835, Everett Papers, Massachusetts Historical Society, where he

nerability to the same spirit many years earlier tempered his impatience with the passionate excesses of a new generation. But no doubt he also remembered what had been at stake in those tumultuous days of the first party system. Now, as the election of 1828 drew near, Madison broke his public silence only to urge his fellow citizens to conduct their political discussions "in a spirit and manner, neither unfavorable to a dispassionate result, nor unworthy of the great and advancing cause of Representative Government."[19]

Madison's dilemma is not hard to discern. On the one hand, he deplored "the lengths into which some of our politicians are running" and "the erroneous constructions of the Constitution" that were the most visible symptom of the partisan madness.[20] As debate over the tariff grew ever more passionate, it was difficult to resist the urge to do what he might to clarify the turbid atmosphere. But he also realized that any public statement from him would be construed as partisan (and its influence correspondingly discounted), and he was extremely reluctant to invite renewed efforts to drag his name into the muck and mire of the presidential campaign. Only when he discovered that he had been wrong in believing that Virginia would stand alone – when, indeed, the antitariff movement began to spread to South Carolina, where it threatened to take on truly alarming proportions – did Madison resort to a strategy that offered a possible escape from the dilemma.[21] He consented to the publication of what became the controversial two letters to Cabell, but he also insisted that they be withheld from the press until after the election. They duly appeared in the Washington *National Intelligencer* on December 22, 23, and 25.

Madison's indictment of Giles and the Virginia legislature offered a dual lesson in history and the familiar perils of popular govern-

---

mentions that his correspondence was "too often tinged with the party spirit of the times."

19 Madison to Francis Brooke, Feb. 22, 1828, in Gaillard Hunt, ed., *The Writings of James Madison* (New York and London, 1900–1910), IX, 310n. Madison's exhortation appeared in the *Richmond Enquirer* on March 4, 1828.

20 Madison to Jonathan Roberts, Feb. 29, 1828, in [Rives and Fendall, eds.], *Letters and Other Writings*, III, 625.

21 For Madison's early concern about the situation in South Carolina, see, for example, Madison to Thomas Lehre (not sent), Aug. 2, 1828, *ibid.*, 635–636.

ment, two matters that were, for him, inseparable. Applying the only standards of constitutionality he deemed valid, he built what he assumed was an unanswerable case. That the framers of the Constitution had intended to vest in Congress the power that disgruntled hotheads now denied to the federal government was obvious; no less obvious was the recognition of that intention by all the parties – Federalists and Antifederalists alike – to the great ratification debate. Everyone had taken for granted that among the objects of the power to regulate commerce was the encouragement of manufactures; as the experience of the postwar years had so vividly demonstrated, this power could not be effectively exercised by the individual state governments; and a fundamental purpose of the Constitution had been precisely to vest this power in a new, more competent federal government. Anyone with a rudimentary knowledge of the confederation era, especially of "the evils which were to be cured" and "the benefits to be obtained" by adopting the Constitution, could hardly miss the point.[22] Indeed, if some Americans in the 1820s had difficulty understanding such elementary matters, their forebears certainly had not. To buttress his case, Madison scrutinized the published records of debates from the state ratifying conventions without finding even the slightest hint of this innovative view that "the encouragement of manufactures" was "not within the general power over trade to be transferred to the Government of the United States."[23] Moreover, subsequent debate in Congress in 1789 clearly revealed that all representatives, including southerners, had correctly understood that the new government not only had the power but was expected by the states to exercise it.[24] And Madison turned yet again to history for "evidence that ought of itself to settle the question." For nearly forty years, the construction of the Constitution that he now defended had been routinely acknowledged and acted upon, "with a concurrence or acquiescence of every State Government" and through "all the vicissitudes of Party" that

22 The quoted material is from "Notes" appended to the second tariff letter to Cabell dated Oct. 30, 1828, in Hunt, ed., *Writings of Madison*, IX, 323n. The full text of the two letters can be found on pages 316–340.
23 Madison to Cabell, Sept. 18, 1828, *ibid.*, 330.
24 Madison to Cabell, Feb. 13, 1829, in [Rives and Fendall, eds.], *Letters and Other Writings*, IV, 15.

marked the era. "No novel construction however ingeniously devised, or however respectable and patriotic its Patrons," he concluded, "can withstand the weight of such authorities, or the unbroken current of so prolonged and universal a practice."[25]

The constitutionality of protective duties had received, in short, "a national sanction not to be reversed but by an evidence at least equivalent to the national will." The cumulative weight of precedent could properly be overturned by only one means: formal amendment of the Constitution. If, on the contrary, "every new Congress were to disregard a meaning of the instrument uniformly sustained by their predecessors for such a period," constitutional government as the Founders had conceived of it was lost.[26] When the standard of constitutionality inadvertently became "the opinion of every new Legislature heated as it may be by the strife of parties, or warped as often happens by the eager pursuit of some favourite object; or carried away possibly by the powerful eloquence, or captivating address of a few popular statesmen, themselves influenced, perhaps, by the same misleading causes," Americans were acknowledging that "every new Legislative opinion might make a new Constitution." It was unlikely, Madison warned, that republican government could long survive under such circumstances, because there would be an end to the stability that was "essential to good Government and good Laws" – a stability, he admonished his countrymen, "the want of which is the imputation which has at all times been levelled aginst Republicanism with most effect by its most dexterous adversaries."[27] And Madison made it clear that he spoke of more than the mutability of laws. The evidence for the constitutionality of the tariff adduced in his letters, he said, "cannot be resisted without destroying all stability in social institutions, and all the advantages of known and certain rules of conduct in the intercourse of life."[28]

25 Madison to Cabell, Sept. 18, 1828, in Hunt, ed., *Writings of Madison*, IX, 333.
26 Madison to Cabell, Mar. 18, 1827, in [Rives and Fendall, eds.], *Letters and Other Writings*, III, 573.
27 Madison to Cabell, Sept. 18, 1828, in Hunt, ed., *Writings of Madison*, IX, 334, 333.
28 Madison to Cabell, Oct. 30, 1828, *ibid.*, 323n-324n.

This fervent concern for stability informed Madison's plea during the late 1820s that his countrymen heed the essential distinction between the exercise of a usurped power and the abuse of a legitimate power. He readily conceded that tariff laws might fall into the second category. Congress's power in this area could be (and, in the judgment of some Americans, obviously had been) abused "by its excess, its partiality, or by a noxious selection of its objects." But "mere *inequality* in imposing taxes," he insisted, was hardly "synonymous with *unconstitutionality*." Unlike the exercise of usurped power, which unequivocally marked a violation of the constitutional covenant (and was therefore a far more serious matter), the abuse of power "cannot be regarded as a breach of the fundamental compact till it reaches a degree of oppression so iniquitous and intolerable" as to justify, in effect, a resort to the natural right of revolution.[29] Madison emphasized this distinction, in no small part because it resolved a looming ambiguity in Jefferson's personal legacy that antitariff politicians were quick to exploit.

Governor Giles had deviously manipulated one of Jefferson's final tirades against "consolidation" – scrupulously marked "not intended for the public eye" – to suggest that the Sage of Monticello had, at the very end of his life, unequivocally proclaimed the tariff unconstitutional.[30] Madison privately admitted that Jefferson's letter to Giles contained "unstudied and unguarded language incident to a hasty and confidential correspondence." He was appalled, however, that Giles and his cronies exploited the ambiguities for their own narrow ends, all the while professing the most profound veneration for his dear friend's memory. They either disregarded the contrary inference to be drawn from the views Jefferson had maintained in "his more deliberate correspondence with others" and had, moreover, "acted on through his whole official life," or even worse, they suggested that Jefferson had suddenly "seen the light" of the

---

29 Madison to Cabell, Mar. 18, 1827, in [Rives and Fendall, eds.], *Letters and Other Writings*, III, 573–574.
30 For a fuller discussion of the so-called "Giles letter" of December 26, 1825, see Dumas Malone, *The Sage of Monticello* (Boston, 1981), 440–441, and Irving Brant, *James Madison: Commander in Chief, 1812–1836* (Indianapolis and New York, 1961), 468–470.

truth that he (and others) had been guilty for decades of supporting usurped power.[31] Madison deemed "monstrous" these partisan efforts to place the Sage of Monticello "in such pointed contradiction to himself." A true friend to Jefferson's memory, he insisted, would read the letter to Giles in light of the cumulative weight of that statesman's words and deeds throughout a long career. And if they did, they would understand that Jefferson had never meant to deny the constitutionality of the tariff, but only to denounce the abuse of that legitimate power.[32]

Perhaps it was best for Madison that the disconsolate and impetuous Jefferson was no longer around to define the precise terms of his own legacy. But even the faintest recognition of that advantage offered Madison little consolation in the wake of the public reaction to his two letters to Cabell. Writing privately to Cabell in February 1829, Madison found rather grim solace only in having had his reservations about going public confirmed. "You see, my good friend, that my disinclination to go into the newspapers was more justified than you were disposed to allow. What is occurring was anticipated, and was a sufficient motive for wishing to avoid the dilemma of leaving a good cause to be borne down by the persevering efforts of zealous partisans, or throwing the defence of it on reluctant though adequate hands."[33] Madison was neither intimidated nor silenced by despair, however. His second public career – and his role as caretaker of Jefferson's memory – had only begun.

II

The distinction between opposition to the tariff as unconstitutional and as inexpedient was not mere semantic nitpicking. As Madison understood, judgments of proper recourse among the aggrieved and disaffected were inescapably linked to the terms of the indictment. And if he regarded the charge of unconstitutionality as a dangerous

31 Madison to Rives, Jan. 23, 1829, in [Rives and Fendall, eds.], *Letters and Other Writings*, IV, 7–8.
32 Madison to Joseph Cabell, Feb. 2, 1829, *ibid.*, 10–11, and Madison to Cabell, Dec. 5, 1828, *ibid.*, III, 659–660.
33 Madison to Cabell, Feb. 2, 1829, *ibid.*, IV, 11.

innovation, he found almost incredible the strange doctrines of resistance that began to accompany that claim in late 1828. Madison's forceful response to what later became the doctrine of nullification had been nicely foreshadowed in his exchange of letters with Spencer Roane in the early 1820s. Reminding Roane that there must always be a provision for terminating disagreements between the federal and state governments about their respective spheres of authority, Madison vigorously denied that this trust – which he insisted the founders had correctly placed in the judicial branch of the general government – could be vested in the states in their individual capacity. The latter mechanism, he objected, would have the potential effect of rendering a different meaning for the Constitution in every state (and hence of reverting, he implied, to the chaos of the Articles of Confederation).[34] Eight years later, however, under the cover of anonymity, the vice president of the United States, John C. Calhoun, articulated in the South Carolina "Exposition and Protest" a formal theory of the Constitution that bore an uncanny resemblance to that very threat.

Calhoun was complying with the request of a special committee of the South Carolina legislature for a principled and systematic indictment of the new tariff legislation of 1828. The vice president – who ten years earlier had been appalled by President Madison's squeamish denial of the constitutionality of the Bonus Bill (and whose admirers would soon have the temerity to ridicule Madison for his alleged inconsistency) – now sent Governor Giles's wave of protest crashing against the very foundations of the Union. Conveniently ignoring Congress's power to regulate commerce, Calhoun argued that the protective system was patently unconstitutional because the national legislature's power to tax was expressly limited to the purpose of raising revenue and could not, therefore, be used instead to encourage particular sectors of the economy at the expense of others. Fortunately, the victims of this unconstitutional system – the southern agricultural states – could defend themselves by exercising individually their sovereign right to nullify the obnoxious laws. According to Calhoun, the Constitution was a compact of the individual states, each of which retained sovereignty within its

---

34 Madison to Roane, June 29, 1821, *ibid.*, III, 223.

borders and hence the right to "interpose" its authority and declare null and void any federal law that it deemed in violation of the original compact. Indeed, since the federal government was a creature of the sovereign states, none of its branches, including the Supreme Court, could properly be the ultimate arbiter of the constitutionality of its actions.

Calhoun even devised a set of formal constitutional procedures for implementing nullification. Once an individual state had suspended operation of an unconstitutional law and received support of its action from one-fourth of all the states, the federal government could appeal the decision to the same authority that had formed the compact – the sovereign states. The nullifying verdict would stand, Calhoun continued, unless three-fourths of the states granted the disputed power by amending the Constitution; in which case the protesting state could acquiesce or withdraw from the Union. Such, in brief, was the ingenious system of constitutional theory and practice that an incredulous Madison branded "a preposterous and anarchical pretension."[35]

The nullifiers were undertaking nothing less than a fundamental redefinition of the Union, and Madison knew it. His essential fear can be simply stated: that a new generation of politicians – intoxicated by partisan ambition and either willfully or carelessly ignorant of the past – would dismantle the achievement of the late 1780s and plunge the republic into the dreadful chaos that adoption of the Constitution had barely averted. Madison redoubled his own efforts to arouse serious interest in what was, after all, the not-so-distant history of the United States, and he missed no opportunity to encourage others to do the same. "I wish your example in tracing our constitutional history through its earlier periods could be followed by our public men of the present generation," he lamented to Rives. "The few surveyors of the past seem to have forgotten what they once knew, and those of the present to shrink from such researches."[36] When another of Madison's young disciples, Nicholas P. Trist,

35 Merrill D. Peterson, *The Jefferson Image in the American Mind* (New York, 1960), 51–66. Madison is quoted on page 56.
36 Madison to Rives, Dec. 20, 1828, in [Rives and Fendall, eds.], *Letters and Other Writings*, III, 664.

began to compile the printed materials that would illuminate "the state of things during the interval between the peace of 1783 and the adoption of the Constitution," Madison gave the project enthusiastic support. "I have long wished for such a work, not only for its future value," he told Trist, "but for the salutary lights it would give to those who were not cotemporaries with those interesting scenes in our Revolutionary drama, and are liable to be misled by false or defective views of them."[37]

As Madison insisted time and again, accurate knowledge of the events of the 1780s – events "now new because they have become old" – was essential for more than providing a guide to interpreting specific clauses of the Constitution.[38] The "novel and complex" nature of the American regime could be understood only by examining "the process of its formation"; and an appreciation of this historical context, he maintained, could alone expose the nullifiers for what they were – deluded souls who unwittingly sought not only to rewrite history and to confer belated victory on the Antifederalists, but to expose the republic once again to the full horrors of the confederation period.[39] When Edward Everett sent Madison in late 1831 a copy of his address to the American Institute of New York, the Virginian praised it as both elegant and "instructive in its general character." "I have read it with the greater pleasure," Madison told the author, "as it goes back to times and scenes in which I was often an actor, always an observer; and which are too much overlooked in discussing the objects and meaning of the Constitution."

A review of the state of our commerce and navigation; of the abortive efforts and conflicting regulations among the states, of the distracted condition of affairs at home, and the utter want of respect abroad, during the period between the peace of 1783 and the convention of 1787, could not fail to open the eyes of many who have been misled, and to cherish in all a love for a constitution which has brought such a happy order out of so gloomy a chaos.[40]

37 Madison to Trist, Dec. 4, 1832, *ibid.*, IV, 227.
38 Madison to Everett, Aug. 22, 1833, *ibid.*, 307.
39 Madison to James Robertson, Apr. 20, 1831, *ibid.*, 171.
40 Madison to Everett, Nov. 14, 1831, Everett Papers, Massachusetts Historical Society. Madison subsequently assisted Everett in his historical research; see Madison to Everett, Jan. 5, 1832 [misdated 1831], *ibid.*

Madison was certain, moreover, that the American people had run out of miracles. If the union of 1787–88 were dissolved – and surely Madison noticed, in this connection, that as early as 1829 Governor Giles was defending the break-up of that Union into four regional confederacies – "an impossibility of ever renewing it" would be "brought home to every mind" simply by remembering "the difficulties encountered in establishing it."[41] The doctrine of nullification, he warned, "would convert the federal government into a mere league which would quickly throw the states back into a chaos out of which not order a second time but lasting disorders of the worst kind could not fail to come."[42] In his more pessimistic moments, Madison elaborated on such disorders: "a rupture of the Union; a Southern confederacy; mutual enmity with the Northern; the most dreadful animosities and border wars, springing from the case of slaves; rival alliances abroad; standing armies at home, to be supported by internal taxes; and federal Governments, with powers of a more consolidating and monarchical tendency than the greatest jealousy has charged on the existing system."[43] The litany of horrors resembled, indeed, a summary of the dangers described in the first nine papers of *The Federalist*.

Madison's bill of particulars against nullification led inescapably to his underlying argument: the theory fundamentally misrepresented the nature of the regime and, put into practice, would subvert the republican achievement of 1787–88. A recurrence to history revealed that the Constitution had not been formed, as the Articles of Confederation had, by the sovereign authority of state governments, but rather "by the people in each of the States, acting in their highest sovereign capacity" through the means of popularly constituted ratifying conventions. The distinction might appear

---

41 Madison, "Outline," Sept. 1829, in [Rives and Fendall, eds.], *Letters and Other Writings*, IV, 20. For the reference to Giles, see Anderson, *Giles*, 227–228.

42 Madison to Richard Rush, Jan. 17, 1829, in [Rives and Fendall, eds.], *Letters and Other Writings*, IV, 5–6.

43 Madison to Andrew Stevenson, Feb. 10, 1833, *ibid.*, 272–273. See also Madison to Mathew Carey, July 27, 1831, *ibid.*, 192. Madison had raised the specter of civil war and its attendant horrors as early as February 1828; see the deleted paragraph in Madison to Francis Brooke, Feb. 22, 1828, Madison Papers, Library of Congress, series one (microfilm).

subtle, but the implications were momentous. The essential point was that the federal Constitution had thus been derived from the same source as the individual state constitutions. Within each state it had, therefore, "the same authority as the Constitution of the State" and was "as much a Constitution, in the strict sense of the term, within its prescribed sphere [i.e., of its delegated powers], as the Constitutions of the States are within their respective spheres." But there was one obvious and essential difference that underlined the precise character of the regime – a distinction that the nullifiers had clearly lost sight of. As a compact "among the States in their highest sovereign capacity" that formed the people of *all the states* into "one people for certain purposes," the Constitution and the laws formed under its authority could not, as Calhoun stipulated, "be altered or annulled at the will of the States individually, as the Constitution of a State may be at its individual will." Aware that controversies would inevitably arise over the legitimacy of some federal laws, the "people of the states" had wisely provided in the Constitution for "a peaceable and authoritative termination" of such disputes. By vesting in the judicial branch of the general government the requisite authority to resolve disagreements about the proper boundary of jurisdiction between the general and state governments, they had adopted the only mechanism consistent with "the object and end of a real Government" – namely, "the substitution of law and order for uncertainty, confusion, and violence."[44]

In effect, Madison asked his countrymen to remember and to honor the plain facts of the case: their forebears had not simply conferred a few additional powers on a federal government that remained nothing more than the creature of sovereign states. Indeed, for the next generation to pretend that the founders had amended the Articles of Confederation without changing the basic structure of federal authority, and to treat the federal government as "a mere league of independent sovereigns," was to deny that the revolution of 1787–88 had ever taken place.[45] By denying federal

44 Madison to Everett, Aug. 1830, in [Rives and Fendall, eds.], *Letters and Other Writings*, IV, 95–97.
45 Madison to Andrew Stevenson, May 2, 1827, Madison Papers, Library of Congress, series one (microfilm).

135

judicial supremacy in the exposition of laws, Calhoun's theoretical formula of resistance, according to Madison, was rooted in fantasy, not history. The "people of the states" had delegated part of their sovereign power to a general government that was supreme within its stipulated sphere of authority, subject to a battery of checks that were clearly demarcated in the Constitution. These checks included, of course, the division of power among different branches of the government, the participation of the people and the states in the election of federal officials, and ultimately, the amendment process. But beyond the modes of recourse contained in those checks, the only remedy for the usurpation or abuse of power was extraconstitutional: a resort to the natural right of revolution. In their misguided attempts to invent additional constitutional checks on federal power, the nullifiers disregarded the fundamental lesson of the 1780s. When a new twist on their basic doctrine appeared in the claim that state judges might effect the nullification of federal law, Madison reminded a correspondent that the state judicial systems "can only be kept in their constitutional career by the control of the federal jurisdiction. Take the linch-pins from a carriage, and how soon would a wheel be off its axle; an emblem of the speedy fate of the federal system, were the parties to it loosened from the authority which confines them to their spheres."[46]

Nullification defied more, however, than the irrefutable history of the formation of the regime; it contravened as well the fundamental tenet of republican government: that the will of the majority must ultimately prevail. On the ground of principle alone, Madison rejected a theory that implied that a single state "may arrest the operation of a law of the United States, and institute a process which is to terminate in the ascendency of a minority over a large majority, in a Republican System, the characteristic rule of which is that the major will is the ruling will."[47] If Calhoun's scheme were an admissible means of resolving disputes about the constitutionality of federal laws, one-fourth of the states would be given the initiative

46 Madison to Cabell, Sept. 16, 1831, in [Rives and Fendall, eds.], *Letters and Other Writings*, IV, 196.
47 Notes on Nullification, 1835–1836, in Hunt, ed., *Writings of Madison*, IX, 588–589.

not only to overturn all valid precedents, but to define fundamental law for the other three-quarters (each of which, according to Calhoun's logic, had an equal right to define constitutionality). "To establish a position and permanent rule giving such a power to such a minority over such a majority," Madison objected, "would overturn the first principle of free Government, and in practice necessarily overturn the Government itself."[48]

If Madison's defense of majority rule in the 1830s seems anomalous against the backdrop of his earlier thought, we must remember, as Marvin Meyers has stated the point, that "Madison's lifelong concern with the dangers of majority rule has sometimes obscured the source of that concern: his prior commitment to popular government."[49] The nullifiers' case was built explicitly on a defense of minority interests against the overbearing force of popular majorities. Madison, of course, had long evinced both a fear of majority faction and a solemn concern for the rights of minorities, as anyone familiar with the *Federalist* well knows. But Madison's preoccupation with the perils of majority rule must not be confused with a rejection of the principle itself. In 1787 and in the last decade of his life, his purpose remained consistent: to minimize the risk of majority abuse without abandoning the cause of popular government, to seek, as he had put it in *Federalist* number ten, "a republican remedy for the diseases most incident to republican government." With the help of David Hume in the late 1780s, he had found a plausible remedy in "extending the sphere" of popular government. And after three decades of rigorous trial, Madison proclaimed the experiment a success. Experience had vindicated the theory that under representative government, power was indeed less likely to be abused by majorities in larger rather than in smaller communities; or in more specific American terms, that popular majorities had proved far more dangerous on the state level, under the Articles of Confederation, than at the federal level, under the Constitution.

48 Madison to Everett, Aug. 1830, in [Rives and Fendall, eds.], *Letters and Other Writings*, IV, 102. See also Madison to M. L. Hurlbert, May 1830, *ibid.*, 73–76.
49 Marvin Meyers, ed., *The Mind of the Founder: Sources of the Political Thought of James Madison*, rev. ed. (Hanover, N.H., and London, 1981), 408.

As early as the summer of 1828, when Madison first grasped the nature of the threat emanating from South Carolina, he offered advice to those who were so fearful of abusive national majorities that nullification and even disunion seemed appropriate modes of resistance. "They would do well to examine," he said, whether "minorities" at the state level would be any more secure against "wrongful proceedings of majorities" within any individual state that might separate from the Union. Lest anyone miss the historical reference, he added that "a recurrence to the period anterior to the adoption of the existing Constitution, and to some of the causes which led to it, will suggest salutary reflections on this subject."[50] The nullifiers appeared to forget, indeed, that "the abuses committed within the individual States previous to the present Constitution, by interested or misguided majorities, were among the prominent causes of its adoption." If Calhoun averred that large republics and national majorities posed the gravest threat to minorities, Madison appealed to history for a compelling refutation of this recrudescence of Antifederalist dogma. "Whatever may have been the just complaints of unequal laws and sectional partialities under the majority Government of the United States," he argued in 1833, "the abuses have been less frequent and less palpable than those which disfigured the administrations of the State Governments while all the effective powers of sovereignty were separately exercised by them."[51]

What troubled Madison most about the nullifiers, in this connection, was their disingenuous pose as defenders of popular government. "Every friend to Republican Government," he demanded, "ought to raise his voice" against the pernicious theme that colored the constitutional theorizing of the dissidents: their "sweeping denunciation of majority Governments as the most tyrannical and intolerable of all Governments." Although they attempted to mask their "anti-republicanism" under the cover of an obsession with overbearing *national* majorities, they were, in fact, espousing the

50 Madison to Thomas Lehre [not sent], Aug. 2, 1828, in [Rives and Fendall, eds.], *Letters and Other Writings*, III, 635–636.
51 Madison to _____, [1833], [Majority Governments], in Hunt, ed., *Writings of Madison*, IX, 522–523.

alarming heresy that "a majority Government is of all other Governments the most oppressive." This doctrine "strikes at the root of Republicanism," Madison charged, "and pursued into its consequences, must terminate in absolute monarchy, with a standing military force; such alone being impartial between its subjects, and alone capable of overpowering majorities as well as minorities." In other words: if the nullifiers rejected as unacceptably oppressive majority government on the federal level — which experience now confirmed was the "least imperfect" form of popular government — they could hardly defend the republican principle anywhere, but especially on the state level, where the danger of majority abuse, contrary to their naive insistence, was palpably so much greater. Thus by threatening to undo the work of the Founders and return "the effective powers of sovereignty" to the individual states, the nullifiers were counterrevolutionaries in every sense of the term. Following the logic of their pseudo-republicanism, it would ultimately be necessary, in order to defend minorities against majorities, to "seek a refuge" in some authority superior to the sovereign will of the people.[52] And the inevitable result, Madison warned, would be authoritarian governments that offered a sorry contrast to the liberal government of the extended republic.

The nullifiers did not, in fact, view their theory as either innovative or heretical. Rather they presented it as a revival of tradition — the honorable tradition established by none other than Jefferson and Madison in the halcyon days of the "Revolution of 1800." Here they followed Giles's lead in rooting protest against the tariff in the constitutional doctrines proclaimed in the late 1790s, when Virginians had led resistance to the Federalists' wanton usurpation of power in the federal government. The sacred texts, of course, were the resolutions adopted by the legislatures of Virginia and her sister state Kentucky in response to the infamous Alien and Sedition Acts, along with the "Report on the Virginia Resolutions," an answer to criticism of its actions that the Virginia legislature approved and had published in early 1800. By the late 1820s, the secret of

52 *Ibid.*, 520–521, 528.

Madison's and Jefferson's involvement in the drafting of the Virginia and Kentucky resolutions, respectively, had been exposed, and Madison's authorship of the Report of 1800 was common knowledge. Much to Madison's chagrin, in short, the nullifiers posed as Madisonians and Jeffersonians of the first order.

There is no reason to doubt the sincerity of the nullifiers in their initial embrace of the two great Virginians. Privately, Madison told anyone who would listen that the antitariff leaders had grossly misconstrued the events of the late 1790s and that claims for his and Jefferson's paternity were therefore absurd. But some of the dissidents were rather slow to get the message. In early 1830, for instance, Senator Robert Hayne of South Carolina, fresh from his great oratorical duel with Daniel Webster, sent Madison copies of his recent Senate speeches as a gesture of gratitude. He appears to have assumed that Madison would support his version of the state rights theory against the nationalist claims of the ex-Federalist from Massachusetts. "The Virginia Resolutions of '98 and your admirable Report," Hayne told Madison, "have almost passed away from the memory of the politicians of the present day. It is this forgetfulness which has led to the alarming assumptions of power on the part of the federal government, and I feel an entire conviction that nothing can save us from consolidation and its inevitable consequence, the separation of the States, but the restoration of the principles of '98."[53]

When Madison responded by disputing Hayne's version of constitutional history and theory, the South Carolinian was stunned. After several months of silence, he told Madison that he still preferred his own interpretation of the principles of 1798 to that of their author and promised to defend his position at some length in a future letter. But five years later, when reviewing his correspondence, Madison scribbled in the margin: "the promised communication has not been made."[54] Once Madison realized that private

53 Robert Y. Hayne to Madison, Mar. 5, 1830, Madison Papers, Library of Congress, series one (microfilm).
54 Madison to Hayne, Apr. 3 or 4, 1830, in Hunt, ed., *Writings of Madison*, IX, 383n-384n; and Hayne to Madison, July 22, 1830, Madison Papers, Library of Congress, series two (microfilm).

rebuke would do nothing to deter Hayne and others from misrepresenting "the principles of '98," not even the scars from his earlier foray into the public arena could prevent him from venturing forth once again. In August 1830, he polished the text of his letter to Hayne, addressed it to Edward Everett, and, with a wish and a prayer, consented to its publication in the *North American Review*.[55]

By this time, the nullifiers had begun to talk of a state's constitutional right to secede from the Union as well as to nullify federal laws. Publicly and privately, seeking in part, no doubt, to clear his reputation for posterity, Madison relentlessly denied any complicity in advancing such errant interpretations of the Constitution. When Trist began to prepare rebuttals of the nullifiers for the press, his mentor fed him leads and inspiration – and sometimes the actual text. It was certainly not the object of the Virginia proceedings of 1798–99, Madison reassured Trist, to "assert a right in the parties to the Constitution of the United States *individually* to annul within themselves acts of the Federal Government, or to withdraw from the Union" – nor, he added, could such meanings be fairly inferred from the documents in question.[56] The nullifiers' errors were legion. They failed to distinguish between "what is declaratory of opinion" and "what is *ipso facto* executory"; the Virginia Resolutions had merely declared that the Alien and Sedition Acts were unconstitutional, in the hope of rallying support for that view in other states, without formally assuming the judicial function and impairing the execution of federal law. The dissidents also failed to distinguish between "the right of *the parties* to the Constitution" and the right "of a *single* party"; the resolutions of 1798 had urged the states to unite against an abusive regime, but said nothing to suggest that an individual state might, by itself, invalidate federal law. And they failed to distinguish between "resorts within the purview of the Constitution" and what Madison called "the *ultima ratio*" of an ap-

55 Madison to Everett, Aug. 1830, in [Rives and Fendall, eds.], *Letters and Other Writings*, IV, 95–106.
56 Madison to Nicholas P. Trist, Feb. 15, 1830, *ibid.*, 61. For a full view of the Madison–Trist collaboration, see Trist's letters to Madison between 1828 and 1833 in the Nicholas P. Trist Papers, Virginia Historical Society. See also draft of Trist to Madison, Mar. 7, 1830, Nicholas P. Trist Papers, Library of Congress.

peal "from a Constitution, cancelled by its abuses, to original rights paramount to all constitutions." The Virginia Resolutions and the Report of 1800 had appealed to popular opinion and the electoral process. They had been intended to accomplish, Madison insisted, exactly what they had, and nothing more: by mobilizing and organizing public opinion, they had contributed to an electoral revolution – "within the purview of the Constitution" – that deposed the offensive party and its unconstitutional policies. But now the nullifiers were misrepresenting as a constitutional right what was in fact a very different, extraconstitutional appeal to the natural right of revolution.[57]

Madison clearly respected the rhetorical talent and intelligence, if not the judgment, of his adversaries. With painstaking care he analyzed the meaning of specific phrases and even words – usually his own, of course – in the relevant documents. But he also understood that the meaning of any document, especially in view of the mutability of language, was rooted in historical circumstance, and it was here that he most regretted the myopic distortion of the popular analogy between 1798 and the present. Madison simply could not comprehend how reasonable men might equate the effects of tariff laws, as unfortunate or inequitable as they might be, with the momentous crisis in republican institutions that had existed three decades earlier. Once again, it was the lack of historical perspective, if not downright ignorance – this time, pertaining to the 1790s rather than to the previous decade – that sustained the passionate energy of the antitariff movement and its constitutional heresies.

"In explaining the proceedings of Virginia in 1798–99," Madison told Rives, "the state of things at that time" had been "too much overlooked."[58] The Virginia Resolutions had addressed a set of public circumstances that bore no resemblance, in kind or degree, to the putative "crisis" of 1830. In 1798 a Federalist Congress had trampled on the fundamental right of Americans to express freely their political views. Madison no doubt remembered his own fearful vulnerability to prosecution under the Sedition Act, which forbade,

57 Madison to Edward Livingston, May 8, 1830, in [Rives and Fendall, eds.], *Letters and Other Writings*, IV, 80.
58 Madison to Rives, Mar. 12, 1833, *ibid.*, 291.

after all, conspiring "with intent to oppose . . . measures of the government" or bringing either Congress or the President "into contempt or disrepute."[59] One congressman, Matthew Lyon of Vermont, had been arrested and sentenced to prison for his outspoken opposition to the Federalist administration, and the federal courts were relentlessly moving against other prominent dissidents. Now the nullifiers were telling Madison that high duties on imported textiles were an equivalent form of oppression. As he lamented in 1833, "we have seen the finest talents, the most ardent zeal, and the most captivating eloquence, indefatigably exerted in painting in the deepest colours all the sufferings, public and private, real and imaginary; and in inculcating a belief that the tariff was the cause, the sole cause of them." No wonder he spoke of "a ferment in the popular mind, almost beyond example" and waited anxiously for "the paroxysm of the fever" to pass.[60]

In truth, Madison the historian had a serious problem on his hands, not so much with his own legacy, but with Jefferson's. The nullifiers generally linked the two men and the two sets of legislative resolutions from the late 1790s. They soon discovered, however, that the Kentucky resolutions and Jefferson's imprimatur were much better suited to their purposes. Unlike Madison, Jefferson was no longer around to refute their claims, and in his case there was much less to refute. Although Madison's denial of Calhoun's and Hayne's construction of the Virginia Resolutions and Report hardly stopped their invocation of those documents, the old man was a nuisance that they hoped would go away. When he did not, some nullifiers pursued the strategy of separating Jefferson from Madison, discrediting Madison (usually on the grounds of senility, the sins of his past, or a combination of both), and building on Jefferson.[61] Madison fought as hard to clear Jefferson's name as he did to clear his own. But this was no easy task. There had been important differences between the two men in the late 1790s, when Madison

---

59 See Ralph Ketcham, *James Madison: A Biography* (New York, 1971), 394.
60 Madison to Professor Davis [not sent], 1832 [1833], in [Rives and Fendall, eds.], *Letters and Other Writings*, IV, 259–260.
61 For an excellent example, see the writings of "Mutius" in the *Richmond Enquirer*, July 23, Aug. 20, 1833.

had struggled to restrain Jefferson from carrying the protest against federal legislation in a direction he could not support; and now, in the early 1830s, Madison had to cover for his friend by playing down Jefferson's momentary sympathy for ideas that were disturbingly similar to nullification.[62] Indeed, chagrined to discover in late 1830 that, contrary to his recollection (and prior assertion), Jefferson had actually used the term "nullification" in his manuscript draft of the Kentucky Resolutions, Madison adamantly refused to concede his friend's memory to the nullifiers.[63]

As Madison advised Trist, it was necessary, when inferring Jefferson's legacy from his words, to make "allowances" for "a habit in Mr. Jefferson, as in others of great genius, of expressing in strong and round terms impressions of the moment."[64] This observation has been quoted so often by scholars who share Madison's admiration for his friend that to call it a euphemism for intellectual sloppiness and irresponsibility might seem perverse. Everyone would agree that in 1798 and 1799 Jefferson employed strong and round terms with a vengeance. His draft resolutions described the Constitution as a compact among the several states, each of which had the right to judge for itself both the constitutionality of federal laws and the appropriate mode of redress when the compact was violated. If the general government overstepped its legitimate bounds, Jefferson asserted, its acts were "unauthoritative, void, and of no force," and "a nullification of the act" was "the rightful remedy." In this connection, indeed, he spoke of "the natural right" – a phrase that Madison would desperately seize upon in the 1830s to separate Jefferson from the South Carolinians, who talked of such a right *under the Constitution* – of every state "to nullify of their own authority all assumptions of power by others within their limits."[65]

62 My discussion of the late 1790s below is drawn from Adrienne Koch, *Jefferson and Madison: The Great Collaboration* (New York, 1950), 174–211; Merrill D. Peterson, *Thomas Jefferson and the New Nation: A Biography* (New York, 1970), 590–625; and Dumas Malone, *Jefferson and the Ordeal of Liberty* (Boston, 1962), 395–424.

63 Madison to Everett, Sept. 10, 1830, in [Rives and Fendall, eds.], *Letters and Other Writings*, IV, 109–110. See also Madison to Trist, Sept. 23, 1830, *ibid.*, 110–111.

64 Madison to Trist, May 1832, *ibid.*, 217–218.

65 My account is drawn from Peterson, *Jefferson and the New Nation*, 613–616, and

Apparently Madison, in 1798, did not see Jefferson's draft before it was on the wing to Kentucky (where the legislature would moderate its language considerably), but once he did, he lost no time alerting Jefferson to the errors and dangers in his logic. Above all, Madison rejected any hint of the notion that the Constitution conferred upon each state legislature the power to act within its borders against federal laws that it judged unconstitutional. His caution was especially evident in the final draft of the resolutions that he was preparing for the Virginia legislature. When a third party carried these draft resolutions to Monticello on their way to Richmond, Jefferson tried to sharpen their edge. Wanting to overcome the impression that the legislature of his own state was doing nothing more than expressing its opinion and urging others to agree (precisely Madison's interpretation, at least in the 1830s), Jefferson proposed adding the phrase, "that the said acts are . . . null, void and of no force, or effect." The resolutions were thus introduced in the legislature, but the original language – "almost certainly at Madison's urging," his biographer, Ralph Ketcham, has noted – was eventually restored.[66] Three decades later, when Madison insisted that the Virginia Resolutions had made no reference to a nullifying power, he pointed to the legislature's deletion of the stronger language (about whose source he remained silent) as firm evidence that nothing more than a declaration of opinion had been intended. But a correspondent soon posed the inevitable questions: Where had the words "null, void and of no force, or effect" come from? Had they been part of Madison's original draft? And if so, did they not contradict what he was now saying about his beliefs in 1798? In a rare lapse of memory, Madison answered the first two queries by saying that he simply could not recall.[67]

Perhaps Madison "forgot," too, what had happened in the following summer of 1799. After the Virginia and Kentucky resolutions failed to arouse the support of other legislatures – indeed, they were generally condemned as irresponsible and unconstitutional,

Ketcham, *James Madison*, 394–397. Jefferson's original draft of the Kentucky Resolutions is conveniently reprinted in Merrill D. Peterson, ed., *The Portable Thomas Jefferson* (New York, 1975), 281–289 (quotations from 281, 286).

66 Ketcham, *James Madison*, 396–397; Koch, *Jefferson and Madison*, 190–191.

67 Brant, *Madison: Commander in Chief*, 483–484.

especially in the northern states where the Federalists were in control – Vice-President Jefferson was determined to renew the protest. Before conferring with Madison at Monticello, he sent his friend proposals for a second round of resolutions. Jefferson apparently wanted the protesting states not only to assert the principle of nullification, but to threaten to detach themselves from the Union if the usurpations of power continued. Fortunately, as Jefferson's biographer Merrill D. Peterson has put it, Madison "came to dinner – a cool breeze in a hot summer – and at once soothed his friend's feelings."[68] Above all, Madison cautioned Jefferson against conveying the false impression that nullification and secession were legitimate procedures within the existing constitutional framework. Since separation from the other states would put an end to the Constitution, placing the people of Virginia in a natural state of revolution, such extreme and potentially violent recourse was unthinkable in the absence of sustained and unbearable oppression.[69] Madison believed that the moment for this kind of drastic action had not arrived and that Jefferson was wrong to anticipate it. After persuading Jefferson to retreat from his extreme proposals, Madison went on, in the months ahead, to draft the Virginia Report in such cautious and guarded terms that only the most partisan nullifier could read them, thirty years later, as if Jefferson had had his way. Indeed, the Report of 1800, read carefully, is not simply a clarification of the meaning of the original resolutions in response to Federalist charges that they overthrew the Constitution; it constituted an answer, as well, to the doctrinal ambiguities and excesses that Madison apparently saw – and doubtless regretted – in even his closest friend.[70]

Madison's memory of these events may have been more acute than he let on. When Thomas Jefferson Randolph asked him in late 1833 if his grandfather had believed that a state had a constitutional right to secede peaceably from the Union, Madison's reply was curiously equivocal. "I do not recollect any precise conversation with him on

68 Peterson, *Jefferson and the New Nation*, 623–624.
69 Ketcham, *James Madison*, 398–399; Koch, *Jefferson and Madison*, 194–207.
70 The interpretation here is my own, and admittedly conjectural, although it is based on the sequence of events described in Koch, *Jefferson and Madison*, as well as on my reading of the document itself.

the question stated," he said, adding that "nothing certainly ever passed between us, which left an impression that he considered a State as having a constitutional or any right to secede from its compact with the other parties, without their consent, or without such a breach or abuse of the compact as absolved the seceding party from the obligations imposed by it."[71] We might note that Madison's reply subtly shifted the focus from Jefferson's views to the impression Madison had gained of those views, in relation, moreover, to what are clearly Madison's views. He did not necessarily misrepresent Jefferson; but he made considerable allowance for the influence he had exerted on his friend during the crisis of the late 1790s. And if he recalled, too, Jefferson's prevailing demeanor just before his death in 1826, Madison may even have been relieved, in the early 1830s, not to have to put his powers of persuasion with him to the test once again.

We might infer something about the continuation of their dialogue, had Jefferson remained alive, by examining more closely the subtlety of Madison's position during the nullification crisis. In a sense, Madison's public and private commentary addressed two concerns and two different audiences. His most important objective was to draw traditional Jeffersonian advocates of state rights away from the heresy of nullification.[72] But he also wanted to moderate and modify the position of several prominent opponents of nullification. He sought, in other words, to invalidate the constitutional claims of the nullifiers without lending his imprimatur to the constitutional history and theory put forth by some second-generation nationalists, the most conspicuous of whom was Webster. To be sure, Madison's fear of the nullifiers was so great that he did not hesitate to lend support to anyone who fought them, including Webster. But if, in the public letter to Everett, Madison's primary purpose was to refute Senator Hayne's misconstruction of the Jeffersonian tradition, he also hoped to stake out a position between Webster and Hayne that

71 Madison to Thomas Jefferson Randolph, Dec. 6, 1833, Cutts–Madison Collection, Library of Congress (microfilm).
72 For an excellent discussion of the quite different strains or varieties of "states' rights," see especially Richard E. Ellis, *The Union At Risk: Jacksonian Democracy, States' Rights, and the Nullification Crisis* (New York, 1987).

offered a clear alternative to both.[73] For the next several years, Madison fought the war against the nullifiers on two fronts, trying to knock sense into the heads of wild-eyed South Carolinians and their sympathizers in Virginia while trying, at the same time, to draw his public allies away from Webster's claim for undivided national sovereignty. This strategy made excellent tactical sense, since Madison worried that excessive claims for national supremacy, although an understandable response to the nullifiers' formula for anarchy, would drive moderate, sensible southerners (like his old friend Jefferson?) into the extremist fold. But the strategy also made sound theoretical sense, because Madison's intermediate position was, in his judgment, the only position in accord with the facts of the case – or, to put it differently, consistent with the history of the formation of the Constitution.[74]

In late 1830, Andrew Stevenson, speaker of the House of Representatives and a relative of Madison's, urged him not to allow the war against nullification to obscure the continuing danger of consolidation. The two men had spent time together at Montpelier just after Madison's letter to Everett appeared in the *North American Review*. Now Stevenson – an opponent of nullification who was nonetheless an ardent defender of the rights of the states – urged Madison to issue a formal statement against abuse of the "general welfare" clause and the continuing threat from those who sought to draw all power into the vortex of the general government.[75] Madison readily complied. He provided Stevenson with a thorough defense of the view that the Constitution, contrary to both the nullifiers and the more extreme nationalists, "rests on a middle

73 Just such a position was presented during the Senate debate in a speech by Edward Livingston of Louisiana, who told Madison that he had derived his principles from a close reading of Madison's writings in the *Federalist* and in the Virginia Report of 1800, as well as from his more personal knowledge of Madison's views. See Brant, *Madison: Commander in Chief*, 479.

74 For valuable discussions of this issue, see *ibid.*, 498–500; Paul C. Nagel, *One Nation Indivisible: The Union in American Thought, 1776–1861* (New York, 1964), esp. 31–32; and Maurice G. Baxter, *One and Inseparable: Daniel Webster and the Union* (Cambridge, Mass., 1984), esp. chaps. 11 and 13.

75 Stevenson to Madison, Nov. 20, 1830, Miscellaneous Papers, New York Historical Society; see also Chapters 2 and 3 of this volume.

ground between a form wholly national and one merely federal."[76] For the remainder of his years, Madison developed this insight in as many ways and in as many different places as he could. When his young friend Rives delivered a powerful speech in the Senate in February 1833 that brilliantly explained the complex nature of a Union that reconciled national supremacy and the reserved rights of the states – a speech that reportedly caused Calhoun to "wince in his seat" – Madison virtually spoke through his disciple's lips.[77] A month later, Madison wrote directly to Rives's colleague Webster, who was fond of describing an organic union that transcended formal contractual arrangements. Although Madison congratulated Webster for the blow he had struck against the nullifiers, he also condemned the Massachusetts senator's refusal to admit that the Constitution had originated in "a compact," and even more specifically in a compact among the people of the states. "It is fortunate when disputed theories can be decided by undisputed facts," Madison lectured Webster, "and here the undisputed fact is, that the Constitution was made by the people, but as imbodied into the several States who were parties to it, and, therefore, made by the States in their highest authoritative capacity." The people of the states had adopted, moreover, "a mixed form" that made them "one people, nation, or sovereignty for certain purposes" but "not so for others," and it was essential that the terms of this original compact be rigorously observed and honored – by nationalists as well as by nullifiers.[78]

The American system of government was, in fact, "emphatically *sui generis*."[79] Perhaps this explained why the members of a second political generation, lacking personal memories of the confederation

76 Madison to Stevenson, Nov. 27, 1830, in [Rives and Fendall, eds.], *Letters and Other Writings*, IV, 121–139, 131. See also Francis Fry Wayland, *Andrew Stevenson: Democrat and Diplomat, 1785–1857* (Philadelphia, 1949).

77 For Rives's speech, see the United States Congress, *Register of Debates*, 22d Cong., 2d sess., Feb. 14, 1833, 492–517. For the report of its effect, see Brant, *Madison: Commander in Chief*, 497–498. See also the correspondence between Madison and Rives for this general period.

78 Madison to Webster, Mar. 15, 1833, in [Rives and Fendall, eds.], *Letters and Other Writings*, IV, 293–294.

79 Madison to Robert S. Garnett, Feb. 11, 1824, *ibid.*, III, 367.

era, were having so much difficulty coming to grips with what their fathers had wrought. As Madison told Webster in 1830, the Constitution had created a regime "so unexampled in its origin, so complex in its structure, and so peculiar in some of its features" that the traditional "political vocabulary" did not "furnish terms sufficiently distinctive and appropriate, without a detailed resort to the facts of the case."[80] The new nationalists were to some extent guilty of the same error as the nullifiers: they failed either to grasp or to accept the fact that the American people had undertaken the unprecedented experiment of dividing sovereignty. They had distributed their sovereign power between two different levels of government, with "the portions surrendered by the States composing the Federal sovereignty over specified subjects" and "the portions retained forming the sovereignty of each over the residuary subjects within its sphere."[81] Those who now denied that sovereignty could be thus divided, Madison privately warned, "must choose between a government purely consolidated and an association of governments purely federal." The Constitution had been a response to the ignominious failure of the second alternative, embodied in the Articles of Confederation, which the nullifiers now appeared hell-bent to revive; but the Constitution represented something quite different as well from the first alternative. Americans in the late 1780s had adopted a unique "modification of political power," distributing that power so as to "avoid as well the evils of consolidation as the defects of federation" and to "obtain the advantages of both."[82]

And the experiment, Madison reminded everyone, was on the whole working splendidly. For nearly half a century, this "new and compound system" had proved successful "beyond any of the forms of government, ancient or modern, with which it may be compared." No wonder, then, that Madison concluded what turned out to be his final assault on the nullifiers with a message that was appropriate for Webster as well:

It becomes all, therefore, who are friends of a government based on free principles, to reflect, that by denying the possibility of a system partly

80 Madison to Webster, May 27, 1830, *ibid.*, IV, 85.
81 Madison to Trist, Feb. 15, 1830, *ibid.*, 61.
82 Madison, "On Nullification," 1835–1836, *ibid.*, 424–425.

federal and partly consolidated, and who would convert ours into one either wholly federal or wholly consolidated, in neither of which forms have individual rights, public order, and external safety been all duly maintained, they aim a deadly blow at the last hope of true liberty on the face of the earth.[83]

Here was an appeal capable, indeed, of rescuing Jefferson from the clutches of the nullifiers and restoring his good sense yet again.

III

During the final six years of his life, amid a sea of personal troubles that threatened to engulf him, Madison could not get the nullifiers out of his mind. At times mental agitation issued in physical collapse. For the better part of a year in 1831 and 1832 he was bedridden, if not silenced, by a joint attack of severe rheumatism and chronic bilious fevers. Literally sick with anxiety, he began to despair of his ability to make himself understood by his fellow citizens. After the appearance of his letter to Everett in the *North American Review*, sympathetic correspondents assured him of its powerful effect on the public mind. Edward Coles reported that he had taken "some pains" during a trip from Albemarle County to Philadelphia to ascertain its reception among those he encountered along the way. Save for "a few hot headed ultra State-right-men about Richmond," it was "not only approved of but highly extolled by all." But if Coles assumed that Madison would be gratified to hear that his publication had done so "much good in enlightening the Community on Constitutional doctrines, and correcting the political heresies of the day," he was doubtless taken aback by the glum and skeptical tone of his mentor's reply. Madison told Coles that he had abundant evidence — including parts of Coles's own letter — to suggest that many readers of his most recent public missive had failed, in fact, to grasp its precise meaning.[84]

83 *Ibid.*, 424–425. See also "Sovereignty," [1835], in Hunt, ed., *Writings of Madison*, IX, 568–573.

84 Edward Coles to Madison, Nov. 4, 1830, in "Letters of Edward Coles," *William and Mary Quarterly*, 2d ser., 7 (1927), 35; Madison to [Coles], Nov. 8, 1830,

Many incidents fed Madison's growing disillusionment and despair. In the late summer of 1831, an antitariff meeting at Orange Court House, within five miles of Montpelier, issued resolutions that Madison deemed "the most extraordinary, though far from the only proof, how little the constitutional branch of the subject is understood by those who take the lead on these occasions."[85] He continued to worry that self-promoting politicians would indulge their ambition by recklessly inflaming the public mind on false issues. The partisan mania that he had philosophically attributed to the election of 1828 had not disappeared, nor had the ignorance and carelessness with which the present generation approached the past. Madison refused to watch helplessly as so much of his own history was twisted and distorted, whether willfully or through negligence. When Ritchie made the silly mistake of saying in the *Enquirer* that Madison's *Helvidius* essays from the mid-1790s had opposed President Washington's proclamation of neutrality, for example, there was a prompt demand from Montpelier for a correction.[86] More serious, when the message announcing President Jackson's veto of an important internal improvements bill misrepresented the position Madison had taken against the Bonus Bill, he protested an error that he generously attributed to "too slight and hasty examination" of his 1817 veto message.[87] But Madison's concern about abuse of the past — and of his own legacy — never wandered very far from the nullifiers. In September 1831 he told Trist that if the antitariff zealots did not soon yield to the force of reason, "the explanation will lie between an impenetrable stupidity and an incurable prejudice."[88]

---

in [Rives and Fendall, eds.], *Letters and Other Writings*, IV, 119. See also Madison to Stevenson, Nov. 27, 1830, *ibid.*, 121.

85 Madison to Trist, Sept. 23, 1831, Madison Papers, Library of Congress, series one (microfilm).

86 Madison to Ritchie, May 24, 1830, in [Rives and Fendall, eds.], *Letters and Other Writings*, IV, 84.

87 Madison to Trist, June 3, 1830, *ibid.*, 87. See also Trist to Madison, May 29, 1830, Trist Papers, Virginia Historical Society; Madison to Cabell, May 31, 1830, in [Rives and Fendall, eds.], *Letters and Other Writings*, IV, 86; and Madison to Van Buren, June 3, 1830, *ibid.*, 88.

88 Madison to Trist, Sept. 23, 1831, Madison Papers, Library of Congress, series one (microfilm).

Neither choice was appealing, but no matter what the source of their obtuse perversity, some of them, he soon despaired, were incorrigible, and he could only hope for saner minds to follow.[89] "The coming generation," he remarked to Trist at the height of the crisis in early 1833, "will look back with astonishment at the infatuation which could produce the present state of things."[90]

By this time, Madison was accustomed to having his own statements dismissed with snide allusions to the date of his birth. He tried to be philosophical – at his age, he told Robert Walsh, "a writer will find his arguments, whatever they be, answered with an 'I wonder how old he is?'" – but he could hardly conceal his irritation in the face of this relentless age-baiting.[91] The general strategy of the nullifiers was, after all, quite transparent: when Madison contradicted them, they seized upon his alleged inconsistencies during a long career in order to cast doubt on the reliability of his present judgment. The charges of inconsistency rankled Madison, especially from critics who were simply too obtuse to understand the subtlety of his constitutional reasoning. "I am far from regarding a change of opinions, under the lights of experience and the results of improved reflection, as exposed to censure," he said, "and still further from the vanity of supposing myself less in need of that privilege than others. But I had indulged the belief that there were few, if any, of my contemporaries through the long period and varied scenes of my political life, to whom a mutability of opinion was less applicable," especially "on the great constitutional questions which have agitated the public mind."[92] Madison's memory of the postwar nationalism of many of the same South Carolinians who now espoused nullification no doubt sharpened his pique. And they were woefully inconsistent in another respect that he noted privately to Trist. "There can be no objection to the reference made to the weakening effect of age on the judgment, in accounting for changes

89 See, for example, Madison to Cabell, Apr. 1, 1833, in [Rives and Fendall, eds.], *Letters and Other Writings*, IV, 294–297.
90 Madison to Trist, Jan. 18, 1833, *ibid.*, 267.
91 Madison to Walsh, Feb. 15, 1831, *ibid.*, 164. See also, for example, Madison to Trist, Feb. 15, 1830, *ibid.*, 66.
92 Madison to C. E. Haynes, Feb. 25, 1831, *ibid.*, 164–165.

of opinion," he remarked bitterly. "But inconsistency, at least, may be charged on those who lay such stress on the effect of age in one case [his own], and place such peculiar confidence where that ground of distrust would be so much stronger." "What was the comparative age of Mr. Jefferson," Madison asked rhetorically, "when he wrote the letter to Mr. Giles, a few months before his death?"[93]

Madison rallied from his yearlong indisposition just as controversy turned to crisis, both in the nation and in Virginia. In late 1832, when South Carolina finally fulfilled its threat to nullify the tariff, all eyes turned to the Old Dominion as the legislature debated whether to support the insurgents. When Thomas Walker Gilmer, the young darling of the antitariff crusade, moved that five hundred copies of the Report of 1800 (which the nullifiers persisted in embracing) be printed, another delegate proposed an amendment: the Report should be printed, but with Madison's recent letter of explication in the *North American Review* attached to it. Gilmer angrily rejected the amendment; he could not support printing "the private fugitive epistles of an individual," adding that it was "useless to lumber the journal with such trash." Another worshipper of Madison's writings from the 1790s, but hardly of their author, declared that "the fabric raised by a youthful Hercules" could not be "thrown down by him in the weakness and decrepitude of old age." And delegate William Brodnax, of Dinwiddie County, pushed even further this argument for disregarding what he called Madison's "subsequent parol interpretations of written State papers." "Nothing can be more improper, instead of looking at the document itself," he charged, than "to be enquiring, thirty years after, of one of the body who adopted it, and when enfeebled by age, as to his construction of it." As Brodnax concluded in wonderfully Madisonian terms, "if this is to be tolerated, there can be no certainty or stability in any public, or official expression of principle upon earth, and politics will cease to be a science."[94]

Perhaps Madison braved a wry grin as he read the report of the

93 Madison to Trist, Dec. 1831, *ibid.*, 207.
94 The legislative debates were reported in the *Richmond Enquirer*. For quoted statements, see Dec. 22, 1832, and Jan. 29, 1833. For a more detailed discussion of events and context, see Brant, *Madison: Commander in Chief*, 493–496.

Brodnax speech in the *Enquirer*. But if he were in a mood to relish irony, he must have enjoyed much more the comments of delegate Wallace, who blasted the youthful arrogance of Madison's many detractors. "His commentary on his own Report," the delegate from Fauquier County complained, "has been tauntingly spoken of as a *mere letter*, by those who were in the feebleness of infancy, when this venerable sage, in the vigor of his perfect manhood, stood on the battlements of constitutional liberty, their ablest and most successful defender." It seemed, Wallace quipped, that "the order of nature is reversed: Youth has become the season of wisdom and experience, and age the period of rashness, *ambition*, and folly."[95]

By a vote of 65 to 45, the delegates decided not to print Madison's letter. In part this was a Pyrrhic victory for the nullifiers, however, since the legislature ultimately denied South Carolina the kind of strong support it wanted, and explicitly denied, too, that the Virginia Resolutions of 1798–1800 supported nullification.[96] And when the politicians in Washington subsequently arrived at the so-called "Compromise of 1833," lowering the tariff and successfully inducing South Carolina to rescind its nullification ordinance, the immediate danger of violent conflict and disunion seemed over. Although Madison was surely pleased by this turn of events, he was also not disposed to celebrate. In fact, he appears to have agreed with the twentieth-century historian Richard E. Ellis that the South Carolina nullifiers, far from being isolated, enjoyed "considerable support among well-placed individuals throughout the South" and "emerged from the controversy secure and unrepentant."[97] In Virginia, to be sure, the battle over the meaning of the Constitution and the security of the Union was far from over. As Rives remarked in the spring of 1833 to Trist, who was about to resign his position as President Jackson's private secretary, "we still want light very much in Virginia, where, I am sorry to tell you, both nullification and secession are much more current, than you seem to imagine at Washington."[98]

Meanwhile, the personal attacks on Madison grew bolder and

95 *Richmond Enquirer*, Jan. 5, 1833.
96 Brant, *Madison: Commander in Chief*, 496.
97 Ellis, *The Union at Risk*, ix, and passim.
98 Rives to Trist, Apr. 15, 1833, Trist Papers, Library of Congress.

more strident. Relying heavily on Robert Yates's published notes of the debates at the 1787 convention, Senator John Tyler, the future president, reminded everyone that Madison had once wanted "to render the States nothing more than the provinces of a great Government, to rear upon the ruins of the old confederacy a consolidated Government, one and indivisible."[99] What good Virginian – indeed, what good Jeffersonian – could embrace *this* authority? By the summer of 1833, copies of Tyler's speech flooded the Old Dominion, and the newspapers were once again a public forum on James Madison, past and present. Regretting the spread of innuendo and distortion, Rives gently told his mentor what no regular reader of the newspapers had to be told: the disciples of the South Carolina school were making nothing less than a systematic effort to destroy his credibility in the state.[100] The elderly Madison, his assailants implied, was a fool, and the Madison of *Publius* fame, a fraud.

We can only wonder at the depth of Madison's pain and anguish as he dutifully scanned the pages of the *Richmond Enquirer* during the summer of 1833. The efforts of one "Mutius," in a long series of articles, to show "that in consequence of the mutations in his faith, Mr. Madison's authority was not of superlative importance and transcendent value" prompted him to send Rives yet another elaborate defense of his consistency.[101] Surely Madison was nauseated by "Mutius's" mendacious denial that he meant any disrespect and by his assurances to readers that he wished the beloved patriarch well. "I was induced to animadvert upon the fluctuating character of his opinions," "Mutius" matter-of-factly explained, "because Mr. Madison's 'authority' is so frequently invoked to sustain a false creed, or strengthen a weak cause. We are in this country," "Mutius" complained, "too apt to become man-worshippers, without

99 Tyler, speech in Senate, Feb. 6, 1833, *Register of Debates*, 22d Cong., 2d sess., 362. On Yates's notes, see Chapter 3 of this volume.

100 Rives to Madison, Oct. 4, 1833, and Rives to Madison, July 28, 1833, Rives Papers, Rosenbach Foundation (transcripts on file at the Papers of James Madison project office, Alderman Library, University of Virginia, Charlottesville).

101 *Richmond Enquirer*, Aug. 20, 1833 (see also Sept. 20, 1833); Madison to Rives, Oct. 21, 1833, in [Rives and Fendall, eds.], *Letters and Other Writings*, IV, 309–323.

due regard to truth or common sense. We have no right to expect or to assert, that any man or set of men are *absolutely perfect in wisdom* or virtue." Madison did not want a nation of "man-worshippers," either. Nor did he consider himself a faultless paragon of wisdom or virtue. But he doubtless shared the views of "Germanicus," a critic of "Mutius," who found it "very singular" indeed that "those who live in the present day, although unborn when the Constitution was formed, understand the views and objects of the framers of that instrument, better than they who formed it!" And Madison could take some cheer in this scribbler's passionate plea to the people of Virginia not to forsake the wisdom of her patriarchs. "The admonitions and instructions of the aged, the able and experienced men of our country," "Germanicus" declared, "should be received, and weighed with great deference and respect. They speak from experience, and, therefore, speak the lessons of truth and soberness."[102]

But "Germanicus's" plea went largely unheeded – or at least Madison thought it did. Writing to Edward Livingston in August 1834, he observed that "party spirit rages with all its vigor, and nowhere more than in Virginia, which is among the States where the scales seem most on a poise."[103] A year earlier he had glumly admitted that his views on the tariff opposed "the dominant opinions in Virginia as well as elsewhere."[104] If it seemed to Madison that fewer and fewer people were willing to listen to him or, even if willing, able to understand what he said, he could not fail to notice that the problem extended to some of his closest followers. He was able to communicate and cooperate quite effectively with both Rives and Trist; but the same cannot be said of his kinsman and former secretary Edward Coles. In the fall of 1834, a series of tense exchanges nearly severed their relationship. When one of Madison's closest associates and self-proclaimed disciples from the next generation failed to understand him – and allowed the spirit of "party" to overwhelm the measured and dispassionate wisdom he called for –

102 For "Mutius," see *Richmond Enquirer*, July 23, 1833; for his critic "Germanicus," see *ibid.*, Aug. 6, 1833.
103 Madison to Livingston, Aug. 2, 1834, in [Rives and Fendall, eds.], *Letters and Other Writings*, IV, 347.
104 Madison to Professor Davis [not sent], 1832 [1833], *ibid.*, 259.

Madison had cause to wonder, indeed, if the Constitution as he knew it were not irretrievably lost.

The trouble between Coles and Madison apparently began in 1831, when the younger man began to draw on Madison's authority in ways that Madison found offensive and for causes that Madison deemed secondary and even trivial. Coles usually chose his causes carefully, but once he did, he was tenacious in their pursuit, especially, as we shall see in a future chapter, when slavery was involved. At a moment when Madison was preoccupied with his struggle against the nullifiers, Coles excitedly summoned his mentor to assist him in disputing a claim – one that Madison judged preposterous – regarding land titles in Coles's adopted state of Illinois. Madison politely chastised his former secretary for his faulty sense of priorities and, less directly, for the importunate tone of his request; he also had to warn him not to violate the strict confidentiality of their correspondence.[105] From Madison's point of view, Coles's problem arose in no small part from his passionate partisanship. The young man indulged his longstanding hatred of Andrew Jackson with little restraint, and by 1834, had managed to convince himself that "King Andrew's" executive usurpations were a colossal threat to the integrity and security of the republic. He felt so strongly, indeed, that he virtually demanded that Madison take a public stand against the evil tyrant.[106]

When Madison repeatedly spurned Coles's call to Armageddon, each man lost patience with the other. Madison tried in vain to convince Coles not only that Jackson's popularity was an anomaly, which suggested that any danger posed by his abuse of patronage would die with his presidency, but also that "the anarchical principle" of nullification was rapidly gaining ground, often in new disguises and most alarmingly in Virginia. Madison was repeatedly urged to speak out against the putative evils of executive usurpation, but not all of Jackson's "Whig" opponents who approached him

105 Coles to Madison, June 12, 1831, in "Letters of Coles," *William and Mary Quarterly*, 2d ser., 7 (1927), 36; Madison to [Coles], June 28, 1831, in [Rives and Fendall, eds.], *Letters and Other Writings*, IV, 187–188.
106 Coles to Madison, Aug. 17, 1834, in "Letters of Coles," *William and Mary Quarterly*, 2d ser., 7 (1927), 40–41.

shared Coles's particular political persuasion. Madison knew that the president's threatened use of force against South Carolina, along with the extreme nationalism expressed in his Nullification Proclamation of December 1832, had irrevocably alienated many staunch defenders of state rights in Virginia, who now displayed considerable sympathy, if not outright support, for the nullifiers. Clearly, Madison had no desire to lend any assistance to this anti-Jackson movement – a coalition of strange bedfellows, indeed, that brought together the "American System" ideologue Henry Clay and Calhoun himself – in part because he feared that the movement would only play into the hands of the nullifiers by lending new strength to their cause. *Here* was the great danger to the republic – "local prejudices and ambitious leaders" in the southern states were spreading a disease that could prove lethal to the Union, while a naive Coles, a slave to his consuming hatred of Andrew Jackson, was caught looking the other way.[107]

Undaunted, Coles dismissed Madison's response to his request as unsatisfactory and utterly irresponsible. Chiding Madison for not seeing that nullification was harmless next to the threat posed by Jackson's exercise of executive prerogative, Coles virtually demanded that Madison perform the necessary service of disavowing the current administration. He brushed off Madison's protestations that no one would listen to him, insisting that the venerable sage exercised tremendous influence over public opinion. And he brusquely made it clear that he would accept no further excuses.[108]

Although neither man gave any ground, they proved able, in the end, to repair the damage to their relationship.[109] But for Madison it must have been an especially unsettling experience. Coles's behavior probably came as no surprise to him, but it was, for that, no less disturbing. Madison knew that Coles had neither the intellectual discipline nor the sound historical sense of his peer Rives, and

---

107 Madison to Coles, Aug. 29, 1834, in Hunt, ed., *Writings of Madison*, IX, 541, 542. See also Brant, *Madison: Commander in Chief*, 512–514.
108 Coles to Madison, Sept. 15, 1834, Edward Coles Papers, Chicago Historical Society.
109 For the respective gestures of conciliation, see Coles to Madison, Oct. 31, 1834, Edward Coles Papers, Chicago Historical Society, and Madison to Coles, Nov. 15, 1834, Edward Coles Papers, Princeton University Archives.

Edward Coles, c. 1831. Lithograph by Albert Newsam, after Henry Inman. (Courtesy of the Historical Society of Pennsylvania, Philadelphia)

he had understood for quite some time that Coles's habit of fixing on a single cause or issue often upset his capacity for balanced judgment. Madison certainly resented Coles's presumptuous approach to invoking his name and authority, and he genuinely feared that Coles, by fanning the flames of passionate opposition to Jackson, was unwittingly strengthening the nullifiers. But Madison also respected the younger man's moral integrity, his noble intentions, and perhaps, too, his determination to think for himself. Madison's troubled relationship with Coles underlines, indeed, both his bitter ambivalence and the larger dilemma that no good republican, not even the last of the Fathers, could escape.

In this connection, his response to Coles's assertion that his views still carried great authority among his countrymen is most revealing. Madison left the point implicit, but if Coles had stopped to think for a moment, he might have realized that Madison's authority had failed to change even his own mind. "May I not appeal, also," Madison asked Coles,

to facts which will satisfy yourself of the error which supposes that a respect for my opinion, even naked opinion, would control the adverse opinions of others? On the subject of the bank, on that of the tariff, and on that of nullification, three great constitutional questions of the day, my opinions, with the grounds of them, are well known, being in print with my name to them. Yet the bank was, perhaps, never more warmly opposed than at present; the tariff seems to have lost none of its unpopularity; whilst nullification has been for some time, and is at present, notoriously advancing with some of my best personal, and heretofore political, friends among its advocates.[110]

Madison did not want this vivid account of his loss of influence to convey the impression that he was bitter and disillusioned – or did he? "It must not be thought," he told Coles, "that I am displeased or disappointed at this result. On the contrary, I honor the independent judgment that decides for itself; and I know well that a spirit of party is not less unyielding."[111]

Four years earlier, Madison had thanked Jefferson's granddaugh-

110 Madison to Coles, Oct. 15, 1834, in [Rives and Fendall, eds.], *Letters and Other Writings*, IV, 367.
111 *Ibid.*

ter, Ellen Randolph Coolidge of Boston, for sending him an advance review of her grandfather's published correspondence. "The reviewer has, I observe, taken particular notice of a letter to me, which presents a view, at once original and profound, of the relations between one generation and another," he wrote. "It must be admitted, as he remarks, that there would be difficulties in reducing it fully to practice. But it affords a practical lesson well according with the policy of free nations."[112] In the midst of his battle with the nullifiers, Madison's thoughts turned once again to his dialogue with Jefferson at the time of the founding of the republic and to the inescapable challenge of accommodating Revolutionary principles and civilized order. He believed that stability, justice, and the preservation of the Union were impossible without deference to the founding generation. And yet the deference could not be – and ought not to be – unthinking or blindly reverential. Indeed, Madison had stated the matter as well as anyone, many years earlier, in *Federalist* number fourteen. "Is it not the glory of the people of America," he had asked, "that whilst they have paid a decent regard to the opinions of former times and other nations, they have not suffered a blind veneration for antiquity, for custom, or for names, to overrule the suggestions of their own good sense, the knowledge of their own situation, and the lessons of their own experience?" The republican faith meant, if anything, that people had the right to form their own government, to make their own judgments, and if they wished, to ignore the weight of tradition and the authority of their ancestors, no matter how revered. Madison's generation had done all of those things, after all; and "to this manly spirit," he had proclaimed in 1788, "posterity will be indebted for the possession, and the world for the example of the numerous innovations displayed on the American theatre, in favor of private rights and public happiness."[113] Now the elderly Madison had no choice but to exhort posterity to be wise enough to understand – and to voluntarily embrace – a priceless legacy that was in danger of being lost forever.

112 Madison to Mrs. E. Coolidge, Apr. 8, 1830, *ibid.*, 69.
113 Jacob E. Cooke, ed., *The Federalist* (Middletown, Conn., 1961 [orig. publ. 1788]), 88.

✳

Within days of Madison's death, his widow, brother-in-law, and other family friends were busy readying his papers for publication. The Father of the Constitution had parried all requests that he personally release his exclusive notes from the 1787 convention, offering several reasons for his decision to make their publication posthumous. As long as any of the delegates remained alive, he felt at least partially constrained by the spirit of the convention's rule of secrecy, according to which they had all spoken freely and in confidence – even though this rule was honored mostly in the breach long before Madison was the only one left. He also voiced the opinion, early on, that publication was best "delayed till the Constitution should be well settled by practice, and till a knowledge of the controversial part of the proceedings of its framers could be turned to no improper account." Ever mindful of his belief that the debates and "incidental decisions" of the Philadelphia convention had no "authoritative character" when it came to expounding and applying particular provisions of the Constitution, Madison apparently sought to minimize the risk that his records would be misappropriated for that kind of use.[114] His overriding purpose, indeed, was to enhance the proper influence of what he hoped his countrymen would receive as a national treasure – a treasure suited, as he put it in 1823, "rather for general and future use than for occurrences of the day."[115]

Writing to Samuel H. Smith four years later, Madison reiterated his belief that publication "posthumous to others as well as myself, may be most delicate, and most useful too." "As no personal or party views can then be imputed," the documents would be "read with less of personal or party feelings, and consequently with whatever profit may be promised by them." Madison apparently believed that if he released his papers while still alive, it was more likely that he

114 Madison to Thomas Ritchie, Sept. 15, 1821, in Hunt, ed., *Writings of Madison*, IX, 71n-72n.
115 Madison to Tench Coxe, Nov. 3, 1823, in [Rives and Fendall, eds.], *Letters and Other Writings*, III, 342.

would be accused of harboring partisan motives, and that the precious documents would therefore suffer the kind of reception that soon greeted, in fact, his public letters on the tariff and nullification. No doubt he also wished to avoid having to respond to endless requests that he clarify and explain not only the views expressed in his speeches at the 1787 convention, but their relevance to present-day controversies. And there was yet another element to Madison's consideration worth noting: his desire to arouse and strengthen feelings of reverence, indeed veneration, among new generations of republicans. He believed that respect for the peculiar dignity that antiquity conferred – so much, as David Hume had taught, a part of human nature – would work to proper advantage if delay lent the papers the requisite appeal. "It is true also," he told Smith, "that after a certain date, the older such things grow, the more they are relished as new; the distance of time like that of space from which they are received, giving them that attractive character."[116]

Madison prepared his last will and testament in the spring of 1835, shortly after Harriet Martineau's visit to Montpelier. He bequeathed to his wife "all my manuscript papers, having entire confidence in her discreet and proper use of them," subject to one qualification that he stipulated at some length:

Considering the peculiarity and magnitude of the occasion which produced the convention at Philadelphia in 1787, the Characters who composed it, the Constitution which resulted from their deliberation, it's effects during a trial of so many years on the prosperity of the people living under it, and the interest it has inspired among the friends of free Government, it is not an unreasonable inference that a careful and extended report of the proceedings and discussions of that body, which were with closed doors, by a member who was constant in his attendance, will be particularly gratifying to the people of the United States, and to all who take an interest in the progress of political science and the cause of true liberty.

It was his desire, Madison continued, that "the report as made by me" should be published under his wife's authority and direction; but "as the publication may yield a considerable amount beyond the necessary expenses thereof," the "net proceeds" were assigned to her,

116 Madison to Smith, Feb. 2, 1827, in Hunt, ed., *Writings of Madison*, IX, 269–270.

and charged with a list of legacies. Out of the fund to be derived from the sale and publication of the convention debates, in other words, fixed amounts were earmarked for specific individuals and purposes. Madison bequeathed two thousand dollars to Ralph R. Gurley, secretary of the American Colonization Society, for the society's use in its ambitious program to colonize American blacks in Africa; fifteen hundred dollars went to the University of Virginia, one thousand dollars to his alma mater in Princeton, New Jersey; another thousand to the College at Uniontown, Pennsylvania; and roughly six thousand dollars was reserved for the education and support of some of his great-nephews and great-nieces. Madison was thus confident enough of the value that his countrymen would place on the manuscript – pecuniary and otherwise – to direct the anticipated proceeds to worthy philanthropic purposes. Obviously he also hoped that publication of his notes would serve another, more personal end, that of providing for his much younger wife, for whose support and comfort, he worried, the rest of his estate might prove inadequate.[117]

Less than a month after Madison's death, his widow had the papers well enough arranged to entertain bids from interested parties. Her son journeyed to New York, she later reported, where he remained "for the purpose of negotiating with the most eminent publishers" while she communicated with additional prospects in other cities. After several months, however, no offer had been made by any publisher "entitled to confidence" that would free her "from heavy and inconvenient pecuniary advances and the risks of impositions and eventual loss."[118] At her son's urging, she rejected a bid from Harper's.[119] The commercial publishers apparently wanted Mrs. Madison to take the financial gamble they themselves would not. "The proposals which have been received," she lamented to

117 Madison's will, Apr. 19, 1835, *ibid.*, 549–550. See also Brant, *Madison: Commander in Chief*, 514. Madison was not oblivious to the possibility of some disappointment, since he stipulated that if the anticipated fund proved insufficient to pay for the whole of the legacies, they should "abate in proportion."
118 Dolley Madison to Henry Clay, Nov. 8, 1836, Cutts–Madison Collection, Library of Congress (microfilm).
119 John C. Payne to William Cabell Rives, Oct. 20, 1836, Rives Papers, Library of Congress, box 54.

President Jackson, "so far from corresponding with the expectations of Mr. Madison when he charged the first of these works with those legacies, have evidenced that their publication could not be engaged in by me, without advances of funds and involving risks which I am not in a situation to make or incur."[120]

Depressed and in poor health, she seized upon a plan formulated by Madison's young friend Trist: the manuscript would be offered instead to the federal government, with the "failure of individual enterprize as the ground of the memorial to Congress for the interposition of the public aid."[121] The original plan called for her to offer the work to the patronage of Congress, requesting its assistance in defraying the cost of the legacies, after which use the stereotype plates would be returned to her. "This would at once allow me to throw them into general circulation on a scale that would remunerate me more in accordance with the expectations entertained by their author, and would also allow the price to be so graduated as to ensure their general diffusion."[122] Although this particular arrangement proved unsatisfactory, the general plan of approaching the government in Washington seemed sound. As Vice-President Van Buren had reassured Rives, "assuming that there is no constitutional [problem] I would think there would be no other difficulty." After all, "the authority to make such purchases appears to have been taken for granted in Genl. Washington's case, & there can be no doubt of the disposition of Congress to favor Mrs. Madison."[123] Both Madison's widow and her brother, John C. Payne, who acted as her agent, worried that the proposal would become enmeshed in partisan politics, with one party trying to lay exclusive claim to the Madison legacy and driving the other to oppose the venture. Nevertheless, they were generally optimistic. Trist was closely connected with the Jackson administration; the president promised to

---

120 Dolley Madison to Andrew Jackson, Nov. 15, 1836, Madison Papers, Library of Congress, series one (microfilm).
121 Payne to Rives, Oct. 20, 1836, Rives Papers, Library of Congress, box 54.
122 Dolley Madison to Clay, Nov. 8, 1836, Cutts–Madison Collection, Library of Congress (microfilm).
123 Van Buren to Rives, Sept. 11, 1836, Rives Papers, Library of Congress, box 54.

help; Rives was a powerful Jacksonian leader in the Senate; and the most influential member of the opposition party, Henry Clay, was willing to do what he could to assure bipartisan support of the project. It remained only to decide on specific financial arrangements.

Using a formula that Coles had gotten from some commercial publishers, the family arrived at the figure of $100,000 for the anticipated three volumes of convention debates. They acknowledged that this figure had not been set by Madison, but they defended it as reasonable. Few in Washington agreed. James Barbour conveyed the sad news that the suggested price had caused considerable embarrassment to members of Congress friendly to the idea of purchasing the debates, and that $30,000 was probably the best that could be gotten. In fact, Barbour made it clear that unless he and others were immediately authorized to accept that figure on behalf of the family, there was the real danger of failure. Payne responded by saying that Dolley would take $50,000. "She has been led into high expectations, because Mr. Madison himself entertained them, and the world at large seemed to confirm the impression received from him; and although an inflexibility on this point should not be inferred, much disappointment of hopes hitherto indulged would follow an acceptance of less." Three weeks later, the widow agreed to take $30,000, provided she retained the foreign copyright. [124]

Only one major hurdle remained: gaining the formal approval of Congress. Senator Calhoun took the lead in opposing the bill, which he promptly branded unconstitutional. The *Register of Debates* recorded some of his sentiments:

The question now before the Senate, Mr. C. said, was whether Congress had the power to purchase the copy-right to Mr. Madison's papers, which, in the present state of political feelings, were regarded of little or no value in the money market. Mr. C. regarded it as truly deplorable, that these invaluable papers, which threw a light upon the constitution which had never been shed upon it before, should be deemed of no value by the public, absorbed with party politics and the low love of gain, so that such a

124 Payne to Rives, Dec. 14, 15, 24, and 30, 1836, *ibid.*; Dolley Madison to Rives, Jan. 15, 1837, *ibid.*, box 55.

work could not be published. But where, Mr. C. asked, was the special power in the constitution for Congress to publish such a work?

Certainly not in the "general welfare" clause, Calhoun maintained, and to make the point he read from Madison's famed Report of 1800, which denied the false interpretation of that notorious clause that supporters of the present bill would need to rely on. Indeed, Calhoun touted the Virginia Report as Madison's greatest constitutional testament and said that Congress would dishonor his name by assenting to an appropriation of money for which the Constitution gave no sanction. "Mr. C. felt that his position in opposition to this resolution was a painful one; but the opinions of Mr. Madison, which were the text book of Mr. C., and of those with whom he acted, demanded that he should not abandon it."[125]

Some of Calhoun's colleagues ventured support of his opposition. Senator John M. Niles of Connecticut agreed that Congress was in effect being asked to pay the legacies in Madison's will, which was obviously wrong, and he added that the American people would have the benefit of the documents in question no matter what Congress did. Besides, he continued, Congress had no business subsidizing and distributing political literature. He did not mean to denigrate the value of Madison's papers, but passage of this bill would set a dangerous precedent for the exercise of a "very extraordinary" and "very dangerous" power.[126] Perhaps buoyed by such support, Calhoun had a bit more to say before the final vote. No doubt he objected vehemently to at least one of the specific legacies in Madison's will, but he left implicit the argument that Congress should not subsidize the antislavery Colonization Society. He did say that it was regrettable that Mr. Madison had chosen to draw his will in the peculiar way that he had. He should have left his papers as a free legacy to the American people. But now Congress was put in the awkward position of being able to honor Madison's memory — and his constitutional principles — only by refusing to purchase and publish the convention notes that he had so conscientiously gathered for posterity. Calhoun said that he was especially eager to display

125 United States Senate, Feb. 1837, *Register of Debates*, 24th Cong., 2d sess., 858–859.
126 *Ibid.*, 863.

John C. Calhoun, Senator. Miniature by Washington Blanchard. (Courtesy of the New-York Historical Society, New York City)

such deference because he would be repaying a personal debt. When young and unwise, he had himself leaned toward the constitutional heresies of consolidation, until the profound teachings of Madison and the principles of 1798 had rescued him from his delusion.[127]

127 *Ibid.*, 866.

An angry and disgusted Senator Rives took the floor to answer Calhoun. An appeal to "strict construction" of the Constitution was utterly inappropriate, he said, and as a friend of Madison and the family he resented any gratuitous commentary on "the private actions of the dead." Henry Clay then made it clear that not all adversaries of the Democratic Party stood with the South Carolinian. Calling the present debate ridiculous, Clay referred to Madison as "the most distinguished, with a single exception, of the patriots of the Revolution." When the final vote was called, the opposition of fourteen senators could not prevent passage of the bill.[128]

128 *Ibid.*, 867, 870–871, 871–872.

5. The Republic Transformed:
Population, Economy, and Society

MADISON'S adamant refusal to discount the threat of the nullifiers after their apparent national defeat in early 1833 – a position that he sustained with such vigor in his correspondence with the wayward legatee Edward Coles – arose from more than his fear of their constitutional heresies. The nullifiers had left a vicious legacy in more areas than Madison cared to count. Of especial concern to him was the popular appeal of their economic analysis, no matter how simplistic and misleading he judged it to be. Madison scorned the battery of economic ideas that had energized opposition to the tariff in his own state as well as in South Carolina. But he could hardly dismiss the potential significance of the noxious trail of fear and recrimination which those ideas had laid. Writing to Henry Clay in the spring of 1833, Madison anxiously decried "the torch of discord, bequeathed by the Convention of South Carolina, to its country" with "the insidious exhibitions of a permanent incompatibility, and even hostility of interests between the South and the North." Of all the misleading ideas put forth by the nullifiers, their ultimate contention – that the economic systems of these two regions of the American republic were so different as to be, at bottom, irreconcilable – threatened the greatest mischief. And in their spurious allegation that a permanent northern majority was now free to victimize, almost at will, an increasingly vulnerable southern minority, the malcontents patently sought to engender "a disgust with the Union" that Madison had been defending for almost fifty years.[1]

Madison agreed with the nullifiers on at least one count: that

---

1 Madison to Henry Clay, Apr. 2, 1833, in [William C. Rives and Philip R. Fendall, eds.], *Letters and Other Writings of James Madison* (Philadelphia, 1865), IV, 568.

their protest was inextricably tied to shifting economic circumstances. When he assessed the origins of the antitariff movement, he pointed to a complex set of variables that included the familiar "sophistry of the passions" as well as the irresponsible ambition of local politicians. But he never denied that the primary source of the political unrest lay in economic conditions. He only quarrelled with the nullifiers about the causes of the distress that fueled their protest. In their monomaniacal indictment of federal laws for promoting manufactures – which they insisted on construing, in Madison's words, as "a system of plunder, wresting the money from the pockets of the Southern agriculturalist and putting it into the pockets of the Northern manufacturers" – the antitariff zealots conjured up a scapegoat for regional economic woes that arose, in fact, from very different and more complicated conditions.[2] As Madison remarked to Joseph Cabell in late 1831, the insurgency would doubtless continue red-hot "while mistaken causes of exaggerated sufferings continue to nourish it; while the tariff, which produced [the protest], is exclusively charged with the inevitable effects of a market equally glutted with the products of the land and with the land itself."[3] And Madison pointed to these mistaken and distorted views in political economy as doubly tragic. They sustained the feverish delusion among growing numbers of southern Americans that he so much feared; they also prevented the insurgents from understanding that current trends actually pointed toward an accommodation, rather than a polarization, of regional economic interests.

Madison's assessment of these matters was rooted squarely in his larger views on political economy. Developed throughout his retirement (and not always in connection with nullification), these views pointed both backward and forward in time. They were, on the one hand, an appropriate capstone to Madison's engagement for almost half a century with some of the most challenging issues of republican theory.[4] Here, as elsewhere, his analysis during the final twenty

2 Madison to Professor Davis, 1832 [1833], (not sent), *ibid.*, 260.
3 Madison to Joseph C. Cabell, Sept. 16, 1831, *ibid.*, 196.
4 For background and elaboration, see Drew R. McCoy, *The Elusive Republic: Political Economy in Jeffersonian America* (Chapel Hill, N.C., 1980), chaps. 1–9.

years of his life was especially reminiscent of his thinking during the critical decade of his career, the 1780s, as we find a remarkable continuity of approach and concern between the two eras. In both periods, moreover, he seemed as preoccupied with the future as with the present. After the Revolution, Madison had often speculated about both the near and the distant future; during his retirement, he gazed unblinkingly at the former as it had materialized in the intervening decades and extended his contemplation of the latter. Although his fundamental values and purposes had not changed, some of his specific views had, and the shifts in his thinking are best understood in a larger context: Madison had gradually accommodated his republican vision both to the relentless logic of social development – which he had analyzed so acutely at the time of the Constitutional Convention – and to a revolution in American political culture that had been no less visible to the young man laboring through a difficult summer in Philadelphia.

Most remarkable of all, the Sage of Montpelier never succumbed to the kind of despair that both the underlying premises of his political economy and the nullification movement might well have engendered. With renewed emphasis on the power of education, especially, his republican faith endured. Harriet Martineau had not been deceived; in the last years of his life, Madison was notable for the guarded, even stoical, optimism with which he pondered the future. And in the realm of political economy, perhaps, that optimism seemed not quite so precariously dependent, as it was in other areas, on a cheerful disposition, wishful thinking, or the mere force of will.

I

Although Madison began soon after he left Washington in early 1817 to question the health of America's economy, his concern quickened once the Panic of 1819 settled into a worrisome depression. The proximate causes of "the present general embarrassments" were not hard to discern, as Madison pointed to the familiar "want of economy in the use of imported articles" among Americans and to the contributing role of banks that had extended more than liberal

173

credit to reckless, and soon heavily indebted, speculators and consumers.[5] As always, the best remedy for these ills was individual frugality and self-restraint; if Americans re-embraced the austerity befitting serious republicans, relief would soon follow. Yet Madison also emphatically believed that the hard times reflected more fundamental structural difficulties in the American economy. If the country continued to be plagued by a problem that reached far back in time – the so-called unfavorable balance of trade, which signified that Americans purchased more from foreigners than they sold to them – the problem lay as much in deficient exports as in excessive imports. By tightening their belts, resisting the lure of luxury, and disdaining the trap of indebtedness, Americans might, by controlling their consumption of foreign goods, begin to alleviate their distress. But individual moral reform could do little to remedy the more serious problem of overproduction and inadequate markets for a burgeoning agricultural surplus. In fact, the virtuous pursuit of traditional republican ideals seemed to exacerbate the dilemma. The ironies were as inescapable as they were cruel.[6]

Madison's vision of a healthy republic – a vision that had captured the fancy and allegiance of large numbers of his countrymen – had always been rooted in nature. He believed that the United States was endowed with natural advantages that not only distinguished it from less favored countries in Europe, but made possible (and plausible) its breathtaking venture in republican government. In 1821, for instance, we find Madison speaking revealingly of "the gifts of nature" in reference to America and of "the limits prescribed by nature" with regard to Holland and Britain.[7] The key, of course, was land; or, more specifically, the astonishingly low ratio of population to land that promised the overwhelming majority of Ameri-

5 Madison to Clarkson Crolius, Dec. 1819, in Gaillard Hunt, ed., *The Writings of James Madison* (New York and London, 1900–1910), IX, 15–16.
6 These issues are developed in a somewhat broader context in Drew R. McCoy, "An Unfinished Revolution: The Quest for Economic Independence in the Early Republic," in Jack P. Greene, ed., *The American Revolution: Its Character and Limits* (New York, 1987), 131–148.
7 Madison to Richard Rush, Nov. 20, 1821, in [Rives and Fendall, eds.], *Letters and Other Writings*, III, 236, and Madison to General LaFayette, 1821, *ibid.*, 239.

cans direct access to the productive resources of nature. This advantage was inestimable. After all, as republican theory taught, only individuals who could feed themselves possessed the full measure of personal independence that supported the kind of political freedom that made self-government possible. America's vast reservoir of unoccupied territory offered the means of sustaining what Madison referred to at the Constitutional Convention as "the safest depositories of Republican liberty," a population of freeholders.[8] Territorial expansion – the diffusion of the republic's increasing numbers across space – was therefore synonymous with the preservation of a Revolutionary order.

But Madison's vision had never been quite that simple or straightforward. If population growth had been central to his thinking since at least the 1780s, his demographic analysis cut several different ways. America's abundance of land – her gift of nature – did more than provide a vital source of moral and social regeneration; by offering such a prodigious supply of subsistence, it also stimulated the population explosion itself. Benjamin Franklin had pondered as early as the 1750s the phenomenal capacity of North Americans to increase their numbers. At the end of the century, the renowned British population theorist T. R. Malthus lent his imprimatur to Franklin's calculations, and Madison doubtless counted himself – with good cause – among those whose independent speculations made Malthus less original than he appeared. Madison clearly regarded America's demographic energy as a source of national strength and therefore pride – what better evidence, after all, of unique natural endowments, a healthy society, and a glorious future than such a rapidly increasing population? When he learned in the early 1820s, for instance, that the British theorist William Godwin was disputing Malthus's claims about the prolific quality of the human species, and denying, in particular, "the increase of the American population from its own stock," Madison could barely contain his rage. Godwin's absurd claim that the demographic growth of the United States was not only exaggerated but due

8 Madison in Constitutional Convention, Aug. 7, 1787, in Max Farrand, ed., *The Records of the Federal Convention of 1787*, rev. ed. (New Haven and London, 1937), II, 203.

"wholly to emigrations from Europe" so rankled the American that he sent Richard Rush an elaborate refutation, which he hoped Rush would employ to good advantage in any conversations he might have on the subject in England. Madison sincerely believed that Malthus had the better of the argument with Godwin, of course, but he was especially irked because no matter what his motives, Godwin's theorizing had a "tendency to disparage abroad the prospective importance of the United States, who must owe their rapid growth to the principle combatted."[9]

Indeed, whenever Madison spoke of America's future importance in the global scheme of things, he adverted to the country's phenomenal growth in population and power that could be traced to its natural advantages. Stimulated by his reading of a recent treatise on the condition of Europe in 1819, Madison belittled claims for England's (and Russia's) future greatness, pointing instead to the mind boggling potential for national growth in the New World. He was confident, for instance, that "the trident" – by which he meant supremacy in commerce and navigation – would "ultimately belong, not to the Eastern, but to the Western Hemisphere," where "the greater and more lasting fund of materials are found for constructing ships, and for bulky cargoes; and consequently for the employment of marines."[10] Writing to the Englishman George Joy in late 1821, Madison's anticipation of a profound shift of power between Europe (especially Britain) and the United States is reminiscent of Franklin's speculations a half-century earlier. And like Franklin, the Virginian pointed, above all, to the undeniable implications of America's demographic explosion. He told Joy that present-day American readers were much less interested in newspaper reports of "what occurs abroad" than formerly, and that European interest in American developments, once negligible, was doubtless growing. "This is a natural consequence of the change going on in the relative growth of this Country," he proudly noted. "If it should continue to prosper

9 Madison to Richard Rush, Apr. 21, 1821, in [Rives and Fendall, eds.], *Letters and Other Writings*, III, 212, 209. Madison's interest in Malthus and Godwin surfaced in several other letters during this period.
10 Madison to Rush, Nov. 21, 1821, *ibid.*, 236. See also Madison to George Joy, Sept. 9, 1834, *ibid.*, IV, 361.

till it reaches a population, which self-love predicts, of 60 or 70 millions," this reversal of both fortunes and attention would be complete. "This is a light in which the people of G. Britain are too proud to view the future," he comfortably observed, "and the people of this country too vain, if that be the epithet, not to regard it."[11]

Nevertheless, if this prolific increase in numbers was emblematic of America's health and future greatness, it also contributed in various ways to a republican dilemma that Madison had first pondered in the years surrounding the Constitutional Convention. Given such a burgeoning population, westward expansion was urgently necessary to defuse the threat of social crowding and, consequently, of political decay. Madison wondered how long such Old World evils could be deferred and also how Americans would eventually cope once the supply of land was exhausted. Fortunately, this problem, while too obvious to be ignored, could be relegated to the rather distant future, especially after the Louisiana Purchase of 1803. The issues raised by a somewhat different train of analysis could not. As the number of people, and hence producers, in a healthy, rural America increased, so too did the size of the agricultural surplus.[12] Vast expanses of fertile land and an industrious republican people were an explosive combination. That farmers in the United States were capable of producing a great deal more than what was necessary to feed even America's mushrooming numbers was obvious. Whether foreign markets sufficient to absorb this prodigious surplus beyond domestic subsistence could be found – and exploited – remained during Madison's retirement what it had been in the 1780s: the question that defined the inescapable challenge for Americans who yearned, for good republican reasons, to remain an industrious and virtuous people on the land. Madison had long assumed, indeed, that without such markets, the United States would be forced to develop extensive public manufactures beyond

11 Madison to George Joy, Nov. 21, 1821, *ibid.*, 241–242.
12 For evidence of Madison's connection of these two matters, see, for example, his letter to Reynolds Chapman on Jan. 6, 1831, in Hunt, ed., *Writings of Madison*, IX, 432, in which he refers to "the increased products [of the land] resulting from the rapid increase of population" that drove prices down and produced considerable distress.

what one modern scholar has appropriately called "the household-handicraft-mill complex of an advanced agricultural society." This was a prospect that he had generally hoped to defer for as long as possible. [13]

Madison had appeared confident in the late 1780s that the markets were there and that Americans could get to them, once a more competent federal government – the one provided for in the Constitution – used its power to undermine the mercantilistic system of commercial restrictions that European governments favored to harass and diminish American trade. Thirty years later, his optimism had all but vanished. A rather grim record of apparent failure notwithstanding, his faith in the efficacy of American commercial coercion remained remarkably strong; the problem, he now suggested, was that adequate markets would not be available even if his ideal world of free trade were somehow secured – which he conceded was an unlikely prospect in any event. Logic suggested that because population (and hence the number of producers) was growing far more quickly in the United States than population (hence the number of potential consumers) in Europe, the imbalance between the volume of the republic's agricultural surplus and the foreign demand would only increase. Put simply and paradoxically, American farmers were too industrious for their own good; they produced too much. As Madison told Rush in 1821, the usually astute Malthus had erred in "assigning for the increase of human food an arithmetical ratio," for in a country "as fertile as the United States" the increase might exceed even the higher geometrical ratio that the Englishman assigned to the increase of population. Indeed, Madison added in reference to Virginia that "a surplus" beyond that ratio, "for which a foreign demand has failed," was "a primary cause of the present embarrassments of this Country." [14]

Glancing back at recent history, moreover, Madison was con-

13 Merrill D. Peterson, *Thomas Jefferson and the New Nation* (New York, 1970), 941. For elaboration see McCoy, *Elusive Republic*, passim, and McCoy, "Jefferson and Madison on Malthus: Population Growth in Jeffersonian Political Economy," in *Virginia Magazine of History and Biography* 88 (1980), 259–276.
14 Madison to Rush, Apr. 21, 1821, in [Rives and Fendall, eds.], *Letters and Other Writings*, III, 209–210.

vinced that these "present embarrassments" underlined the failure of Americans after the War of 1812 to adjust to a fundamental shift of international conditions. To the extent that American commerce had thrived during the period between the adoption of the Constitution and his presidency, it had profited directly from extraordinary circumstances abroad – and, he might have added, from the distress of other peoples. Madison did not have to be reminded that the long years of war in Europe had created many vexing diplomatic problems for the neutral United States, problems that ultimately dragged the fledgling republic, during his own administration, into the war. But the Napoleonic wars had also provided a basis, however precarious and ephemeral, for the unparalleled expansion of American commerce and withal, for the prosperity of American farmers – at least until Madison and Jefferson had resorted to their dubious experiments in peaceable coercion. Indeed, the hard times of the confederation era had abruptly ended with the explosion of trade in the early 1790s. By the early years of the nineteenth century, the value of America's direct export trade had tripled.[15] But the conditions that had underwritten this buoyant prosperity were hardly permanent – and who could wish that they were? Madison hardly wanted his countrymen to root for a renewal of the horrid conflagration that had brought so much misery to Europeans for the better part of two decades, no matter how advantageous it might be for American farmers and merchants. The point, rather, was that Americans must recognize that a stable, productive, and peaceful Europe simply would not demand the same volume of exports that it had absorbed during the wrenching dislocations of war. And this simple fact spelled serious trouble for Madison's vision of an agrarian paradise. Glutted markets for the American surplus meant falling prices and flagging industry at home; and as he noted to Tench Coxe in 1819, if peace continued in Europe, "as ought to be the wish of all, nothing but seasons extensively unfavorable [i.e. in Europe] can give us an adequate market for . . . our grain crop." No matter how

---

15 See, for instance, Douglass C. North, *The Economic Growth of the United States, 1790–1860* (New York, 1961), 36–38, 221, and 249; and Curtis P. Nettels, *The Emergence of a National Economy, 1775–1815* (New York, 1962), esp. chaps. 3–6 and 10–11.

Americans weighed the situation, apparently it took catastrophe –
either civil (in the form of war) or natural (in the form of poor
harvests and famine abroad) – to make their economy work. [16] A year
later, Madison bluntly expressed his "anticipation of a decreasing
market for all our great staples for exportation." [17]

Overproduction, clogged foreign markets, falling prices: here,
Madison knew, was the essential explanation for the depressed economy in Virginia and in the other older areas of the South – including, of course, the hotbed of nullification, South Carolina. [18] By the
early 1830s he was inspired to refute, often in elaborate detail,
the spurious, alternative case against the tariff as the primary or even
the sole culprit. All the fulminations in the world against protective
legislation were futile, he argued, because even outright repeal of
the tariff would do little or nothing to alleviate the distress that
sparked the anguished complaints. Madison's analysis of the crisis
never wandered very far from his familiar concern about glutted
markets for a booming surplus, and his train of thought brought to
light yet another irony in his broader vision of a republican political
economy. Rather than being compatible elements of a coherent
vision, territorial and commercial expansion, it now seemed, were
effectively contradictory. [19]

Madison still believed that rapid settlement of the American
frontier – strongly typified by the opening of extraordinarily profitable land in Louisiana and the southwestern territories just after the
War of 1812 – served the invaluable purpose of accommodating the
surge in population growth which might otherwise force the development of advanced manufactures and threaten the republican character of the United States. But this "safety valve" of westward expansion also threw vast amounts of cheap, fertile land into the market,

16 Madison to Tench Coxe, Feb. 12, 1819, in [Rives and Fendall, eds.], *Letters
   and Other Writings*, III, 116–117.
17 Madison to Coxe, Mar. 20, 1820, *ibid.*, 170.
18 Madison's analysis of the economic background of the antitariff movement had
   ample validity. See, for instance, the relevant discussion in William W. Freehling, *Prelude to Civil War: The Nullification Controversy in South Carolina, 1816–
   1836* (New York, 1966).
19 See, for instance, Madison to Reynolds Chapman, Jan. 6, 1831, in Hunt, ed.,
   Writings of Madison, IX, 432.

which had the unfortunate consequence of bringing the value of land in older parts of the South tumbling down. Moreover, westward expansion only hastened and exacerbated the dilemma of glutted markets for the products of the soil. Bringing more and more rich land under cultivation increased the size of an ever more unmanageable surplus and made the predicament of eastern farmers, who had to compete with the new producers, especially acute. As Madison summarized his argument in the early 1830s, "the depression felt is mainly and palpably the result of the great fall in the value of land and in the price of its produce; and this double fall is as palpably the result, in the former case, of the quantity of cheap and fertile land at market in the West, and in the latter case, of the increase of the produce of the land beyond any corresponding increase in the demand for it." Since this unfortunate situation was the inevitable consequence of bringing a prolific, mobile, and enterprising people into contact with abundant, fertile land – the essence of Madison's formula for a republican paradise – the irony could hardly have been greater.[20]

Diagnosis of a malady was one thing, prescribing a cure quite another. Was there a solution to the problem of economic distress in the older regions of the South? Madison realized that his analysis of the crisis might leave the impression that for the good of his own state especially, development of the West should be restricted and emigration there restrained. Although he generally hastened to disavow that inference, he did not blink the complexity of the problem, and at times his disclaimers lacked conviction. He assured Nicholas Trist in 1828, for instance, that "nothing would be further from my wishes than to withhold at proper prices, a fair supply, of the National Domain to Emigrants, whether of choice or of necessity." "But how can it be doubted," he quickly added, "that in proportion as the supply should be reduced in quantity or raised in price, emigration would be checked and the price of land here [in Virginia] augmented."[21] When assessing the causes of Virginia's plight a few years later, his ambivalence was even more pronounced.

20 Madison to Professor Davis, 1832 [1833], (not sent), in [Rives and Fendall, eds.], *Letters and Other Writings*, IV, 261.
21 Madison to Trist, Jan. 26, 1828, in Hunt, ed., *Writings of Madison*, IX, 303.

"The great and adequate cause of the evil" was "the rapid settlement of the W[estern] and S[outh] W[estern] Country" – "if that be indeed an evil," he reflected, "which improves the condition of our migrating citizens and adds more to the growth and prosperity of the whole than it subtracts from a part of the community."[22] Indeed, had access to the West been obstructed in the past, or were it possible to restrict it now, the value of land and labor in the Old Dominion would be much higher; but the first scenario was "an idea at which an enlarged patriotism revolts," and the second could occur only "at the expense of every philanthropic feeling."[23] A young visitor to Montpelier in November 1827 appears to have caught the drift of Madison's argument without heeding its qualifications. Jesse Burton Harrison's memoranda of his conversations with Madison included the following assessment of his host's reflections on manufactures: "He also observed that it is more to the interest of Virginia and the South that the Northern people should turn [to] manufactures and eat our corn and wheat, and consume our products, than be induced from overstocked population at home to emigrate to the West, there to make for market rival produce to ours, to glut the foreign markets. He thought that the encouragement to Western emigration by Government had gone quite far enough for the welfare of the seaboard."[24]

Virginia's and the South's particular interests aside, Madison indeed believed that economic conditions in the United States – and in Europe and Latin America as well – would lead inescapably to the rapid growth of manufactures. All political economists, including Madison, agreed that manufactures were the logical, indeed necessary, means of employing a surplus population whose labor was no longer needed on the land. In perhaps the most thorough and mature statement of his political economy, which appeared in an unsent letter of the early 1830s, Madison explained clearly just why his original vision of a predominantly agricultural republic was – and,

22 Madison to Thomas R. Dew, Feb. 23, 1833, *ibid.*, 501.
23 Madison to Professor Davis, 1832 [1833], (not sent), in [Rives and Fendall, eds.], *Letters and Other Writings*, IV, 261–262.
24 Harrison, "Private notes of conversation with Mr. Madison in 1827," in Burton Harrison Papers, Library of Congress, series 3, box 6.

in retrospect, perhaps always had been – highly problematic. Every-one understood, he said, that in the "thickly-settled countries" of the Old World, "the application of labour" to manufactures arose naturally from the presence of "a surplus [of labor] beyond what is required for a full cultivation of a limited soil." Too many people, too little land to accommodate all of them: here was the dilemma – and the dynamic – that forced the development of manufactures in the crowded societies of Europe. Although conventional wisdom had it that the United States, as a young and sparsely populated re-public, was not vulnerable to the same kind of pressure, the truth was more complex: the presence of vast reservoirs of fertile land in North America, Madison argued, actually generated its own mo-mentum toward the same end. "In the United States, notwithstand-ing the sparseness of the population compared with the extent of the vacant soil," he reflected, "there is found to be a growing surplus of labourers beyond a *profitable* culture of it; a peculiarity which baffles the reasonings of foreigners concerning our country, and is not sufficiently adverted to by our own theoretic politicians."[25]

The emphasis on *profitable* cultivation was Madison's. Given the continuing abundance of land, it was easy to imagine the over-whelming majority of Americans happily remaining farmers for gen-erations to come. But given the reality of market conditions, these prospective agrarians would have to remain primitive subsistence farmers, detached from the civilizing influence of commerce – hard-ly the stuff of a healthy republic – rather than the industrious, surplus-producing farmers who had always graced the Jeffersonian vision. "Whatever be the abundance or fertility of the soil," Madison remarked, "it will not be cultivated when its fruits must perish on hand for want of a market."[26] Here, again, was the rub: the inescap-able need to find markets that could sustain the industry and full employment of a large rural population, no matter how great the natural treasure in vast supplies of land. "Our country must be a manufacturing as well as an agricultural one, without waiting for a

25 Madison to Professor Davis, 1832 [1833], (not sent), in [Rives and Fendall, eds.], *Letters and Other Writings*, IV, 265.
26 Madison, "Majority Governments," [1833], in Hunt, ed., *Writings of Madison*, IX, 525.

crowded population," Madison concluded a few years before his death, "unless some revolution in the world or the discovery of new products of the earth, demanded at home and abroad, should unexpectedly interpose."[27]

Madison's anticipation of increased manufacturing – in all regions of the United States – surfaced very early in his retirement. In the sorry aftermath of the Panic of 1819, he was confident that manufactures would receive a valuable boost from "the cheapness of food, of materials, and of labour" that resulted "from the cessation of the foreign demands" for surplus produce.[28] Who could doubt that glutted foreign markets and a depressed economy would stimulate productivity in other areas, "for which the labor turned off from the land will be a ready fund?"[29] And the perverse adherence of European governments to the outmoded principles of commercial restriction – which further limited access to foreign markets for American producers, and hence their capacity to purchase foreign manufactures in return – only promised to accelerate the transition. Both England and France, he observed in 1819, were pursuing misguided policies designed to promote national self-sufficiency, with the inevitable result that their trading partners, especially the United States, "must plough less and manufacture more."[30] Along with most Americans, Madison had customarily looked east toward the markets of Europe in search of commercial opportunity. In the early 1820s, however, he began to look south instead, and as he did, he saw even further reason to expect a profound shift in the character of his nation's economy.

The revolutions for independence in Spanish America reached their height during the early years of Madison's retirement. These manifestations of anticolonialism warmed the hearts of many proud republicans to the north, but with his characteristically sharp eye

27 Madison to Professor Davis, 1832 [1833], (not sent), in [Rives and Fendall, eds.], *Letters and Other Writings*, IV, 265.
28 Madison to Richard Rush, Dec. 4, 1820, *ibid.*, III, 195.
29 Madison to George Joy, Nov. 25, 1820, in James Madison Papers, Library of Congress, series two (microfilm).
30 Madison to Rush, May 10, 1819, in [Rives and Fendall, eds.], *Letters and Other Writings*, III, 129. See also Madison to Rush, Aug. 12, 1820, *ibid.*, 181.

Madison saw potential linkages and ramifications that were truly global. As "young nations which are entering into the commerce of the world," he observed in 1822, the new republics of Latin America were "still more agricultural than the United States." Moreover, by "narrowing the room for our present staples in foreign markets," they would "hasten and extend the application of our industry to manufactured articles." Madison was not the only American to suggest that political revolution in this oppressed part of the Western Hemisphere would unleash the productive energy of potentially formidable rivals to the United States in the agricultural export trade to Europe. Rather than lament or even fear this competition, however, he calmly put the best light he could on the consequences of such a happy change of circumstance for America's New World neighbors, who were, after all, following the North American example. The "growing markets" of these young republics, liberated from the Spanish monopoly, would call for manufactures, and Madison believed that "our comparative vicinity will favor supplies from our workshops." In a curious sense, in other words, the Hispanic-American republics would now occupy the former role of the youthful United States as the most efficient supplier of produce and raw materials for European markets, while an older America began to assume a posture toward them that resembled Britain's former commercial relationship with its colonies in North America. "Whatever advantage therefore may accrue to a nation from a combination of manufacturing with agricultural industry," Madison concluded, "will in our case be forwarded by the independent rank assumed by our fellow inhabitants of this hemisphere."[31]

For all of these reasons, in sum, the United States appeared well on its way toward becoming a manufacturing society. Madison did not doubt that with every passing year more and more Americans who might once have expected to own and till their own land would instead find themselves laboring for wages in workshops and factories – if, indeed, they were fortunate enough to find secure employment of any kind. To that extent, the problematic and disturbing future that he had envisioned as a young Revolutionary in the 1780s

31 Madison to Mathew Carey, Oct. 25, 1822, Madison Papers, Library of Congress, series two (microfilm).

was now, more than ever, hardly "too remote to claim attention."[32] And if Madison's analysis of the relationship among labor, markets, and employment led him to accept the rapid development of manufactures as inevitable, even natural, his reasoning here had definite policy implications. Those implications affected, in turn, his larger view of the prospects for a stable federal Union.

As we have seen, Madison tenaciously defended the constitutionality of federal tariff laws that were designed to encourage and accelerate the transition toward a manufacturing society. But his assessment of the tariff on grounds of policy, as opposed to constitutionality, was another matter; here, along with Nicholas Trist and William Cabell Rives, his young disciples in the crusade against nullification, he firmly rejected Henry Clay's extravagant vision of an "American System" that included high levels of protection. As early as 1820 Madison expressed the desire to push "a middle course" between doctrinaire free traders and zealous advocates of the tariff, urging a spirit of judicious compromise both "in the National Councils and in the public opinion."[33] After perusing a copy of Clay's celebrated congressional speech on promoting manufactures, Madison assured the Kentuckian that he had always believed in necessary "exceptions" to the "general rule" in political economy that left "to the judgment of individuals the choice of profitable employments for their labour and capital." Therefore he continued to support, as he had since his earliest days in Congress in 1789, a moderate tariff. But Madison also warned Clay not to forget that exceptions to a rule were by definition limited – involving in this case, for example, articles necessary for public defense or "of a use too indispensable to be subjected to foreign contingencies."[34] What the Virginian called his "true policy" on the tariff, therefore, lay "between the extremes of doing nothing and prescribing everything; between admitting no exception to the rule of 'laissez faire' and converting the exceptions into the rule."[35]

32 Note on Suffrage, 1829–1830, in [Rives and Fendall, eds.], Letters and Other Writings, IV, 29.
33 Madison to Tench Coxe, Mar. 20, 1820, ibid., III, 171.
34 Madison to Henry Clay, Apr. 1824, ibid., 430–431.
35 Madison to Frederick List, Feb. 3, 1829, ibid., IV, 12.

Madison readily conceded that no theorist had yet provided comprehensive guidelines for policymakers in this delicate area; "I know not a better service that could be rendered to the science of political economy," he commented in 1824, "than a judicious explanation of the cases constituting exceptions to the principle of free industry, which, as a general principle, has been so unanswerably established."[36] Contrary to the assertions of an increasing number of militant free traders among his fellow Virginians, Madison affirmed the constitutionality of even the lavish support of domestic manufactures that Clay advocated. But he vigorously disputed the wisdom and expediency of multiplying the exceptions to the rule of "free industry," which were bound, he believed, to inflame sectional acrimony. "In every doubtful case," he advised, "the Government should forbear to intermeddle," a caution especially applicable when "one part of the community would be materially favoured at the expense of another."[37] And given his assumptions about the logic of social and economic development, Madison simply saw an extravagant tariff as superfluous. He believed that most of the desired changes would take place anyway, "without a legislative interference."[38]

We should recall that Madison had once viewed these changes as largely deleterious – indeed, as something to be evaded or postponed for as long as possible. Wary of the intentions of his rival in the Treasury Department in 1792, for example, he had typically argued that a resort to manufacturing in the United States "ought to be seen with regret as long as occupations more friendly to human happiness, lie vacant."[39] But now he saw the vacancies all filled; and if he regarded the emergence of a manufacturing society as necessary, he also saw potential advantages and benefits in what he had once categorically shunned as degeneration. Back in the early 1790s Madison had talked boldly of the superior strength of a young

36 Madison to Thomas Cooper, Mar. 22, 1824, *ibid.*, III, 429.
37 *Ibid.*, 430.
38 Madison to Clay, Apr. 1824, *ibid.*, 431.
39 Madison, "Republican Distribution of Citizens," Mar. 3, 1792, in William T. Hutchinson et al., eds., *The Papers of James Madison* (Chicago, Charlottesville, 1962–), XIV, 256.

agricultural country in relation to an older manufacturing nation. The American republic, he had then proclaimed, was all the more powerful and independent because of its simple agricultural economy. Its exports consisted of "necessaries" – food and raw materials – upon which its customers depended for their very survival. By contrast, England exported to the United States frivolous luxuries, the consumption of which fluctuated wildly with every whimsical shift of fashion and fancy. Such abject dependence on foreign customers for employment and hence subsistence, Madison had boasted, marked "the lowest point of servility." If Americans decided to favor shoestrings and slippers rather than wear buckles on their shoes, to use his favorite example, the thousands of Britain's laboring poor in the buckle industry would suffer grievously. In any test of commercial strength, therefore, the younger, self-sufficient country would surely prevail over the vulnerable manufacturing nation.[40]

But thirty years later, after pondering America's chronic economic instability, Madison had appreciably changed his position. As he noted repeatedly to several correspondents in the 1820s and 1830s, the unbalanced nature of America's foreign trade reflected an underlying structural problem, one that actually put the young republic at a disadvantage. The demand for America's exports, he said, never exceeded "what may be deemed real and definite wants," but its manufactured imports were generally "objects neither of necessity, nor utility; but merely of fancy and fashion, wants of a nature altogether indefinite."[41] He still believed that a nation exchanging necessary and useful articles for foreign luxuries had a definite advantage over its trading partners during exceptional circumstances, such as war or "a contest of prohibitions and restrictions." But the advantage was reversed, he now admitted, during "the ordinary freedom of intercourse."[42] Beyond a point, there was nothing the United States could do to increase the demand for its agricultural

40 For elaboration and documentation, see McCoy, *Elusive Republic*, chap. 6 (quoted material on p. 142).
41 Madison to Clarkson Crolius, Dec. 1819, in Hunt, ed., *Writings of Madison*, IX, 17.
42 Madison to Richard Rush, May 1, 1822, in [Rives and Fendall, eds.], *Letters and Other Writings*, III, 266, and Madison to Clay, Apr. 1824, *ibid.*, 433.

surplus abroad – after all, people only needed to eat so much – which effectively limited the opportunities for profitable employment in a simple agricultural society. The foreign demand for Britain's manufactures, on the other hand, knew no such natural limit; in a modern commercial society, consumer demand for foreign conveniences and luxuries was largely a matter of taste or fashion, not biology, and this ostensibly boundless, "artificial" demand could sustain the industry and employment of an ever greater number of citizens in the more advanced, manufacturing country. All too often, indeed, Americans' gluttonous consumption of British imports, "consisting so much of articles superfluous to us, but giving bread to those who prepare them," gave vivid evidence of the point.[43] The ultimate inference to be drawn from Madison's train of logic marked the distance he had traveled since the early 1790s: a manufacturing America would not only be commercially stronger and more independent, but much better able, above all, to provide employment for its growing numbers.

In this connection, although Madison never appears to have explicitly concluded that the United States should manufacture luxuries on an extensive scale – which would have turned his position from the early 1790s completely on its head – he now displayed little patience with those who thoughtlessly repeated the classical shibboleths decrying luxury and refinement. In 1822, for instance, he politely chastised the author of a booklet entitled "The Moral Instructor" for failing to appreciate some of the ways in which luxury was a necessary means of promoting happiness, even (and perhaps especially) in a republic that had so little difficulty providing the basic necessities of life. Madison told Dr. Jesse Terry that it was a mistake to place so many articles of "general" and "innocent" use as Terry did in the category of "noxious luxuries." Even more important, Terry should recall that a society that shunned the production of such items would experience severe difficulties. Since "the labor of part of the community, especially with the aids of machinery," was sufficient "to provide the necessaries and plainest comforts of life for the whole," it was obvious, Madison said, that "the remaining part must either be supported in idleness or em-

43 Madison to C. C. Cambreleng, Mar. 8, 1827, *ibid.*, 566.

ployed in producing superfluities, from the sale of which they may derive their own necessaries and comforts."[44] In order to avoid the moral snare of idleness, unemployment, and even starvation, in other words, a republican people had to produce superfluities as well as necessaries, exploiting the opportunities for employment that human folly and fashion made possible.

Madison's characteristically optimistic cast of mind was considerably subdued by the ominous drift of national politics in the 1830s. But hoping to discover advantages in changes he had once found alarming, his tendency to seek reassurance in the consequences of this inevitable shift toward manufactures only quickened. And we might say that he found the greatest benefit where help was needed most. At the height of the nullification crisis, when cause for despair about the future of the Union was greatest, Madison took considerable comfort in the thought that an "important alleviation" of the raging sectional discord was silently "in embryo." Here he pointed hopefully to what he called the imminent "assimilation of the employment of labor in the South to its employment in the North." In early 1833 he pointed to "the certainty" that "unless agriculture can find new markets for its products, or new products for its markets," a large portion of the labor of the South (and here he referred explicitly to slave labor) would be diverted from "the plough and the hoe to the loom and the workshop." If the tariff conflict was rooted in the different interests, real and imagined, of industry and agriculture, in other words, the underlying source of friction was bound to diminish steadily as prevailing economic conditions forced the southern, as well as the northern, states into manufacturing. Therefore if the nullifiers stopped moaning and whining long enough to see the true cause of their distress – an unmarketable agricultural surplus – they might also glimpse the foolishness of their charge that the northern and southern economies were utterly and permanently at odds.[45]

During the last few years of his life, especially, Madison had a message for his fellow southerners about their economic future that he missed few chances to deliver. "When we can no longer convert

44 Madison to Dr. Jesse Terry, Jr., Jan. 30, 1822, *ibid.*, 258.
45 Madison to Henry Clay, Apr. 2, 1833, *ibid.*, IV, 567–568.

our flour, tobacco, cotton, and rice into a supply of our habitual wants from abroad," he insisted in 1833, "labor must be withdrawn from those articles and made to supply them at home."[46] That this change would soon overtake Virginia and South Carolina, making the dangerous controversy over the tariff irrelevant, Madison always appeared confident. That he was desperately looking for silver linings wherever he might find them, however, is no less clear, because he also proffered another economic scenario that traveled a rather different route to the same political destination: a reinvigorated and flourishing Union, united and secure under the Constitution. Madison speculated that once northern manufactures were able to succeed without "obnoxious aids" like a high tariff − which he expected to be the case very soon − they would quickly displace foreign products in southern markets. And this change, he hoped, would solidify the Union by forming the basis for what he called "internal exchanges which are beneficial to every section."[47] In this event, "the source of discord" − regional differences in patterns of employment − could actually become "a bond of interest," and "the difference of pursuits," he reasoned, "more than equivalent to a similarity."[48]

Sometimes Madison appeared to want to have it both ways; the destination of a strong Union, after all, always mattered more than the particular economic path to that end. No matter which scenario he favored, the irony is striking. During the last few years of his life, Madison looked to the "dismal science" of political economy − which a half-century earlier had done as much to chasten as to support his republican optimism − to confirm his unyielding faith in the future. We might say that his commitment to a familiar Jeffersonian ideal was no less fervent, but that the ideal was no longer so firmly rooted in the familiar Jeffersonian world of commercial agriculture that Madison, in fact, now deemed largely obsolescent. And in convincing himself, if not most of his fellow Virginians, that the republic might endure even the kinds of demographic and economic changes that had once seemed so threatening, he offered superb proof of what

46 *Ibid.*, 568.
47 Madison to Benjamin F. Papoon, May 18, 1833, *ibid.*, 298.
48 Madison to Clay, Apr. 2, 1833, *ibid.*, 568.

Harriet Martineau called "his inexhaustible faith" that "a well-founded commonwealth" might be immortal. Believing, as she said, that "the principles of justice in which such a commonwealth originates never die out of the people's heart and mind," Madison allowed nothing – certainly not the specter of an industrial society – to erode his confidence that the American people were, for now and forever, capable of self-government.[49]

II

When the elderly Madison traced the consequences of social and economic change, the crux of his concern remained, as it had been forty years earlier, essentially political. Indeed, he often made explicit the connections between polity, economy, and society. In 1829, for instance, while attending the Virginia Constitutional Convention, he observed that "it is a law of nature, now well understood, that the earth under a civilized cultivation is capable of yielding subsistence for a large surplus of consumers beyond those having an immediate interest in the soil" – a human surplus derived from an agricultural surplus that would, he added, only "increase with the increasing improvements in agriculture, and the labour-saving arts applied to it." Of this surplus population, moreover, "a large proportion" was "necessarily reduced by a competition for employment to wages which afford them the bare necessaries of life." Since this proportion – "being without property, or the hope of acquiring it" – could not be expected to sympathize sufficiently with the rights of property holders, Madison posed the inevitable question about their political status. Could (and should) they be entrusted with the full responsibilities of citizenship, including the right to vote, even if they clearly lacked the independence traditionally demanded of the republican citizen?[50]

Madison's ultimate fear was of a society in which "this unfavoured

49 Harriet Martineau, *Retrospect of Western Travel* (London and New York, 1838), I, 191.
50 Note on Suffrage, 1829–1830, in [Rives and Fendall, eds.], *Letters and Other Writings*, IV, 28.

class of the community" would actually constitute a majority of the population. He appears to have conceded that such a situation did not yet obtain in most parts of America, but he worried, in the meantime, about the danger that arose from "a dependence of an increasing number on the wealth of a few," which in the United States, he said, meant "the connexion between the great capitalists in manufactures and commerce" and the "indigent labourers" employed by them.[51] Individuals who lacked "a sufficient stake in the public order and the stable administration of the laws" – above all, those who did not own land – posed the most conspicuous threat to "the rights of property or the claims of justice," Madison believed, since they would naturally (and understandably) be drawn toward schemes that might promise to relieve their distress. As examples of such recourse, some of which were hardly unknown in America, he mentioned "agrarian laws and other levelling schemes" as well as "the cancelling or evading of debts, and other violations of contracts."[52]

Madison's fear of the desperation that might accompany landless poverty lays bare the fundamental assumption of his political theory – that justice was defined largely in terms of defending property rights. It recalls, as well, the enduring influence on his thinking of the turbulent years just after the American Revolution. When Madison observed in the early 1820s that "a just and free Government" must effectively guard "the rights both of property and of persons," he repeated the idea, in its conventional formulation, that had guided his analysis during the 1780s.[53] Madison continued to believe that republican governments must protect the rights of property, as well as of persons, for reasons that doubtless seemed to him too obvious to elaborate. As the Scottish philosopher and historian David Hume had emphasized, justice and property were insep-

---

51 *Ibid.*; Note on Suffrage, referring to Madison's speech of Aug. 7, 1787, circa 1821, *ibid.*, 24.
52 Note on Suffrage, 1829–1830, *ibid.*, 29; Note on Suffrage, circa 1821, *ibid.*, 22–23.
53 *Ibid.*, 22. For exceptionally lucid and telling insight into the consistency of Madison's views in this area, see J. R. Pole, *Political Representation in England and the Origins of the American Republic* (Berkeley, Calif., 1966), esp. 314–338 and 374–375.

arable because together they defined the necessary underpinnings of civilized order. As Madison observed during his retirement, the "rules of justice" shaped and enforced laws that encouraged industry ("from which property results") by "securing the enjoyment of its fruits." And since that enjoyment consisted not merely in the immediate use of property, "but in its posthumous destination to objects of choice, of kindred or affection," these just laws also bound generations and communities across time. Indeed, the stakes were so high that Madison could not help but wonder: how would stability and civilization fare, once a majority of the population in a postagricultural republic came to have an interest, "real or supposed," in pursuing "measures of injustice"?[54]

Madison wrestled with this question more than once during his later years, but it is not surprising that he gave it his most concentrated attention when reviewing some of his papers from the 1780s. Relatively early in his retirement, probably in 1821, he was moved to record a change in his views on the broad subject of property and suffrage. In a speech to the Constitutional Convention on August 7, 1787, he had endorsed, albeit tentatively, a property qualification for those who would elect members of the House of Representatives. But in the early 1820s, Madison attached to his record of that speech a memorandum, which asserted that "these observations do not convey the speaker's more full and matured view of the subject"; he added that "he felt too much at the time the example of Virginia," where stiff property qualifications for suffrage had been in place.[55] Actually, Madison's analysis of the relevant issues appears to have changed very little, except that he was now, perhaps, somewhat more solicitous of the rights of the disadvantaged and less willing to limit their influence in government. If something had changed in the intervening thirty-five years, it was not Madison's basic principles or his assumptions about the impact of population growth on the structure of American society; the change had occurred, rather, in the thrust of his countrymen's political ideas and expectations. And what Madison formally acknowledged in his 1821 memoran-

54 Note on Suffrage, circa 1821, in [Rives and Fendall, eds.], *Letters and Other Writings*, IV, 22–23.
55 *Ibid.*, 21–22.

dum was the justice, as well as the necessity, of accommodating the aggressively democratic aspirations of the American people.

To be sure, Madison found the specter of an impending property-less majority no less threatening — both to stability and to the legitimate rights of the propertied classes — than he had as a young man. He continued to believe, therefore, that "some shield" against the danger "would not be out of place in a just and provident system of Government." But he could no longer endorse the traditional stratagem of confining the right to vote to independent citizens who had a firm interest in upholding property rights and the claims of justice — in other words, "to freeholders and to such as hold an equivalent property." The objection to this regulation, Madison conceded, was obvious: "It violates the vital principle of free Government, that those who are to be bound by laws ought to have a voice in making them." Looking to the future, moreover, this violation "would be strikingly more unjust as the lawmakers [i.e., those with freehold property or the equivalent] became the minority." And if, contrary to the claims of justice, this restriction were some-how enforced, it would hardly serve the cause of order and good government, anyway. Rather, "it would engage the numerical and physical force in a constant struggle against the public authority, unless kept down by a standing army, fatal to all parties." Once the threat of public disorder and extralegal assaults on property from this disenfranchised majority resulted in authoritarian government, and perhaps even some kind of police state, obviously all was lost. To put the matter bluntly, so restricted a suffrage would be utterly inimical to republican government, in practice as well as in theory.[56]

Madison cited two other possible modifications of the franchise designed to protect the rights of property as well as persons. First, one might confine the right of suffrage for one branch of the government to property holders, and for the other branch to those without property — an option that he summarily rejected as unequal, unfair, and inexpedient. Alternatively, one might limit the right of elect-ing one branch to freeholders, and admit everyone to a common right with property owners in electing the other branch. This partic-

56 *Ibid.*, 25.

ular arrangement made more theoretical sense, Madison argued, and such an experiment had been tried in at least two states. In New York, however, it had been abandoned, and in North Carolina the results remained unclear. And since a "satisfactory" trial of the plan would have to be "continued for no inconsiderable period" – until, in fact, "the non-freeholders should be the majority" – Madison put little hope in this approach. After all, who could deny by the early 1820s that the obvious trend throughout the American states was to broaden, rather than restrict, the franchise? Certainly not Madison. "Should experience or public opinion require," he acknowledged, "an equal and universal [i.e., white adult male] suffrage for each branch of the Government, such as prevails generally in the United States," republicans would have to look elsewhere than to suffrage restrictions for "a resource favourable to the rights of landed and other property, when its possessors become the minority."[57]

What potential "resources" remained? Madison mentioned two options that held the same substantive appeal for him now as they had in the 1780s: increasing the size of the electoral districts in representative assemblies, and prolonging the representatives' terms of service. Paraphrasing one of the central arguments of *Federalist* number ten, Madison noted in the early 1820s that "large districts are manifestly favourable to the election of persons of general respectability and of probable attachment to the rights of property over competitors depending on the personal solicitations practicable on a contracted theatre." A little political engineering, in other words, could minimize the likelihood of obscure, unpropertied men, adept in the vicious arts of electioneering and bent on pursuing schemes of injustice, coming to power – without formally restricting their right to vote or hold office. "Although an ambitious candidate of personal distinction might occasionally recommend himself to popular choice by espousing a popular though unjust object," Madison added, this misfortune would only "rarely happen" in many large districts at the same time. And the second measure – lengthening the terms of service for legislators – promised to promote equally salutary ends. Ideally, it would render the government "more stable in its policy,

57 *Ibid.*, 25–26.

196

and more capable of stemming popular currents taking a wrong direction, till reason and justice could regain their ascendancy."[58]

But Madison's retreat continued; he was uncertain that "even such a modification as the last" would be deemed admissible by the aggressively democratic heirs to America's Revolutionary heritage who were now taking their place at the center of the political stage. Given the prevailing ethos, he admitted, "universal suffrage and very short periods of election within contracted spheres" might well be required "for each branch of the Government." Madison doubtless regretted this prospective erosion of even the most modest vestiges of an eighteenth-century world of politics that had so clearly shaped his understanding of the good republic, a world that cherished the virtues of balance, order, and a just hierarchy; but he never hesitated to acknowledge the legitimacy, as well as the likelihood, of just such a transformation in values. And in this bold new republican world, he realized, security against injustice would have to be derived from means other than either suffrage restrictions or the institutional tinkering that "Publius" had advocated in the 1780s.[59]

But practically speaking, Madison now wondered, were there any such options? Pointing to "the ordinary influence possessed by property, and the superior information incident to its holders," he put some stock in the authority that a propertied elite wielded by its very presence. He also adverted to security from two other sources: "from the popular sense of justice, enlightened and enlarged by a diffusive education; and from the difficulty of combining and effectuating unjust purposes throughout an extensive country." As the latter clause suggests, the central insight of "Publius," if not all of his specific methods, was alive and well in the 1820s. Madison believed, above all, that the Union he had helped create forty years earlier — the extended republic of diverse interests — offered advantages, now more than ever, that distinguished it from "small communities where a mistaken interest or contagious passion could readily unite a [propertyless] majority of the whole under a factious leader, in trampling on the rights of the minor [i.e. propertied]

---

58 *Ibid.*, 26–27.   59 *Ibid.*, 27.

party." Faced with the irrepressible democratization of politics in a republic undergoing momentous, and no less inexorable, economic and social changes, Madison continued to place his faith largely where it had rested ever since the Philadelphia convention – in the extended sphere of republican government, and in the peculiar "distribution and organization of its powers."[60]

If there was a new twist to Madison's thinking, it reflected more a shift of emphasis than of approach: he directed ever more of his attention and energy to securing the republican benefits of what he called here "a diffusive education," which, he believed, might "enlighten" and "enlarge" the "popular sense of justice." Madison showed his commitment to promoting education in the United States during his retirement most notably, of course, in his partnership with Jefferson in establishing and nurturing the University of Virginia.[61] Both Virginians saw the twin causes of education and republicanism as inseparable. If nothing else, Madison argued, the power of America's republican example throughout the world was contingent on demonstrating both the will and the capacity to promote "establishments for the advancement and diffusion of knowledge." As he suggested in 1822, the American people owed it not only to themselves, but "to the cause of Free Government," to prove that their political institutions were "as favorable to the intellectual and moral improvement of man" as they were "conformable to his individual and social rights." "What spectacle can be more edifying or more seasonable," he inquired of a correspondent, "than that of liberty and learning, each leaning on the other for their mutual and surest support?"[62]

Along with many of his countrymen, moreover, Madison regarded progress in education as immensely significant precisely because it promised to supply a necessary measure of wisdom and stability once the independent, landed majority disappeared. As a

---

60 *Ibid.*, 27, 23.

61 For a succinct discussion of Madison's role in the early history of Jefferson's University of Virginia, see Irving Brant, *James Madison: Commander in Chief, 1812–1836* (Indianapolis and New York, 1961), 450–460.

62 Madison to W. T. Barry, Aug. 4, 1822, in [Rives and Fendall, eds.], *Letters and Other Writings*, III, 279.

potentially boundless reservoir of virtue, education assumed the attractive form of an alternative to the natural but evanescent treasure of abundant land. Indeed, when Madison discussed the theoretical and practical importance of improvements in education, he described a system of public institutions that would address the relevant needs of all social classes in the United States, now and in the future. What was urgently needed, he believed, was a plan of education "embracing every class of citizens, and every grade and department of knowledge."[63]

Although Madison's vision of a multi-tiered educational system was clearly pegged to a corresponding hierarchy of class, in which a person was educated according to his role and status, it is important to note that he anticipated considerable mobility, across generations, among those ranks. For that reason, Madison dismissed short-sighted objections among those who were currently poor to public support of elite institutions of higher learning, and among those who were rich to public support of education for the common people. In "Governments like ours," he averred, "a constant rotation of property results from the free scope to industry, and from the laws of inheritance" – which meant that "the rich man, when contributing to a permanent plan for the education of the poor, ought to reflect that he is providing for that of his own descendants; and the poor man, who concurs in a provision for those who are not poor, that at no distant day it may be enjoyed by descendants from himself." Doubtless thinking of the unstable Virginia society he knew best, Madison added that it did not "require a long life to witness these vicissitudes of fortune."[64] Thus he believed that only a preoccupation with the putative sovereignty of the living generation – and with the narrow interests of its constituent classes – obscured the presence, in the broadest sense, of a common good in fostering education at all ranks of society and all levels of learning.

At the top of Madison's educational pyramid were the "learned institutions" – such as Jefferson's new university – that gave "to the human mind its highest improvements, and to every country its truest and most durable celebrity." Although only a relatively few (and therefore privileged) individuals received the immediate benefit

63 *Ibid.*, 277.   64 *Ibid.*, 278–279.

of their resources, the impact of public colleges and universities on all classes of society, and on the cause of good government, was immense. "They throw that light over the public mind which is the best security against crafty and dangerous encroachments on the public liberty," Madison noted. As if that were not enough, they also served as "the nurseries of skilful teachers" for the lower schools, which would draw their pupils from all social ranks. And most important, they served as training schools "for the particular talents required for some of the public trusts, on the able execution of which the welfare of the people depends." Who could even begin to measure the significance of higher education in this last connection? Learned institutions "multiply the educated individuals," Madison wrote in 1822, "from among whom the people may elect a due portion of their public agents of every description; more especially of those who are to frame the laws; by the perspicuity, the consistency, and the stability, as well as by the just and equal spirit of which the great social purposes are to be answered." Despite rapidly mounting evidence to the contrary, Madison apparently still hoped that political leaders in America, especially in the new and dangerous age that loomed, might be drawn from the ranks of the ablest and most virtuous – which meant largely from among those who had received the benefits of a liberal education at these institutions of higher learning.[65]

Madison's overriding commitment to good government and to "the great social purposes" also nourished, albeit differently, his commitment to educating the common people. "Those who are without property, or with but little," he remarked, "must be peculiarly interested in a system which unites with the more learned institutions a provision for diffusing through the entire society the education needed for the common purposes of life."[66] The crucial point, of course, was that these common purposes were quite different in America than they were elsewhere, because in a republic with unrestricted suffrage, even the propertyless had to behave wisely and responsibly as citizens. Madison's support for educating the poor was part of a larger, distinctively American pattern of belief at the time. The United States in the early nineteenth century presented a

65 *Ibid.*, 277.   66 *Ibid.*, 278.

striking contrast to England, where the propertied elite vehemently opposed educating ordinary laborers for fear of arousing their ambition and making them unfit or unwilling to fulfill the menial roles expected of them; such hostility to mass public education, at least on the level of theory, was barely articulated in North America. If some scholars have argued that the well-to-do in the United States were no less elitist than their British counterparts – that they shared the same narrow purposes, but took the contrary position because they were confident that education could be used to dampen ambition, enforce social control, and keep unruly proletarians in their proper place – we should note that Madison does not fit this interpretative paradigm at all well.[67] His case reminds us that at least some conservatives wanted to broaden, not restrict, the horizons of the laboring classes in order both to enrich their humanity and to enhance the character of their public vision. For better or worse – and Madison may not always have been entirely sure which – they were, indeed, republican citizens with no little power and influence.

Madison's concern with the education of the poor in America became increasingly evident in the early 1820s. He applauded, for instance, the opening of libraries for apprentices in urban areas, especially since the "proportional numbers" of this valuable class of youths "must increase as our population thickens"; he hoped that their "morals and their understandings" would be vastly improved by having "a proper assortment of Books always at hand."[68] Since Madison expected the younger, less densely populated areas of the country to assume before long a similar character, his attention to the educational needs of the indigent was not limited to the relatively crowded areas of the East. When an acquaintance in Kentucky solicited his help in devising an appropriate system of education, he urged the legislators of that western state to broaden the curriculum

---

67 For an excellent discussion of this and other relevant issues, see Carl F. Kaestle, "Between the Scylla of Brutal Ignorance and the Charybdis of a Literary Education: Elite Attitudes Toward Mass Schooling in Early Industrial England and America," in Lawrence Stone, ed., *Schooling and Society* (Baltimore, 1976), chap. 7, as well as Kaestle, *Pillars of the Republic: Common Schools and American Society, 1780–1860* (New York, 1983), esp. chap. 3.

68 Madison to Solomon Southwick, Apr. 21, 1821, in [Rives and Fendall, eds.], *Letters and Other Writings*, 216–217.

for the poor beyond the traditional subjects of reading, writing, and arithmetic to include something more ambitious and less immediately practical: geography. Madison wanted teachers to use a globe and maps, a concise geographical grammar, and even "a planatarium of the cheapest construction" because, he said, "no information seems better calculated to expand the mind and gratify curiosity." The knowledge of "the characters and customs" of foreign countries thus imparted would "weaken local prejudices and enlarge the sphere of benevolent feelings." And once opened, the minds of the poor might push ahead on their own. "A knowledge of the Globe and its various inhabitants, however slight," he contended, might well "create a taste for books of travels and voyages," out of which, in turn, "might grow a general taste for history – an inexhaustible fund of entertainment and instruction." Madison wanted to develop in all Americans, no matter how humble their status, not just the habit of reading, but of reading well, because "any reading not of a vitious species," he told his Kentucky friend, would be "a good substitute for the amusements too apt to fill up the leisure of the labouring classes."[69]

Madison's faith in the ameliorative power of education was far from boundless; as we shall see in a later chapter, for instance, he didn't believe that either white or black Americans could be educated out of their racial antagonisms. As much stock as he placed in education, he never regarded it as a panacea for all of the republic's ills, present or prospective. Had he been tempted to do so, he would have stumbled on the central question posed by his analysis of social development, a question for which education, in the end, offered no answer: how would America's burgeoning population be employed? In the expansive and more mature republic of the 1820s and 1830s, he suggested, too many people and too few jobs was a grim prospect not just for the lower classes, but for the most learned scholars as

69 Madison to Barry, Aug. 4, 1822, *ibid.*, 280. For additional evidence of Madison's approach to education, see Thomas W. Gilmer to Madison, Aug. 31, 1830, in Madison Papers, Library of Congress, series one (microfilm), and Madison to Gilmer, Sept. 6, 1830, in Hunt, ed., *Writings of Madison*, IX, 407–409.

well. College graduates might be well-cultivated and humane, ready to serve the most valuable professions and the public; whether American voters would elect them to serve in government, of course, remained to be seen. But Madison also wondered about another potential disappointment: their ability to win public office aside, would the best and the brightest be able to support themselves at all? Less than a year before his death, Madison answered a nephew's request for advice on choosing a profession with both avuncular encouragement and a rather stern warning. Young Richard Cutts favored a career in law, which his uncle approved; but Madison also exhorted him to study as assiduously as he could, saying it was impossible to prepare too much for any of the professions. As he wrote in the fall of 1835, this advice, "at all times commendable," was particularly apposite when "the great and increasing number of our universities, colleges, and academies, and other seminaries, are already throwing out crops of educated youth beyond the demand for them in the professions and pursuits requiring such preparations." Since this was "likely to be more and more the case," moreover, only the few who distinguished themselves from the herd of capable candidates would receive "the expected rewards." With hard work, Madison hoped, Cutts might succeed in the crowded, competitive world of his chosen profession.[70]

Although Madison apparently saw glut everywhere, even in the market for the most skilled and learned forms of labor, he understood that the crisis of employment hit hardest at a different level of society. "To provide employment for the poor, and support for the indigent," he observed in 1820, "is among the primary, and, at the same time, not least difficult cares of the public authority" — even, he added, in such a relatively favored country as the United States.[71] Working men who studied geography in the primary schools and developed a taste for history might become better people and citizens; but would they find a way to eat? As Madison never tired of

70 Madison to Richard D. Cutts, Sept. 12, 1835, in [Rives and Fendall, eds.], *Letters and Other Writings*, IV, 383–384.
71 Madison to Rev. F. C. Schaeffer, Jan. 8, 1820, *ibid.*, III, 162.

saying, competition for scarce employment in a highly developed and productive society — even one with an abundance of land — inevitably drove down wages and provoked widespread suffering and despair. This paradox of poverty amidst plenty, of large numbers of miserable people somehow being unable to take advantage of the abundance that society was now capable of generating, concerned Madison as much as it did the many thinkers in Europe who also pondered the phenomenon — including one with a zealous faith in education who paid a personal call on him during his retirement. Robert Owen was a successful, indeed a fabulously wealthy British industrialist whose disenchantment with conventional society had transformed him into the consummate philanthropist and reformer. In 1825, he came to Montpelier eager to win Madison's support of his visionary projects.

So eclectic that it defies easy summary, Owen's thought was unmistakably radical: he repudiated the prevailing ethos and institutional structure of what Madison understood as modern commercial society. Often couched in the most extravagant terms, Owen's protest was fueled more by moral indignation than by dispassionate economic analysis, but he blamed the vicious system of commercial exchange, in which people were encouraged to buy cheap and sell dear, for the unconscionable inequality and injustice that characterized all civilized countries, especially his native Britain. By the mid-1820s, when he journeyed to the United States in the hope both of spreading his ideas and of establishing an alternative community at New Harmony, Indiana, Owen had embraced education as the remedy for everything that ailed mankind. He fervently believed that all distinctions among men, of whatever kind, were the product of circumstance rather than nature, and that the exploitative spirit of competition that poisoned modern society could be traced not to man's natural tendencies, but to vicious institutions. Owen's creed might be reduced to the simple maxim that man's character was formed *for* him, not *by* him; environment, he therefore insisted, was everything. Arrange properly the "circumstances" — Owen's favorite term — and men could be completely transformed. Once better institutions were in place and children educated differently, a healthier society organized around the ethos of perfect equality and cooperation, rather than privilege and competition, would flourish.[72]

Although we know very little of what Madison and Owen said to each other at Montpelier, inferences about their dialogue can rest on more than mere conjecture, thanks largely to Madison's young friend Nicholas Trist. Trist had met Owen at about the same time as Madison, at Monticello, where the great philanthropist had called on Jefferson; and he quickly became a passionate convert. Devouring every issue of the *Harmony Gazette* that he received from Indiana during the next few years, Trist promptly forwarded them, with glowing accolades, to Madison. In early 1827 he wrote excitedly to his mentor about "some speculations" in the *Gazette* under the title "Wealth and Misery" (written by Owen's son and chief disciple, Robert Dale Owen). "To my mind," Trist told Madison, "they have proved as satisfactory as any thing I ever read; and have established beyond a doubt that the appalling evils which are impending over England are inherent in the commercial principle of distribution." Under this principle, Trist was convinced, "every individual of the productive class, whose bread depends on the exchange which he shall receive for the objects produced by him" was in "constant danger of starvation." The reason was paradoxical, perhaps, but undeniable: "the wonderful discoveries and improvements of this wonderful age" had made the production of those objects "as cheap almost as the elements," far too cheap "to get a living by producing them." And as long as society remained organized around "the commercial principle of distribution," Trist implied, the irony was unavoidable: technological innovations and greater productivity were bound to impoverish and demoralize ever larger numbers of men.[73]

---

72 Of the many works on Owen that shed light on his brief American career, see esp. John F. C. Harrison, *Quest for the New Moral World: Robert Owen and the Owenites in Britain and America* (New York, 1969) and Arthur Bestor, *Backwoods Utopias: The Sectarian Origins and the Owenite Phase of Communitarian Socialism in America, 1663–1829*, 2d ed. (Philadelphia, 1970 [orig. publ. 1950]), chaps. 4–8.

73 Trist to Madison, Mar. 25, 1827, Nicholas P. Trist Papers, Virginia Historical Society. For more on Trist's involvement with both Owens, see Richard

Owen's personal charisma had apparently done little to arouse Madison's interest in Owenism; although the *Harmony Gazette* came regularly to Montpelier, he did not bother to read the "Wealth and Misery" pieces until Trist forced them on his attention. Like Trist and Owen, Madison found Britain's crisis of poverty and unemployment "full of instruction," but his inferences were substantially different. The diseases that Owen proposed to eradicate, Madison told Trist, were simply "too deeply rooted in human society to admit of more than great palliatives." Madison clearly thought that Owen exaggerated the problems inherent in commercial society and that he ignored the best remedy for Britain's distress — "a freedom of commerce among all nations." But for Madison the problem with Owenism lay much deeper, because the British reformer failed to understand that the system he decried, and many of the specific difficulties he proposed to cure, were rooted not in deficient and corrupting institutions, but rather in the natural proclivities of man.[74]

By claiming, like the French *philosophe* Helvétius, to be able to make new men merely by improving the environment that formed their characters, Owen was in effect equating human nature with "the force of education and habit." As Madison complained to Trist, "custom is properly called a second nature; Mr. Owen makes it nature herself." And Madison left his specific assessment of human nature implicit (but unambiguous) in his gentle dismissal of Owen's remedy at New Harmony. As he reminded Trist, this fanciful remedy clearly implied "that labour will be relished without the ordinary impulses to it; that the love of equality will supersede the desire of distinction; and that the increasing leisure, from the improvements of machinery, will promote intellectual cultivation, moral enjoyment, and innocent amusements, without any of the vicious resorts for the ennui of idleness."[75] Madison, the child of the Enlightenment, could go only so far with Owen who, like William Godwin

---

William Leopold, *Robert Dale Owen: A Biography* (Cambridge, Mass., 1940), chap. 4.

74 Madison to Trist, Apr. 1827, in [Rives and Fendall, eds.], *Letters and Other Writings*, III, 576–577.

75 *Ibid.*

and others before him, carried its premises and broad legacy in a utopian direction. Like Owen, Madison believed that education could improve man's condition and the character of society and, to that extent, the chances for republican success as the United States turned ever more toward manufacturing. But unlike Owen – and unlike Trist, whom the two men now shared as a disciple – Madison did not think that education could literally re-form either man or society, not even in the corner of the world where nature had been most generous.

✳

When Madison died, on June 28, 1836, his young friend Trist was unable to attend the burial ceremony at Montpelier. In fact, he was no longer living in the United States. Three years earlier, after flirting with the notion of moving to the Owenite community of New Harmony, Trist had resigned his government post in Washington in order to accept appointment as the American consul in Havana. His four-and-a-half-year stint in Washington had been an exciting time. In addition to performing his duties as a clerk in the State Department, Trist had served in 1831 as President Jackson's private secretary and thereafter found himself a trusted confidante of the chief executive. Since he had also served informally and quite effectively as a conduit between Madison and the inner circles of power, especially in the war against the nullifiers, his decision to leave Washington in the spring of 1833 might seem puzzling. Indeed, explaining his imminent departure to Madison, Trist confessed to some feelings of guilt about abandoning his country amid a national crisis that might well determine the destiny of the Union. But Trist's journey to Cuba was hardly an aberrant departure from the larger pattern of his life. His "Havana speculation," as he called it, was but one of many initiatives in an anguished search for the financial and personal independence that seemed always to elude him – and that would continue to elude him until his death almost forty years after Madison's.[76]

76 The only thorough biographical treatment of Trist – and it is far from complete

Born in Albemarle County, Virginia, in the same year that witnessed what his father's friend, Thomas Jefferson, later called "the Revolution of 1800," Nicholas Philip Trist had ties to Madison and Jefferson that went back several generations. His grandmother, Eliza House Trist, had helped her mother run the Philadelphia boardinghouse frequented by the two Revolutionaries when political duty called them to that city; and Eliza's brother, Samuel House, had also served during the 1780s as the Madisons' tobacco sales agent. In 1803, shortly after President Jefferson appointed Eliza's son, Hore Browse Trist, to office in the newly acquired territory of Louisiana, tragedy struck: Nicholas's father succumbed to yellow fever, leaving his widow and two infant sons alone on the southwestern frontier. Although Nicholas's mother remarried in Loui-

---

or adequate – is Robert Arthur Brent, "Nicholas Philip Trist: Biography of a Disobedient Diplomat," unpublished Ph.D. dissertation, University of Virginia, 1950. I have pieced together the following sketch of Trist from extensive research primarily in his papers at three different archives: the Library of Congress, the Virginia Historical Society, and above all the Southern Historical Collection at the University of North Carolina, Chapel Hill. Quotations in the text may be found, in order, in the following specific documents: Trist to William Cabell Rives, Nov. 11, 1833, in William Cabell Rives Papers, Library of Congress, box 51; Martha J. Randolph to Trist, July 1, 1822, in Trist Papers, Southern Historical Collection, Univ. of North Carolina, box 1; Virginia Randolph to Trist, Apr. 13, June 5, and Aug. 3, 1823, in Trist Papers, Library of Congress; Eliza House Trist to Trist, Nov. 28, 1818, ibid., and Dec. 20, 1818, in Trist Papers, Southern Historical Collection, Univ. of North Carolina, box 1; Mary Tournillion to Trist, Nov. 19, 1818, ibid.; Hore Browse Trist to Trist, Aug. 17, 1820, ibid.; Trist to Thomas Mann Randolph, May 14, 1821, ibid.; Trist to Virginia Randolph, Jan. 1, June 13, Feb. 22, 1823; Jan. 3, 1824; Oct. 1, 1823; Mar. 10, Jan. 16, 1822, ibid., boxes 1 and 2; Trist to William Wirt, July 1, 1828, ibid., box 2; Trist to Andrew J. Donelson, Oct. 19, 1828, in Andrew J. Donelson Papers, Library of Congress, box 2; Trist to "My Friends," Nov. 2, 1828, in Trist Papers, Library of Congress; Trist to Virginia R. Trist, Jan. 27, 1829, in Trist Papers, Southern Historical Collection, Univ. of North Carolina, box 2; Trist to Andrew Jackson, Apr. 12, 1830, in Trist Papers, Library of Congress; Jackson to Trist, Sept. 15, 1831, ibid.; Trist to Virginia R. Trist, Sept. 18, 1831, in Trist Papers, Southern Historical Collection, Univ. of North Carolina, box 2; Trist to Madison, May 3, 6, 1833, in Trist Papers, Virginia Historical Society; Trist to Jesse B. Harrison, Mar. 10, 1836, in Burton Harrison Papers, Library of Congress, box 6; and R. D. Owen to Trist, Apr. 25, 1834, in Trist Papers, Library of Congress.

siana and raised the boys there, the Trist family ties to Virginia and to Monticello, reinforced by frequent visits, grew stronger. "You were born and have almost grown up under our eyes," Martha Randolph, Jefferson's daughter, told Nicholas in 1822. He formalized the bond two years later by marrying her daughter, Virginia. For the next two years, Nicholas studied law with his grandfather-in-law and served informally as his secretary. On the morning of July 4, 1826, he watched Thomas Jefferson die.

The family connection notwithstanding, Nicholas's courtship of Jefferson's granddaughter had been protracted, in part because the young man's career prospects were so unsettled. Everyone – his mother, his grandmother, his brother, and his sweetheart – urged him to prepare for a career in one of the professions. Nicholas was proud (unduly proud, his brother warned him) of having been born in Virginia and wished to make his permanent home there, especially after his bride-to-be began to fret that she might be separated from her family. But as she was the first to remind him, there was no future for him – or for many others – pursuing her grandfather's elusive dream of rural independence in the "ancient dominion" of Jefferson's dying days. In April 1823 she told Nicholas: "I never think of you having a profession, independant of the changes of wind and weather, time and tide, which seem to govern the fortunes of Agriculturalists, without satisfaction." Two months later, after drought and the Hessian fly had wreaked further havoc on farmers in Albemarle, she added that "my wonder greatly increased that any one, who has an alternative, should entrust their peace of mind to the wind and weather of so capricious a climate as ours seems to be." Virginia Randolph blamed nature and climate for an agricultural depression whose causes, as Madison would have told her, were more complicated; but she knew that her grandfather's dream had gone sour, and that the vaunted independence of a sturdy yeomanry now seemed a cruel joke. "Heaven knows, I never wish to see you *harrassed* and *worn out* with the management of a farm," she told Nicholas; "the life of a 'saddle bag' lawyer is, I believe, far less laborious and more independent."

But Trist was less sure about what he should do with his life. In 1818 he had enrolled in the military academy at West Point, hoping both to find an answer to that question and to remedy what all of his close relations told him were disturbing personal weaknesses. Decrying "the want of stability in your character," his grandmother urged him to overcome "your early propensities to carelessness and extravagance"; his mother bluntly expressed the hope that West Point would instill discipline and purpose in his life, "for my dear child, you have passed the last three years in such a desultory manner that you would have become unfit for any pursuit." But Nicholas apparently had rather a rough time of it at West Point, succeeding academically but offending tutors and fellow students alike by his reluctance to defer to authority and by his fierce pride at having been born in Virginia. His younger brother, Browse, chided him for his arrogance, and toward the end of Nicholas's tenure at the academy disdained tact as well as punctuation: "I wish you to tell me candidly, and without the least disguise, what you propose doing for yourself in the world, as you inherit no fortune that I know of, you will have to struggle like others to support yourself, what means you intend to embrace, in order to accomplish this undertaking, is the object of my enquiries."

Trist moved forward on two fronts. Despite the "great aversion" he felt for a career in the law ("which was assigned me by the partiality of a mother"), he began shortly after leaving West Point to read systematically in the appropriate texts. But clearly he hoped never to have to rely on this profession for security and independence. If agriculture was a dead end in the Old Dominion, it was an alluring prospect elsewhere. While studying law in the early 1820s, Trist turned the bulk of his energy in a different direction: exploiting his inheritance and family ties in Louisiana, he set himself up as a planter in the Baton Rouge area. He did not intend to make a permanent home there; he had no thought, he assured his future wife, of whisking her off to this distant and godforsaken frontier. He sought only to make a quick killing, a financial windfall that would provide the fortune they needed to enjoy a dignified independence (ideally in Albemarle County) for their life together. With a fortune, he would not only have the privilege of "caring for no man, beyond his *merits*"; he would also have full command of his time, which would be devoted to philosophical and other worthy pursuits. He confessed to Virginia: "I should like very well to be independent of the *world*, in every respect, and even to have qualities that would give me some little degree of mastery and empire over the vulgar herd."

Trist was more than confident that Louisiana was the place to begin pursuing this version of the republican dream. The southwest had claimed the lives of both his father and his grandfather (who had died in New Orleans in 1784), but now he would wreak familial revenge by cashing in on the extravagant promise this frontier afforded any good man who, as Nicholas put it, arrived there "with forty or fifty slaves." Such a fellow, he assured Virginia, "is certain with industry and economy, of securing in a few years such an independence as will make him comfortable the rest of his life." In fact, Louisiana was so much the land of opportunity that it offered the answer to her grandfather's economic predicament. Trist repeatedly urged Virginia (and her mother and brother) to persuade Thomas Jefferson to transport his slaves to the rich lands of the southwest, where they might labor to recoup the fortune that had disappeared at Monticello. The old man would have none of the idea.

Much to his surprise, Trist found the life of a Louisiana planter disappointing. Caterpillars and a hurricane ravaged his crops; his stepfather was a temperamental neurotic who, when not flogging his slaves, tried to cheat Trist and his brother out of their inheritance; and in general Trist found uncertainty where he had expected to find security and success. As he wrote to Virginia in the fall of 1823, "the making of money" in Louisiana was now "the most difficult of *all* things." They married a year later despite the transparent failure of his scheme. Meanwhile, Nicholas had undergone some important personal changes. In the course of his lonely nights of reading in Louisiana, he had discovered writers and thinkers who moved him – above all, William Godwin. "Much as Godwin has been abused by the *holy holy*, most *holy* men, of this and the old world," he wrote to Virginia, "he is one of the *very* few authors I ever read, who have served to make me a 'better man.' He has made me *reflect upon*, and consequently *see*, the dangerous tendency of those high flying notions of chivalry and honor, which I had got, God knows where; and might have made me miserable for life." A few months earlier Nicholas had confessed to his lover – to whom he had entrusted care of his pistols – that it was "a source of no small regret to me that I have been sufficiently engaged in duels to be debarred from all offices" in his native state. When Trist met Robert Owen at Monticello a few years later, he was prepared to place his new faith in Reason in the hands of a man who gave dazzling shape, indeed, to Godwin's enlightened radicalism. But Trist's private dilemma was no less pressing. He still had to find a way to make money in the grubby world that Owen promised to transform.

Nicholas persisted in his study of the law, but he was hardly surprised, license in hand, to discover that this was not the career for him. He professed to have an intellectual passion for the subject; what he couldn't stomach was the life of a practicing attorney in Virginia. Trist panicked whenever he had to speak in public, which he rightly believed made him less than ideally suited for the profession. He described his problem as "altogether physical" – "a defect" that was founded not "in diffidence and modesty" ("for I err rather in the other extreme") but "in my nerves, which, when the moment for speaking arrives, get into such a state as to deprive me of even the power of articulation." For a few years after his grandfather-in-law's death, he pondered possible ways to make a living in the law without doing most of the things lawyers were expected to do. But when the family was forced to sell Monticello, and the future seemed ever more bleak, Trist scaled down his ambitions and did what was necessary: exploiting his connection to the Jefferson family, he pursued patronage.

A month before Andrew Jackson won the election of 1828, Trist wrote to his old chum from West Point, Jackson's nephew Andrew Donelson, that he would soon assume the office of a clerk in the Department of State. He explained to Donelson: "It is a mere clerkship; and some of my friends are, I believe, surprised at my seeking such an employment; but it was the best of two evils. After devoting much time and hard study to the Law, and becoming passionately fond of it, *as a study*; I found, engrained in me, an unconquerable repugnance to the practice: but my circumstances required that I should pursue some calling from which to derive a support for my family." Hence his successful venture as "an applicant for some employment in the Federal Government." Shortly before leaving for Washington, Trist sent yet another long letter to Robert Dale Owen and Frances Wright, his friends at New Harmony. He reminded

Nicholas P. Trist, c. 1820s. (From the collection of Mrs. Joseph C. Cornwall; photograph courtesy of Barry Bienstock)

them of the need to protect his anonymity as a member of their radical, avant-garde movement by keeping secret his authorship of the communications they occasionally chose to publish in their newspapers. "I can't be *one of you*," he lamented, "and therefore must remain one of the silent herd."

Within a few months of winning his sinecure in Washington,

Trist was optimistic that his personal fortunes were moving in the right direction. He told his wife that his brother, Browse, who was still managing their investment in Louisiana, was coming east in the spring "for the purpose of purchasing negroes"; their sugar plantation, Nicholas assured her, "will soon make me an independent man." Meanwhile, he began lobbying in Washington for an office for Browse, who was no less eager to win "a fortune" by multiple means. Apparently things did not go quite as well as Nicholas had hoped in early 1829, since he was soon pressing his connections for a higher-paying post in the government. He had gotten his "mere clerkship" because Secretary of State Henry Clay wanted to help ease the financial distress of Thomas Jefferson's daughter, Nicholas's mother-in-law, who lived with the Trists; now Nicholas lost no chance to remind everyone, including President Jackson, that his desire for more money was "as much for Mrs. Randolph as myself." Two years later he agreed to replace Donelson as Jackson's secretary, an important job with a low salary, only with the president's promise that he would "not suffer in a pecuniary point of view." In September 1831 Nicholas wrote to his wife: "Old Hiccory is all kindness. After repeatedly offering me money, and desiring me to call upon him when I wanted it, the other day [he] put into my hands a note enclosing a check for $300." The president also promised to improve Nicholas's situation as soon as the right office came open. Two years later he was on his way to Havana.

Since Trist suffered from more than a mild case of hypochondria, he was doubtless sincere in thinking that Cuba would be "of infinite service to my constitution as well as pocket." He told Madison a month after accepting the job: "The more I hear, the more I am satisfied that it would have been next to madness in me to suffer such an opportunity for acquiring independence to pass unimproved; and the more I am satisfied also, that instead of danger, my constitution will be much benefitted." But once in Havana he continued to suffer from all the familiar complaints – coughing, indigestion, and a general malaise – and was no longer sure what kind of climate best suited his delicate constitution. By early 1836 he was consulting physicians and talking of returning to Washington. In March, his old friend Jesse Burton Harrison, an ambitious, well-educated Virginian who had removed to New Orleans in search of greater opportunity, sought his advice on how to secure a diplomatic post. Trist warned him of the stiff competition. There was "nothing in the shape of a *place* – high or low, profitable or ruinous" for which there was not a plethora of aspirants; indeed, "there seem to be thousands," Trist said, "who think that if they can but once get *office* – no matter what – they are made men." Speaking of his own case, he ruefully admitted that he had been "altogether disappointed in the expectation" that had brought him to Havana, that "of *making money*."

But Trist remained in Cuba – for another nine years, as it turned out. Perhaps he took some comfort in the thought that he had little cause, at least according to Robert Dale Owen, to regret his decision not to move to New Harmony. Writing from what remained of his father's utopian enterprise in the spring of 1834, Owen described for Trist a dismal scene: "I found this place, on my arrival last summer, if not in a declining, yet scarcely in an improving state. Houses, fences, &c. going much to decay, little sociability, or apparent desire of improvement among the citizens, and even a little of that aristocratical spirit of class which is so ludicrous, yet so frequently found, in a country village." Trist was soon extending his fortune-hunting energies beyond the Cuban consulate. In April 1836 he wrote to his wife that he had decided to buy land and Negroes in the Spanish colony. When Madison died two months later, his grieving legatee was preparing to set himself up – yet again – as a sugar planter.

6. Accommodation: The Old Dominion

NICHOLAS TRIST remained a wanderer in search of a home – the proverbial rolling stone who gathers no moss, as he described himself in 1858 – long after he quit Havana.[1] In that respect he little resembled his mentor, who somehow managed to call the same place home for all of his eighty-five years. Unlike Madison, who remained economically as well as emotionally tied to the place of his birth, Trist drifted from job to job, indeed from place to place. He returned briefly to the State Department in the mid-1840s, winning a fleeting moment in the national limelight and a place for his name in American history books by courageously defying the recall orders of President James K. Polk and negotiating the end of the Mexican War. Despite the controversy surrounding his behavior as a diplomat, it was even possible for Trist, if for no one else, to fantasize briefly about a Trist presidency. But he soon lapsed into relative obscurity, resuming the earlier pattern of his career. In 1851 he hatched an ambitious and characteristically abortive plan to get rich quick in California; three years later, friends in Virginia had to talk him out of pursuing yet another fortune-hunting scheme, this time to patent and then market an invention, apparently a washing machine. Meanwhile, he moved from Pennsylvania to New York and then back again. Employed at a modest salary by a railroad company in Philadelphia when the Civil War broke out, Trist reluctantly hit the patronage trail he knew so well. Appeals to the Lincoln administration were unsuccessful; but in 1870, largely in recognition of his unrewarded service in the

1 Martin Gordon, Jr., to Winfield Scott, Oct. 13, 1858, Nicholas P. Trist Papers, Library of Congress. It is clear that this letter was written by Trist himself. My reconstruction of Trist's career is based primarily on my reading in the manuscript collections cited in footnote 76 of the previous chapter.

Mexican War, and with the crucial assistance of Senator Charles Sumner, the seventy-year-old Trist was appointed postmaster in Alexandria, Virginia, by President Ulysses S. Grant. Four years later, Thomas Jefferson's private secretary, as he was identified in a Mathew Brady photograph from the period, died happily in the state where he had been born.[2]

Trist's ultimate return to his native soil provided a fitting close to his life. Yet just as clearly the move came forty years too late, and it also left him about a hundred miles too far north. Although Trist outgrew the fatuous conceit that native Virginians constituted a master race of sorts, he never broke the habit of reminding others where he had been born. Writing from Albemarle County in the summer of 1833, just before leaving for Cuba, he proclaimed to a correspondent: "I am here in my native mountains – a very healthy and delightful region, the finest, perhaps, every thing considered, in the Union."[3] Later he would write wistfully of perhaps one day being able to make his home, again, in those salubrious hills where he, along with Jefferson and Madison, had been born. But only belated recognition of his national service made even a rough approximation of that dream possible. During Madison's lifetime and well beyond, Trist's emotional ties to the Old Dominion proved insufficient to keep him, and later to bring him, where he fiercely insisted he belonged.

Trist's decision to pursue opportunity elsewhere made him, ironically, a typical Virginian. As both he and Madison knew all too well, the economic distress of the post-1819 years prompted thousands of citizens, young and old alike, to flee the commonwealth. Writing to his betrothed in early 1823, Trist, loyal in spirit if not in

2 See, for example, Trist to General Winfield Scott, July 26, 1851; Trist to Robert B. Minturn, Sept. 30, 1852; Frank Ruffin to Trist, Feb. 23, 1854; George W. Randolph to Trist, Mar. 6, 1854; Martin Gordon, Jr., to Winfield Scott, Oct. 13, 1858; Edward Coles to Edward Bates, Apr. 16, 1861; and Coles to Abraham Lincoln, July 15, 1862, all in Trist Papers, Library of Congress. In 1871, Grant also signed a bill awarding Trist a substantial lump-sum payment as belated remuneration for his Mexican mission; see Robert A. Brent, "Nicholas P. Trist: A Discredited Diplomat Vindicated," in John B. Boles, ed., *America: The Middle Period; Essays in Honor of Bernard Mayo* (Charlottesville, Va., 1973), 256–264.
3 Trist to R. J. Cleveland, July 29, 1833, Trist Papers, Library of Congress.

Nicholas P. Trist, c. 1870. Photograph by Mathew Brady or assistant. (Courtesy of the Library of Congress, Prints and Photographs Division)

body, blasted this "moving mania" as mindless. "These emigrants abandon comforts which are not the work of a few years, or even of a generation, to live in a log house the rest of their days," he complained, adding that their children, "debarred from the advantages of education" in so many "tracts of forest in the new states," were making "a retrograde from even the small degree of civilisation" that their parents had attained. Of course, Trist was writing from Louisiana, where, he had to admit, things were not altogether bleak or primitive; the state had reached what he called "a certain degree of polish," and more important, it proffered economic opportunities that were nothing short of dazzling.[4] If Trist was pursuing the elusive dream of republican independence almost a thousand miles from where he hoped to enjoy it, at least he expected to return home. Clearly others did not. Another of Thomas Jefferson's grandsons, Francis Eppes, saw removal to the alluring southwestern frontier as not only reasonable, but urgently necessary in the face of Virginia's moral and economic decline. "I see no ties," he told Trist in 1828, "which should bind any descendant of our grandfather to this state. The people are cold to his memory, the soil is exhausted, the staple reduced almost to the prime cost of the material." Under these circumstances, indeed, "what inducement is there to remain? Our children may grow rich under a different system, but *we* will never witness better times here."[5] Apparently Eppes saw nothing incongruous about blaming the commonwealth's moral decline on "noxious exhalations from the eastern states" – here he referred to the "Yankee notions" and "Yankee practices" of a "leaden-hearted, copper-souled race of tin peddlars" whose migration to Virginia from the North had "poisoned our atmosphere" – and in the next breath proclaiming his desire to go "where I can make more money." Eppes trekked with his family to Florida; at one point, Trist considered following him.[6]

For neither man did the decision to abandon Virginia have anything to do with moral reservations about the commonwealth's system of labor and society. If anything, they were seeking better opportunities to exploit slave labor. When Trist, the disciple of Robert Owen, worried about the deteriorating character of his na-

4 Trist to Virginia Randolph, Feb. 22, 1823, Nicholas P. Trist Papers, Southern Historical Collection, University of North Carolina at Chapel Hill.
5 Francis Eppes to Trist, Mar. 2, 1828, *ibid.*
6 Francis Eppes to Trist, Nov. 7, 1826, *ibid.* See also Trist to A. J. Donelson, May 20, 1829, Trist Papers, Library of Congress. For an especially perceptive assessment of the plight of young Virginians in this period, see Jan Lewis, *The Pursuit of Happiness: Family and Values in Jefferson's Virginia* (New York, 1983).

tive state, his concern was focused not on the untoward effects of slavery, but on the sudden proliferation of evangelical Christians, whom he described as a horde of barbarians; in 1827 he begged Madison to take up the cause of preserving Virginia's greatest distinction, her principles of religious freedom, in the face of this recrudescent threat to the Enlightenment.[7] But other Virginians who condemned their state's economic and moral decline placed the blame not on Yankee "tin peddlars," as Eppes did, or on crusading evangelicals (who could doubtless be traced to New England, too), as Trist did, but rather on matters closer to home and to Virginia's indigenous past.

At least a few young men, including Edward Coles (to whom we shall return in the next chapter), abandoned their native state in large part to escape complicity with the abominable institution of slavery. Among an older generation, Thomas Mann Randolph – the husband of Thomas Jefferson's daughter, Martha – also found it ever more difficult to live with the peculiar institution. In 1818 Randolph recounted for Trist the tragic story of a Virginia slave who sought dignity in suicide; two years later, while serving as governor of Virginia, he brooded about "the new morality which tolerates perpetuity of slavery." As Randolph's alienation from home and even family deepened in the 1820s, he became preoccupied with images of bloodshed, and began to talk in terms of holocaust and civil war. In 1821, he wrote to his future son-in-law at West Point: "You have chosen the military profession in a country which can scarcely ever have war, unless against revolted slaves, whose Blood will never stain your sword."[8] Some of Randolph's children, unlike Trist, shared their father's (and grandfather's) despair about slavery.

7 Trist to Madison, May 6, 1827, Nicholas P. Trist Papers, Virginia Historical Society.
8 Thomas Mann Randolph to Trist, Nov. 22, 1818, Trist–Burke–Randolph Papers, Alderman Library, University of Virginia; Randolph to Trist, June 5, 1820, and May 6, 1821, Trist Papers, Southern Historical Collection, University of North Carolina at Chapel Hill. On Randolph, see William H. Gaines, Jr., *Thomas Mann Randolph: Jefferson's Son-in-Law* (Baton Rouge, La., 1966), and George Green Shackelford, "Martha Jefferson and Thomas Mann Randolph, Jr.," in Shackelford, ed., *Collected Papers to Commemorate Fifty Years of the Monticello Association of the Descendants of Thomas Jefferson* (Princeton, N.J., 1965), 45–66.

After witnessing slave auctions at Monticello the year after Thomas Jefferson's death, Mary Jefferson Randolph could not bring herself to describe the horror of what she had seen; she reflected that it would be better "to submit to any personal inconveniences however numerous and annoying . . . than to live in a state of society where such things as this are of daily occurrence." Everyone was pouring out of Virginia, she told her sister, Ellen Randolph Coolidge, who had moved with her husband to Boston, because the state had become uninhabitable in almost every conceivable way.[9]

Madison doubtless heard a great deal in this despondent vein from many young Virginians during his retirement, some impelled by a strong antipathy to slavery and others not. None, however, could have offered a more bitter and categorical indictment of the Old Dominion than did a member of his own generation, his old friend and correspondent Francis Corbin. In the years just before he died in 1821, Corbin vented his anger and despair in a series of rambling, barely coherent letters to Madison. Everything, it seemed, had gone sour in Virginia, and Corbin was especially disturbed by the character of the people. Luxury and effeminacy – the dreaded bane of "fashion" – were sweeping the countryside; many of "our intelligent Negroes," Corbin averred, "are far superior in mind, morals, and manners to those who are placed in authority over them."[10] It was now "manifest to all," he lectured Madison, that "the morals of our people have inconceivably deteriorated, are daily deteriorating more and more, and require instantaneous reformation, by some means or other." But since decadence had become equivalent to "the customs and usages" of the people, Corbin found no cause for optimism, especially because this moral decline was inseparable from economic decline – and from the unavoidable effects of slavery.[11]

Indeed, Corbin thrust on Madison the formal proposition, with Virginia as his prime evidence, that "Farming and Slavery are incompatible with one another."[12] "Without industry, carefulness,

9 Mary Jefferson Randolph to Mrs. Joseph Coolidge, Jr., Jan. 25, 1827, Ellen Wayles Coolidge Correspondence, Alderman Library, University of Virginia.
10 Corbin to Madison, Oct. 10, 1819, in James Madison Papers, Library of Congress, series one (microfilm).
11 Corbin to Madison, Nov. 13, 1820, ibid.
12 Corbin to Madison, Sept. 24, 1818, ibid.

and frugality," he contended, "no Farmer ever did, or ever can prosper in any Country. But where there is Negro slavery there will be laziness, carelessness, and wastefulness. Nor is it possible to prevent them." Corbin admitted that slavery was for the moment profitable in the cotton and sugar states, but elsewhere it proved expensive, unrewarding, and vexatious, the source of "neverending violence to our feelings."[13] As he told Madison in 1820, "the profits of my Estate will not do more this year than pay the expences of it, our burthensome Taxes included. I suppose yours will hardly do more." Corbin's patience had run thin; even at the ripe age of sixty-one, he was prepared to abandon home in search of a better life, if not for himself then at least for his nine children. "If I could see my way clear to any *safe* and moderately productive mode of investing the proceeds of my property here," he confided to Madison, "I would, old as I am, migrate to the free North, where my sons, uninfluenced by false pride, might engage in honest pursuits for an honest livelihood." Corbin did not want his children to prolong the futility of his own agricultural endeavors; but if they remained in Virginia, he saw no viable alternatives for them. "Here we have nothing but the Profession of the Law," he told Madison, "and this, in addition to its being a meagre and miserable Profession, is, generally speaking, a vile and vicious one."[14]

Corbin's disdain for the law as it was practiced in Virginia anticipates Trist's disgust after his own awkward skirmishing at the bar. But unlike Trist (or Eppes), when the older man spoke of escaping from a state that denied viable employment to its young people, he looked to the north, where his sons might find free soil and "honest" labor, rather than to the south, where slave labor promised great speculative profits and new fortunes. Indeed, Corbin expressed contempt for the speculative temperament that characterized so many young Virginians, who disdained tradition, place, and continuity across generations, he said, for the quick profits of the marketplace. It mattered profoundly whether landed property was in the hands of those "who are attached to it by a thousand infantile recollections and cordial feelings, or of those who only estimate it by the number

13 Corbin to Madison, Oct. 10, 1819, *ibid.*
14 Corbin to Madison, Nov. 13, 1820, *ibid.*

of Dollars it cost, and are ever ready to part with it for a few more Dollars than they gave."[15] Since Virginia was no longer what it had once been, and certainly not what his (and Madison's) generation had envisioned during the heady days of the Revolution, Corbin found it ever harder to think of the Old Dominion as home. Only under such disheartening circumstances could he think of becoming a migrant himself.

Madison could hardly ignore the drift of his friend's stream of letters: Corbin's gloom deepened with each passing year. In 1819 he told Madison: "It is impossible, I think, that the present state of things can last. We must either abandon all the pure morality of Republicanism, or the gross and glaring immorality of slavery. They cannot co-exist many years longer."[16] A year later he bluntly inquired: "What, my dear sir, is to become of us?"[17] Corbin did not live long enough to find out; but three months before he died, his despair extended to the American Union. Believing that vice was its own punishment, Corbin predicted of slavery that "punished we shall be most severely before we have done with it, or it with us." The "decree of Fate" was clearly written: controversy over slavery would work its way "through the Skin of our present Confederation" and completely divide one part of the Union from the other. For this reason Corbin had even come to regret his cooperation with Madison at the Virginia ratifying convention of 1788. Reminding Madison of Cicero's maxim that a wise man changes his opinions often, a fool never, Corbin announced that he was no fool: "I confess then to *you*, my dear sir, that my opinions are changed as to our present *form* of Federal Government." Corbin took what was for Madison an unthinkable step – he recanted the commitment to the Constitution that he had made during the ratification debates. In 1787, he told Madison, his "youthful fancy" had been tickled with "our chimerical Project" of an expansive republic. But now he knew better than to think that "new states might be comprehended within it 'ad infinitum'." He therefore believed that the sections should separate at once, peacefully, rather than postpone and make dangerous what was transparently unavoidable: disunion.[18]

15 Corbin to Madison, Oct. 10, 1819, *ibid.*   16 *Ibid.*
17 Corbin to Madison, Nov. 13, 1820, *ibid.*
18 Corbin to Madison, Mar. 3, 1821, *ibid.* See also Corbin to Madison, May 13,

Madison may have responded to Corbin in more letters than the few that have survived. Whether this is the case, or whether he was inexplicably and uncharacteristically laconic, we have only a fragmentary indication of how he reacted to his friend's orgy of despair. It is hardly surprising that Madison did everything he could to comfort Corbin, even urging him to come to Montpelier, where they might share "a bottle of the old Bachelor" and "cast an eye at the reverse of the medal which has presented you with such a group of gloomy features in our national affairs." (Madison never got the chance to exercise his genial charm face to face, since Corbin died within a few weeks of receiving the invitation.)[19] Nor is it surprising that Madison, offering further evidence of his temperamental aversion to despair, was considerably more sanguine about the condition of both Virginia and the Union. At the risk of appearing to qualify his categorical denunciation of the evils of slavery, for instance, Madison gently suggested that even "under all the disadvantages of slave culture" that Corbin had cited, "much improvement" was "practicable," especially where slaves were "held in small numbers, by good masters and managers." Madison claimed to have seen as much in his own neighborhood. And doubtless disturbed by Corbin's talk of deserting Virginia and reinvesting his wealth elsewhere, Madison cautioned him not to exaggerate "the cares and vexations" incident to the business of a slaveholding planter. Did Corbin really think, Madison wondered out loud, that he would be any less vulnerable to pecuniary distress and uncertainty as a commercial stockholder – or even as the owner of large landed property somewhere in America "where there are no slaves"?[20]

Above all, what is striking is how vigorously Madison disagreed with his friend about the pattern and direction of change in their native state. So far from sharing Corbin's belief that the morals and manners of the people had declined, Madison could even describe the character of Virginia, in letters to other correspondents at this

---

1821, and Robert Corbin to Madison, June 1, 1821 (in which Madison is informed of his friend's death), *ibid.*

19 Madison to Corbin, May 21, 1821, in [William C. Rives and Philip R. Fendall, eds.], *Letters and Other Writings of James Madison* (Philadelphia, 1865), III, 225.

20 Madison to Corbin, Nov. 26, 1820, *ibid.*, 193–194.

time, as having improved dramatically since the days of the American Revolution and his own youth. Clearly, Madison detested slavery as much as Corbin did, but he had also made his peace with the Old Dominion in a way that his friend had not. And if the elderly Corbin was prepared to seek a new home, the Sage of Montpelier obviously found such recourse unnecessary, even unthinkable.

Virginia had become so much a part of Madison by the end of his life that it is difficult to think of him as anything but deeply committed to the state, irrevocably wed to the countryside that aroused passionate loyalty even among "natives" like Trist who found it inconvenient to stay. He appears to have been just the sort of person Corbin idealized, someone attached to the land – to place – "by a thousand infantile recollections and cordial feelings." Yet Madison's attachment to Virginia had not always been so readily forthcoming. The serenity and composure of the patriarch gives little hint of a troubled past, when a younger Madison had wrestled with a dilemma, not unlike Trist's anguished search for republican independence, that had nearly uprooted him. In fact, Madison had once shared Corbin's bleak assessment of the commonwealth and had been just as willing, even anxious, to escape. If we are to place the elderly Madison's accommodation of the Old Dominion in perspective – and assess its significance – we must, therefore, take a brief journey back in time, to a period when feeling at home in Virginia had been anything but easy or natural.

I

Following his graduation from the College of New Jersey in September 1771, the twenty-year-old Madison, with his father's permission, had lingered in Princeton for almost seven months. Perhaps he anticipated the culture shock that awaited his homecoming. As a student, Madison had learned from more than his books and tutors; he had seen different parts of British America for the first time and had fraternized with students from all over the colonies, from New England to Georgia. His collegiate years in the Middle Colonies introduced a provincial youth to a cosmopolitan world beyond Virginia, and what he discovered was a rich and wonderful world of

226

learning and liberty that he simply could not get enough of. Madison returned home imbued with new, often harshly critical perspectives on where he had spent the first eighteen years of his life.[21]

No sooner was the graduate re-ensconced in Orange County than he began to brood and complain that home now seemed unbearably dull to him. Trapped in what he called "an Obscure Corner" of the North American world, Madison found himself abruptly cut off from the intellectual stimulation he had savored and now sorely missed. He could only implore his friends to take pity on him, to keep him well informed and well supplied with the newspapers, pamphlets, and books that so rarely penetrated the hinterland that now reclaimed him. In early 1773 Madison opened a correspondence with his closest friend from college, William Bradford, by apologizing for the paucity of news and stimulation he would be able to provide. Since Bradford had returned home to "the Fountain-Head of Political and Literary Intelligence" – Madison's description of the city of Philadelphia – the Virginian warned him that he "must expect to be greatly [the] loser on that score by our Correspondence."[22] At least Madison discovered some solace in his provincial captivity: unlike Bradford, he would not have to "suffer those impertinent fops that abound in every City" to divert him from his "business and philosophical amusements." "I am luckily out of the way of such troubles," he reminded the Pennsylvanian; and Madison knew that Bradford was surrounded by these bothersome creatures, who "breed in Towns and populous places, as naturally as flies do in the Shambles, because there they get food enough for their Vanity and impertinence."[23]

Nevertheless, it seems clear that if Madison had to choose between few books and no fops in splendid rural isolation, or many books and a few fops amid the temptations of urban corruption, he would doubtless suffer the fops. By early 1774 he was planning a

21 For elaboration and context, see Irving Brant, *James Madison: The Virginia Revolutionist, 1751–1780* (Indianapolis and New York, 1941), 72–103, and Ralph Ketcham, *James Madison: A Biography* (New York, 1971), 25–67.

22 Madison to Bradford, Apr. 28, 1773, in William T. Hutchinson et al., eds., *The Papers of James Madison* (Chicago, Charlottesville, 1962–), I, 84.

23 Madison to Bradford, Nov. 9, 1772, *ibid.*, 75–76.

trip north. As he bluntly told Bradford, "I want again to breathe your free Air." Pre-Revolutionary Virginia may have been spared the impertinence of urban fops, but it was hardly a bastion of wholesome virtue – at least not in Madison's eyes. Rather, the Old Dominion was in a sorry condition, and the young graduate desperately needed a gulp of Bradford's "free air" in order to mend his constitution and confirm his principles. "I have indeed as good an Atmosphere at home as the Climate will allow," Madison told Bradford, "but have nothing to brag of as to the State and Liberty of my Country." Elaborating his view of the Virginia countryside surrounding Montpelier, Madison paid especial attention to the plight of dissenters from the established Anglican church, who presently endured fierce repression and even imprisonment. The militant cadence of his language revealed the moral vehemence of his feelings:

Poverty and Luxury prevail among all sorts: Pride ignorance and Knavery among the Priesthood and Vice and Wickedness among the Laity. This is bad enough. But It is not the worst I have to tell you. That diabolical Hell conceived principle of persecution rages among some and to their eternal Infamy the Clergy can furnish their Quota of Imps for such business. This vexes me the most of any thing whatever. There are at this [time?] in the adjacent County not less than 5 or 6 well meaning men in close Goal for publishing their religious Sentiments which in the main are very orthodox. I have neither patience to hear talk or think of any thing relative to this matter, for I have squabbled and scolded abused and ridiculed so long about it, [to so lit]tle purpose that I am without common patience. So I [leave you] to pity me and pray for Liberty of Conscience [to revive among us].[24]

Madison admired Pennsylvania precisely because the colony's principled tradition made such a dismal scene impossible. "You are happy in dwelling in a Land," he told Bradford, where the public "has long felt the good effects of their religious as well as Civil Liberty." Indeed, the commitment to freedom of conscience in William Penn's province encouraged the virtual antithesis of what Madison saw in his native Virginia: "Foreigners have been encouraged to settle amg. you. Industry and Virtue have been promoted by mutual emulation and mutual Inspection, Commerce and the Arts

24 Madison to Bradford, Jan. 24, 1774, *ibid.*, 106.

have flourished." And Madison could not "help attributing those continual exertions of Gen[i]us" that appeared among Bradford's people "to the inspiration of Liberty and that love of Fame and Knowledge which always accompany it." Whether the Old Dominion could shake free from the shackles of religious bondage – a bondage, Madison said, that "debilitates the mind and unfits it for every noble enterprize" and "every expanded prospect" – remained to be seen. In the meantime, he had little choice but to seek his quota of "free air" elsewhere, away from home.[25]

Madison found the time and opportunity to take one long, deep breath between early April and late June of 1774, when he escaped Virginia. He journeyed first to Philadelphia, where he enjoyed a reunion with friends and heard the shocking news of the closing of Boston harbor. He then continued north through Princeton, New York City, and finally Albany before turning back toward home. He left no record of his motives for extending his trip beyond the familiar Philadelphia-Princeton axis. No doubt he was curious to see more of America, and perhaps to observe conditions and institutions very different from those he had grown up with. But whatever it was that drew him to the Hudson River valley of upstate New York, the attraction proved persistent. Ten years later he would return as a committed veteran of a republican Revolution and, if anything, even more disillusioned with the prospect of settling down in Virginia.[26]

It was after the Revolution, indeed, that Madison's dilemma of choosing a vocation and a place to pursue it became critical. Although he now had cause to hope for a promising career in public life – a career that he clearly relished – he could neither expect nor wish actually to earn a living in politics, which was not yet considered an honorable calling; a republican statesman, after all, had to have independent means of support. Much like Trist in the 1820s, Madison in the 1780s wanted to find a source of income – ideally a fortune – that would confer just such independence; and

25 Madison to Bradford, Apr. 1, 1774, ibid., 112–113. See also Madison to Bradford, Dec. 1, 1773, ibid., 101.
26 Ketcham, Madison: A Biography, 59–60, and Brant, Madison: Virginia Revolutionist, 132–133.

like Trist, too, he studied law but rejected its practice, in part because he thought that he lacked the requisite physical stamina and talent for public speaking. Explaining his reluctance "to make a professional use" of his law studies, Madison told Edmund Randolph in the summer of 1785, "My wish is if possible to provide a decent & independent subsistence, without encountering the difficulties which I foresee in that line." But there was an important difference between Madison and Trist. The veteran of a republican revolution expressed another wish, which was "to depend as little as possible on the labour of slaves."[27]

Madison's access to his family's wealth in land and slaves after the Revolution was more than sufficient to support him comfortably; that was never his problem. Indeed, in the early 1780s the Madisons owned 118 slaves, the largest such holding in Orange County, and James Madison senior had just presented his son with a handsome gift of 560 acres of the Montpelier estate.[28] But apparently the young Virginian could not square his patrimony with the dictates of republican conscience, for he was also engaged in a principled search for some satisfactory alternative to the life of an Orange County planter. Madison told Randolph that his desire for a decent subsistence apart from slavery had aroused his interest in "several projects from which advantage seemed attainable."[29] And as he bluntly wrote to a friend in Kentucky, he had "no local partialities" that would keep him "from any place which promises the greatest real advantages" – which meant that he was quite ready, if necessary, to leave his family and move elsewhere, even if that meant burying

---

27 Madison to Edmund Randolph, July 26, 1785, in Hutchinson et al., eds., *Papers of Madison*, VIII, 328.

28 Irving Brant, *James Madison: The Nationalist, 1780–1787* (Indianapolis and New York, 1948), 324. For the reference to the Madison family's slaveholdings, see John Thomas Schlotterbeck, "Plantation and Farm: Social and Economic Change in Orange and Greene Counties, Virginia, 1716 to 1860," unpubl. Ph.D. diss., The Johns Hopkins University, 1980, chap. 1, p. 16. Schlotterbeck's marvelous dissertation is immensely helpful in placing Madison in at least one of the contexts, often neglected, that nurtured and sustained him.

29 Madison to Randolph, July 26, 1785, in Hutchinson et al., eds., *Papers of Madison*, VIII, 328.

James Madison in 1783. Miniature by Charles Willson Peale. (Courtesy of
the Library of Congress, Rare Books and Special Collections Division)

himself in the wilderness.[30] Hoping to keep Madison in the state and to gain a congenial neighbor, Jefferson tried to persuade him to settle down in Albemarle County; he even described a particular spot that he had picked out for him, 140 acres of decent land "with a small indifferent house on it," two miles from Monticello, where Madison might conduct "a farm of experiment and support a little table and household." The nature of Jefferson's proposed "experiment" is not clear, but we might note that such a modest estate was hardly conducive either to an opulent lifestyle or to slave labor.[31] Yet as Jefferson soon learned, when Madison talked of independence, he had something rather more ambitious in mind. Some of the "projects" from which Madison sought "advantage" in the mid-1780s remain obscure, but most of them appear to have involved land speculation on a significant scale.

Shortly after Jefferson extended his invitation to become an experimental farmer in Albemarle, in fact, Madison took another "ramble" into the northern states, an extended journey that repeated a good portion of his route from ten years earlier, up the Hudson River from New York to Albany and then on into the wilderness of the Mohawk River valley. Accompanied by the marquis de Lafayette, the young Virginian saw what he quickly proclaimed one of the most attractive frontiers in America – good soil, well watered, open to immediate settlement – a land of opportunity, he believed, for both settlers and speculators. Madison intended to become one of the latter. Here, he thought, as he began to buy as much of this choice land as he could, was his chance to build an independent fortune and to free himself from his family's plantation – and from slavery.[32]

Before his Mohawk fever ran its course, Madison even attempted to involve Jefferson directly in the speculation. Madison's partner in this ambitious enterprise was another young Virginian, James Monroe, but neither man had enough available cash to do more than buy modest tracts of land. Madison's hope was to use Jefferson's private credit in Paris, where his friend was now serving as Ameri-

---

30 Madison to Caleb Wallace, Aug. 23, 1785, *ibid.*, 350.
31 Jefferson to Madison, Feb. 20, 1784, *ibid.*, VII, 428.
32 For elaboration, see Brant, *Madison: Nationalist*, 324–342.

can minister to France, to help them all borrow huge sums from French investors; the time was ripe, he assured Jefferson, for "adventurers" to make a killing investing in upstate New York.[33] Madison obviously hoped to clear enough profit from this one vast undertaking to support himself comfortably, through its judicious investment, for the rest of his life, and to do so with a clear conscience; development of a frontier was not inherently exploitative, after all, and it was obviously preferable to exploit land, not slaves, if profit seeking in a just cause – in this case, an honorable independence – was unavoidable. But the scheme aborted. Jefferson did not have the credit with French investors that Madison assumed he did, and efforts to find alternative sources of the necessary capital proved just as disappointing. Ten years later, Madison sold his 900 acres in the Mohawk valley for a neat profit; but the fact remained that he had never been able to buy enough land to realize his dream. Notwithstanding his best efforts, he thus found himself no less dependent on Montpelier and on slave labor. Indeed, as Madison's biographer Irving Brant appropriately observed of his situation by the late 1780s, "For better or worse, he was yoked to the Virginia plantation for the rest of his life."[34]

So after 1789, when Madison continued to pursue avidly the career in public life that the Revolution had opened, he did so in a subtly but significantly different context. The apparent collapse of his many "projects" left him with an ambiguous and ultimately tragic inheritance. Privately, at least, Madison appears not to have lost sight of the tensions and even contradictions that characterized the Old Dominion and perforce his own life. Sometime in late 1791 or early 1792, for instance, he displayed remarkable insight and candor about the peculiar character of southern institutions and values. As he prepared to organize opposition to what he deemed the aristocratic and monarchical designs of counter-Revolutionary Federalists, most of whom were northerners, Madison also began to fill a notebook with political scribblings that are notable for their

33 Madison to Jefferson, Aug. 12, 1786, in Hutchinson et al., eds., *Papers of Madison*, IX, 97–98. See also Madison to Monroe, Mar. 19, 1786, *ibid.*, VIII, 505, and Madison to Ambrose Madison, Aug. 7, 1786, *ibid.*, IX, 89.
34 Brant, *Madison: Nationalist*, 342.

attention to slavery even when he was treading on familiar ground. When he reviewed the "various instances" that illustrated "the danger of oppression to the minority from unjust combinations of the majority," he included an instance that had not figured prominently in his analysis of this matter in the years surrounding the Philadelphia convention: "the case of Black slaves in Modern times."[35] And he scribbled at some length on a subject that, while rarely discussed publicly in the United States, was clearly vital to an understanding of American politics: the "Influence of domestic slavery on Government." Indeed, Madison discussed thoroughly – for himself – the general proposition that "in proportion as slavery prevails in a State, the Government, however democratic in name, must be aristocratic in fact."

According to Madison, "all the antient popular governments" had been "aristocracies," since the majority of the people had been slaves and power had been exercised "for the most part by the rich and easy." Under these circumstances, "the power lies in a part instead of the whole; in the hands of property, not of numbers." Turning to modern times, moreover, he concluded that "the Southern States of America" were also, by the same principle, "aristocracies." In Virginia, black slaves were "an instance" that illustrated perfectly "the danger of oppression to the minority from unjust combinations of the majority"; and the aristocratic character of the government was only increased "by the rule of suffrage, which requiring a freehold in land excludes nearly half the free inhabitants, and must exclude a greater proportion, as the population increases." Madison estimated that at present, the disenfranchised – which is to say, the slaves and the white non-freeholders combined – amounted to nearly "3/4 of the State"; hence the power actually lay in the hands of only a small fraction of the people. Indeed, "were the slaves freed and the right of suffrage extended to all, the operation of the Government might be very different." And Madison's broader conclusion is just as striking: "the slavery of the Southern states," he argued, "throws the power much more into the hands of property, than in the Northern States. Hence the people of property in the former are much more contented

35 Notes for the *National Gazette* Essays, ca. 19 Dec. 1791 – 3 March 1792, in Hutchinson et al., eds., *Papers of Madison*, XIV, 160.

with their establishd Governments, than the people of property in the latter."[36]

Scholars have generally ignored these fragmentary scribblings, in part because they have only recently been brought to light by the modern editors of Madison's papers. But they are remarkable for several reasons. They indicate, first of all, that Madison saw clearly the relevance of slavery to his political theory and to the political complexion of the United States. He was fully prepared – privately, at least – to integrate slavery into his analysis of both republicanism and American society. They also indicate that Madison saw just as clearly what some recent scholars have seen: that by reducing the potential for challenge and insurgency from the lower ranks of society, slavery crucially affected the political posture and vision of republican elites.[37] Finally, Madison's reflections on slavery and republicanism convey the measure of his intellectual integrity. Racism could not obscure for him a central truth of American politics: since black slaves had to be considered people in any meaningful analysis of the character of modern governments, the regimes in the southern states, including Virginia, may have been "democratic in name," but they were, in fact, far less democratic than northern state governments. Indeed, the proper label for them was aristocracy.

Yet what is most striking and significant about these reflections is, of course, that they remained private; they were never formally integrated into Madison's political theory, not in 1792 and not later. Much of the material in Madison's notebook was reproduced, sometimes verbatim, in a series of essays in the *National Gazette* designed to mobilize, on principled grounds, the opposition to Alexander Hamilton; but the comments concerning "the influence of domestic slavery on Government" quoted here were omitted from the printed essays. The reasons are not hard to discern. Few of Madison's southern constituents were willing to introduce slavery

36 *Ibid.*, 160, 163–164.
37 The most forceful statement may be found in Edmund S. Morgan, *American Slavery, American Freedom: The Ordeal of Colonial Virginia* (New York, 1975). For indirect evidence that Madison was still thinking in these terms toward the end of his life, see the report of Madison's conversation with visitors to Montpelier in the *Richmond Enquirer*, June 28, 1833.

into national political discussion, nor would they appreciate a candid admission of the aristocratic character of their governments; and surely Madison was no less reluctant than they to supply his political adversaries with such potent ammunition. Indeed, for both Madison and the swelling ranks of his southern supporters, slavery would remain the great unacknowledged presence in the republican equation – which meant that for the remainder of Madison's career, northern Federalists eager to expose Jeffersonian pretense and hypocrisy, and not Madison himself, would publicly discuss the issue in these terms.

We might say that Madison gradually accommodated his sense of personal identity and republican purpose to a dimension of his own – and American – life that he proved no more able to change than to approve of. This meant that he had to defer coming to meaningful terms with personal and public issues that he had once seemed willing to engage. As we shall see in the next chapter, Madison consistently did what he thought prudent and feasible to contain the horrid effects of slavery and to make possible its eventual demise. But he was also becoming ever more firmly bound to his native soil and its conventions. Or, to put it more harshly, the mature statesman eased comfortably enough into the life of a Virginia planter that the Revolutionary of the 1780s had resolved to avoid. His political career became no less dependent on evading the implications of the political analysis that he had committed to his notebook in the early 1790s.

By the time Madison began to receive Francis Corbin's anguished missives during the early years of his retirement, his perspective on Virginia clearly reflected the extent to which faith and vision could color perception. To be sure, he continued to acknowledge the shortcomings of the commonwealth and its people; in 1818, for instance, as president of the Agricultural Society of Albemarle, Madison minced few words condemning Virginians for their carelessly exploitative approach to the land and to nature more generally.[38] But as he made amply clear in a long letter to Robert Walsh

38 "Address to the Agricultural Society of Albemarle, Virginia," May 1818, in [Rives and Fendall, eds.], Letters and Other Writings, III, 63–95, esp. 76–77, 93–94.

the following year, he was, on the whole, more than pleased by the progress his native state had made in the moral scale of things. Weighing the overall condition of Virginia in the early nineteenth century against what it had been during his youth, Madison saw change that cheered rather than depressed the soul. Walsh, who was preparing his rebuttal of foreign slanders against the United States, had asked Madison to help him defend Virginia's reputation. We may presume that Corbin would have spurned any such request, but the Sage of Montpelier proved more than willing to comply. He summed up his position in a single sentence: "With respect to the moral features of Virginia, it may be observed, that pictures which have been given of them are, to say the least, outrageous caricatures, even when taken from the state of society previous to the Revolution; and that so far as there was any ground or colour for them then, the same cannot be found for them now."[39]

Madison's memories of what he had found upon his return home from Princeton in the early 1770s were hardly too dim to recall. But now he insisted that the evils of late colonial Virginia were grossly exaggerated, especially by foreigners, and that the Revolution had changed everything, anyway. Indeed, Madison spoke as if the Revolution had literally re-formed the commonwealth. Carefully examining for Walsh the primary causes "tainting the habits and manners of the people under the Colonial Government," he began with slavery, which he was quick to make primarily the responsibility of an imperial government that had defeated the colonists' efforts to stop the importation of slaves. Madison proudly noted, in this connection, that "one of the first offsprings of independent republican legislation" in his state had been "an act of perpetual prohibition [of the slave trade]." Perhaps recalling his own youthful indictment of luxury in the colonial commonwealth, Madison also cited as a primary source of corruption "the too unequal distribution of property, favored by laws derived from the British code, which generated examples in the opulent class inauspicious to the habits of other classes." Here the abolition of entails and the rule of primogeniture – again, by a republican legislature – had done much to rectify the problem. And so the list of causes went: the "indolence" and "irreg-

39 Madison to Walsh, Mar. 2, 1819, *ibid.*, 122.

237

ular lives" of many of the established Anglican clergy; the "source of contagious dissipation" provided by British, chiefly Scottish, factors in the tobacco trade; "the rule of septennial elections for the Legislature" – all were part and parcel of a corrupt British world that the Revolution had all but obliterated. As Madison reminded Walsh, "with the exception of slavery, these demoralizing causes have ceased, or are wearing out."[40]

Even in the case of slavery, moreover, the problem had "lost no small share of its former character." No impartial observer could doubt, Madison insisted, that "the actual condition of slaves in Virginia" was "better, beyond comparison, than it was before the Revolution":

The improvement strikes every one who witnessed their former condition, and attends to their present. They are better fed, better clad, better lodged, and better treated in every respect; insomuch, that what was formerly deemed a moderate treatment, would now be a rigid one, and what formerly a rigid one, would now be denounced by the public feeling.[41]

And what accounted for this salutary change in the moral sensibility of those who continued to own property in human beings? Madison cited two great causes of amelioration: again, the abolition of entails and primogeniture, which meant that slaves were generally held in smaller numbers by individual holders of them (a circumstance, Madison believed, that was conducive to their more humane treatment), and above all "the sensibility to human rights, and sympathy with human sufferings, excited and cherished by the discussions preceding, and the spirit of the Institutions growing out of" – what else? – the Revolution. If a youthful Madison had envied his friend Bradford's good fortune to have been born a Pennsylvanian, a mature Madison told Walsh, another denizen of Philadelphia, that Virginia had in effect closed the moral gap. "On the whole," Madison observed, "the moral aspect of the State may, at present, be fairly said to bear no unfavorable comparison with the average standard of the other States. It certainly gives the lie to the foreign calumniators whom you propose to arraign."[42]

In making this systematic case for moral progress in his native

<hr>

40 *Ibid.*, 122–124.   41 *Ibid.*, 124, 121–122.   42 *Ibid.*, 122, 124.

state, Madison ultimately turned his attention to the issue that had, more than any other, defined his republican faith: freedom of conscience. He described the improvement in the commonwealth's religious life as momentous, especially when gauged by "the number of religious teachers, the zeal which actuates them, the purity of their lives, and the attendance of the people on their instructions." And the cause of this renaissance in religion was no less clear. Madison remembered both the outrageous persecution of dissenters that had aroused his fury in the years just before the Revolution and the epochal triumph that he had enjoyed in the Virginia legislature a scant twelve years later; for him, there was no greater monument to the American Revolution than the Act for Establishing Religious Freedom that marked one of his own greatest personal achievements. Indeed, the disestablishment of the Anglican church in Virginia had exploded, once and for all, the crippling myths that civil government could not stand without the support of established religion and that the Christian religion – and morality more generally – would perish without legal provision for its clergy.[43] Viewed in this light, the Virginia that Madison contemplated during the early years of his retirement offered unambiguous evidence not of the declension that so demoralized Corbin, but of impressive republican progress.

Madison's optimism clearly reflects the extent of his faith in the transforming effects of a Revolution that had, among other things, given his own life meaning. His career – his very identity – were so fused with the Revolution and its legacy that, on the simplest level, to accept Corbin's view of Virginia would be an admission of failure no less personal than profound. As Harriet Martineau would so shrewdly discern, Madison's faith in republicanism constituted what she called "political religion," a form of personal piety that had the effect of "sustaining the spirit through difficulty and change."[44] Madison's perspective on his native state, and indeed on many matters during his retirement, emerged in no small part from his passionate commitment to preserving the moral force of America's republican example. His defense of Virginia in 1819 was obviously

43 Ibid., 124–125.
44 Martineau, Retrospect of Western Travel (London and New York, 1838), I, 198.

quickened by his sensitivity to foreign, especially British, criticism. Yet there is no reason to question his sincerity, nor should we lose sight of his primary concern in caring about what others in Europe believed about his native state. His defense of post-Revolutionary society transcended any simple pride or provincial insecurity; keeping faith with republican progress in America, including Virginia, was Madison's way of defending the cause of republicanism itself and, most important, of preserving its potential influence in other parts of the world.

The Sage of Montpelier would need his republican faith in abundance when, at the age of seventy-eight, he formally reentered public life for the only time during his retirement. In the spring of 1829 he was selected to represent his state's senatorial district at the constitutional convention scheduled to convene later that year. The Virginia convention of 1829–30, Madison's final constitutional gathering, was charged with nothing less than the delicate and demanding task of revising the political framework of the state in whose republican progress he had invested so much.

II

Among the delegates who converged on Richmond in October 1829, Madison was the sole survivor of the 1776 convention that had drafted the original state constitution which reformers now hoped to replace. That constitution had aroused considerable controversy from the very beginning, as many Virginians, led by Thomas Jefferson, had objected vehemently to its ostensibly unrepublican provisions for suffrage and representation. According to the author of the Declaration of Independence, voting in state elections was restricted by a freehold requirement that excluded the majority of the men who had fought in the Revolution and paid taxes. Even worse, representation in the House of Delegates was apportioned by county (and in the Senate by district) – which implicitly took into account the distribution of property, especially in slaves – rather than by white population alone; and this arrangement effectively gave the older Tidewater region of the state far more power in the government than its numbers (of free citizens, that is) warranted. This constituted an inequity that only increased with time, as the newer parts of the state, west of the Blue Ridge mountains, attracted their due share of white population, the Tidewater suffered economic decline (and reduced population growth), and the slave population remained generally concentrated in the east.

Jefferson had not been alone in objecting to this constitution, which he criticized in the *Notes on Virginia* and continued to oppose publicly for the rest of his life. In 1784 Madison had himself sponsored a bill in the House of Delegates calling for a new convention. That such a gathering did not actually convene until after Jefferson's death is an effective measure of the power wielded by Virginians who had no interest in change and of their determination to protect their privileged position. By the late 1820s western Virginians were seeking to dismantle a system of government that consistently refused to meet their legitimate needs (for internal improvements, for instance) and that unjustly protected, in their judgment, the minority interests of eastern slaveholders. Their principal demand at the 1829 convention was that representation be based on white population alone, which they defended as the only formula consistent with pure republicanism; other reformers (not always the same people) were just as eager to abolish freehold suffrage in favor of what had become common throughout the United States, universal white manhood suffrage. Easterners, on the other hand, feared that a reformed state government controlled by power-hungry westerners would impose a grievous tax burden on their slave property – or worse. They generally resisted all calls for significant reform, contending instead for representation by population and taxation (i.e., property) combined, as well as for retaining necessary suffrage restrictions.[45]

45 For fuller accounts of the convention and its background than I can provide in this quick summary, see, among many possible secondary sources, Alison Goodyear Freehling, *Drift Toward Dissolution: The Virginia Slavery Debate of 1831–1832* (Baton Rouge, La., 1982), 36–81; Dickson D. Bruce, Jr., *The Rhetoric of Conservatism: The Virginia Convention of 1829–30 and the Conservative Tradition in the South* (San Marino, Calif., 1982); and Robert Paul Sutton, "The Virginia Constitutional Convention of 1829–1830: A Profile Analysis of Late Jeffersonian Virginia," unpubl. Ph.D. diss., Univ. of Virginia, 1967. An excellent brief summary of the convention can be found in chap. 3 of Claude H. Hall, *Abel Parker Upshur: Conservative Virginian, 1790–1844* (Madison, Wisc., 1964), 30–66.

The extent of Madison's influence in the convention is difficult to judge. According to one delegate, who pleaded with him at a critical juncture not to side with the reformers, he held the very fate of the commonwealth in his hands: "All eyes are turned upon you, and every step you take and every word you utter are watched by the whole state."[46] Madison spoke briefly at the opening of the convention, when, according to a correspondent for a New York newspaper, his voice "betrayed the feebleness of age, and, like his whole frame, trembled with agitation and apparent embarrassment."[47] After that, Madison did not say very much at all, at least not in the formal proceedings, but what he did say – and do – caught everyone's attention. By the time he delivered his only major speech, on December 2, neither faction appeared confident of his support. Early in the convention, as chairman of an important committee, Madison had initially voted with the westerners in favor of white representation for the lower house of the legislature – which prompted eastern critics, who felt betrayed, to make snide comments about "the fatuity" and "vacillating conduct" that came with "putting old men in active life."[48] Later, however, in the committee of the whole, Madison moved away from his apparent support of the reformers, which prompted them, in turn, "to regret his inconsistency as much on his own account, as for the effect it has on our cause."[49]

As usual, Madison himself saw more method and consistency in his actions than did his contemporaries (and some later scholars). As he explained not long after the convention adjourned, his primary goal had not been to support one or the other of the two factions, but rather "to promote a compromise of ideas between parties fixed in their hot opinion by their local interests, and threatening an abortive result to an experiment closely connected with the tranquillity of the State, and the capacity of man for self-government."

46 Joseph Cabell to Madison, Dec. 3, 1829, in Madison Papers, Library of Congress, series one (microfilm).
47 Reprint from New York *Commercial Advertiser*, in *Richmond Enquirer*, Oct. 20, 1829.
48 Hugh Blair Grigsby, Diary at Virginia Convention (#4), Oct. 4–31, 1829, in Grigsby Papers, Virginia Historical Society, pp. 54–55, 91–92.
49 J. A. G. Davis to Nicholas P. Trist, Dec. 15, 1829, in Trist Papers, Library of Congress.

Indeed, if Madison had a single lesson to teach this rising generation of politicians, it was the need to see beyond the most passionate, immediate differences of interest and opinion in order to sustain stable republican government – a lesson that he had learned especially vividly, of course, at Philadelphia in 1787. Madison was careful to record for posterity his preferred stance on every issue faced by the 1829 convention. But as a delegate he was also mindful of what he called "the known will and *meditated* instructions" of his Piedmont constituents and, even more, of the dreadful consequences that would attend any failure to reach some satisfactory consensus. Both concerns, especially the latter, gradually pushed him toward greater accommodation of eastern positions than he might have preferred as a matter of principle alone.[50]

Madison never doubted the very real danger that the convention might abort. For several months he had listened to enough menacing talk of Virginia dissolving into two separate states, and eventually he identified what appeared to him to be the more intransigent, and perhaps desperate, of the contending factions. The convention received a wave of petitions from eastern constituencies threatening disunion and violence if the reformers prevailed; as one terrified associate of Madison's complained, "*our western* people," whom he described as "*sui generis*," were fanatical in their campaign to grind down the east.[51] Madison had initially supported in committee the white basis for representation in part because he hoped to encourage a general disposition among both sides to compromise. But his gambit only aroused the implacable fury of the easterners; a Norfolk delegate who followed his lead in the committee was even forced, by angry constituents denouncing his "treason," to resign from the convention. Instead of the desired conciliatory spirit, in other words, Madison confronted passionate fanaticism and the ever more frightening likelihood of utter impasse. With some obvious

50 Douglass Adair, ed., "James Madison's Autobiography," in *William and Mary Quarterly*, 3d ser., 2 (1945), 208. Madison apparently composed the final version of this document sometime after 1833.
51 Cabell to Madison, Dec. 3, 1829, in Madison Papers, Library of Congress, series one (microfilm). See also Irving Brant, *James Madison: Commander in Chief, 1812–1836* (Indianapolis and New York, 1961), 463–464, and Ketcham, *Madison: A Biography*, 638, for references to the threat of disunion in the state.

reluctance, he shifted the balance of his position accordingly.[52] In later explaining his behavior at the convention, Madison appropriately adverted to "the necessity of securing an effective and tranquil result by indulging the party, whose defeat would have been most pregnant with danger."[53]

In his speech of December 2, amid this mounting fear that the convention might actually collapse, Madison couched his concerns of the moment in the larger context of his longstanding republican concerns. If conditions had changed since the 1780s, his broad perspective and fundamental principles had not. The reformers at the convention were doubtless disappointed when he firmly defended the right of Virginia's eastern slaveholders to have their "peculiar" interests in some way protected "in the basis and structure of the Government itself." Reminding the delegates that governments were instituted to protect both "the rights of persons" and "the rights of property," Madison once again became "Publius," fearful of unrestrained majoritarian democracy: "In Republics, the great danger is, that the majority may not sufficiently respect the rights of the minority." Easterners were understandably apprehensive that if power were exercised by a western majority with little or no interest in slave property, profound injustice might be done to the owners of such property. Madison therefore urged the western delegates to acknowledge and to respect this legitimate concern. And if "the most apposite and effectual security that can be devised" was to somehow "incorporate that interest into the basis of our system," Madison was confident that he knew the best way to achieve this balance. He eagerly supported earlier proposals to borrow from the federal Constitution the apportionment mechanism by which five slaves were considered the equivalent of three free persons. Here, he confidently believed, was a remedy for the fever of political antagonism that jeopardized the integrity of the Old Dominion.[54]

52 Brant, *Madison: Commander in Chief*, 463. See also Hugh Blair Grigsby's diary, Oct. 4–31, 1829, in Grigsby Papers, Virginia Historical Society, pp. 91–92.

53 Adair, ed., "Madison's Autobiography," in *William and Mary Quarterly*, 3d ser., 2 (1945), 208.

54 For a printed text of the speech, see [Rives and Fendall, eds.], *Letters and Other Writings*, IV, 51–53. The original draft in Madison's hand, which contains

Madison's enthusiasm for the "three-fifths clause" is immensely revealing for a number of reasons, all of which confirm the extent to which he was attempting to use the wisdom of the past, and the lessons of the 1780s, to resolve the convention's urgent dilemma. He lauded the so-called "Federal number" for "its simplicity, its certainty, its stability, and its permanency." And he raised, indeed dwelled upon, a relevant issue that appears not to have moved many of his fellow delegates in 1829 on either side of the great debate. Most of them tended to consider slaves strictly as property and thus to approach from that premise the question of whether they should be represented in the government. But Madison deliberately cast his advocacy of the three-fifths clause in a more complex light. Speaking of "the coloured part of our population," he issued a solemn reminder: "It is due to justice; due to humanity; due to truth; to the sympathies of our nature; in fine, to our character as a people, both abroad and at home, that they should be considered, as much as possible, in the light of human beings, and not as mere property." It was as human beings, after all, that "they are acted upon by our laws, and have an interest in our laws," and to that degree, he concluded, they should be "considered as making a part, though a degraded part, of the families to which they belong."[55]

The point bears emphasis: the reformers explicitly likened the slaves to cows and horses – to property. In suggesting that slaves be considered members of white families in a way that cattle obviously could not, however, Madison reminded the delegates of the essential difference between draught animals and slaves, the latter of which were, in fact, more analogous politically to women, children, servants, and other dependent nonvoters. If Virginia's bound laborers "had the complexion of the Serfs in the north of Europe, or of the Villeins, formerly in England" – in other words, if they were "of our own complexion" – much of "the difficulty" and confusion would be removed: clearly, they would be included in any counting of human heads for representation. "But the mere circumstance of complex-

only a few minor differences, has recently been added to the Madison Papers, Library of Congress, series 7.

55 Speech in convention, Dec. 2, 1829, in [Rives and Fendall, eds.], *Letters and Other Writings*, IV, 53, 52.

ion," Madison insisted, could not deprive the blacks "of the character of men," no matter how debased their present status in law. Here he turned on its head the logic of the reformers, who professed to be defending pure republican principles. Madison was suggesting, indeed, that the "white basis" approach to representation, which must necessarily treat slaves exclusively as property (and therefore not entitled to any representation), was in fact, among other things, a statement of false — and blatantly unjust — principle.[56]

This train of analysis was hardly a fresh discovery for the elderly Madison. Forty years earlier, in *Federalist* number fifty-four, he had defended the three-fifths clause at much greater length in remarkably similar terms. Opponents of the Constitution in 1788 had reasoned that because slaves in the southern states were "considered merely as property, and in no respect whatever as persons," they ought not to be represented in the federal government. But Madison had pointed out that in both fact and principle this distorted "the true state of the case." Slaves actually partook of both qualities, "being considered by our laws, in some respects, as persons, and in other respects, as property." Since Madison's position in 1829 was clearly based on similar reasoning, this earlier elaboration of the argument deserves close attention:

In being compelled to labor not for himself, but for a master; in being vendible by one master to another master; and in being subject at all times to be restrained in his liberty, and chastised in his body, by the capricious will of another, the slave may appear to be degraded from the human rank, and classed with those irrational animals, which fall under the legal denomination of property. In being protected on the other hand in his life and in his limbs, against the violence of all others, even the master of his labor and his liberty; and in being punishable himself for all violence committed against others; the slave is no less evidently regarded by the law as a member of the society; not as a part of the irrational creation; as a moral person, not as a mere article of property.[57]

Madison drew the inescapable inference: "The Federal Constitution therefore, decides with great propriety on the case of our slaves,

56 *Ibid.*, 53.
57 See Jacob E. Cooke, ed., *The Federalist* (Middletown, Conn., 1961 [orig. publ. 1788]), 367–368.

when it views them in the mixt character of persons and of property," not only because this was their "true character," as "bestowed on them by the laws under which they live," but also because *these are the proper criterion*" (emphasis added). Only under "the pretext" that the laws had somehow transformed the Negroes into animals could they be denied any place in "the computation of numbers"; and everyone understood that if the blacks had their full rights restored and ceased to be slaves, they "could no longer be refused an equal share of representation with the other inhabitants."[58] They were, after all, human beings, "moral persons," and not "a part of the irrational creation"; and forty years later, in 1829, Madison deemed it ever more urgent that this simple fact be acknowledged, through the three-fifths clause, in the structure of Virginia's republican government. Indeed, the beauty of the "three-fifths" formula as he conceived of it was precisely its subtle versatility. It would do more than protect the legitimate property interests of eastern slaveholders. It would also formally recognize what the pragmatic accommodation of circumstance should never obscure, even more, perhaps, in 1829, when the faint murmerings of a proslavery argument were audible, than in 1788: the self-evident truth of the humanity of the slaves.

By the time of this December 2 speech Madison had cast himself, whether consciously or not, in the avuncular role of peacemaker that the venerable Benjamin Franklin had played so well at the 1787 convention. He appropriately concluded with perhaps the most vivid reminder of the enduring relevance of the 1780s. In a moving tribute to the momentous cause that engaged the labor of the delegates, a cause that loomed large in the eyes of men everywhere, Madison spoke of past triumphs and of his own resilient optimism. "The Convention is now arrived at a point where we must agree on some common ground," he remarked, "all sides relaxing in their opinions, not changing, but mutually surrendering a part of them."

In framing a Constitution, great difficulties are necessarily to be overcome; and nothing can ever overcome them but a spirit of compromise. Other nations are surprised at nothing so much as our having been able to form Constitutions in the manner which has been exemplified in this country.

58 *Ibid.*, 368.

The Virginia Constitutional Convention of 1829–30. Madison is pictured speaking, at center, surrounded by his colleagues. Watercolor by George Catlin. (Courtesy of The New-York Historical Society, New York City)

Even the Union of so many States is, in the eyes of the world, a wonder; the harmonious establishment of a common Government over them all, a miracle. I cannot but flatter myself, that, without a miracle, we shall be able to arrange all difficulties. I never have despaired, notwithstanding all the threatening appearances we have passed through. I have now more than a hope – a consoling confidence that we shall at last find that our labours have not been in vain.[59]

More than a month later Madison was still clinging to little more than his indomitable faith. As he wrote to a friend in Pennsylvania, "Our Convention is now in the pangs of parturition. Whether the result is to be an abortion, or an offspring worthy of life, will shortly be determined."[60] The delegates eventually proved able to give birth to something, even if it was, in the eyes of many Virginians, of

59 Speech in convention, Dec. 2, 1829, in [Rives and Fendall, eds.], *Letters and Other Writings*, IV, 54–55.
60 Madison to C. J. Ingersoll, Jan. 8, 1830, *ibid.*, 57.

dubious character. Madison was doubtless disappointed that in the aftermath of his speech, the easterners sustained enough momentum to go considerably beyond his "Federal ratio" and to secure provisions in the new constitution that in effect guaranteed their firm control of both houses of the legislature. And privately he made it quite clear that he was disappointed that the Convention had not gone further than it had in extending the suffrage to non-freeholders. Although Madison was, by his own account, acutely "aware of the danger of universal suffrage in a future state of society such as the present state in Europe," he also believed that the vote should be extended, as a matter of principle, "so far as to secure in every event and change in the state of Society a majority of people on the side of power." In his retrospective account of the convention, he emphasized the central point. Notwithstanding his principled fears of the danger of majority oppression, that risk was preferable to accepting "a Government resting on a minority," which he deemed "an aristocracy not a Republic." After all, such a regime "could not be safe with a numerical and physical force against it"; it would demand for its security "a standing Army," an "enslaved press," and "a disarmed populace."[61]

The new constitution contained, in sum, some major disappointments. But in the end Madison chose to see his larger faith in the delegates vindicated rather than betrayed, and, considering the alternatives, he professed to be satisfied, even pleased, with the outcome of the convention. Forwarding a copy of the constitution to a professor at the University of Virginia, he described it as "very much a compound of compromising ingredients. It is pudding, with some good plumbs in it at least."[62] Some of Madison's biographers have suggested that beneath his outward equanimity, he was deeply disillusioned by his experience at the Convention.[63] Perhaps so. Certainly had he wished to, he might have seen ample evidence that a

61 See esp. Adair, ed., "Madison's Autobiography," in *William and Mary Quarterly*, 3d ser., 2 (1945), 208.
62 Madison to Prof. Long, Mar. 30, 1830, in Madison Papers, Library of Congress, series one (microfilm).
63 See esp. Ketcham, *Madison: A Biography*, 640; and Brant, *Madison: Commander in Chief*, 466–467.

slaveholding clique, hostile to the liberal spirit of republicanism and to any notions of emancipation, had a stranglehold on the Old Dominion. But this appears not to have been at all his preferred – or, I believe, sincere – interpretation of the ultimate significance of the convention.

Shortly after returning to Montpelier from Richmond, Madison sketched that upbeat interpretation in a revealing letter to the marquis de Lafayette, who had expressed considerable interest in the deliberations. Citing the extraordinarily complex "sources of jealousy and collisions which infected the proceedings throughout," Madison emphasized how difficult it had been to arrive at even a fragile consensus. He explained that for responsible delegates, "every concession of private opinion, not morally inadmissible, became necessary, in order to prevent an abortion discreditable to the body and to the State" – a miscarriage, he added, that would have inflicted "a stain on the great cause of self-government." At the time Madison wrote, the amended constitution awaited popular ratification, and although people from both camps were less than entirely pleased, he was hopeful that it would be approved. After all, it "alleviates greatly where it does not remove the objections" that had been "justly urged" by the westerners, while the easterners, who had opposed any change, could regard the result "as an obstacle to another Convention which might bring about greater and more obnoxious innovations." And if Madison were right, that the constitution had enough "good plumbs" to win the people's support, the success of the convention presented nothing less than another chapter in the American vindication of republicanism. "The *peculiar* difficulties which will have been overcome," he told Lafayette, "ought to render the experiment a new evidence of the capacity of men for self-government, instead of an argument in the hands of those who deny and calumniate it." Even in the most trying circumstances, in other words, reason had eventually triumphed over passion. The convention had not aborted; social and political order had been preserved; and Virginia had remained a community capable of overcoming its "peculiar" difficulties – which meant that the champions of self-government everywhere now had fresh cause, if not in this case to celebrate, at least to be reassured. Madison even boasted to Lafayette, for good measure, that "the Convention was composed of the *elite* of the community, and exhibited great talents in the discussions belonging to the subject."[64]

This was by no means an absurd or utterly farfetched interpretation of the evidence. As an assessment of the convention, however, it was also far from inclusive or sufficient. Madison's republican faith, his stoical optimism, and his concern for world opinion were together so strong that he almost instinctively placed the most favorable construction on what was, at best, an ambiguous record. Given what was at stake, he was simply unable to consider, much less confront, even the thought that his state's constitutional convention buttressed the case of those who might doubt or disparage "the capacity of men for self-government." Nowhere is this more starkly clear than in a subsequent paragraph of the letter to Lafayette, in which Madison sought to explain why the delegates had failed to do something that the Frenchman had both desired and apparently expected.

"Your anticipations with regard to the slavery among us," Madison wrote, "were the natural offspring of your just principles and laudable sympathies" – principles and sympathies that he clearly shared. But the Virginian sorely regretted having to say that it had been impossible even to broach the subject of emancipation at the convention. Indeed, Madison spoke of the "morbid" and "violent" sensibility against any such discussion among those delegates who had "the largest stake" in the institution – the same delegates, he might have added, whose peculiar interests and demands had necessarily been indulged on the issue of representation. "I scarcely express myself too strongly in saying," he concluded, "that any allusion in the Convention to the subject you have so much at heart would have been a spark to a mass of gunpowder."[65]

Remarkably, however, even this disappointment failed to

64 Madison to General La Fayette, Feb. 1, 1830, in [Rives and Fendall, eds.], *Letters and Other Writings*, IV, 59–60.

65 *Ibid.*, 60. Lafayette was not alone in expressing this concern to Madison. During the convention he received a plea from a forty-one-year-old South Carolinian, who called herself "the Pilgrim Stranger," to do what he could to leave the door open to gradual emancipation in Virginia. See Harriet Livermore to Madison, Oct. 22, 1829, in Madison Papers, Library of Congress, series one (microfilm).

dampen Madison's faith in the future. As he told Lafayette, "it is certain, nevertheless, that time, the 'great Innovator,' is not idle in its salutary preparations. The Colonization Society are becoming more and more one of its agents. Outlets for the freed blacks are alone wanted for a rapid erasure of the blot from our Republican character."[66] In the case of slavery, Madison's vision, fueled by an optimism that now rested on little more than simple faith in time, ran so far ahead of reality that he could even appear to take the freedom of the blacks for granted. And as Harriet Martineau would note after her visit to Montpelier five years later, Madison's bizarre and incongruous faith in colonization, expressed here so vividly to Lafayette, was all that kept him from plunging into total despair. The convention of 1829, we might say, pushed Madison steadily toward the brink of self-delusion, if not despair. The dilemma of slavery undid him.

66 Madison to Lafayette, Feb. 1, 1830, in [Rives and Fendall, eds.], *Letters and Other Writings*, IV, 60.

7. Despair: The Peculiar Institution

A S AN AGRICULTURAL REFORMER, Madison touted
the general superiority of oxen and even mules to horses,
especially behind the plow. But like most Virginia planters, he admired a good horse for other reasons. Visitors reported
that his daily routine at Montpelier began in earnest when he
mounted his favorite, "Liberty," for an inspection of the plantation.
Liberty had grown old in his master's service, and the pampered
animal was petted, fed, and stalled alone. Apparently a free spirit of
sorts, he was also indulged. One of Madison's nieces remembered
that Liberty "well deserved his name," there being "not a gate which
he could not open" nor "any outrage which cattle could commit"
that the Negroes at Montpelier did not ascribe instead to him. "Mr.
Madison in his humorous way, often repeated these amusing and
generally false tales of his disused horse," she recalled, but "never
curtailed his freedom."[1]

Madison bought and sold horses throughout his life, though not
always without the vexing complications that commercial transactions can bring. In 1791 Thomas Jefferson badly needed a good
saddle horse, and Madison sold him one for the price of twenty-five
pounds. When the creature became sick and died almost immediately, however, the two friends vied in their efforts to do one
another justice. An embarrassed Madison wanted to cancel the sale
or, at the least, appoint a mutual friend to review the case and arrive
at a fair settlement. Jefferson would have none of this, and insisted
on making full payment for something that had proved of no use to
him. "It being impossible to entertain a doubt that the horse I
bought of you was fairly sold, & fairly bought, that his disorder was

---

1 Mary Cutts Memoir, Cutts–Madison Collection (microfilm), Library of
Congress.

of the instant, & might have happened years after as well as when it did," Jefferson wrote, "I should as soon think of filching the sum from your pocket, as of permitting the loss to be yours." He promptly remitted a check for twelve dollars more than the agreed price.[2]

Over forty years later, in the fall of 1834, Madison's involvement in another horse trade did not turn out so well. This time he exchanged horses with a kinsman from Point Coupée, Louisiana, William Taylor, who was visiting family in the Old Dominion. Apparently one of Taylor's horses was deemed too wild for the trip home, and Madison accepted the horse in exchange for one of his own dependable plough horses that was better suited for a long overland journey. Before leaving Virginia, Taylor assured Madison that he would profit nicely from this little trade: "The horse you got of me, is too valuable to put to the plough or Waggon, and too unsafe for your carriage. I would therefore recommend your swapping him away which can be done to advantage at the Court House. You ought to get two good plough horses for him."[3]

But neither man got what he bargained for, and both seemed less than eager to display the generous spirit that defused the awkward tension of Madison's 1791 mishap with Jefferson. Months later, Taylor reported from Louisiana that Madison's substitute horse had become so weakened by "a complaint" that it had conked out on the road. Taylor attributed the horse's problem to its having been over-fed on small grain, presumably before the trip, but Madison had an alternative explanation — "the known effect of limestone water on horses unused to it" — that clearly placed responsibility on conditions encountered during the journey. At the same time, the Virginian was prepared to inform his kinsman of his own unhappiness with the exchange, because Taylor's former horse had hardly "answered expectation." Madison's overseer had reported "a slight damage" in the rambunctious animal on the morning of its arrival,

2 Madison to Jefferson, Jan. 11, 1791, and Jefferson to Madison, Jan. 12, 1791, in William T. Hutchinson et al., eds., *The Papers of James Madison* (Chicago, Charlottesville, 1962–), XIII, 352–353, 354–355.

3 William Taylor to Madison, Oct. 10, 1834, in James Madison Papers, Library of Congress, series one (microfilm). This letter is filed incorrectly under Oct. 10, 1824.

but this supposed minor injury was in fact a serious wound, no doubt sustained during one of the creature's many fits of wildness. The horse remained lame for several months, during which time it could not be sold; and once recovered, it commanded a poor market price. Indeed, the horse's "known freaks have attached such a character to him" that Madison could get only $100, including "a special guaranty, not only of his soundness, but of his being tractable and safe in harness." Thus by his own account, Madison had "not only lost the services of a superior plough horse during the crisis of seeding my wheat"; he had also been "at the expense of keeping in pampered idleness for an half year" this beautiful but ungovernable creature.[4]

Madison presented his side of this unhappy story in the draft of a letter that he prepared to send to Taylor in the spring of 1835. For some reason, however, he chose to omit the paragraph describing the controversy over the horses.[5] Perhaps he was embarrassed by the petulant tone of his remarks and wanted to present instead more of the conciliatory spirit that had animated his handling of the problem with Jefferson forty years earlier. He also had a more compelling reason to think better of his quibbling about commercial decorum and the market value of horses. The deleted paragraph followed discussion of another disagreement, also of a commercial nature, and the curious juxtaposition of the two matters – which Madison appeared to discuss in parallel and equivalent terms – could hardly have escaped his notice. The two horses, in fact, had been incidental to the commercial transaction that the two kinsmen had recently negotiated. Taylor had written not to complain primarily about the sick horse, but about another piece of allegedly damaged goods that he had received from the retired statesman. Madison referred to her simply as the "Negro woman Betty."

Madison's sale of sixteen slaves to his kinsman Taylor in the fall of 1834 was an event that, as another relative recalled twenty years

4 Madison to Taylor, April 1835, *ibid.* I have deduced the details and circumstances of the Taylor-Madison transaction largely from this single source.
5 *Ibid.* The paragraph in question is literally marked: "omitted in letter sent."

later, "gave him much trouble" — "in connection therewith," indeed, Madison had remarked that "'it had caused him to break in on fixed principles.'"[6] Madison had apparently resolved not to participate in the trafficking of human lives, a practice that assumed new and systematic forms in his native state during the last few decades of his life. Put briefly, many of his fellow Virginians who did not themselves move to the more inviting cotton and sugar fields of the Southwest discovered great profit in marketing their mobile property there. Professional slave traders appeared in Washington and northern Virginia during the early decades of the nineteenth century, and by the 1830s visitors to Fredericksburg, less than fifty miles from Montpelier, could find slave pens containing over a hundred chattels awaiting transport to the New Orleans market.[7] Even closer to home, horses were not the only commodities on display at Orange Court House, where slave auctions were regularly held and one of the finest hotels was kept by a professional trader. A British traveler to Madison's area of Virginia, who dined "most luxuriously" at this hotel in the spring of 1834, reported that upon witnessing slave auctions for the first time, some people vomited. Most natives, of course, were better inured to the abominable activities of the "nigger traders," as they were called, but a certain squeamishness still prevailed. The professional traders were ideal scapegoats for the conspicuous evils of the system, and they were often socially ostracized, no matter how vast their wealth; such was the case, according to the British traveler, with a fabulously rich trader in Warrenton, Virginia. He hastened to add, however, that the hotel owner in Orange, by contrast, "had all the profits of the business without its odium."[8] In any event, impecunious slaveholders of the most delicate sensibilities could avoid the professionals altogether by selling their chattels privately and directly to the purchasers; like William Taylor, many deep South planters came to the Chesapeake to buy and carry back the human capital that, as

6 John Willis to Edward Coles, Dec. 19, 1855, in William Cabell Rives Papers, Library of Congress, box 87.

7 Frederic Bancroft, *Slave-Trading in the Old South* (Baltimore, Md., 1931), 23–26.

8 E. S. Abdy, *Journal of a Residence and Tour in the United States of North America* . . . (London, 1835), II, 215, 210–215.

Nicholas Trist had once tried to persuade Jefferson, could be put to much better use outside of Virginia.[9]

Madison's reluctant involvement in this less offensive form of the slave trade arose at least in part from his determination to avoid more extensive and regular consort with the professionals. As a Virginia planter during the less-than-halcyon days following the Panic of 1819, Madison suffered repeated disappointments and mounting indebtedness. In the early 1820s nature conspired with bad markets to wreak havoc on his fortunes. Alternating drought and heavy rains, not to mention early frosts and the ravages of insects, drove him by the spring of 1825 to beg a loan – unsuccessfully – from Nicholas Biddle and the Bank of the United States. Three years later, he began to resort to the least objectionable alternative to pursuing additional credit, which was to part not with his human property, but with as much of his "superfluous land" as he thought he could.[10] As he later explained to Edward Coles, he had been forced to sell at least three of his farms "in order to avoid the sale of Negroes." But Madison only found himself, as a result of this strategy, in the midst of a cruel and ironic predicament. As he steadily sold off his outlying lands, his slaves were crowded onto the remaining and rapidly dwindling Montpelier acreage, which hardly needed their labor and which proved barely sufficient for their support. It may not have been exactly what Malthus had envisioned, but as Madison and his slaves (in his words, "concentered and increasing as they are") found themselves huddled together on an ever more unproductive estate, a subsistence crisis was scarcely unimaginable. Under these circumstances, Madison reported to Coles, describing his recent dealings with Taylor, "I have yeilded to the

9 See Allan Kulikoff, "Uprooted Peoples: Black Migrants in the Age of the American Revolution, 1790–1820," in Ira Berlin and Ronald Hoffman, eds., *Slavery and Freedom in the Age of the American Revolution* (Charlottesville, Va., 1983), 143–171.

10 Madison to Richard Cutts, Sept. 13, 1824, Cutts–Madison Papers, Massachusetts Historical Society; Madison to Nicholas Biddle, Apr. 16, 1825, in Gaillard Hunt, ed., *The Writings of James Madison* (New York and London, 1900–1910), IX, 221–222; Madison to Jefferson, Feb. 24, 1826, *ibid.*, 244; and Madison to ? , (draft), June 4, 1828, Cutts–Madison Papers, Massachusetts Historical Society.

257

necessity of parting with some of them to a friend and kinsman who I am persuaded will do better by them than I can." By this transaction, Madison added, enclosing a check for over two thousand dollars, he was finally able to repay the money he owed his young friend.[11]

Writing to their niece Mary Cutts shortly after the sale, an irritable Dolley Madison did not mince words: "Your uncle is very poorly."[12] As Madison's former slaves began the long trek to their new home in the southwest, their old master doubtless took comfort in the thought that, as he told Coles, they "gladly consent to be transferred" to their new owner.[13] It may be difficult to take seriously the proposition that slaves would gladly consent to being sold "down the river" to Louisiana, especially away from a humane master. But before we dismiss Madison's claim as self-serving, we might ponder the testimony of a northern visitor to Virginia, hardly an apologist for southern slaveholders, who reported the following summer that Chesapeake slaves no longer considered it a great evil to be sent to the deep South unless separation of family were involved. "The increasing poverty of the planters in Virginia, and their consequent inability to furnish a comfortable support for their slaves," wrote Ethan Allen Andrews, "increase the desire on the part of both master and slave to remove to a land of greater abundance." Andrews even recounted a recent case of runaway slaves asking a trader in Fredericksburg to purchase them from their masters, so they might escape Virginia and be sent to a better life in New Orleans.[14]

More than Madison's conscience was gnawing at him in the autumn of 1834. As Dolley reported to his niece, he was still not able to pay his debts. Notwithstanding his anxious hopes, "the sale he made of his Negroes who wanted to go with Taylor did not enable

11 Madison to Coles, Oct. 3, 1834, in Madison Papers, Library of Congress, series one (microfilm).
12 Dolley Madison to Mary E. Cutts, Oct. 1834 [mislabelled 1831], in Cutts–Madison Collection (microfilm), Library of Congress.
13 Madison to Coles, Oct. 3, 1834, in Madison Papers, Library of Congress, series one (microfilm).
14 Ethan Allen Andrews, *Slavery and the Domestic Slave-Trade in the United States* (Boston, 1836), 118–119, 167.

him to do so, and fell short of paying several thousand dollars." Madison was so depressed, she wrote, that "he still talks of the last resort, 'the House in Washington.'" Here she referred to property that the Madisons owned in the nation's capital, a house to which she would ultimately repair after her husband's death. Mired in debt and surrounded by slaves whom he could barely support (but whom he was determined, on principle, not to sell), Madison may even have worried that he might not die at Montpelier after all.[15]

On the day before Christmas, Taylor wrote to Madison to say that the Negroes had arrived safely and were in good condition. But three weeks later, in a second letter, he represented "the condition of the girl Betty as annulling her sale"; and on that account, he declined to pay any part of his note for eight hundred dollars, the balance due on the general purchase. "This information was not less unexpected than regretted under every aspect," a distraught Madison told Taylor, "particularly as it disappointed me altogether of a resource which was needed and confidently relied on." He was soon applying for another bank loan. Madison seemed genuinely puzzled, as well as aggrieved, by Taylor's abrupt action. He hoped that Betty's complaint, the precise nature of which he could only infer from Taylor's oblique manner of alluding to it, would be found "according to medical information" to be "neither permanent nor incurable." He was also quick to remind his kinsman that "no want of health was known to the overseer or to any other white person here, nor was it indicated by presumed inquiries at the time of [her] being selected." Indeed, Madison and Taylor both knew that purchasers of young female slaves were especially concerned about disease and fertility and that close inspection procedures before the sale were therefore common. Moreover, as Taylor himself had admitted, Betty was well during the long journey "and for some time afterwards."[16]

---

15 D. Madison to Cutts, Oct. 1834, in Cutts–Madison Collection (microfilm), Library of Congress.

16 Madison to William Taylor, April 1835, in Madison Papers, Library of Congress, series one (microfilm). For the reference to Madison's loan application, see Madison to ? , April 6, 1835, *ibid.* And for the reference to the rigorous inspection procedures that normally attended the purchase of young female slaves, see Bancroft, *Slave-Trading in the Old South*, 108.

Clearly, Madison thought he was being cheated, and he especially resented Taylor's unilateral and summary attempt to dispose of the issue: "I certainly should have readily concurred in any arrangement that might be eventually due to the peculiarity of the case," he complained, "and am still." His suggestion was that the dispute, "in all its circumstances," be submitted to the decision of "two of our common friends, each of us appointing one and a third to be named by them in the event of disagreement." In a sad and tragic understatement of the dilemma that now confronted him, Madison emphasized his "readiness to terminate a matter which may possibly involve considerations of humanity, as well as a pecuniary one."[17]

On the fate of Betty, the surviving Madison papers are silent.

I

If Madison had often found it necessary to suggest that slaves in the United States, as a legal abstraction, could partake of the qualities of both persons and property, Betty was a concrete and painful reminder that they had to be one or the other, that there was really no choice, and that no decent person could be comfortable in a society that pretended otherwise. His own "fixed principles" against selling slaves acknowledged the essential difference from selling horses, appearances and the laws of commerce notwithstanding; and those private principles were reminiscent of a younger Madison at the Philadelphia convention, who had contended, even while acknowledging the need to protect the property rights of slaveholders, that it would be "wrong to admit" in the explicit language of the Constitution "the idea that there could be property in men."[18] On the level of principle, in fact, Madison's antislavery credentials can be fairly described as impeccable. Throughout a long public career (and an even longer life) he never wavered for a moment in utterly condemning the institution. His categorical opposition to slavery generated an unyielding commitment to abolishing it in the United

---

17 Madison to Taylor, April 1835, in Madison Papers, Library of Congress, series one (microfilm).
18 Max Farrand, ed., *The Records of the Federal Convention of 1787*, rev. ed. (New Haven, Conn., 1937), II, 417.

States – for him, the question was never if, but rather when and how. Indeed, there was as little ambiguity in the Sage of Montpelier as there had been in the young Revolutionary of the 1770s and 1780s: slaves were human beings, entitled to all the natural rights enumerated in the Declaration of Independence, and republican justice demanded that those rights be restored. It is hardly surprising that several months after the sale to Taylor and only a year before his death, Madison's principled indictment of slavery – "acknowledging, without limitation or hesitation, all the evils with which it has ever been charged" – was so strong and spirited that it deeply impressed the British abolitionist Martineau.[19]

As Martineau doubtless sensed, his opposition to the institution included a profound sense of the grievous wrongs inflicted on the slaves themselves. Yet to the extent that Madison regarded slavery as a matter of urgent moral concern during his retirement, sympathy for the blacks was neither the only nor the most compelling source of his concern. On this issue, as on others, it is simply impossible to separate Madison's perspective from the broader imperatives of his republican faith and from the irrepressible sense of mission which that faith engendered. Slavery was wrong and regrettable for so many reasons that many Americans, including Madison, simply took its manifest evils for granted. According to the standard indictment, the institution, in addition to oppressing its innocent victims, undermined the moral integrity of those who were not slaves. Slavery bred contempt for honest labor and thus for the character trait of industry, so essential to a republican people; moreover, it encouraged idle masters to indulge their worst passions and to practice the habits of tyranny. Slavery also weakened a republic militarily, rendering it especially vulnerable to hostile invasion. Even economically, many Americans believed, slavery, as a relatively unproductive form of labor, constituted a source of weakness rather than strength.

For Madison, however, placing slavery on the road to ultimate extinction was urgently necessary for other, even more pressing reasons. As he suggested in 1819, in words also reminiscent of statements he had made at the Philadelphia convention three dec-

19 Martineau, *Retrospect of Western Travel* (London and New York, 1938), I, 191.

261

ades earlier, slavery raised the ominous specter of a regional polarization of American politics that might jeopardize his generation's greatest achievement, the Union of the states. Parties, he knew, would exist in the United States as long as its government remained free; but if slavery endured and "a state of parties" founded on "geographical" boundaries took firm root, what, he worried, would "controul those great repulsive Masses from awful shocks against each other?"[20] And if that were not enough reason to erase "the blot" or "the stain" (two of Madison's favorite ways of referring to slavery) from the republic, there were compelling international considerations as well. Madison never doubted, above all, that the persistence of the peculiar institution significantly impaired the moral force of America's republican example in the rest of the world.

This latter concern lay at the heart of Madison's determination to end slavery in America. The idea was hardly his alone, but for him it had especially strong resonance. Put simply, Madison had everything staked on his belief that the republican revolution in North America marked a decisive turning point in human history. He was confident that the mere presence of the republic had altered the balance of political force throughout the world; as empirical evidence of man's capacity to govern himself, the United States affected the minds of men everywhere and had thus become, by his reckoning, a vital presence in the domestic politics of all nations. Even more than the American war for independence, the great revolution in France had defined the contours of a titanic struggle between the forces of republicanism and the forces of monarchy, a contest that was truly international in scope, extending throughout Europe and ultimately into the southern portion of the Western Hemisphere; and especially after the tragic demise of the French Revolution, Madison knew that the essential battle must continue, sometimes on the battlefields or even on the barricades, but always in the arena of public opinion. He never doubted that the American republic was the central figure in this great drama. He knew, to use the obvious example, that the "newborn nations" of Latin America, which had embarked on "the same great experiment of self-government," were

20 Madison to Robert Walsh, Nov. 27, 1819, in Hunt, ed., *Writings of Madison*, IX, 12.

"alive to what they owe to our example, as well in the origin of their career as in the forms of their institutions."[21] And even in Europe, where its influence was less tangible, the United States continued to make an important difference. A month into his retirement, for instance, Madison assessed the turbulent state of "British affairs," which appeared "to be approaching, if not already in, a paroxysm." Here the American beacon was especially salutary, he said, for it was necessary to counteract the deleterious influence of "the horrors of the Revolutionary experiment in France" (without which, indeed, the present crisis in Britain would already have issued "in some radical change" for the better). "But for the Republican example in the United States," Madison asserted, the British crisis "would as certainly issue in the invigoration of the monarchical system."[22] Ultimately there was no way to separate the battle for men's minds and the progress of politics, in Europe as much as in America. And in the shining example of the United States, men everywhere found inspiring testimony to what was humanly possible – as long, that is, as they could overlook or discount the great stain of slavery.

Ever since Samuel Johnson had posed the inevitable question in the 1770s – "how is it that we hear the loudest yelps for liberty from the drivers of Negroes?" – the game had been on.[23] When the taunts came from the British, of course, Americans were not surprised; nor should we be surprised that they tried unpersuasively to deflect blame for the institution onto the slave traders and corrupt British officials, including the king, who were said to have forced slaves down the throats of innocent colonists. That Madison gave credence to this fatuous delusion – which was based entirely on the efforts of some colonial assemblies, especially Virginia's, to limit the importation of slaves just before the Revolution – is a depressing measure of the extent to which Revolutionary anglophobia (and the pressure of guilt) could overcome good sense. Even the subsequent emergence of the British as leaders in an international movement against slavery

21 Madison to John Quincy Adams, Dec. 9, 1827, in [William C. Rives and Philip R. Fendall, eds.], *Letters and Other Writings of James Madison* (Philadelphia, 1865), III, 602.
22 Madison to W. H. Crawford, April 24, 1817, *ibid.*, 40.
23 Johnson as quoted in John Chester Miller, *The Wolf by the Ears: Thomas Jefferson and Slavery* (New York, 1977), 8.

failed to impress Madison. In 1826, when he complained privately that "the taunts to which this misfortune [slavery] exposes us in Europe are the more to be deplored, because it impairs the influence of our political example," he could not resist adding that the jibes came "with an ill grace from the quarter most lavish of them, the quarter which obtruded the evil, and which has but lately become a penitent, under suspicious appearances."[24] For Madison, it was just as ironic, and hardly coincidental, that the loudest yelps for liberty now came from the defenders of kings.

Whether the taunts were in English or some other language, Madison never doubted that they came overwhelmingly from the lips of the enemies of republicanism. He believed, too, that they were causing great harm, not by wounding the pride of Americans, who were used to enduring insults from certain quarters, but by vitiating the essential cause of American influence abroad. Lafayette bombarded his American friends with evidence of the problem and with pleas to do something about it. Were it not for "that deplorable Circumstance of Negro Slavery in the Southern States," he told Jefferson in 1821, "Not a word Could be objected, when we present American doctrines and Constitutions as an example to old Europe." The French veteran of both America's and his own country's revolutions, who professed to feel "an inexpressible delight in the progress of every thing that is Noble minded, Honourable, and Useful throughout the United States," kept stumbling against slavery, that "Great draw Back Upon my Enjoyments." As Europe's most prominent and vigorous proponent of the republican cause, he found himself stymied every step of the way by this lingering embarrassment, which "Raises a Sigh, or a Blush, according to the Company, American or foreign, where I Happen to Be." Indeed, "this wide Blot on American Philant[h]ropy is ever thrown in My face," he complained, "when I indulge my Patriotism in Encomiums, otherwise Undisputable."[25]

Lafayette understood, of course, that "the plague" could not be

---

24 Madison to Lafayette, Nov. 1826, in Hunt, ed., *Writings of Madison*, IX, 266.
25 Quoted material may be found in Lafayette to Jefferson, July 1, 1821, and June 1, 1822, in Gilbert Chinard, ed., *The Letters of Lafayette and Jefferson* (Baltimore, 1929), 407, 408–409.

cured overnight, but he wanted assurances from his American friends "that progressive and earnest Measures Have Been adopted to attain, in due time," so "desireable" and "necessary" an object as a general emancipation. Madison, for one, was unstinting in giving Lafayette such assurances, no matter how discouraging the circumstances, because he shared the Frenchman's belief that "Prudence as well as Honor" demanded evidence of progress in the fight against slavery.[26] If nothing else, both men sorely needed that evidence to parry the thrusts of the taunters. The American patriarch never stopped cherishing the hope, as he put it in 1831, "that the time will come when the dreadful calamity" would cease, "thus giving to our Country the full enjoyment of the blessings of liberty and to the world the full benefit of its great example."[27]

Too often, though, Madison seemed content merely to savor the hope. Along with some of his more outspoken contemporaries, virtually all twentieth-century observers, even his admirers, have expressed disappointment with his actual record in the war against slavery, especially toward the end of his life. There was too much that he did not say or do, and much of what he did say and do has struck critics as wrongheaded at best and hypocritical at worst – and of course racist. During the Missouri crisis, for example, Madison subscribed to the notion of "diffusion," popular among southerners, according to which the expansion of slavery into the western territories offered the best means of improving the condition of the slaves and hastening their emancipation. Modern scholars (and students) have almost uniformly treated this idea with contempt; some have gone so far as to characterize Madison's position during the Missouri crisis as in effect "proslavery."[28] And if his support of diffusion, in the minds of some, made him a proslavery expansionist, his avid defense of colonization, in the eyes of critics less generous than

26 *Ibid.*, 409.

27 Madison to R. R. Gurley, Dec. 28, 1831, in Hunt, ed., *Writings of Madison*, IX, 469.

28 See, for instance, Don E. Fehrenbacher, who writes that "the pro-slavery pronouncements of Jefferson and Madison signalized the depth and unity of southern commitment to slavery by 1820. The Missouri crisis had strikingly revealed just how solid the South could be on this issue." *The Dred Scott Case: Its Significance in American Law and Politics* (New York, 1978), 110.

Harriet Martineau, exposed additional limitations of judgment, vision, and perhaps character. By refusing to consider a general emancipation of the slaves except under the condition that they be colonized abroad – a practical impossibility as well as a profound injustice, everyone would now agree – Madison made emancipation itself impossible and perforce excused his own and his society's inaction.[29]

Almost two centuries later, indeed, a battery of troubling questions pursue scholars and students alike. If Madison truly deplored slavery, why didn't he do what we know he should have done? Why didn't he, like Abraham Lincoln and the other Republican heroes of the 1850s, at least advocate the geographical restriction, rather than the extension, of slavery, especially since he had done so earlier in his career? Going further, why didn't he accept and attempt to prepare his countrymen for the only just solution to the problem they could no longer afford to ignore? For his society, that solution was plainly a general emancipation and incorporation of the blacks into the republic as full citizens, and for Madison personally, it was just as clearly a firm commitment to freedom, not merely a better life under slavery, for his own bound laborers. And why didn't he seem to appreciate the true urgency and full depth of the crisis? Why, in sum, didn't this sage and honest statesman understand – and publicly acknowledge – the need for swift and effective action against slavery?

It is no small irony, perhaps, that Madison's apparent failure to confront adequately his country's most serious problem was tied to his reluctance to provide further ammunition for its critics; if his concern about world opinion aroused his opposition to the institution and energized his faith that it must die, it may at the same time have inhibited his admission of the full extent of the evil and contributed to his informal policy of relative public silence. But Madison's dilemma went much deeper than fear of conceding too much to the enemies of republicanism in Europe. To a remarkable extent, he remained a prisoner of his republican idealism and the

29 See, for example, the parallel analysis of Jefferson's support of colonization in Robert McColley, *Slavery and Jeffersonian Virginia*, 2d ed. (Urbana, Ill., 1973), 129–130.

optimistic temperament that sustained it, both of which made it exceedingly difficult for him to acknowledge the near hopelessness of his country's predicament. As Martineau shrewdly discerned, something close to blind faith in the American project (which she called Madison's finest characteristic) kept the patriarch going. That same faith, however, also rendered him incapable of admitting, perhaps even to himself, that a catastrophe was inherent in the founding of a republic of slaveholders and that his own heroic efforts were for that reason tragically flawed. Here was a man, after all, who as president in the summer of 1814, amid an invading army and the burning ruins of his own government, had managed somehow to keep a republic running on faith alone. Such a man, flushed with success, was unlikely to admit that slavery posed an insoluble problem, that it presaged, in fact, the unavoidable ruin of the republican dream that had now sustained him for almost half a century.

During his retirement as much as in the 1780s, moreover, Madison's idealism remained securely lashed to the anchor of an underlying conservatism. His tenacious confidence that the republic might fufill its destiny by surmounting even this most imposing obstacle of slavery hardly meant that he saw no limits to what republican citizens in America might accomplish or overcome. In his concern for public order, in his tendency to seek not perfection, but the least imperfect alternative, and above all in his firm belief that revolutions in human nature were impossible in this world, Madison accepted even republican man for what he was. Refusing to abandon fundamental ideals and principles, he embraced what prudent judgment told him was, under the circumstances, the least dangerous and impractical course of action. On no issue are these conservative inclinations of a republican idealist more apparent, and of more consequence, than on slavery.

Madison had little choice but to swallow whatever reservations he might have had about the logic of diffusion, for instance, because he knew that the consequences of restricting the movement of slaves into the West would be disastrous — for the slaves, for the whites, and above all for the Union. He neatly broke down "the Missouri question," as he called it, into two separate questions, one of constitutionality and the other of expediency. As we have seen, his position on whether the Constitution conferred on Congress a power to restrict slavery in the federal territories was somewhat guarded and ultimately flexible.[30] His position on Missouri as "a question of expediency and humanity" appears to have been rather more firm. The correct answer to this question, he told Robert Walsh, "depends essentially on the probable influence of such restrictions on the quantity and duration of slavery, and on the general condition of slaves in the United States."[31]

The drift of Madison's reasoning can be summarized as follows. Now that the importation of slaves from outside the United States was permanently prohibited, any growth in the number of slaves in the country was limited to the natural increase of those already there. This had not always been true, of course; when the old Congress had closed the Northwest Territory to slaves in 1787, "the importation of slaves was rapidly going on, and the only mode of checking [the increase of their numbers] was by narrowing the space open to them." Hence Madison's support of restriction at this early stage of his career. After 1808, however, diffusing a relatively fixed population of slaves across a larger area would not add to the numbers or to the aggregate misery of black sufferers. Here Madison had to reject, though to my knowledge he never explicitly did, the Malthusian logic of restrictionists, who contended that diffusion, by increasing the supply of available subsistence to the black population, would indeed increase their numbers by accelerating the rate of natural growth; if anything, Madison appears to have believed that in "a dispersed condition," the rate of generative increase among the slaves would likely diminish.[32] The important point for Madison

30 For a discussion of constitutionality, see Chapter 3 of this volume.
31 Madison to Robert Walsh, Nov. 27, 1819, in Hunt, ed., *Writings of Madison*, IX, 12.
32 *Ibid.*, 10. My inference about Madison's view on "comparative rates of generative increase" is based largely on the question he raises for Walsh in this letter. For a sampling of the invocation of Malthus in discussions of diffusion, see the congressional debates on Missouri, in Joseph Gales, comp., *Debates and Proceedings in the Congress of the United States, 1789–1824* (Washington, D.C., 1834–1856), 16th Cong., 1st sess., I, esp. 207, 1087, 1132–1133, 1209, 1392, 1532.

was that diffusion would substantially improve, in all respects, the condition of what he chose to see as this fixed population of slaves. Their standard of living would be generally higher amid western prosperity (than it would be, say, in depressed Orange County toward the end of his life), and they would be better treated because individual masters would own fewer of them, on average, than if the entire slave population were forced to remain among a smaller number of potential slaveholders in the East. As a general proposition, Madison repeatedly contended that the treatment of slaves was harshest when they were held in large numbers and most humane when in small.

Moreover, by "intermixing" this fixed black population with "greater masses of free people," diffusion would greatly ease tension between the two races and reduce fears about the consequences of emancipation. Under these propitious circumstances, while "the moral and physical condition" of the slaves was improving, "partial manumissions" would be more likely to occur among relaxed masters whose individual investment in slave property would also be relatively small. In this way nothing less than progress toward "a general emancipation" could be substantially "accelerated."[33] In effect, Madison and the diffusionists proposed to encourage throughout the country the same kinds of conditions – especially a low density of slaves relative to the white population – that had recently allowed citizens in Pennsylvania, New York, and New Jersey, imbued with the spirit of the Revolution, to proceed safely toward abolition.

Skeptics today can poke holes in this logic almost at random, as they did in Madison's own time, even when the theory was accorded a modicum of respect. Consider the following revealing example. In late 1820, Jefferson baldly and rather smugly presented the diffusion argument to Lafayette as something close to self-evident truth. He even tossed in a gratuitous dismissal of the restrictionists' sincerity as humanitarians and abolitionists. "All know," Jefferson wrote, "that permitting the slaves of the South to spread into the West will not add one being to that unfortunate condition, that it will increase the happiness of those existing, and by spreading them

33 Madison to Walsh, Nov. 27, 1819, in Hunt, ed., *Writings of Madison*, IX, 10.

over a larger surface, will dilute the evil every where, and facilitate the means of getting finally rid of it, an event more anxiously wished by those on whom it presses than by the noisy pretenders to exclusive humanity." But Lafayette would not buy this bill of goods, even from Jefferson. He politely but firmly demurred: "Are you Sure, My dear Friend, that Extending the principle of Slavery to the New Raised States is a Method to facilitate the Means of Getting Rid of it? I would Have thought that By Spreading the prejudices, Habits, and Calculations of planters over a larger Surface You Rather Encrease the difficulties of final liberation." When Jefferson did not rise to the challenge, his old comrade was insistent: "Let me Confess, My dear friend, I Have Not Been Convinced, and the less as I think More of it, By Your Argument in favor of dissemination." He added that "One is I believe More Struck with the evil when Looking Upon it from without."[34]

Although Lafayette would appear to have much the better of this argument, it is essential to try to understand why Madison and Jefferson, among many others, believed what they did. Of course, diffusion can be dismissed as a rationalization of naked self-interest, especially among Virginians, who were generally anxious about their eroding power in the Union relative to their old adversaries, the "eastern" states of New England, and who certainly understood the pecuniary advantages of a territorial demand for their surplus slaves. But in Madison's case, such crude explanations ring hollow. It is revealing that he never advanced the diffusion argument with the same vehemence and certainty as did Jefferson and many southerners in Congress. He may have had some quiet doubts about whether the geographical extension of slavery would, in fact, so readily promote its demise.[35] Reading as widely as he did, Madison

34 Jefferson to Lafayette, Dec. 26, 1820, and Lafayette to Jefferson, July 1, 1821, and June 1, 1822, in Chinard, ed., *Letters of Lafayette and Jefferson*, 402, 407, 409.
35 Compared to Jefferson, indeed, Madison's articulation of the diffusion argument is conspicuously tentative. In early 1819, before the Missouri question had exploded, Madison sketched out the diffusion argument in the draft of a letter to Robert Walsh but deleted the paragraph in the letter actually sent; see Madison to Walsh, Mar. 2, 1819, in Madison Papers, Library of Congress, series one (microfilm). Nine months later, responding to Walsh's specific re-

Marquis de Lafayette, c. 1825. Portrait by Matthew H. Jouett. (Courtesy of the National Portrait Gallery, Smithsonian Institution, Washington, D.C., John Hay Whitney Collection)

---

quest for guidance on the Missouri question, Madison presented the diffusion argument (before he read or knew of Walsh's mocking refutation of the idea in the pamphlet he was writing) in the form of a series of questions rather than as direct affirmation; see Madison to Walsh, Nov. 27, 1819, in Hunt, ed., *Writings of Madison*, IX, 10. Writing to President Monroe at the height of the encountered several powerful refutations of the argument, and one suspects that only the most dogmatic temperament could have sustained complete confidence in the theory under such assault.[36] However, Madison never questioned his conviction that the alternative to diffusion – closing the West to slavery – would most certainly have catastrophic repercussions. And given that choice, he seemed quite willing to take his chances, and the necessary leap of faith, with diffusion.

What was likely to happen if the restrictionists had their way? Madison shuddered to think of the consequences if slavery were confined to those parts of the South where it already existed – if, in other words, southern whites continued to migrate to the federal territories, as they surely would as their numbers increased in the East, while blacks were forced by the federal government to stay put. Already, even with the Southwest open to slaves, many white Virginians correctly sensed a dramatic increase in the proportion of black faces surrounding them. East of the Blue Ridge Mountains, the census returns identified a disquieting pattern of change: in 1790, whites had outnumbered blacks; by 1800, blacks were a majority; by 1820, they outnumbered whites by more than sixty thousand.[37] The trend was more than evident in Madison's own

crisis, Madison admitted that in forming his response to the questions involved he had "certainly felt all the influence that could justly flow from a conviction, that an uncontrouled dispersion of the slaves now in the United States was not only best for the nation, but most favourable for the slaves, also both as to their prospects of emancipation, and as to their condition in the mean time"; see Madison to Monroe, Feb. 23, 1820, *ibid.*, 25. And in a letter to Lafayette after the first phase of the crisis had passed, he briefly presented the case for diffusion without explicitly endorsing it; see Madison to Lafayette, Nov. 25, 1820, *ibid.*, 36–37.

36 Madison read at least Walsh's pamphlet, which included a blistering assault on the logic of diffusion, and even among his close friends and correspondents, including Lafayette and Edward Coles, he might have encountered the same response. A vivid example of Coles's contempt for diffusion, written a few years after the Missouri crisis, can be found in the handwritten draft of his newspaper essay "To the Citizens of Illinois," No. 2, Edward Coles Collection, Historical Society of Pennsylvania, box 2, file 12.

37 Carl N. Degler, *The Other South: Southern Dissenters in the Nineteenth Century* (New York, 1974), 15.

Orange County, where the proportion of blacks in the population surged from forty-five percent in 1790 to almost sixty percent in 1820.[38] Madison knew that Virginians, especially, were frightened by the specter of restriction because they had no desire, as one of them commented to President Monroe at the height of the Missouri dispute, to be "dammed up in a land of slaves."[39] If northern advocates of restriction hoped that under such straitened conditions southerners would somehow be induced to free their slaves, few southerners, including Madison, took this idea seriously.

On the contrary, placed in such unenviable circumstances, southern Americans would confront a much greater potential for slave resistance and insurrection – always a horrifying prospect for whites in a slave society – and those conditions would just as surely provoke draconian measures of slave discipline and repression. Madison clearly believed that stimulating such fears, thereby triggering the unavoidable response, was no way to improve the condition of the slaves or to promote manumissions; by reducing whites to an ever smaller minority in the older parts of the South, restriction would most likely unleash instead a devastating cycle of repression, resistance, and violence, thereby inflaming rather than defusing the dilemma of slavery. And who wanted the Old Dominion, in the worst case scenario, to relive the horrors of Santo Domingo, the former French colony in the Caribbean where, amid just such a racial imbalance several decades earlier, a bloody war of reprisals and extermination had been the price both races had paid for an end to slavery?

Madison clearly believed, moreover, that the triumph of restriction would likely entail the worst of all sacrifices, that of the Union itself. To one correspondent he posed a question whose answer he thought obvious: "Will the aggregate strength, security, tranquillity, and harmony of the whole nation, be advanced or impaired by lessening the proportion of slaves to the free people in particular

38 John Thomas Schlotterbeck, "Plantation and Farm: Social and Economic Change in Orange and Greene Counties, Virginia, 1716 to 1860" (unpubl. Ph.D. diss., The Johns Hopkins University, 1980), 84.
39 Spencer Roane to James Monroe, Feb. 16, 1820, in "Letters of Spencer Roane, 1788–1822," *Bulletin of the New York Public Library* 10 (1906), 174–175.

sections of it?"[40] His question only hinted at the heart of the matter. He knew that concentrating the slave population in a limited area would provoke convulsions; he also knew that his fellow southerners were unlikely to remain loyal to a federal government that was grossly insensitive to their racial predicament, not to mention their rights, prosperity, and self-esteem. As it was, many prominent Virginians passionately resisted the compromise that eased the crisis, greeting the news of President Monroe's support of it with outraged incredulity. By the terms of this accommodation, Missouri was permitted to enter the Union as a slave state – a major Southern victory – and slavery was prohibited only in the territories north of a fixed line of latitude. How would Virginia's leaders react if northern restrictionists, defying (and doubtless ridiculing) the logic of diffusion, succeeded in preventing altogether the geographical extension of slavery? In 1820, Madison praised fellow Virginians who, understanding "the injury threatened to the nation," supported the compromise; but he knew, too, that the numbers of such "cool and candid" citizens would likely evaporate if the restrictionists succeeded in establishing their principle as national policy. If Madison had lived to witness the winter of 1860–61, he would have been inconsolable – but hardly surprised.[41] If nothing else, diffusion, not restriction, offered the best hope that the Union would survive longer than slavery, long enough, perhaps, to resolve the dilemma of slavery without violent upheaval. In any event, Madison was never confused about his priorities.

One of the strangest documents to be found among Madison's papers, in this connection or any other, is a fictional essay that he apparently composed shortly after the Missouri crisis. Bearing the title "Jonathan Bull and Mary Bull," this little parable about the origins and resolution of a marital squabble between young Jonathan (the North) and Mary (the South) Bull – descendants of old John Bull (England) – was a thinly veiled allegory of the recent sectional

40 Madison to Walsh, Nov. 27, 1819, in Hunt, ed., *Writings of Madison*, IX, 10–11.
41 See Glover Moore, *The Missouri Controversy, 1819–1821* (Lexington, Ky., 1953), 232–256. For the quoted material, see Madison to Monroe, Feb. 23, 1820, in Hunt, ed., *Writings of Madison*, IX, 25.

argument. Madison's playful contribution to what was by then a familiar genre of "John Bull" satire apparently remained nothing more than a private source of personal amusement while he was alive; not until the 1850s, when the collector into whose possession it had fallen published it in the midst of an even more serious sectional crisis, did the allegory receive any public notice. Drawing serious inferences about Madison's views on slavery from this whimsical flight of fancy requires, of course, the exercise of prudent caution. Interpreted with restraint, his unlikely literary foray can illuminate his general cast of mind at the time of the Missouri crisis, and especially his larger scale of priorities. It may also betray a way of thinking about slavery that is less clearly expressed in his more formal statements.

Mary's problem is her black left arm, the result of a stain accidentally received from "a certain African dye" when she was a child. Although this stain had not prevented the consummation of a happy and fertile union with Jonathan – who bore only scattered spots and specks of the same dye, which he was able gradually to remove – trouble later arose when Jonathan, in a fit of passionate spite over imagined grievances, insisted on reserving the lands of one of their children about to come of age (Missouri) for the tenants of his own estate. Seized by this "perverse humour," moreover, "he looked at the black arm, and forgot all the rest," taunting Mary and even threatening divorce unless she immediately got rid of the offensive stain. Fortunately, Mary was able to control her own passions. She calmly and politely lectured Jonathan, correcting his every misimpression and, when appropriate, gently chastised him for his callous and ungenerous attitudes. Speaking through Mary, Madison's southern Americans had a great deal to say, indeed, to their northern partners in republican marriage. For example:

You ought surely, when you have so slowly and imperceptibly relieved yourself from the mortifying stain, although the task was comparatively so easy, to have some forbearance and sympathy with me, who have a task so much more difficult to perform. Instead of that, you abuse me as if I had brought the misfortune on myself, and could remove it at will; or as if you had pointed out a ready way to do it, and I had slighted your advice. Yet, so far is this from being the case, that you know as well as I do that I am not to be blamed for the origin of the sad mishap; that I am as anxious as

275

you can be to get rid of it; that you are as unable as I am to find out a safe and feasible plan for the purpose; and, moreover, that I have done every thing I could, in the mean time, to mitigate an evil that cannot as yet be removed.[42]

Mary happily carries the day "with this tender and considerate language." Jonathan, who had "a good heart as well as a sound head and steady temper," promptly regains his lost composure, and the couple's bickering soon ends "in an increased affection and confidence between the parties."[43]

Clearly Madison wanted Mary and Jonathan to live happily ever after – and had enough faith to hope that they might. But we find no mention of what might happen to the black arm. Somehow the need to confront that lingering problem was deferred or lost in the shuffle of the more pressing need to reconcile the feuding lovers and save their happy union. The humanity of the slaves is utterly lost in the allegory, of course, and on the surface, at least, we also find not even the slightest hint of another vital dimension of the institution, one that Madison only rarely addressed. His allegorical depiction of the slaves as a source of unmitigated weakness – a "mortifying stain," a "misfortune," a "sad mishap," an "evil" – simply ignores the immense productivity of their labor, indeed blinks the historical fact that they had played, and continued to play, a central role in the economic development of a continent. Perhaps the plot of the allegory made the point well enough, though indirectly. As Jonathan's reconciliation with his comely wife at least made plain, Mary's "weak" arm had apparently never kept her from being a healthy and attractive partner. And in his happy ending, Madison could continue to describe, with obvious pride, an extraordinarily prosperous union, black arm and all.

II

During the nineteen years of his retirement, Madison did not dodge Mary's implied challenge, as he struggled to find what she de-

42 The essay is printed in [Rives and Fendall, eds.], *Letters and Other Writings*, III, 249–256 (block quote from 252–253).
43 *Ibid.*, 256.

manded of both Jonathan and herself: a safe and feasible means of eliminating the stain of slavery. His fullest statement on this subject appropriately came in the summer of 1819, amid the Missouri controversy, when he responded at length to a request for his thoughts from a Philadelphia antislavery writer, Robert J. Evans. In characteristically disciplined, even methodical, fashion, Madison posited three essential conditions for "a general emancipation of slaves." The process must be gradual; it must also be "equitable, and satisfactory to the individuals immediately concerned"; and above all, it must be "consistent with the existing and durable prejudices of the nation." Madison expected little disagreement from Evans on the first point, since it was intuitively obvious that any abrupt or reckless attempt to extirpate a "deep-rooted" and "widespread" evil could only produce ruinous confusion and disorder. On the second point, Madison indicated that the master's consent would in most cases require financial compensation for the loss of property which, after all, was "guaranteed by the laws" and "recognised by the Constitution"; the consent of the slave, in turn, required "that his condition in a state of freedom be preferable, in his own estimation, to his actual one in a state of bondage." Each party must voluntarily consent, in other words, not only to emancipation, but to its consequences as well. And in that connection, the third condition required lengthier explanation, because to Madison it meant that "the freed blacks ought to be permanently removed" from those parts of the United States "occupied by, or alloted to, a white population."[44]

Although Madison's position on removal was straightforward, its subtlety also bears some emphasis. He believed that if the freed blacks were allowed to remain, the cure for slavery would be worse than the disease, not because blacks were innately inferior or unworthy of American citizenship, but because current "and probably unalterable prejudices" among the whites precluded any peaceful and just accommodation between the two races. Mary and Jonathan Bull might eventually find some way of gently removing the black stain of slavery from Mary's arm; but in real life, the arms of the former slaves would always remain black, and as long as distinctions of color were not only permanent but generally considered signifi-

44 Madison to Robert J. Evans, June 15, 1819, *ibid.*, 133–138 (quotes from 133–134).

cant by the whites, serious conflict must be expected if the two races remained together. Madison believed that his judgment on this matter was based on more than idle theory. His fellow Americans, in all parts of the Union, were every day providing incontrovertible evidence of their unwillingness to accept former slaves as their equals. They generally refused to extend to free blacks, whose natural right to liberty had at least been restored, anything approaching a just measure of social and political rights; even in a state like Massachusetts, Madison observed, where slavery had quietly vanished after the Revolution and there were few former slaves to absorb (and probably more overt sympathy for them than elsewhere in the Union), degrading prohibitions and restrictions still obtained. Treated in such fashion, moreover, free blacks tended to behave in ways that only reinforced the prejudice; generally idle and dissolute in their manners, according to Madison, they were "every where regarded as a nuisance, and must really be such as long as they are under the degradation which public sentiment inflicts on them." Indeed, the logic of Madison's analysis clearly identified the underlying source of the problem. He never referred to any intrinsic inadequacy of the blacks; their degraded condition stemmed rather from this "repugnance of the whites" to the continuance of the blacks among them, which was in turn "founded on prejudices, themselves founded on physical distinctions, which are not likely soon, if ever, to be eradicated."[45]

Such prejudices might not be rational, and they might be regrettable as well; but Madison saw no choice but to respect them as an insurmountable obstacle to what he called "a thorough incorporation" of the two races. He was careful never to present these prejudiced attitudes as his own. Unlike his friend Jefferson, he did not advance the tentative suspicion that blacks were by nature inferior to whites in their physical and mental endowments. Nor did Madison identify the danger of proliferating sexual relations between the two races as an important reason for separating them; again unlike Jefferson, he never voiced any personal concern about "amalgamation," which would allegedly debase whites by mixing their blood with that of a primitive race.[46] Madison simply accepted white prejudice

45 *Ibid.*, 134; Madison to Lafayette, 1821, *ibid.*, 240.
46 See the discussion of this latter point in Miller, *Wolf by the Ears*, 64. Augustus

against blacks as a part of American culture that was, for the time being at least, impervious to change or reform. And under these circumstances, emancipating the blacks without removing them was a formula not for progress, but for disaster. It would mean little or no improvement in their condition, a likely indulgence in reciprocal hatreds and violence, and the danger of even greater injustice. As Madison put the case to Evans:

The objections to a thorough incorporation of the two people are, with most of the whites, insuperable; and are admitted by all of them to be very powerful. If the blacks, strongly marked as they are by physical and lasting peculiarities, be retained amid the whites, under the degrading privation of equal rights, political or social, they must be always dissatisfied with their condition, as a change only from one to another species of oppression; always secretly confederated against the ruling and privileged class; and always uncontrolled by some of the most cogent motives to moral and respectable conduct. . . . Nor is it fair, in estimating the danger of collisions with the whites, to charge it wholly on the side of the blacks. There would be reciprocal antipathies doubling the danger.[47]

Emancipation without removal, in short, would consign the free blacks to the degraded and dangerous status of a permanent underclass. At their worst, Madison feared, race relations would deteriorate into a war that could have no real winner.

Reading Madison's letter, the philanthropist Evans might well have wondered: given the Virginian's conditions for emancipation, and given his underlying pessimism about how whites were bound to treat free blacks (and how blacks, in turn, would respond to their public degradation), was there, in fact, any practical way to emancipate the slaves? Madison had faith that there was, and he believed that Americans were obliged to keep searching until they found it. He specifically praised, as a promising point of departure, the plan of the recently organized American Colonization Society, which was

---

Foster, the British diplomat who visited both Montpelier and Monticello in the early nineteenth century, commented on the strength of Jefferson's belief in black inferiority but did not attribute similar feelings to Madison; see Richard Beale Davis, ed., *Jeffersonian America: Notes on the United States of America Collected in the Years 1805–6–7 and 11–12 by Sir Augustus John Foster, Bart.* (San Marino, Calif., 1954), 148–150.

47 Madison to Evans, June 15, 1819, in [Rives and Fendall, eds.], *Letters and Other Writings*, 134.

to establish on the west coast of Africa a colony for American blacks who were already free or who might, as Madison put it, be "*gratuitously* emancipated.*" The language of his endorsement of the A.C.S. is revealing. Since this plan was consistent with all of Madison's stipulated conditions, he deemed it worthy of "encouragement from all who regard slavery as an evil, who wish to see it diminished and abolished by peaceable and just means, and who have themselves no better mode to propose." But if the logic of the society's approach to the problem was sound, its current scope was also woefully inadequate. Madison told Evans that the colonizing approach, if it were ever to become "a commensurate remedy for the evil," would somehow have to be extended beyond the present small numbers to "the great mass of blacks." It would also have to embrace a fund sufficient to defray "the enormous sums required to pay for, to transport, and to establish in a foreign land, all the slaves in the United States, as their masters may be willing to part with them." Without blinking an eye, Madison pointed to the federal government as the necessary agency of colonization (with a suitable amendment of its powers, of course); and he also thought that the staggering cost of a general emancipation and relocation could be taken from a "providential" source under the control of that same national agency. Here he referred to America's great treasure of vacant land, its western territories, "the vendible value of which," by Madison's calculations (he even toted up the figures for Evans), would be sufficient to meet the challenge.[48]

In Madison's scheme of things, indeed, the western lands – the traditional panacea for many Jeffersonians – continued to offer answers to America's most pressing problems. Both as an outlet for diffusion and as a source of the revenue that would finance colonization, the frontier, by extending hope for a slave-free America, remained his solace for the future. In his letter to Evans, Madison acknowledged – and then itemized – the many practical difficulties that stood in the way of a successful program of emancipation and colonization; but he remained optimistic, and above all he did not want potential obstacles to discourage the necessary search for "a remedy for the great evil under which the nation labors." The only

48 *Ibid.*, 134–136.

difficulty Americans could not overcome, apparently, was their racial prejudice. Until someone came up with a better idea, therefore, colonization remained worthy of Madison's — and everyone's — sincere hopes and stout encouragement.[49]

Founded in 1816, the American Colonization Society instead aroused immediate controversy. Free blacks vehemently protested what they feared was a cynical scheme to force them back into slavery in Africa, making it clear that few would volunteer for "redemption" in their native land. White critics, including outspoken northern opponents of slavery like the Philadelphia Quaker Roberts Vaux, quickly dismissed the society as part of a devious effort to strengthen the institution. This strong skepticism reflects both the ambiguous purposes of the society and the diverse character of its sponsors. It drew substantial support from New England clergymen and other old-line Federalists, particularly from the upper South and the border states, for whom it formed part of what scholars now call the "Benevolent Empire" of reform organizations that began to proliferate in the second and third decades of the nineteenth century. Together with Bible and religious tract societies, temperance organizations, and Sunday school unions, the A.C.S. proposed to reform (or in this case actually remove) troublesome elements of disorder in American society, whether they be drunkards, infidels, unruly frontiersmen — or free blacks. And for evangelical reformers of this stripe, colonization was doubly beneficial, because the resettled blacks, under proper white tutelage, would spread to the "Dark Continent" of Africa the beneficent forces of a civilized Christianity.

The society also attracted the support of many southern Jeffersonians, from Madison and President Monroe to second-generation leaders like Henry Clay of Kentucky, who espoused the enlightened, antislavery convictions of the Revolutionary era. Like Madison, the organization was not explicitly racist; it made no argument for innate African inferiority, instead attributing the degraded status of free blacks to the impact of ineradicable white prejudice. Nevertheless, by emphasizing that degradation and making it central to the rationale for their program, the colonizationists were effectively ac-

49 *Ibid.*, 138.

cepting, and perhaps unwittingly strengthening, that prejudice. More important, the blacks themselves clearly resented the tone and thrust of this putative "humanitarian" message – which insisted that they must leave the United States, for their own, America's, and Africa's good – and whites like Vaux had good reason to doubt that there was anything inherently antislavery about colonization. Indeed, for largely expedient reasons, some southern founders of the society, including Clay, explicitly separated its program from any broader scheme of emancipation. And it didn't take long for critics to realize that colonization could attract the support of many southerners who had no interest in promoting manumissions. Since free blacks were generally considered a serious threat to the security of slavery – they were accused of fomenting slave resistance and rebellion, and it was thought that their very presence suggested to slaves that freedom was possible for people with black skins – getting rid of such troublemakers was a project that might even appeal to the staunchest defenders of the peculiar institution. Extreme critics of colonization thus eventually took the position articulated so vehemently in the early 1830s by the abolitionist William Lloyd Garrison who, recanting his own earlier involvement in the society, branded it a consummate fraud, fundamentally racist and proslavery in character.[50]

Since Madison must bear the burden of association with an institution (and an idea) that still carries a strong measure of this stigma, his support of colonization merits further scrutiny. It is important to note, first of all, that he did not come slowly to this position late in life; his close ties to the A.C.S. were neither a repudiation of previous commitments nor a belated response to changing circumstances in Virginia (or the United States) in the early nineteenth century. Colonization or removal as a condition of emancipation was an old idea that reached as far back as a 1691 Virginia statute and the activities of Pennsylvania Quakers in the early eighteenth century. During the Revolution, the Virginia

---

50 My discussion here is derived principally from George M. Fredrickson, *The Black Image in the White Mind: The Debate on Afro-American Character and Destiny, 1817–1914* (New York, 1971), chap. 1, and esp. P. J. Staudenraus, *The African Colonization Movement, 1816–1865* (New York, 1961), chaps. 1–6.

House of Delegates had debated a plan of gradual emancipation specifically tied to colonization.[51] Madison formally endorsed the principle in 1789, just after the launching of the new federal government, when a Quaker physician living in Philadelphia, William Thornton, placed before him an ambitious plan to establish a self-governing commonwealth for former American slaves on the west coast of Africa. In a private memorandum of approval, Madison advanced ideas identical to those he espoused to Evans three decades later. And in Madison's case, there was never any ambiguity about the larger purpose of colonization, assuming it could be made practicable: in 1789 as in the 1820s, he talked not of ridding the country of a nuisance and a threat both to slavery and general social order – the free black population – but of making possible a general emancipation. Indeed, in his memorandum to Thornton, Madison pointed directly to the concerns that would later wed him to the ill-fated American Colonization Society.[52]

If "an asylum" for American blacks in Africa (or elsewhere) could in fact be provided, Madison argued in 1789, it would be a boon precisely because it might "prove a great encouragement to manumission in the Southern parts" of the United States. More broadly, it might "even afford the best hope yet presented of putting an end to the slavery in which not less than 600,000 unhappy negroes are now involved." Madison reported to Thornton that although the laws in most southern states currently permitted masters, "under certain precautions," to free their slaves, he was not confident that this happy legal climate would endure. (Madison was doubtless thinking primarily of Virginia, where the legislature had recently been flooded with petitions to repeal a liberal manumission law that had gone into effect in 1782.) If the Revolutionary wave of idealism and emancipation had indeed crested, the primary problem, according to Madison, was the unsatisfactory condition and disappointing behavior of the liberated blacks; he suggested to Thornton that the progress of emancipation in the South was "rendered precarious by

---

51 See Katherine Harris, "The United States, Liberia, and their Foreign Relations to 1847," unpubl. Ph.D. diss., Cornell University, 1982, 29–38.
52 See Gaillard Hunt, "William Thornton and Negro Colonization," *Proceedings of the American Antiquarian Society*, n.s., XXX (1920), 32–61.

the ill effects suffered from freedmen who retain the vices and habits of the slaves." Even if the liberal laws stood, he worried that many humane masters would refrain from acting, precisely because experience now suggested that manumission promoted "neither the good of the Society, nor the happiness of the individuals restored to freedom."[53]

But as Madison would again suggest thirty years later, this unhappy situation, appearances notwithstanding, was actually not the fault of the blacks. In order for emancipation to be "eligible as well to the Society as to the Slaves," he argued, "a compleat incorporation of the latter into the former should result from the act of manumission." The former slaves, in other words, could themselves achieve happiness – and be well behaved enough to satisfy others that their freedom was a blessing to society – only if they escaped degradation and were fully "incorporated" or integrated into the republic. This was "rendered impossible," however, not by any intrinsic failings of the blacks, but "by the prejudices of the Whites, prejudices which proceeding principally from the difference of colour must be considered as permanent and insuperable." For the abolition of slavery to go forward, Madison told Thornton, "some proper external receptacle" had to be provided "for the slaves who obtain their liberty." Without it, he reasoned, widespread emancipation could never occur – at least not voluntarily on the part of the whites.[54]

Unlike some of his fellow colonizationists, in sum, Madison's antislavery motives and purposes are unimpeachable. He never supported colonization because he wanted to deport free blacks; he consistently supported it because he wanted to eradicate slavery. And since his analysis never explicitly led to the conclusion that blacks were inherently deficient or inferior, perhaps it is misleading to consider his formal position, in any meaningful sense of the term, "racist." Yet clearly the case is more complex. Madison's references to the free blacks, especially during his retirement, were often laced with a quiet but unmistakable hint of contempt. He was just as quick to describe the former slaves as a nuisance, in sweeping and

53 Madison, "Memorandum on an African Colony for Freed Slaves," ca. 20 October 1789, in Hutchinson et al., eds., *Madison Papers*, XII, 437–438.
54 *Ibid.*, 438.

categorical terms, as he was to blame their degradation on the whites. By portraying the free blacks largely as helpless victims of white prejudice, of course, Madison wanted to absolve them of blame; but he also unwittingly dehumanized them, making them irresistible targets of even his own inadvertent contempt, a quiet contempt that was never fully obscured by his formulaic invocation of white prejudice as the explanation for their degradation. In 1823, for instance, the New England clergyman Jedidiah Morse forwarded to Madison a printed list of questions pertaining to slavery. When Morse asked Madison to comment on "the general character" of free blacks "with respect to industry and order, as compared with that of the slaves," the Virginian's response was typically blunt: "Generally idle and depraved; appearing to retain the bad qualities of the slaves with whom they continue to associate, without acquiring any of the good ones of the whites, from whom [they] continue separated by prejudices against their colour and other peculiarities."[55] Five years later, writing to a fellow colonizationist, Madison gave his blessing to all judicious plans "for removing from our country the calamity of its black population."[56]

We might say that Madison had every reason to want to believe that free blacks behaved in contemptible ways, no matter whose fault it was, and especially to believe that there was no way for them to behave otherwise. The temptation for American republicans to dehumanize the victims of an institution that embarrassed them was inevitable. Indeed, Madison lived long enough to see some of his fellow southerners attempt to escape their predicament by beginning to do just that, literally: making their peace with slavery as a matter of principle, proslavery apologists would seek to deny blacks their entitlement, as human beings, to the natural right to liberty. For Madison, this escape was unconscionable. He remained loyal to his Revolutionary ideals, but he could bear the moral burden of his own and his country's dilemma only by believing, first, that the majority of whites were simply incapable of overcoming their preju-

---

55 Answers to Questions Concerning Slavery, [1823], in Hunt, ed., *Writings of Madison*, IX, 134.
56 Madison to C. Sigourney, Sept. 25, 1828, in Madison Papers, Library of Congress, series one (microfilm).

dice against blacks, and second, that the blacks themselves would be just as incapable, if turned loose as free men in such a hostile environment, of overcoming the degrading effects of that racism. By rendering the immediate pursuit of justice for the blacks utterly impractical and indeed dangerous, this formulation of the problem only compounded the national predicament. But these beliefs, as articles of negative faith that explained and even justified a posture of cautious restraint, also eased considerably Madison's personal dilemma, awkward and uncomfortable as it was.

Two years after his memorandum to Thornton, in which he had described in wholly negative terms the condition of free blacks in the Chesapeake, Madison stumbled upon evidence with quite different implications. Traveling with Jefferson through the remoter regions of upstate New York, he encountered, near Lake George, "a free Negro" whose case clearly interested him. In his notebook Madison recorded, with no elaboration, the following terse description of the man:

He possesses a good farm of about 250 Acres which he cultivates with 6 white hirelings for which he is said to have paid about 2 1/2 dollars per Acre and by his industry & good management turns to good account. He is intelligent; reads writes & understands accounts, and is dextrous in his affairs. During the late war he was employed in the Commissary department. He has no wife, and is said to be disinclined to marriage; nor any woman on his farm.[57]

Here was a capsule description of nothing less than Madison's and Jefferson's ideal citizen: the industrious, intelligent, fiercely independent yeoman farmer. Had the two Virginians in fact found evidence of what free blacks were capable of accomplishing not just anywhere, but within the confines of the United States? Perhaps. But Madison appears to have been strongly impressed by something else: this man's striking penchant for solitude, and the obvious isolation of his farm — and indeed his success — from the surrounding pressures of hostile white society.

57 Madison, "Notes on Lake Country Tour," May–June 1791, in Hutchinson et al., eds., *Madison Papers*, XIV, 27.

＊

Not long after Madison retired to Montpelier, a young Scottish heiress met and fell in love with his republic. He would eventually come to know her quite well. Frances Wright exuded energy and idealism, and she found during a two-year visit to the United States almost everything she wanted in a healthy society but had not found in Europe: dignity, simplicity, and equality. After returning to England in the summer of 1820, she published an account of her experience, under the title *Views of Society and Manners in America*, that constituted a paean to the republic she adored. The flattery struck even some Americans as excessive. Although the author's passionate hatred of slavery was evident throughout the book, it did little to dim the glow of her general portrait. Indeed, on the origins and development of the institution, no American could have offered a more labored defense of the colonists' good intentions and relative innocence. According to Wright, they had done everything possible to prevent the importation of slaves. Now their republican sons and daughters – slaveholders included – were anxious to complete the task of eradicating this regrettable imposition.[58]

Only at the end of her book did Wright register significant unease. Notwithstanding her "secret reluctance" to visit the southern states – "the sight of slavery is revolting everywhere," she explained, "but to inhale the impure breath of its pestilence in the free winds of America is odious beyond all that the imagination can conceive" – she seemed particularly fond of Virginians. In Washington she had met an eminent native of the Old Dominion who bluntly confirmed what she had inferred from the conversation of others: as committed as they were to ending slavery, many Virginians were also disheartened by "the slender success" of philanthropic efforts to remedy the evil. Wright repeated verbatim this man's remark: "Look into the cabins of our free negroes," he had told her, and "you will find there little to encourage the idea that to

58 Frances Wright, *Views of Society and Manners in America*, ed. Paul R. Baker (Cambridge, Mass., 1963 [orig. publ. 1820]), esp. 37–44. For elaboration of Wright's background and her experience in America, see esp. Celia Morris Eckhardt, *Fanny Wright: Rebel in America* (Cambridge, Mass., 1984).

impart the rights of freemen to our black population is to ameliorate their condition, or to elevate their character."[59]

Wright had apparently peeked into enough cabins to concede the empirical point, for she agreed that "the free negroes of Maryland and Virginia form the most wretched and consequently the most vicious portion of the black population." Indeed, she allowed that "the most casual observation is sufficient to satisfy a stranger of the truth of this statement. I have not seen a miserable half-clad negro in either state whom I have not found, upon enquiry, to be in possession of liberty." But the conclusion that some Virginians were now clearly tempted to draw from this evidence – that "to emancipate the African race would be to smite the land with a worse plague than that which defaces it already" – she found "revolting." Of course slaves were generally ill-prepared for freedom, and it was hardly surprising that, in an unsupportive climate, free blacks became a public nuisance. "To their untutored minds," Wright explained, "the gift of freedom is only a release from labour. Poor, ignorant, and lazy, it is impossible that they should not soon be vicious." No wonder Virginia lawmakers, seeking to protect the commonwealth from "the increasing weight of black pauperism," now required citizens to remove from the state any slaves they chose to manumit. But north of the Potomac, Wright found sufficient evidence of the improving character of free blacks (even though they formed "the least valuable portion of the population" there) to convince her that they could, in time, be re-formed everywhere into "useful" members of society. Education was the idealistic Scot's answer to the dilemma of American slavery; and she was confident that once Americans committed themselves to a general emancipation, a national commitment to educating and improving the blacks would emerge as well.[60]

Wright was plainly worried, however, that southern planters talked a better game than they played. In fact, they seemed to be doing very little to encourage what "they profess to think not only desirable but inevitable," and this hesitation to pursue emancipation, she warned, increasingly invited "the scorn of mankind." She chose to place her ultimate faith in the sons of Virginia – whose

59 Wright, *Views of Society*, 267–268.   60 *Ibid.*, 268–269.

history recorded "so many acts of heroism and disinterested generosity" – to dash this threat of inertia and "eradicate the Egyptian plague which covers her soil." After all, "a servile war" was "the least of the evils" which might befall the Old Dominion. "The ruin of her moral character, the decay of her strength, the loss of her political importance, vice, indolence, degradation" – here were "the evils" awaiting Virginians should they fail to act.[61]

Four years later, Wright returned to the United States, this time in the tow of a distinguished new friend and confidante, the marquis de Lafayette. Although he was more than twice her age, Lafayette's relationship with Frances and her sister Camilla invited malicious gossip that his interest in the Wrights was more than avuncular. While the old hero celebrated his return to America with a spectacular public tour, Frances kept a respectable distance and renewed her own, much briefer acquaintance with the republic. Her concern about slavery quickened. As her mild disillusionment with southern planters verged on disgust, she had no choice but to make exceptions of individual heroes. She spent several delightful days with Jefferson at Monticello, where she doubtless ventilated her concerns. Before leaving, she wrote to a friend that the prejudice against mixing the two races, whether absurd or not, was so deeply rooted in the American mind that emancipation without expatriation seemed impossible.[62]

Wright was plainly in the market for new heroes. Returning to Washington, she encountered another foreign visitor, Robert Owen, whose public lectures announced preparations for the utopian undertaking at New Harmony. Wright already shared Owen's dislike of inequality and the destructive effects of competitive individualism; intrigued by his scientific approach to a new system of society in which cooperation and benevolence would revolutionize human relations, she quickly became his pupil. At the same time, her unease about racial prejudice in America turned ever more bitter. Rapidly losing patience with the whites' irrational fear of associating with blacks, a fear that energized support for colonization, Wright soon joined her enthusiasm for Owen's communitarian reform and her commitment to emancipation.

61 *Ibid.*, 268, 269–270. 62 Eckhardt, *Fanny Wright*, 84–85.

Frances Wright, c. 1824. Portrait by Henry Inman. (Courtesy of The New-York Historical Society, New York City)

In early 1825, after a brief visit with the Madisons at Montpelier, Wright journeyed west to Harmony, Indiana, in time to see for herself the remarkable success of Owen's predecessor, the German pietist George Rapp. Inspired by the example of his thriving and exceptionally moral settlement, she conceived an ambitious plan for her own experimental community, one that would utilize the cooperative methods of Rapp and Owen to promote the emancipation of slaves. Her plan was complex; its essence was to create an environment where slaves could work for the purpose of purchasing their own freedom, all the while developing the necessary skills to support themselves once free. She was confident that under the correct management, the profits of cooperative slave labor would be sufficient to meet the cost of emancipation within as little as five years, and that in a properly structured environment, the education of the blacks would erase from their character and behavior all the unfortunate vestiges of enslavement. Once she had demonstrated the success of her methods, moreover, these kinds of communities would rapidly proliferate. With the aid of other philanthropists, and perhaps public land grants, she would thus ignite a general emancipation of the slaves in the United States. Even in the flush of her revolutionary enthusiasm, however, Wright was willing to be practical on at least one vital point. She attached to this scheme a general proposal for colonization. Deferring reluctantly to prevailing American prejudices, Wright told the planters that their slaves would enjoy freedom apart from white society, not as part of an integrated republic. She well knew that they would be deaf to any calls for emancipation without this reassurance.[63]

When Wright forwarded a copy of her prospectus, via Lafayette, to the Madisons, she took care to convey her profound concern not only for the slaves, but also for their masters, who were now exposed, she said with an eye on Latin America, to a juggernaut of emancipation sweeping the Western Hemisphere.[64] She was hardly bashful about soliciting Mr. Madison's approval of her plan; but the best she could get was a polite letter of guarded, skeptical support. Measuring her plan against the standards he had established for Robert Evans six years earlier, Madison was quick to remind Wright that "the physical peculiarities" of the slaves in the United States precluded "their incorporation with the white population"; for that reason, he applauded her scheme not only for requiring the volun-

63 *Ibid.*, 104.
64 Wright to Dolley Madison, July 26, 1825, in Madison Papers, Library of Congress, series one (microfilm).

tary concurrence of the slaveholders, but above all for contemplating "the removal of those emancipated, either to a foreign or distant region." Madison also praised her proposed course of education for the slaves. What he called into serious question, albeit gently, were her Owenite assumptions about the practicality and advantages of cooperative labor. Wright was confident that the lure of freedom would stimulate prodigious labor from the slaves; Madison said he was not satisfied "either that the prospect of emancipation at a future day" would "sufficiently overcome the natural and habitual repugnance to labour" common to all men or that there was "such an advantage of united over individual labor" as the young Scot took for granted. Wright's ambitious plan could not possibly work as advertised, according to Madison, because it was based on faulty assumptions about human nature: the slaves, especially under a system in which there would be no direct, commensurate relationship between an individual's exertions and his immediate rewards, could not realistically be expected to produce enough of a surplus to earn their freedom in a brief space of time. Her extravagant expectations had been falsely encouraged by the success of cooperative labor in religious communities like Rapp's; but her community, he pointed out, would not have the advantage of the extraordinary discipline that religious enthusiasm (and charismatic leadership) could provide. So while Madison congratulated Wright for her dedication to the cause of ending slavery, he also advised her to scale down both her expectations and the initial scope of the experiment.[65]

A year later, Madison reported to Lafayette that he was awaiting news of the progress of their young friend's experimental community called "Nashoba," located in a remote part of western Tennessee. He said that he hoped his letter of encouragement had conveyed to Wright the full measure of his respect "for her fine genius and exalted benevolence." But it must have been obvious to Lafayette that Madison held little enthusiasm for the experiment. Wright's plan had properly "contemplated a provision for the expatriation of her Eleves," Madison reported, but she had failed to specify that provision, from which he inferred "the difficulty felt in devising a

65 Madison to Miss Frances Wright, Sept. 1, 1825, in [Rives and Fendall, eds.], *Letters and Other Writings*, III, 496, 497.

satisfactory one." As he conceived of the task of emancipation, in fact, Wright's energy was misdirected; the principal challenge was not to make emancipation economically feasible, it was to guarantee that the slaves could be satisfactorily removed once they were free. According to Madison, manumissions in the United States were already keeping pace with the available outlets, and their increase was checked only by a present inability to expand the number of satisfactory receptacles for emancipated slaves, whether in Africa, the Caribbean (especially Haiti, where some American blacks were now seeking refuge), or even in the far western removes of the United States itself. If only this obstacle were removed, Madison sighed to Lafayette, "all others would yield to the emancipating disposition."[66] The inescapable inference was that masters held on to their chattels not because slaves were economically necessary — certainly not in Virginia — but rather because responsible whites, for sound reasons, were unwilling to create and unleash in their midst a dangerous black underclass.

Indeed, if emancipation were merely a problem of economics, Madison said he had a solution that made far more sense than Wright's in any case. "What would be more simple, with the requisite grant of power to Congress," he asked Lafayette, "than to purchase all female infants at their birth, leaving them in the service of the holder to a reasonable age, on condition of their receiving an elementary education." A little quick math indicated that "the annual number of female births may be stated at twenty thousand, and the cost at less than one hundred dollars each, at the most; a sum which would not be felt by the nation, and be even within the compass of State resources." But this plan, too, would instantly founder on the larger problem of racial adjustment. "No such effort would be listened to," Madison reminded Lafayette, "whilst the impression remains, and it seems to be indelible, that the two races cannot co-exist, both being free & equal." The "great sine qua non," therefore, for Fanny Wright and for everyone, was to discover "some external asylum for the coloured race."[67]

Madison probably sensed where Wright was heading with

66 Madison to Lafayette, Nov. 1826, in Hunt, ed., *Writings of Madison*, IX, 265.
67 *Ibid.*, 265–266.

Nashoba, and under the spell of Owen, she soon took her community in bold and unorthodox directions. Owen had issued from New Harmony on July 4, 1826 – the fiftieth anniversary of American independence – his own very personal "Declaration of Mental Independence." All human misery, he announced, could be traced to the pernicious influence of a great trinity of evils under which even republicans in America, for all their admirable progress, still suffered: private property, irrational systems of religion, and conventional marriage. Wright agreed, and she was soon explaining the mission of Nashoba in just these terms. "While we endeavour to undermine the slavery of colour existing in the North American Republic," she announced, "we essay equally to destroy the slavery of mind now reigning there as in other countries." Wright was no longer willing to play the colonization game. Racial prejudice, after all, was merely one part of the mental slavery – that encumbering tangle of irrational and repressive custom – from which Americans awaited liberation. Praising sexual passion as the noblest of all human passions, she also wrote boldly and optimistically of miscegenation. Indeed, mixing the races became Wright's answer to America's dilemma, and her goal at Nashoba was now to educate black and white children together so that future generations might behave better and more freely.[68]

Writing to the Madisons from France in late 1827, Lafayette gently tried to explain what had happened to their young friend. Miss Wright had abandoned colonization, he said, because she now believed that it was utterly impractical and that a fresh approach to the task of eradicating slavery was therefore necessary. Once Americans faced up to the futility of colonization, they would have to tackle their true challenge, which was not to relocate millions of people in Africa or other distant areas, but rather "to soften and finally do away prejudices of colour." This she sought to promote at Nashoba "by the experiment of common education."[69] Madison politely replied that he already knew of Miss Wright's dramatic change of plan. On her new endeavor he characteristically passed no explicit judgment of his own, citing instead the daunting force of

68 Eckhardt, *Fanny Wright*, chap. 6 (quotation from 151).
69 Lafayette quoted in *ibid.*, 164.

public opinion. "With her rare talents & still rarer disinterested-ness," he told Lafayette, "she has I fear created insuperable obstacles to the good fruits of which they might be productive by her dis-regard or rather defiance of the most established opinion & vivid feelings. Besides her views of amalgamating the white & black population so universally obnoxious, she gives an eclât to her no-tions on the subject of Religion & of marriage, the effect of which your knowledge of this Country can readily estimate."[70]

Time would prove Madison prophetic on a number of counts. Nashoba quickly collapsed, failing as an experiment both to end slavery and to demonstrate the efficiency of cooperative labor. And Wright's search for a new theater in which to promote Owen's gospel of collective work and human improvement carried her next to New York City where, as part of a radical workingmen's move-ment, she just as promptly became, for many American republicans less imaginative than she, the notorious "Red Harlot of Infidelity." Meanwhile, at Montpelier, Madison quietly redoubled his efforts to promote colonization. If anything, the range of alternatives ap-peared to be narrowing.

✳

During the last five years of his life, Madison saw little reason to change his assessment of what was and was not possible in the United States. The emergence in the northern states of a radical abolitionist movement, calling optimistically as Wright had for an end to prejudice, was hardly a sign of a revolution in public opinion. While the movement drew strong support from many free blacks, it involved only a very small, albeit quite visible and vocal, minority of white Americans, and it elicited a reaction that emphatically confirmed the contrary disposition of most northerners. In general, efforts to improve the condition of blacks with an eye toward prepar-ing them for full-scale citizenship met sustained and often violent resistance, especially if classroom integration of white and black

70 Madison to Lafayette, Feb. 20, 1828, in Hunt, ed., *Writings of Madison*, IX, 311.

pupils was involved. New England offered no exception to the pattern. In 1832, for instance, a black student at Wesleyan College withdrew rather than face continuing harassment from his fellow scholars. In both New Haven and Canterbury, Connecticut, in the early 1830s, townspeople vehemently opposed the establishment of lower schools that would, they charged, attract undesirable blacks from other states and undermine the peace – and of course the property values – of their communities. In Canterbury, the career of Prudence Crandall, a young Quaker schoolmistress, offered tragic evidence of a general pattern in northern public opinion. When Crandall admitted a Negro to her successful boarding school for girls, most of the other students promptly withdrew. Undaunted, she announced plans to open a new school exclusively for blacks. An outraged town selectman voiced prevailing sentiment when, stridently insisting that America's Negro underclass must be colonized in Africa, he vowed that Crandall's "nigger school" would never be tolerated in Canterbury. The town made good on his threat; after a protracted siege of legal and even physical harassment (which included dumping manure in the children's drinking water), Crandall finally abandoned the school in the fall of 1834.[71]

Visiting the United States in the early 1830s, Alexis de Tocqueville was struck by the enduring depth and virulence of white prejudice throughout the United States. Modern scholars have amply confirmed his judgment. Madison, of course, had arrived at a similar conclusion on his own, long before, but as an avid reader of American newspapers in this tumultuous period he could only have become more convinced that one national option was indeed foreclosed. He could never endorse a plan for emancipating the slaves and allowing them to remain in the United States, even if such a plan were politically feasible (which it clearly was not), because he had no less reason to doubt its deleterious consequences both for the blacks and for the republic. And under these circumstances, Madison must have asked himself countless times, just what were the alternatives to supporting colonization? Some of his fellow southerners had, in fact, discovered one, and Madison found it so

---

71 Leon F. Litwack, *North of Slavery: The Negro in the Free States, 1790–1860* (Chicago and London, 1961), esp. chap. 4 (quotation from 128).

abhorrent that he actually became president of the American Colonization Society.

If a significant change in public opinion concerning slavery and race relations was occurring in the United States toward the end of Madison's life, it was probably taking place in the South, not the North. Frances Wright had reported after her initial visit to America that the consensus among planters was that emancipation was not only desirable but inevitable. The traveling secretary of her friend Lafayette, Auguste Levasseur, gained a similar impression during the great tour of 1824–25 (no doubt in part because he wished to), happily concluding that there was virtually no dissent in the United States on the basic wrongness and injustice of slavery. During his yearlong trip through twenty-four states, Levasseur reported, he had heard only one warped young American defend the institution in positive terms, and at an evening gathering of neighboring planters at Montpelier, the conversation about slavery had been most reassuring. Levasseur was confident that slavery could not exist much longer in Virginia, "because all enlightened men condemn the principle of it, and when public opinion condemns a principle, its consequences cannot long continue to subsist."[72] The naiveté of that judgment requires no comment; but more important, if Levasseur had made his visit to Virginia a decade later, he might have been hard-pressed to make even that statement. By the time of Madison's death, indeed, many "enlightened" critics of slavery could still be found, but their voices were now openly contending with those of more than one young dissenter.

Matters came to a head for Virginians, including Madison, in the aftermath of a crisis they had long dreaded. The year 1831 saw not only the appearance of Garrison's *Liberator* hundreds of miles to the north, but shortly thereafter the first, and only, organized slave rebellion of any consequence in the Old Dominion. Under the leadership of a black prophet, Nat Turner, slaves in Southampton County struck boldly and violently for their freedom in the early morning hours of August 22. Almost sixty whites and over a hundred blacks

72 A. Levasseur, *Lafayette in America in 1824 and 1825; or, Journal of a Voyage to the United States*, trans. John D. Goodman (Philadelphia, 1829), I, 204–225 (quotation from 222).

lost their lives in the abortive insurrection and its bloody aftermath. Shocked into action of a kind, the Virginia legislature during its 1831–32 winter session anxiously debated appropriate responses to the recent turmoil. Some legislators seized the occasion to advocate gradual emancipation, developing in fulsome detail the argument that Virginia must rid itself of a crippling and dangerous institution. Others, however, counselled caution, sometimes suggesting that slavery was not necessarily such a curse, or even immoral, and always resisting efforts to implement immediate plans for ending it.

The House of Delegates eventually adopted a compromise resolution, antislavery in tone, that expressed support for *future* legislative emancipation. Many antislavery Virginians, including Madison, chose to interpret the debate and its outcome as an encouraging sign of progress. In the aftermath of a severe and threatening crisis, after all, Virginia's leaders had demonstrated the courage, finally, to address the underlying problem. Madison's young friend, the colonizationist Jesse Burton Harrison, rejoiced that "the public mind of Virginia" had permitted, indeed encouraged, open debate on a topic "never before thought fit to be mentioned but in a whisper." Pointing explicitly to Madison's renewed optimism about colonization, Harrison eagerly anticipated the future: "The possibility of ridding Virginia of the evil of slavery in our generation, in that of our children, or of our grandchildren," he exulted, "is suddenly made the legitimate object of temperate debate."[73]

Notwithstanding this general optimism, however, Madison also confronted evidence of a most ominous development, one that could hardly have caught him completely unawares. He had consistently asserted his belief in the good intentions of Virginia's slaveholders; it was clearly part of his political faith that they genuinely wanted to free their slaves, because they knew that the institution was morally indefensible, and that given the right opportunity, they would promptly act on those principles. The problem, he repeatedly insist-

73 Harrison, "The Slavery Question in Virginia," in *American Quarterly Review*, December 1832, reprinted in Fairfax Harrison, ed., *Aris Sonis Focisque* (privately printed, 1910), 337–400 (quotations from 337). For the most recent scholarly study of the larger crisis, with a novel (and perhaps overdrawn) interpretive twist, see Alison Goodyear Freehling, *Drift Toward Dissolution: The Virginia Slavery Debate of 1831–1832* (Baton Rouge and London, 1982).

ed, was not the lack of an emancipating disposition; it was the temporary absence of satisfactory outlets or "receptacles" for the prospective freedmen. As long as colonization was in its infancy, Madison could rationalize the failure of more masters to act as a prudent response to obstacles that awaited removal. But he surely must have wondered: what would happen if the obstacles proved permanent and colonization turned out to be a pipe dream? Or, more immediately, what would happen if Virginians merely decided that it was — if they concluded, in other words, that since the program was utterly impractical, the blacks were here to stay? Obviously they wouldn't embrace Frances Wright's response. They would likely accept the necessary permanence of slavery and proceed from there.

Several months after the Turner rebellion, in the midst of the legislative debates, Madison told the secretary of the American Colonization Society, Ralph R. Gurley, that he was greatly pleased by the society's progress. It had overcome many of the difficulties that had once caused him to be less sanguine than others who, he happily admitted, were now "found to have been the better judges." "Many circumstances at the present moment," he added, "seem to concur in brightening the prospects of the Society and cherishing the hope that the time will come when the dreadful calamity which has so long afflicted our Country and filled so many with despair, will be gradually removed, & by means consistent with justice, peace, and the general satisfaction."[74] Indeed, for the next few years the Virginia legislature did seriously consider various means of supporting the colonization of its free blacks in Liberia. But Madison also soon learned that not all of the legislators, or their constituents, shared his optimism — or for that matter, his hopes. A year after he had showered Gurley with optimism, Madison opened a letter from Thomas Roderick Dew, a professor of political law, barely thirty years old, at William and Mary College. Professor Dew solicited his

74 Madison to Gurley, Dec. 28, 1831, in Hunt, ed., *Writings of Madison*, IX, 468–469. Several decades later, Edward Coles observed that the legislative debates had indeed cheered Madison into believing that Jefferson's "march of time" toward an inevitable emancipation was moving more rapidly than anticipated. See Coles to Robert C. Winthrop, Aug. 5, 1856, in "Letters of Edward Coles," *William and Mary Quarterly*, 2d ser., 7 (1927), 166.

elder's candid assessment of his recent pamphlet on the "slave question," which he enclosed. He especially wanted Madison's response, he said, to his analysis of the futility of colonization.[75]

Historians have often pointed to Dew's pamphlet as an immensely significant barometer of a broader shift in public opinion in Madison's state, and they have generally assumed, as well, that his arguments were enormously influential at the time. Madison surely sensed their potential importance and influence, because Dew vigorously challenged the practicality of all deportation schemes, ultimately dismissing colonization as "a *stupendous piece of folly.*" After laying out the many insurmountable problems in both Virginia and Africa, moreover, he advanced arguments which, if not always an explicit endorsement of slavery, called into serious question virtually all of the traditional charges against the institution. Dew specifically denied that slavery was the primary cause of Virginia's economic woes, pointing instead to the dreaded federal tariff. And on a more theoretical level, he explicitly attacked the well-known antislavery arguments in Jefferson's *Notes on Virginia.* He even proceeded to suggest ways in which, contrary to traditional wisdom, slavery actually supported, rather than undermined, republicanism. If Madison had read between the lines, in fact, he might have discerned a proposed solution to the problem in political economy that had long troubled him. Black slavery offered, Dew at least hinted, a happy way of defusing dangerous conflict between a propertyless majority and a propertied minority; with blacks performing all low and menial tasks, the working class was removed from the political equation, and whites enjoyed a measure of equality that would otherwise be impossible. Indeed, when Dew cautiously concluded "that the time for emancipation has not yet arrived, and perhaps it never will," readers might well wonder if this situation were so unfortunate after all.[76]

75 Dew to Madison, Jan. 15, 1833, in Madison Papers, Library of Congress, series one (microfilm).

76 Dew's pamphlet is conveniently reprinted in Drew Gilpin Faust, ed., *The Ideology of Slavery: Proslavery Thought in the Ante-Bellum South, 1830–1860* (Baton Rouge, La., 1981), 21–77 (quotations from 46, 77). Dew's suggestion that slavery in effect solved the "working class" problem in a republican society was explicitly developed in other of his writings; see Allen Kaufman, *Capital-*

A month after he received Dew's letter and a copy of his pamphlet, Madison wrote to Gurley again, this time accepting election as president of the American Colonization Society.[77] Four days later, Madison responded to Dew. He told the professor that he had found "much valuable and interesting information" in the pamphlet, "with ample proof of the numerous obstacles to a removal of slavery from our country, and everything that could be offered in mitigation of its continuance." But he could concur neither in many of the data from which Dew reasoned nor, more important, in the conclusion to which he had been led. Madison readily conceded "the inadmissibility of emancipation without deportation." He acknowledged as well "the impracticability of an immediate or early execution of any plan that combines deportation with emancipation." But he still "yielded," he said, "to the expediency of attempting a gradual remedy" of this shape, and he proceeded to explain, in some detail, why.[78]

Madison reviewed the familiar litany of practical objections to colonization, in each case offering reasons why he refused to despair. His pattern was to admit the existence of present difficulties but to deny that they were insurmountable. Madison had always insisted, for example, that the consent of the blacks themselves was a necessary condition of their removal. At present, however, blacks who were already free had "a known repugnance" to leaving their homes in America, and among the slaves one found "an almost universal preference of their present condition to freedom in a distant and unknown land." No matter: these unfortunate "prejudices" merely reflected the blacks' understandable distrust of the favorable accounts of Liberia they presently received "through white channels." Once they had access to similar testimony of the wondrous joys of life in Africa from members of their own race, their attitude would change: "By degrees truth will find its way to them from sources in

ism, Slavery, and Republican Values: Antebellum Political Economy, 1819–1848 (Austin, Tx., 1982), chaps. 5 and 6.

77 Madison to R. R. Gurley, Feb. 19, 1833, in Madison Papers, Library of Congress, series one (microfilm).

78 Madison to Dew, Feb. 23, 1823, in [Rives and Fendall, eds.], *Letters and Other Writings*, IV, 275.

which they will confide," Madison reassured Dew, "and their aversion to removal may be overcome as fast as the means of effectuating it shall accrue."[79]

Actually, gaining the voluntary consent of the blacks was not high on Dew's list of the problems that attended colonization. Madison understood that he was far more worried, for instance, about the awesome task of replacing the labor force that would be lost with the blacks, and he went to some lengths to explain how Virginia might overcome the gradual loss of its present working class and eventually replace it. The process would be slow, Madison conceded; it would be attended with "much inconvenience," and it might not even be "certain in its result." But look at the alternatives, he demanded. Considering the tone of Dew's pamphlet, Madison risked a great deal when he asked of his plan, with all of its risks: "Is it not preferable to a torpid acquiescence in a perpetuation of slavery, or an extinguishment of it by convulsions more disastrous in their character and consequences than slavery itself?"[80]

Dew had in fact encouraged moderate Virginians to confront an unavoidable choice, but he presented a quite different assessment of the available options. The professor clearly suggested to his fellow Virginians that they had inherited from their Revolutionary forbears a principled indictment of slavery and a moral commitment to emancipation and that this legacy had become an almost unbearable burden. The older generation had comforted itself by thinking that eliminating the foreign slave trade was virtually equivalent to abolishing the institution. When reality intruded, they had quickly turned to yet another naive delusion: the idea that this internally proliferating population of slaves could somehow be freed and then relocated to the other side of the world. But once the present generation faced up to the absurdity of colonization, Dew suggested, they would have to choose. Either they could become abolitionists of a different stripe who, like Frances Wright and those other noisy eccentrics from up North, objected to conventional barriers of prejudice, or they could defend more aggressively the institution and the society they had inherited, benefitted from, and most important, could not change. It was not a difficult choice: the latter course of

79 *Ibid.*, 276–277.   80 *Ibid.*, 277.

action, which Madison condemned as "torpid acquiescence" in perpetual slavery, required only a clarification of principle, that blacks, by virtue of their racial inferiority, were not quite human and entitled to liberty after all. So much for the Enlightenment. Above all, Dew sought to expose and to cure the epidemic of self-delusion in the Old Dominion: it was no longer possible for anyone with an ounce of sense, he earnestly believed, to genuflect to the Revolutionary fathers' antislavery principles by embracing that "stupendous piece of folly," colonization.

Madison clearly understood what was at stake. Perhaps he doubted some of his own reassurances about the potential for colonization to succeed, for he ended his discussion of the subject with an extraordinary admission. "In my estimate of the experiment instituted by the Colonization Society," he confessed to Dew, "I may indulge too much my wishes and hopes, to be safe from error." He then explained why he could do nothing else: "But a partial success [of colonization] will have its value, and an entire failure will leave behind a consciousness of the laudable intentions with which relief from the greatest of our calamities was attempted in the only mode presenting a chance of effecting it."[81] Madison knew that if his fellow Virginians gave up on colonization, they were likely to follow the treacherous path that Dew was now lighting. Faith in colonization, and a determination to overcome the obstacles that the young professor so powerfully described, were necessary not only to sustain whatever slim momentum there was in the direction of emancipation; such faith and determination were also necessary, in a larger sense, to sustain moral opposition to slavery itself, indeed to keep alive among the American people a principled commitment to the substance of their republican revolution. Madison conceded that colonization might ultimately prove futile; but it was also, in his prudent judgment, the only responsible and honorable way of keeping faith with the Revolution. Because even if colonization failed completely, as Dew predicted, its supporters might be remembered as much for what they had not done – which was not to betray the precious legacy bequeathed to them from the eighteenth century – as for what they had done, which was to pursue justice as best they

81 *Ibid.*

could in an imperfect world. Madison could believe, therefore, that their "laudable intentions" might at least garner for the colonizationists the esteem of posterity.[82]

We might note that Dew was not the only of Madison's correspondents in this period to condemn colonization. A few months later, on July 4, 1833, William Turpin wrote to remind Madison of something else the venerable patriarch was not doing and to chastise him for being remiss. Turpin was eighty years old — like Madison, an aging child of the Revolution. Although he wrote now from New York, this native southerner had lived for almost sixty years in South Carolina and thus knew slavery from intimate experience. Some thirty-three years ago, he told Madison, moral conviction had impelled him both to emancipate his own chattels and to advocate the cause of all oppressed Africans. Now he wrote to his "esteemed friend" in Virginia to denounce colonization and to urge him to see matters in their true light. Turpin attacked colonization not because, like Dew, he thought it impractical, but rather for many of the same reasons it has drawn the enmity of later generations of Americans. He insisted, for example, that proponents of colonization were generally insincere and even disingenuous. They professed to want to improve the condition of the blacks (and perhaps, in some cases, to end slavery as well) by sending them to Africa; but "many of the head Promoters of this cruelty" had openly acknowledged to Turpin the actual truth, "that their sole object was to rid the Country of the Free Blacks." To that end, the racist Colonization Society even encouraged individual states to pass oppressive and unjust laws that, by making life miserable for free Negroes, would persuade them to abandon "their Birthright inheritance, their native Country." The gently outspoken Turpin had once told Thomas Jefferson that he was the advocate of the slaves "on paper, only"; now he warned Madison that the United States, by dragging its heels, was in jeopardy of soon having only Brazil and Cuba for company among slaveholding nations. The difference between Jefferson (and Madison) and himself, Turpin said, was that he had "come up to the

82 In view of "posterity's" ultimate contempt for colonization, of course, this expectation can only be described as perversely ironic.

Point Required by god himself," for which, he added, he had been "blessed with complete peace and happiness in mind."[83]

Turpin's challenge could not have taken Madison by surprise, since this was hardly the first time he had had such sentiments thrown in his face. And Madison well knew that, by the early 1830s, Turpin was articulating the position of other northern abolitionists with whom he did not correspond (and about whom he appears to have said very little directly). Madison understood and doubtless respected the profound sense of moral urgency that inspired Turpin and the new breed of abolitionists; but in view of the disturbing direction of change in southern public opinion, especially, he now tended more than ever to blame their misguided, if sincere, idealism for compounding the problem of slavery. Many years earlier, in 1791, Madison had cautioned an antislavery Quaker zealot not to petition the Virginia legislature for even a gradual emancipation law because he thought such pressure "likely to do harm rather than good." He had predicted that strident calls for immediate action, rather than expedite what both men wanted, would only lend strength to reactionary efforts "to withdraw the privilege now allowed to individuals, of giving freedom to slaves" or, at the least, to "clog it with a condition that the persons freed should be removed from the Country." (As Madison later scribbled in the margin, referring to an 1806 Virginia statute that imposed precisely the latter condition, "it so happened.")[84] Now, in the 1830s, Madison was similarly worried about the unintended consequences of the activities of imprudent, if well-meaning, antislavery zealots like Turpin. What they unwittingly did, he lamented, was drive frightened southerners to tighten the chains on blacks and, even worse, to defend the institution in ways that betrayed the fundamental articles of America's republican faith.

Charles Jared Ingersoll later reported that when he had visited

---

83 Turpin to Madison, July 4, 1833, in Madison Papers, Library of Congress, series one (microfilm). Some of the biographical detail is taken from a subsequent letter from Turpin to Madison, Dec. 25, 1833, *ibid.*
84 Madison to Robert Pleasants, Oct. 30, 1791, in Hutchinson et al., eds., *Madison Papers*, XIV, 91–92.

Madison at Montpelier but a few weeks before the patriarch's death, his host had talked at length about the many "deplorable effects of the abolition excitement." According to Ingersoll, Madison had pointed specifically to Professor Dew — who by this time had been rewarded with promotion to the presidency of William and Mary — as evidence of the point that the abolitionists were inadvertently encouraging southerners "to imagine that slavery is right and useful."[85] In 1841, Ingersoll told his fellow United States senators that he remembered Madison saying of "modern Abolition" that, "to it alone, we owe not only the lamentable arrest of onward emancipation; but, till it intruded, no Governor in Carolina extolled slavery as a happy balance of her Government, no Virginia professor vindicated its moral advantages."[86] Ingersoll despised the abolitionists, and he clearly hoped to use Madison's putative testimony to discredit them; but there is no reason to think that he fundamentally misrepresented (even if he exaggerated) his host's opinions. If Madison actually came to believe that the abolitionists were solely responsible for the unhappy developments he described, then his self-delusion had entered yet another phase. If he merely believed that strident attacks on colonization like Turpin's made voluntary emancipation far less likely, and even encouraged southerners to defend the institution as a matter of principle, he was surely right.

Madison replied to Turpin's "friendly letter" by emphasizing that the blacks must voluntarily consent to colonization before it could proceed, and he reviewed many, though not all, of his reasons for continuing to support the project. "Whatever be the difficulties it has to encounter," he asserted, "I can not but regard it as an experiment worthy of the partiality I feel for it." On the one hand, it might offer "a happy introduction to blessings for Africa, at present promised from no other source." Even more important, of course, it would be "a benefit" to the United States as far as it succeeded, and Madison believed it might "possibly succeed to an extent, & lead to other successful experiments, all founded on the *consent* of the Blacks, which taken together, may be of the greatest benefit to both

85 "Visit to Mr. Madison," from Washington *Globe*, reprinted in *Richmond Enquirer*, Aug. 19, 1836.
86 *Congressional Globe*, 27th Cong., 1st sess., June 1841, X, Appendix, 73.

the Blacks & the Whites" – the latter of whom, he reminded Turpin, "will not consent to mix their blood with that of the former." Especially since "it appears impossible for two such distinct races to occupy the same Country in amity & peace," indeed, he could "discern no evils attending the colonizing experiment which ought to forbid it."[87]

Turpin never bothered to answer Madison's rebuttal. He took several months even to acknowledge receipt of the latter's "kind letter." On Christmas day, however, the reformed slaveholder wrote with serene confidence that God had "raised up" some forty million conscientious people, in all parts of the world, who were eager to join him in vindicating the cause of the oppressed Africans. Their numbers, he assured Madison, were daily growing.[88]

Thirty years later, during the American Civil War, an elderly Harriet Martineau had occasion to reflect once again on her pilgrimage to Montpelier in the winter of 1835. She remembered that despair had not come easy to a man of such "cheerful and sanguine temper" as Madison. Yet slavery had in fact pushed him to the very brink of despair, and by his own admission only the Colonization Society now stood between him and the loss of all hope. "Rather than admit to himself that the South must be laid waste by a servile war, or the whole country by a civil war," Martineau observed to her readers in 1862, "he strove to believe that millions of negroes could be carried to Africa, and so got rid of." It was hardly necessary, she added, to comment on "the weakness of such a hope."

Apparently Madison had been willing to present more of his misgivings about colonization to Martineau than he had to Turpin. She recalled, for instance, that he had described "the unwillingness of the negroes to go, so that he had just sold some of his slaves [to his kinsman Taylor], instead of compelling them to emigrate." He had also complained, as president of the Colonization Society, of the difficulty "of getting an African colony to receive batches of immi-

87 Madison to Turpin (marked "private"), Aug. 9, 1833, in Madison Papers, Library of Congress, series one (microfilm).
88 Turpin to Madison, Dec. 25, 1833, *ibid.*

307

grants, at the rate of two or three cargoes a year." Especially when Madison seemed so aware of these imposing logistical and moral problems, it was difficult for Martineau to explain how "a man so honoured and beloved" could persist in "inviting confidence" in such a "delusive scheme" as colonization. Perhaps he simply had too much invested in the fate of this grand but tragically flawed republic. "Not only is a statesman attached to his own work," she mused, "but American statesmen of his generation had that attachment exalted to passion, by the emotions of fear, hope, and pride, which they had passed through."

Now, in 1862, as the killing went on, Martineau well remembered her own feelings on that pleasant winter day almost thirty years before. "It was as painful as it was strange," she recalled, "to listen to the cheerful old man, as he proved that there was no chance for his country, except from a scheme which he, as its President, found unmanageable."[89]

III

What chance was there for Madison's own slaves? As he agonized over colonization and the republic's predicament in the early 1830s, the Sage of Montpelier continued to grapple with this private dimension of a larger public dilemma. His reluctant accommodation of the institution would leave him, at his death, with approximately one hundred slaves to dispose of. Would they, at least, have restored to them their natural right to liberty?

Straightforward logic suggested they would not. If Madison were unable to find an appropriate way to free them while he was alive, there was little reason to think that his death would significantly alter the circumstances that restrained him. True, he had no children to provide for in his will, nor were his debts so burdensome as to make emancipation economically impossible (as had been the case with his friend Jefferson). But Madison still had to be concerned

89 Harriet Martineau, "The Brewing of the American Storm," *Macmillan's Magazine* 6, no. 32 (June 1862), 98–99. I am indebted to Charles Royster for bringing this essay to my attention.

about the assets of his relatively youthful wife, whom he expected to outlive him by more than a few years; and his death would hardly cancel the obligation he felt to assess realistically the effect of emancipation on his slaves. He still had to anticipate what freedom would mean for human beings whom he knew intimately and about whom he cared deeply.

Above all, if his slaves were to be freed, they would have to be removed from the state, as dictated by Virginia statute, and from the vicinity of white Americans elsewhere, as directed by other state laws forbidding their migration and by his own analysis of the debilitating effects of white prejudice. But as Madison lamented to Martineau, his own slaves were no different from virtually all other blacks in the United States, slave or free: they expressed "horror" at the thought of going to Liberia, their most promising refuge, and as a matter of principle he would not consider involuntary deportation. Perhaps Madison understood that his slaves could appreciate the advantages of freedom but still have good reason, when the "practical" alternatives were so unappealing or fraught with uncertainty, to prefer remaining where they were. Indeed, Madison well knew that some of his slaves had been at Montpelier even longer than he and that their generational ties to the community ran almost as deep as his own. During his visit to Madison in 1825, Lafayette had spent a great deal of time at the log cabin of another retiree, "Granny Milly," reputedly 104 years old, who lived happily with her daughter and granddaughter, the younger of whom was almost seventy.[90] Such longevity was not unusual in the black community at "Walnut Grove," a short distance from the big house; Madison reported to a correspondent in the mid-1820s that there were at Montpelier at least four black women "not less than eighty" and that recent deaths included a Negro man nearly one hundred, another at age ninety, and a married couple of at least eighty.[91] As he took stock of his slaves in the early 1830s, Madison saw that a majority were either like Granny Milly, "superannuated," elderly and often infirm, or too

90 See Mary Cutts Memoir, Cutts–Madison Collection (microfilm), Library of Congress.
91 Madison to Charles Caldwell, July 22, 1825, in [Rives and Fendall, eds.], *Letters and Other Writings*, III, 493.

young to be responsible for their own welfare. Others had intermarried with slaves belonging to his neighbors and would be reluctant, under any circumstances, to leave their families. If emancipation were to take into account the preferences of the slaves, in other words, and if its purpose was to promote their welfare and happiness, Madison had ample reason to be cautious.

Notwithstanding these and other practical difficulties, however, Madison could not ignore the imperatives of justice. He also appreciated the importance of a final statement on his part not only for clearing his own conscience but for securing as well his reputation and indeed his legacy. He did not need to be reminded that other principled slaveholders, most notably General Washington, had included in their wills a provision for emancipation and that the same might be expected of him. This was more than a private act, a means of doing justice to loyal servants; it was a profoundly important public gesture, an unequivocal statement of opposition to slavery that Madison, too, very much wished to make. Indeed, if Madison wished to vindicate his character in the eyes of posterity, Edward Coles told him in early 1832 that he had no choice but to do what duty and consistency, as well as his own exemplary character, "imperiously" required. "Not to restore to your slaves that liberty and those rights which you have been through life so zealous and able a champion," he warned his mentor, would be "a blot and stigma" on an otherwise spotless career.[92]

Coles in effect asked Madison to do what he, Coles, had already done under very different circumstances: to clear his conscience by severing all personal ties to the institution. If we take into account the broad outline of Coles's extraordinary career, it is highly appropriate that he became a critical figure in Madison's final deliberations about the disposition of his slaves. Born in 1786 at "Enniscorthy," his father's estate not far from Charlottesville, Coles was raised to be a Virginia planter. While a student at William and Mary College during President Jefferson's second administration, however, young Coles developed a principled and passionate hatred of slavery. He resolved not to continue ownership of the slaves whom

92 Coles to Madison, Jan. 8, 1832, in "Letters of Coles," *William and Mary Quarterly*, 2d ser., 7 (1927), 37.

his father was planning to bequeath to him, though he kept his intentions secret until his father's death in 1807. He then discovered the full extent of his predicament. Coles wanted to free his slaves, but he quickly encountered both the recent 1806 Virginia law (which would require, in the absence of a special petition, their removal from the state within a year) and the hostility of his family and neighbors. He toyed with the notion of attempting to circumvent the 1806 law by employing his Negroes as laborers on his Virginia farm without formally emancipating them until his death; but he found that even his friends were "indignant at the idea" and threatened to harass both him and his prospective hirelings as "pests of society." Coles reluctantly decided that he would have to leave the Old Dominion.[93]

His plans were temporarily shelved, however, when he accepted President Madison's offer to become his private secretary in the White House. Under the circumstances, slavery was neither man's primary concern, but, as Coles later recounted, "Mr. Madisons treatment of me was such as to put me entirely at my ease, and enabled me to converse freely with him on all subjects." And Coles had conveyed to Madison not just the intensity of his own principled beliefs about slavery, but his profound surprise that "just men" and "long sighted politicians" could hesitate to act decisively against this odious blot on America's republican pretensions. By his own later account, Coles had even taunted the president. "On occasions of seeing gangs of Negroes, some in irons, on their way [from Washington] to a southern market," he had taken "the liberty to jeer" his boss "by congratulating him, as the Chief of our great Republic, that he was not then accompanyed by a Foreign Minister" and

93 "Emancipation of the Slaves of Edward Coles," 1827, Edward Coles Collection, Historical Society of Pennsylvania, box 2, file 11. This manuscript collection is the best source of information about Coles and his career. It contains a long autobiographical letter that Coles apparently drafted in 1844 (cited here as "Edward Coles Autobiography"). The best published account of Coles can be found in Clarence Walworth Alvord, ed., *Governor Edward Coles* (Springfield, Ill., 1920), which includes E. B. Washburne, *Sketch of Edward Coles, Second Governor of Illinois . . .* (Chicago, 1882). See also Kurt Edwin Leichtle, "Edward Coles: An Agrarian on the Frontier," unpubl. Ph.D. diss., University of Illinois at Chicago Circle, 1982.

therefore "saved the deep mortification of witnessing such a revolting sight in the presence of the representative of a nation, less boastful perhaps of its regard for the rights of man, but more observant of them."[94] Like Samuel Johnson almost fifty years before, Coles could not bear to hear, without protest, the "loudest yelps for liberty" issue from the lips of the holders of slaves.

But if Coles found Madison's apparent toleration of slavery frustrating, he also never lost his respect for the older man. In 1844, remembering their days of intimacy, he tried to explain why his hero had stoically endured his jeers and remained a slaveholder. On the one hand, Madison's principles were "sound, pure, & conscientious," and his feelings, "sensitive & tender in the extreme." Coles asserted of Madison, indeed, that "to give pain always gave him pain" and that "no man had a more instinctive repugnance to doing wrong to another than he had." Yet, "from the force of early impressions, the influence of habit & association, & a certain train of reasoning, which lulled in some degree his conscience, without convincing his judgment (for he never justified or approved of it)," Madison, much to his secretary's regret, had "continued to hold Slaves."[95]

Coles had not. Perhaps disappointed by Madison's response to his prodding, he wrote to Jefferson in 1814, explaining his unwillingness to remain in Virginia. He further implored the Sage of Monticello to do what Madison apparently could not: lead a public crusade for a general emancipation of the slaves. But Jefferson protested that he was simply too old to be of much help and instead urged Coles to remain in his native state and organize the movement himself. Coles later described Jefferson's response as "in perfect accordance with his character, in fine harmony with his philanthropic republicanism, & in every way worthy of the renown[ed] author of

94 "Edward Coles Autobiography," Coles Collection, Hist. Soc. of Pa., box 2, folder 13. Excerpts from that document, including this one, are reproduced and placed in sound context by Ralph L. Ketcham, "The Dictates of Conscience: Edward Coles and Slavery," *Virginia Quarterly Review* 36 (1960), 46–62. I have followed Ketcham's transcription of the excerpt on page 52.
95 *Ibid.*

the Declaration of American Independence"; but the younger man also respectfully declined the challenge.[96] He was not eager to abandon his family and friends, nor did he relish the life of the expatriate on some remote western frontier; but he would rather bear anything, he vowed, than continue to own slaves. Indeed, not long after receiving Jefferson's reply, Coles told his friend Nicholas Biddle that nothing could induce him even to remain among slaves "except the hope of being in some degree instrumental in ameliorating their condition." If only he were up to that noble and heroic task! "Oh that I had talents and acquirements to become the champion of humanity!" he exclaimed to Biddle. "But having only the power to perceive its wrongs, and feel its sufferings, without the capacity of relieving it, all that I can do is to preserve my principles, and save my feelings, by flying from the scene of its oppression."[97]

In 1819 Coles moved to the new state of Illinois, emancipating en route ten of the slaves whom he had inherited. He gave 160 acres of land to each head of a family and also provided for the education of the young. At the dramatically contrived moment of emancipation, when Coles scrutinized the release of "the long pent up spirit of man," he explained to his former slaves the full measure of the burden he now placed on them. They would have to behave in such a manner "as to show that the black race were not inferior to the white, and were equally qualified to enjoy all the blessings, and perform all the duties, incident to freedom."[98] Coles eagerly informed Madison of what he had done, and Madison relayed his guarded congratulations: "You are pursuing, I observe, the true course with your negroes, in order to make their freedom a fair

---

96 "Edward Coles Autobiography," Coles Collection, Hist. Soc. of Pa., box 2, folder 13. At the time, Coles seemed rather less satisfied with Jefferson's response, though scholars have tended to exaggerate Coles's hostility to his famous correspondent. The best analysis of the exchange is in Dumas Malone, *The Sage of Monticello* (Boston, 1981), 320–323; for a different though somewhat misleading slant, see esp. David Brion Davis, *The Problem of Slavery in the Age of Revolution, 1770–1823* (Ithaca, N.Y., and London, 1975), 180–183.
97 Coles to Biddle, April 6, 1815, in Nicholas Biddle Papers, Library of Congress.
98 "Emancipation of the Slaves of Edward Coles," 1827, Coles Collection, Hist. Soc. of Pa., box 2, folder 11.

experiment for their happiness. With the habits of the slave, and without the instruction, the property, or the employments of a freeman, the manumitted blacks, instead of deriving advantage from the partial benevolence of their Masters, furnish arguments against the general efforts in their behalf." Unfortunately, however, there was one thing that no philanthropist, including Coles, could ever overcome, and by raising this matter Madison gently conveyed his pessimism about Coles's great experiment: "I wish your philanthropy could compleat its object, by changing their colour as well as their legal condition. Without this, they seem destined to a privation of that moral rank & those social participations which give to freedom more than half its value."[99]

Did subsequent events vindicate Madison's reservations? Coles seemed unable to make up his mind. Eight years later, he proudly insisted that his former slaves had more than fulfilled his optimistic expectations, and after seventeen more years he saw no reason to alter this judgment. Their exemplary behavior was empirical proof, he said, that blacks were not innately inferior to whites, that they could, indeed, take advantage of the blessings of freedom. Generally industrious and even prosperous, his people had led sober, orderly, and moral lives. "It affords me pleasure to state," Coles wrote in 1844, "that the Negroes followed the advice I gave them when I restored to them their long lost liberty, & have uniformly & without exception conducted themselves with great propriety; never to my knowledge, by word or deed given just cause of offence, or for any violation of law been brought before a Court of Justice." Many had joined religious congregations, in fact, and one had even become "an active & useful clergyman in the Baptist church."[100] Writing to this man and his wife in 1837, Coles congratulated them for having acted so as "to sustain my conduct, & confirm my opinions of the unity & equality of man & of his capacity to govern himself, & best promote his own happiness." Indeed, he assured them, "you both

99 Coles to Madison, July 20, 1819, in *Bulletin of the Chicago Historical Society* 1 (1934), 3–4, and Madison to Coles, Sept. 3, 1819, in Hunt, ed., *Writings of Madison*, VIII, 455.

100 "Emancipation of the Slaves of Edward Coles," 1827, in Coles Collection, Hist. Soc. of Pa., box 2, folder 11, and "Edward Coles Autobiography," *ibid.*, box 2, folder 13.

Edward Coles, Emancipator. A romanticized depiction of Coles at the
moment of freeing his slaves on the Ohio River in 1819, this celebratory
mural remains on display today in the capitol building at Springfield,
Illinois. (Courtesy of the Illinois State Historical Library, Springfield)

have well fulfilled your parts, and have in every respect maintained
as fair a character under your brown faces, as the fairest of your fair
faced neighbours."[101]

Nevertheless, notwithstanding their apparent success, Coles also

101 Coles to Robert and Kate Crawford, Feb. 7, 1837, in Edward Coles Papers,
Princeton University Archives. Crawford had apparently not left all of his past
behind him; in his letters to Coles, he addressed him: "Dear Master." See
Crawford to Coles, Oct. 23, 1840, *ibid*.

firmly believed that his former slaves should migrate to Liberia. According to his view of things, Illinois was far from a hospitable and supportive environment in which they might develop their full potential, and some elements of the historical record would certainly bear him out. During 1823–24, as the second governor of Illinois, Coles had barely succeeded in defeating a serious campaign to legalize slavery in the state. Some of his former slaves had been cheated and swindled out of their wages by predatory, racist whites, and Coles himself endured in the 1820s what he called "persecution" for his antislavery beliefs and his support of free blacks. Illinois had adopted a savage black code from its inception as a state, and matters were hardly improving; in 1829, a new law would prohibit marriage between the races under penalty of stripes, fines, and imprisonment.[102] Among his former slaves, however, Coles got nowhere with his promotional campaign for Liberia. In 1827, he observed that even though he had offered to go to Africa himself and provide personal assistance, they were "so happy & content where they are, that they seem reluctant to change their situation." He still hoped that "with further reflection, and a better understanding of what their condition would be there, compared with what it is here, that they may yet be disposed to emigrate."[103]

As an activist in the American Colonization Society, Coles did everything he could to persuade all free blacks, not just his former slaves, that happiness and fulfillment awaited them on a different continent. It is difficult to tell just when Coles became an ardent colonizationist, but he later asserted that he had been "among the first to advocate the establishment of a colony on the coast of Africa for the removal to & settlement of our Negro population." After all, he explained in 1844, "races of men that differ so much in appearance as the White & Black man" would "never, till man changes his nature, associate as equals, & live in harmony & social intercourse." In the United States, generations of slavery had only exacerbated

102 Theodore Calvin Pease, *The Frontier State, 1818–1848* (Chicago, 1922), 47–49.
103 "Emancipation of the Slaves of Edward Coles," 1827, in Coles Collection, Hist. Soc. of Pa., box 2, folder 11.

these natural prejudices, making it impossible "that the oppressed race will for ages to come, if they ever do, possess, in such a community, equal political, personal, & social rights." Since Coles knew "the disadvantages & indignities" to which his former slaves and their posterity would be subjected, even in free states like Illinois, and since he never doubted, either, "the advantages they would have, & the enobling position they would occupy, in a Country exclusively their own, & especially in that one which god had alloted to their race," he had persisted in his efforts to get his people to emigrate to Africa. He apparently agreed with Madison that one of the necessary ways of overcoming this unfortunate black prejudice against Liberia was to arrange for testimony that the blacks would trust. Coles thus offered to subsidize a visit to Liberia by Robert Crawford, his former slave who had become a minister, so that Crawford might "write a full & faithful account" of his observations, which Coles could then publish "for the information of his black brethren generally." Although Coles was apparently still trying in 1844, he reported that Crawford "has not yet acceded to my proposition, being, as he says, so fully engrossed & happily occupied in attending to his Family, his Farm, & his Congregation." Coles knew when he was beaten, but he refused to change his mind about what his former slaves should have done for their own good: "Although they have succeeded well, enjoyed their freedom, & led happy lives, I still believe it would have been best for them & their posterity if they had removed to a Country exclusively occupied by people of their own colour."[104]

Madison and Coles, in sum, had no quarrel on the issue of colonization. In the early 1830s they both assumed that Madison's slaves, once liberated, should go to Liberia; indeed, writing in December 1831 to Jefferson's grandson, a member of the Virginia legislature during its momentous debates, Coles could even describe, with palpable horror, the uninviting alternative of having

104 "Edward Coles Autobiography," *ibid.*, box 2, folder 13. For evidence of Coles's fundraising for the Colonization Society, see, for instance, his letter to Henry Clay, Jan. 20, 1829, in American Colonization Society Papers, Library of Congress (microfilm), reel 5.

eventually to turn loose upon society "this ignorant, immoral, & degraded race."[105] Coles understood, of course, that Madison's task was far more onerous than what he himself had faced almost two decades earlier. Madison had almost one hundred slaves to free, not ten; he was eighty years old, not thirty; and he was married, not single. Like Turpin, however, Coles knew first-hand the personal joys and exquisite satisfaction that came with clearing one's conscience, and he assured Madison, in effect, that where there was the will there could be found a way. Yes, there were numerous difficulties to anticipate and remedy, and he further agreed with Madison that General Washington's example had in some respects been "injudicious." By explicitly providing in his will for the freedom of all of his slaves, old and young, at the time of his wife's death, Washington had created an impossible situation for his widow, one that Mrs. Madison must be spared. But Coles offered many specific hints about how Madison might avoid or mitigate these kinds of problems, and he offered no end of encouragement and inspiration. He was confident that he had won his case.[106]

Apparently he had not, because when Madison completed his will in the spring of 1835, he included no provision for emancipating his slaves. The relevant section – a syntactical disaster – read simply: "I give and bequeath my ownership in the negroes and people of colour held by me to my dear wife, but it is my desire that none of them should be sold without his or her consent, or in case of their misbehaviour; except that infant children may be sold with their parent who consents for them to be sold with him or her, and who consents to be sold."[107] Madison made the final revisions of his will shortly after he had sold sixteen of his slaves to his kinsman Taylor. By his testimony, he did so with their consent, after failing to gain their consent to become pioneers in Liberia. Despite Coles's confidence, Madison obviously failed to resolve to his own satisfaction the many problems both men foresaw attending the posthumous emancipation of his slaves. Surely his primary concern was for his wife. But it is

105 Extract, Coles to Thomas Jefferson Randolph, Dec. 29, 1831, in "Letters of Coles," *William and Mary Quarterly*, 2d ser., 7 (1927), 106.
106 Coles to Madison, Jan. 8, 1832, *ibid.*, 37–38.
107 Hunt, ed., *Writings of Madison*, IX, 549.

also plausible to infer that Madison may have been more interested in the actual welfare of his slaves than he was either in clearing his conscience or in using them to make a political statement. Perhaps the will attests to Madison's humanity, in other words, as well as to his conservatism. Contrary to appearances, by providing for his slaves as he did, Madison may have given greater evidence of his concern and respect for them than he would have, had he merely released them into a hostile white world or, for that matter, subjected them to involuntary deportation.[108]

Coles, of course, would have summarily rejected any such interpretation. By the time of Madison's death, the young maverick, now almost fifty years old, had finally settled down, living happily in Philadelphia with his young and quite wealthy bride. When he first learned of Madison's failure to free his slaves in his will, Coles was incredulous. What had gone wrong? His initial response was quite generous: he placed a great deal of the blame on himself. Back in 1831, he recalled, he had mentioned Madison's intentions in confidence to his own brother-in-law, Congressman Andrew Stevenson, whom Coles now inferred had talked Madison out of doing what Coles had convinced him to do. In melodramatic language, Coles accepted responsibility for the tragedy. He continued to hope that a secret codicil to the will, freeing the slaves at Mrs. Madison's death, might still be discovered; but if Mr. Madison "has not done something of the kind, his friends & especially the future admirers of his character will never cease to regret he ever knew Mr. S[tevenson]." As "the personal friend of both, & as the unfortunate link between them," Coles said he would always consider his unwitting complicity in this sad affair as "the most painful & calamitous indiscretion of my life."[109]

Even when Stevenson, through his wife, Coles's sister, vehemently denied this allegation, Coles was unmoved. He was angry at Madison for having imposed on his widow the disagreeable task of selling many of the slaves that his estate could not support, but he

108 I am indebted to Robert Allison, currently a graduate student in the History of American Civilization program at Harvard University, for suggesting this line of thought.

109 Extract, Coles to Sarah Coles Stevenson, July 28, 1836, in "Letters of Coles," *William and Mary Quarterly*, 2d ser. 7 (1927), 107–108.

was far more determined to place primary responsibility for the tragedy on anyone *but* Madison. He insisted to his sister, therefore, that Madison's startling reversal of intention could only be explained by the interference of others, including her husband. And a sickening tragedy it was. Coles had gone to Montpelier to comfort the widow shortly after the great man's death. He described for Mrs. Stevenson what he had seen:

Reports had gotten abroad that she (Mrs. Madison) wished to sell many of them (her slaves) & every day or two (while I was at her house in Aug:) a Negro trader would make his appearance, & was permitted to examine the Negroes. It was like the hawk among the pigeons. The poor creatures wd: run to the house and protest agst. being sold, & say their old master had said in his will that they were not to be sold but with their consent. She sold while I was with her a woman and 2 children to her Nephew Ambrose Madison who lives near her. The woman protested agst. being sold & the more so as her husband was not sold with her.[110]

Whether he knew it or not, Coles had already found a better scapegoat than Stevenson. Dolley Madison, his own cousin – and the daughter of Quaker parents who had freed their slaves at the time of the Revolution – was the obvious alternative villain. When Coles spoke of the affair in his long autobiographical letter of 1844, he said that he still found Madison's will "inexplicable." Within a few years, however, he was accumulating evidence of a plausible explanation. Madison's widow died in 1849; that same year, Coles "fell in" at the Warm Springs with none other than William Taylor, who told him that Robert Taylor of Orange Court House had drawn up Madison's will and that Madison's favorite niece, Mrs. Willis (who was at Madison's bedside when he died), had told him (William Taylor) that Madison had mentioned to Robert Taylor his wish to free his slaves but that he had found too many difficulties in the way of doing so during his wife's life. Madison had finally decided, therefore, not to free them in his will, but he had also told Robert Taylor that "Mrs. Madison knew his wishes & views and would carry them into effect at her death." Coles took eager note of William Taylor's rendition of the story, and when he mentioned it to Henry Clay in Philadelphia two months later, Clay, who had been close to

110 Extract, Coles to S. C. Stevenson, Nov. 12, 1836, *ibid.*, 108–109.

Madison's widow, confirmed that she had indeed told him "that her Husband expected her to free his slaves at her death." Coles made a formal memorandum of the two conversations.[111]

From there the story fell logically into place. In late 1855 Coles wrote directly to Mrs. Willis for confirmation of what he had heard from William Taylor. Although she recalled no such conversation with the gentleman from Point Coupée, Louisiana, she was able to substantiate the gist of his remarks. Madison had made his intentions abundantly clear to his intimates, she said, and she had good reason to think, moreover, that he had conveyed them formally to his wife in "a sealed paper," witnessed by several people on the day Madison was buried, but of which "nothing more was ever heard."[112] This was more than enough for Coles. A year earlier, when telling the historian Hugh Blair Grigsby about his conversations with Taylor and Clay, Coles had made note of the fact that despite the explicit provisions of Madison's will, "his Negroes were sold, not only without their consent, and without having misbehaved, but singly and separated from their families."[113] Armed with Mrs. Willis's testimony, he carried his case against Dolley Madison even further. Coles confidently assured William Cabell Rives, who was preparing a biography of their mentor, that Madison had most certainly "intended to free his Negroes, *and died under the impression he had done so.*" He exhorted Rives to bring this truth to public light, charitably adding that he should be as "little harsh to the guilty parties as the disclosure of the circumstances would permit."[114]

But the larger needs of history had to take precedence over any private feelings. Writing in 1857, Coles told Rives not to forget "that the time is coming, and that it will be an enduring time too," when a biographer of James Madison would "be censured by posterity" if he omitted "to mention so important a fact, one so essential to a complete knowledge of his feelings and principles." Coles was

---

111 Memorandum, "Warm Springs Sep: 1849," in Coles Papers, Princeton University Archives.

112 Coles to Mrs. Nelly C. Willis, Dec. 10, 1855, *ibid.*, and John Willis to Coles, Dec. 19, 1855, in Rives Papers, Library of Congress, box 87.

113 Coles to Grigsby, Dec. 23, 1854, *ibid.*, box 85.

114 Coles to Rives, Feb. 3, 1857, *ibid.*, box 89.

especially anxious, it seems, because there had recently been published in Philadelphia a "most extraordinary" and erroneous assertion about Madison's will, claiming that it had directed that his Negroes be sold. Since this misimpression had been published in a form and manner "likely to find its way into history," Coles tried to impress upon Rives the urgency of his mission as Madison's biographer, indeed "the necessity of your noticing his views and wishes about freeing his slaves, and by giving the facts to make known to posterity this the most characteristic and consistent act of his private life." It would be more than a shame, Coles suggested – it would be a tragedy – if Madison's legacy were misappropriated "in the fervor of partisanship."[115]

115 *Ibid.*

8. Legacy: The Strange Career of William Cabell Rives

DWARD COLES was confident that he had known James
Madison well enough to explain him to anyone who had
not – or for that matter, to virtually anyone else who had.
By the second half of the 1850s, as controversy over slavery in the
western territories took center stage in national politics, more than
his mentor's provision for his servants cried out for interpretation
and clarification. Coles the historian was busy establishing the general case that excluding slavery from the federal territories had been
the undisputed policy of all the Founding Fathers, and that any
other policy – especially the notorious Kansas–Nebraska Act of
1854 which, by substituting the dubious mechanism of popular
sovereignty, left the region potentially open to slavery – represented
a rank betrayal of this heroic tradition. In his *History of the Ordinance
of 1787* published in 1856, Coles even insisted that Thomas Jefferson was chiefly responsible for the antislavery provisions of the now
legendary Northwest Ordinance. (This was not an easy case to sustain, since the author of the Declaration of Independence had not
been a member of the old Confederation Congress – indeed, he had
been in Paris for several years – at the time the law was passed.) As
much as the Constitution itself, Coles suggested, Mr. Jefferson's
ordinance, with its exclusion of slavery from the territory northwest
of the Ohio River, articulated "the great principles on which our
Government is founded."[1]

But here Coles encountered a potential difficulty with Madison,

---

1 Coles's "History," which ultimately took the form of a brief pamphlet, was
initially read before the Historical Society of Pennsylvania; Clarence Walworth
Alvord, ed., *Governor Edward Coles* (Springfield, Illinois, 1920), 376–398, quotation from 398. Merrill D. Peterson discusses the context of Coles's tract in *The
Jefferson Image in the American Mind* (New York, 1960), 189–209.

whose view of that ordinance and of the larger issue of the geographical extension of slavery was considerably more complex. A chance
sequence of events brought this problem to Coles's attention in the
mid-1850s. In order to pay gambling debts, Madison's dissolute
stepson, Payne Todd, had sold some of Madison's manuscripts to a
professional collector in Washington, James C. McGuire, who subsequently published a volume of selections that happened to include
Madison's letter to Robert Walsh during the Missouri controversy in
1819. As we have seen, Madison's discussion both of the constitutionality of restricting slavery in the territories and of the broader
intentions of the framers was not what Walsh had expected or
certainly wished to see.[2] Now Coles shared that surprise. He
promptly decided that McGuire had tampered with the document,
since some passages, as printed, made Madison display what Coles
called an "ignorance or recklessness" that was utterly "disreputable
to him." Indeed, an indignant Coles sniffed that he simply had "too
much respect" for the great man to believe that he could have
written some of the fatuous sentences in the letter that McGuire had
published.[3]

Actually, of course, Madison had – McGuire's transcription of the
document contained no serious distortions or inaccuracies. Whether
Coles ever made this discovery is not clear, but if his response to the
misunderstandings he had with Madison while his hero was still
alive (and therefore able to set him straight) are any indication, he
would not have changed his mind about the fundamental issue,
anyway.[4] Coles knew what Madison's legacy should be, and hence
properly was, no matter what the elder statesman might have actually said on any given occasion. A cynic might suggest that Coles

2 For Madison's reflections, see Chapter 3 of this volume, pp. 108–113.
3 Coles to William Cabell Rives, Mar. 1, 1858, in William Cabell Rives Papers,
   Library of Congress, box 90. See also Coles to Rives, June 19, 1857, *ibid.*, box
   89. Coles apparently harbored doubts as well about Madison's authorship of the
   "Jonathan Bull and Mary Bull" parable, also published in the 1850s. Coles told
   Rives that McGuire's editing of some of Madison's letters to Coles, himself,
   produced omissions and errors that aroused his general suspicions. I have confirmed the accuracy of the passages in McGuire's transcription of Madison's letter
   to Walsh that Coles disputed by comparing them with the original.
4 See Chapter 4 of this volume, pp. 157–162.

was worshipping his own mythical image of Madison, or, even worse, disingenuously manipulating the past to serve the needs of the moment. Neither charge rings entirely true. Coles was simply so confident that he understood the true spirit of Madison's character and vision that he often overlooked the subtle complexity of his old friend's approach to issues that could not be reduced to the simple terms Coles preferred. And in this particular instance, Coles's personal investment in the cause of a free West only confirmed his commitment to an unambiguous version of the legacy. In late May of 1860, when news arrived in Philadelphia that the national Republican convention had nominated Abraham Lincoln of Illinois for president, a crowd of local admirers rushed to Coles's home and serenaded him, in honor of his role, almost forty years earlier, in having prevented the legalization of slavery in the nominee's state. Coles himself seemed no less impressed by his symbolic connection to Lincoln. When the president-elect passed through Philadelphia nine months later, an infirm Coles went to the trouble of calling upon him – and promptly had his pocket picked in the press of the crowd. An eyewitness reported that Lincoln received Coles warmly, assuring him that he was remembered fondly – indeed held in universal esteem – throughout the state he had once served as governor.[5]

Since the Republican party perfectly embodied the antislavery impulse of the Madison legacy as he preferred to construe that legacy, Coles did not hesitate to vote for Lincoln. Neither did Nicholas P. Trist, another native Virginian residing in Philadelphia, who walked arm-in-arm to the polls with Coles on election day. Although both men eagerly cast their ballots for the Republican candidate, they apparently did so for somewhat different reasons. Trist cared less about the cause of excluding slavery from the western territories than he did about defending the larger cause of the Union. Two months before the election, he had admitted that many friends of his youth were conceding that "our experiment in Republican Government" was "a failure." But the sixty-year-old

5 Both events are described by Trist; see Trist to James Parton, May 31, 1860, and Trist's preface to letter from Coles to Lincoln, July 1862, in Nicholas P. Trist Papers, Library of Congress.

325

Edward Coles, c. 1860. Portrait by Edward B. Marchant, originally in the possession of the Pennsylvania Colonization Society. (Courtesy of the Historical Society of Pennsylvania, Philadelphia)

Trist appropriately resisted despair by turning to a familiar source of guidance and inspiration.[6] In December of 1860 he began publish-

6 Trist, Notes of a Speech, Sept. 16, 1860, *ibid.* (in volume labelled "Notes, Extracts, etc.").

ing in a New York newspaper extracts from Madison's instructive letters to him at the time of the nullification crisis of the early 1830s, letters in which the Father of the Constitution had pronounced "Calhounism," as Trist coined the term, a colossal heresy. Explaining his vote for Lincoln, Trist pointed out that as a confirmed free trader he was hostile to the Republican party's protective tariff plank but that he would gladly swallow higher duties in the interest of promoting a sound understanding of the Constitution. He felt an overwhelming obligation, he said, to do whatever was necessary to "dethrone" Calhounism – which, reminiscent of his mentor, he branded "*Anarchy*, systematized Anarchy" – from its control of the federal government and, just as important, "from its seat of empire over the Southern mind." Indeed, in March 1861, with Lincoln safely ensconced in office amid the looming shadows of war, Trist said he would risk "a fifty years civil war, before a dissolution of the Union."[7] He soon discovered that a mere four-year war, as the actual price of Madison's Union, was no bargain.

As Madison's self-appointed legatees, Coles and Trist were members of a privileged group who had been on close personal terms with the patriarch during his later years. Their network extended south from Philadelphia. Coles's anxious concern about McGuire's "editing" of Madison's writings was communicated to yet another heir, William Cabell Rives, who had contracted with the federal government in late 1856 to organize and to prepare for the press the considerably larger collection of Madison's papers purchased from his widow shortly before her death in 1849. When Rives combined his own biographical project with this editing task, Coles took even greater interest in helping him publicize the Madison legacy. Rives was as fiercely loyal to the memory of Madison as Coles, remarking that he would disdain this imposing and financially unrewarding editorial chore "but for my admiration for the character of Mr. Madison & the desire I feel that his wisdom & services should be properly appreciated by the world."[8] After transporting the manu-

7 Trist, letter to "The World" (N.Y.), begun Nov. 1, 1860 (never completed), and Trist to Winfield Scott, Mar. 14, 1861, *ibid*. See also Trist to Edward Bates, July 17, 1862, *ibid*.
8 W.C. Rives to Alfred Rives, Dec. 12, 1856, in Rives Papers, Library of Congress, box 34. Rives lobbied hard for a good salary from the government when

scripts from the State Department in Washington to Castle Hill, his estate in Albemarle County, Rives was soon "up to his eyes" in these priceless papers, happily renewing his acquaintance with the "old worthies" from another age.[9] Having known Rives for quite some time, Coles had no reason to doubt his sincerity or his honesty or for that matter to suspect his motives. But Coles also knew that Rives had remained in Virginia. He still owned slaves. And he had once been a fervent Jacksonian. No wonder Coles was anxious that Madison's first biographer get his subject right for posterity.

Rives proved to be the most interesting and revealing of Madison's legatees. Unlike Coles and Trist, who fled their native state in search of opportunity elsewhere, he stayed where Madison would have stayed and played out the legacy there. In effect, Rives followed the advice he had himself given in 1828 to another young Virginian, who was pondering a move to Missouri, not to break his ties to his native soil: "*Plant* yourself, then, where you are, strike your roots as deep, & stretch them as wide as you can, & draw sentiment & support from all the sympathies, personal, political & professional, with which you are surrounded."[10] Rather than seek his fortune further south, as Trist initially had, or on the free soil of the northwestern frontier, as Coles (and one of Rives's own brothers) had, Rives plunged his roots deep into the Piedmont soil and, for better or worse, wrestled with the economy and the culture of the Old Dominion, including its peculiar institution. Somehow he managed to retain not only Madison's loyalty to the state, but much of his optimism about its future as well, all the while supporting, as best he could, the burden of his mentor's legacy. Indeed, as Madison's editor and biographer from early 1857 until his death in the spring of 1868, Rives could hardly have avoided thinking about Madison and the meaning of his legacy if he had tried. He never considered voting for Lincoln in 1860.

---

negotiating his editing services; see his letter to the same son on Dec. 8, 1856, in the Alfred Landon Rives Papers, Manuscript Department, Duke University Library.

9 Judith Rives to Alfred Rives, Jan. 15, 1857, *ibid.*

10 Rives to T. W. Gilmer, April 22, 1828, in Rives Papers, Library of Congress, box 44.

Rives was a Virginia-based Unionist who venerated a Madisonian tradition that Madison himself would have recognized and in all likelihood embraced. He defended a conservative, antislavery conception of republicanism and worshipped the Constitution, historically interpreted, of which Madison and other Virginians had been the principal architects only a few years before his birth in 1793. Struggling to project Madison's eighteenth-century vision of government forward into the second half of the nineteenth century, however, Rives endured the pressure of circumstances that the venerable patriarch, even in his final years, had only barely glimpsed. In that sense Rives suffered a fate that mortality had mercifully spared his mentor. If his perspective on many seminal issues proved remarkably faithful to Madison's, the unfolding of his career also revealed the full measure of their mutual dilemma. As a Virginia-based nationalist, Rives honored Madison's memory in a way that Coles and Trist, as expatriates, could not; but it was Rives who unwittingly exposed all of the evasions and accommodations that Madison had been moved to embrace in the quiet desperation of his final years. Rives's story, and perforce Madison's, was ultimately one of tragedy, not triumph. In Rives's strange career, indeed, Madisonianism eventually unravelled, laying bare the tragic underside of a noble – and profoundly flawed – legacy.

I

In his own time, Rives was far and away the most prominent and politically influential of Madison's legatees. His name would have been familiar to anyone with even a casual knowledge of national affairs during the three decades preceding the Civil War. Today he is virtually unknown. His name is recognized by few historians other than those who specialize in antebellum politics; archivists who handle his papers regularly mispronounce his name; and students hearing his name correctly pronounced promptly misspell it as "Reeves."

Rives's present obscurity reflects the erratic and ultimately disappointing trajectory of his political career. He emerged as a major figure in national politics in the years just before Madison's death, when he seemed destined to ascend to the highest ranks of leadership in the Democratic party and even succeed to the great "Virginia Dynasty." But something went awry. Perhaps the trouble began as early as the fall of 1834, when Rives made the mistake of trying to advise President Jackson on the crisis with France – a matter about which Rives, as a recent minister to that country, knew a great deal – and made a bad impression by counseling patience and diplomacy. At the 1835 Democratic national convention Rives was abruptly maneuvered out of the vice-presidential nomination, which was generally expected to be his, in favor of a man whose principal claim to distinction was having allegedly killed the great Indian chief Tecumseh in hand-to-hand combat during the War of 1812. From there his career went into a slow but steady decline.[11] He became alienated from his own party, from many of his fellow Virginians, and increasingly from the concept of party loyalty itself – indeed, from "the mad dominion of party," as he revealingly referred to it in 1839.[12] Somehow Rives managed to hold onto his seat in the Senate, off and on, well into the 1840s, and his inevitable gravitation to the rival Whig party brought a second stint as minister to France during the Taylor/Fillmore administration. By the mid-1850s, however, Thomas Jefferson's former law student had effectively been retired from public life. Many Americans deferred, rhetorically at least, to his wisdom and experience, but he wielded little power, and he knew it. No wonder he turned to history – and to Madison – for solace.

11 See esp. John Niven, *Martin Van Buren: The Romantic Age of American Politics* (New York, 1983), 376–419, for the fullest account of Rives's decline. Valuable context is also provided in Major L. Wilson, *The Presidency of Martin Van Buren* (Lawrence, Kansas, 1984), and James Roger Sharp, *The Jacksonians Versus the Banks: Politics in the States After the Panic of 1837* (New York and London, 1970), chap. 9. The most thorough account of Rives's role in the "Conservative" insurgency within the Democratic Party during the Van Buren administration, an account that emphasizes Rives's aversion to the institutionalization of party and his self-conscious adherence to eighteenth-century republican values, is Jean E. Friedman, *The Revolt of the Conservative Democrats: An Essay on American Political Culture and Political Development, 1837–1844* (Ann Arbor, Mich., 1979).

12 The quoted phrase is from one of Rives's Senate speeches, reported in the *National Intelligencer*, Feb. 12, 1839.

William Cabell Rives, c. 1839. Lithograph by Charles Fenderich. Admirers of Rives who purchased this likeness found printed at the bottom an extract from one of his Senate speeches: "In taking this course, I know full well, Mr. President, I am to incur the anathemas of Party. But I can never forget that I have a COUNTRY to serve, as well as a PARTY to obey." (Courtesy of the Library of Congress, Prints and Photographs Division)

Rives had become a Madisonian in the late 1820s. While it would be going too far to say that the young congressman underwent a fundamental transformation during these years, Madison's influence on Rives was both palpable and profound. Many circumstances brought the two men together, including Rives's earlier close ties to Jefferson, who had introduced his young pupil to John Adams in

1814 as "an éleve of mine in law, of uncommon abilities, learning and worth" who "will be in the zenith of his fame and usefulness" when "you and I shall be at rest with our friends of 1776."[13] Madison appears to have shared Jefferson's high expectations for Rives, with whom he developed a close relationship during his retirement years. Castle Hill – which Rives inherited after his marriage in 1819 to Judith Walker, a granddaughter of Jefferson's guardian, Thomas Walker – was less than twenty miles from Montpelier, which encouraged frequent visits; Madison customarily paid a call, for instance, during his journeys to and from Charlottesville for meetings of the board of visitors of the new university.[14] As a staunch Jeffersonian, of course, Rives had always venerated Jefferson's "junior partner," but their extensive personal contact, especially after the senior partner's demise in 1826, infused new meaning into the relationship. Rives's political persuasion was never quite the same. Most important, his career diverged significantly from the path he appeared to have been traveling.[15]

After several terms in the Virginia House of Delegates, the young lawyer and planter had first run for Congress in 1823 as a fervent advocate of pure Jeffersonianism – which is to say, of state rights and of the agrarian society that the elderly Jefferson, especially, anxiously sought to preserve in the Old Dominion. In the waning years

13 Jefferson to Adams, May 18, 1814, copy in Rives Papers, Library of Congress, box 42.
14 See, for example, Madison to Rives, July 1, 1828, *ibid.*, box 44. In her manuscript autobiography, Rives's wife, Judith, described the visits between Montpelier and Castle Hill and commented that Rives's and Madison's collaboration on the affairs of the university, "by bringing them into closer relations, cemented the intimacy already established between them." This document is in box 103 of the Rives Papers in the Library of Congress; see the paragraphs beginning on page 54.
15 There is no biography of Rives, a remarkable lacuna in the historiography of politics in antebellum America. The single best source is a partial life, which covers his career in national politics through 1844. See Raymond C. Dingledine, "The Political Career of William Cabell Rives," unpub. Ph.D. diss., University of Virginia, 1947. Commenting on the close friendship that developed between Rives and Madison during the mid and late 1820s, Dingledine appropriately observes that "Madison, more than Jefferson, became his political godfather" (p. 107).

of the Monroe administration, sounding a great deal like the increasingly doctrinaire and provincial Sage of Monticello himself, Rives had blasted the predatory manufacturing interests of the northern and eastern states, who were seeking, he charged, to victimize the southern states by "arbitrarily transferring wealth and property from one class of the community to another." Rives told his prospective constituents in Amherst County that tariff (and internal improvement) laws were not merely "partial and unequal"; they were unconstitutional as well, patent violations of the sacred compact ratified in the late 1780s – and secured in the glorious "Revolution of 1800" – that had provided for a federal government of strictly limited powers. Appropriately, he vowed as their representative to protect Virginians from their northern enemies and to resist this alarming "spirit of self-aggrandizement" in "our national councils."[16]

Once in Congress, Rives behaved just like the Virginia particularist and the ardent proponent of state rights that he had advertised himself to be. An outspoken and bitter critic of President John Quincy Adams and an early supporter of Andrew Jackson, he became a partisan zealot, opposing with great alacrity just about every administration initiative. In early 1826, for instance, Rives spearheaded congressional opposition to President Adams's and Secretary of State Henry Clay's proposal to send American delegates to Central America to meet with leaders from the new Latin American republics, branding this "Panama Mission" an "extraordinary and dangerous project," part and parcel of the dreaded "American System."[17] (Writing to Lafayette about the controversy several months later, Madison, who very much supported American participation in a hemispheric conference, bemoaned the "mortifying scenes" produced by the fever of party spirit in Congress.)[18] By early 1827, the partisan Rives was passionately resisting what he considered "a strong, steady, and increasing proclivity to monarchy" in the federal

16 See Rives, Address to Citizens of Amherst County, Mar. 1823, in Rives Papers, Library of Congress, box 119, and Address to Citizens of Albemarle County, April 1823, *ibid*.
17 Rives to T. W. Gilmer, Mar. 27, 1826, printed in *Tyler's Quarterly Historical Magazine* 5 (1923–24), 227. See also Rives's speeches in Congress at this time.
18 Madison to Lafayette, Nov. 1826, in Gaillard Hunt, ed., *The Writings of James Madison* (New York and London, 1900–1910), IX, 264.

government.[19] He had only been a young boy at the time, but for Rives, this was the crisis of 1798–1800 revisited; and as the election of 1828 approached, he took the lead in mobilizing the Old Dominion in defense of the sacred principles of the pure Jeffersonian faith. By this time, however, Jefferson himself was gone, and only Madison remained to help Rives refine his understanding of that faith. This made all the difference in the world.

Under Madison's tutelage in the late 1820s, Rives outgrew the provincial extremism of his youth. Above all, he abandoned the notion that federal tariff laws were unconstitutional, which clarified considerably his broader conception of the Jeffersonian tradition of "state rights." By early 1829, as we have seen in an earlier chapter, Rives decried not only the abusive treatment of Madison in the newspapers, but the extreme rhetoric of protest against the tariff that came from Georgia and especially South Carolina.[20] He emphatically condemned "the assumption of novel and extravagant doctrines" and the threat of "violent and disorganizing measures," imploring other Virginians not to follow the lead of deep South extremists. Rives now believed that the constitutional theory of these fanatics was unsound, and he also placed the matter in another revealing context: he had decided that Virginia must consider itself a northern, as much as a southern, state. Doubtless thinking of debate over the slave trade at the Constitutional Convention, when the South Carolinians had insisted on leaving the nefarious commerce open for at least another twenty years, Rives denied that there had ever been a cordial congeniality of feeling between Virginia and her southern neighbors. More important, looking to the future, he insisted that "there is, and must be, a variance of policy & interest on several important questions." These differences included "the *final* destination of our black population" – Rives was confident that slavery would prove to be an evanescent phenomenon in the Old Dominion – as well as "the direction of our industry and pursuits" –

19 Rives's Feb. 20, 1827, speech in the House of Representatives, as reported in *Register of Debates*, 19th Cong., 2d sess., 1270. For elaboration of these views, see Rives's private correspondence throughout 1826, 1827, and much of 1828, especially his letters to Thomas Walker Gilmer of Albemarle County.
20 See Chapter 4 of this volume, pp. 119–123.

here he assumed that Virginia, unlike the cotton states, would soon turn to manufacturing – and "our relations with our sister states & the Union." Writing from Washington on New Year's Day, 1829, the congressman neatly summarized his new perspective: "My experience here, and every day's reflection, convinces me that the clear interest of Virginia is to look to the North rather than the South, for friendly connections and allies, in all her moral, political, and commercial transactions."[21]

Rives believed, indeed, that "the encouragement of manufacturing industry" among Virginians was imperative and should therefore become "a most important point" in the policy not of the federal government in Washington, but of the state legislature in Richmond. The "best security" for Virginia's fidelity to the Union, he told one of the delegates, was precisely to give her "every possible *interest*" in the preservation of close ties with her northern neighbors. And Rives was convinced, above all, that "the great desideratum in Virginia politics" was "prudence, moderation, forecast, & *practical* counsels." He did not doubt that ambitious, scheming politicians from the deep South, using the tariff issue as leverage, would attempt to dismember the Union. Whether they would be able "to get their own people to go along with them" was unclear; "but at all events," he pleaded, "let not Virginia go with them." For Rives, there was only one way for the Old Dominion to honor her past, as well as her destiny. "Her interest," he insisted, "must ever be to remain in that union, of which she may be considered, emphatically, the founder."[22]

These ideas mark the first clear expresssion of what we might call the "Madisonized" Rives. Like his mentor, Rives began to conceive of a Virginia that was as much northern as southern, that would have extensive manufactures and no slaves (indeed no blacks), and that above all would endure as a vital pillar of the most precious republican legacy of all: the Union of 1787. If Rives had his way, loyal Virginians would continue to honor the Constitution as it had been understood at the time of its founding, solemnly respecting the

21 Rives to W. M. Rives, Jan. 1, 1829, in Rives Papers, Library of Congress, box 45.
22 Rives to W. M. Rives, Jan. 8, 1829, *ibid*.

Jeffersonian tradition of a federal government of limited powers and the genuine doctrine of state rights; but they would also oppose base perversions of that legacy which jeopardized the fundamental achievement of the Revolutionary generation. Like Madison, Rives also began to display an intense suspicion of passionate partisanship in politics. He made a fetish of prudence and moderation – in effect, Madisonian reason and restraint – as the essence of republican state-craft. In all of these ways, Rives's response to the emergence of the nullification movement in the late 1820s, a response decisively shaped by Madison's presence, became the crucible in which his mature political identity was forged.

Since Rives was abroad as American minister to France during most of Jackson's first administration, the significance of his revised posture was not immediately apparent. But not long after his return to the United States in the fall of 1832 at the height of the nullification crisis, the newly Madisonized Rives emerged with unmistakable clarity, much to the surprise – and horror – of some of his fellow Virginians. Perhaps there is no better measure of the distance that Rives had traveled since his early years in Congress than the sudden deterioration of his relationship with Thomas Walker Gilmer, once his political protégé and close friend. During the heyday of his opposition to the Adams administration, Rives had groomed the even younger Gilmer (to whom he was connected by marriage) as his potential successor in Congress, drilling him on the politics of state rights and Adams-hating.[23] Gilmer soon became a leader of the faction in Virginia politics most sympathetic to the South Carolina incendiaries. Following Rives's return from France in late 1832, Gilmer helped arrange his old adviser's election to the United States Senate. When some Virginia legislators balked at voting for Rives, complaining that the returning diplomat was equivocal on the tariff issue – he declined, they charged (correctly), to condemn it on constitutional as well as on expedient grounds – Gilmer reassured them that his friend could be trusted. But two

23 The Rives–Gilmer relationship can best be followed in their correspondence of this period; see, for instance, the letters printed in *Tyler's Quarterly Historical Magazine* 5 (1923–24), 223–237; 6 (1924–25), 6–15 and 97–105; and 7 (1925–26), 203–207.

months later, Senator Rives took an emphatic stand in Washington against the South Carolina dissidents and committed the unpardonable sin of voting for President Jackson's "Force Bill" – for which acts, Gilmer and others noted with unconcealed disdain, he was showered with praise from a most disreputable colleague, the personification of New England Federalism himself, Senator Daniel Webster of Massachusetts.

An enraged Gilmer, who had recently dismissed Madison's public letter against nullification as "trash," found Rives's behavior inexplicable, a disgraceful betrayal, he said, of the pure Jeffersonianism that Rives had preached to him during the Adams administration. The two men publicly fell out, and at the courthouse in Charlottesville in early July 1833, their feud erupted into violence. Gilmer showed his contempt for Rives by trying to pull his nose (a ritual maneuver known among Virginians as "the Lieutenant Randolph outrage," after the man who had recently pulled President Jackson's nose); the senator responded by allegedly biting Gilmer's thumb before striking him with his horsewhip. After fisticuffs of a sort ensued, the diminutive Rives returned home to Castle Hill with a black eye – a badge, as it were, of Madison's influence and of his legatee's embattled status in his native state.[24]

Rives had gotten a rude taste of what he would be up against in Virginia politics for the rest of his career. As he attempted to articulate and defend a Madisonian strain of republicanism, he had always to contend with an alternative version of the past and hence of the future, one that embraced a very different understanding of both the Union and Virginia's republican heritage. Gilmer's perspective, like Thomas R. Dew's, pointed unmistakably toward a defense of slavery and toward an extreme doctrine of state rights that weakened, and sometimes defied, Rives's and Madison's commitment both to the principles of the Enlightenment and to the Constitution as the anchor of a national republican community. Indeed,

24 See Dingledine, "Political Career of William Cabell Rives," chap. 5, esp. 179–202. The hilariously complicated affair of the nose-pulling brawl – hardly an amusing or trivial matter to the principals – can be followed in the July and Aug. 1833 issues of the *Richmond Enquirer*; see esp. July 26 and Aug. 9. I am indebted to Kenneth Greenberg of Suffolk University for enlightening me on the significance of nose-pulling in antebellum Southern culture.

carried to its extreme, this alternative perspective could even attempt to drape the mantle of paternal orthodoxy over elements of southern society that Rives, like Madison, rejected as a matter of principle. In the end, the battle was over more than the meaning of the Constitution and America's republican revolution; it marked a dispute over what it meant to be a loyal Virginian. The courthouse brawl with Gilmer proved to be only the first skirmish in a war that Rives courageously waged for the next three decades.

In 1850 and again ten years later, Rives locked horns with the heirs of the nullifiers, a new generation of extremists – primarily but not exclusively from the deep South – who agitated secession and dreamed of a southern confederacy, often in the name of Jeffersonian orthodoxy. He continued to dispute their constitutional ideas, and he also fought their recruiting efforts in the Old Dominion by insisting that Virginia had much less in common with the cotton states than with its northern and western neighbors. When Rives developed these familiar themes, Madison was never far from his mind. In 1860, in order to buttress the argument that Virginia was heading in a very different direction from the cotton states of the deep South, Rives publicized one of his mentor's most important teachings in political economy. He published a "pregnant extract" from an 1833 letter in which Madison had explained that glutted markets for Virginia's agricultural surplus would inevitably stimulate the development of extensive manufactures; this situation did not obtain, according to Rives, where cotton, for which the demand was "universal and constantly progressive," was the staple crop.[25] Rives eagerly promoted the development of railroads and the general cause of economic diversification in his native state, especially in the 1850s, when, according to at least one twentieth-century economic historian, Virginia did in fact begin to assume more and more the character of a northern state.[26] He also remained confident that slavery, which he had always regarded as morally indefensible,

25 See *Letter from the Hon. William Cabell Rives to a Friend, On the Important Questions of the Day* (Richmond, 1860), 14–16. For the expression of similar views during the crisis of 1850, see especially Rives to Alexander Rives, Mar. 27, 1850, in Rives Papers, Library of Congress, box 29.
26 See Avery Odell Craven, *Soil Exhaustion as a Factor in the Agricultural History of Virginia and Maryland, 1606–1860* (Urbana, Illinois, 1925), esp. 122–160.

would eventually disappear from the Old Dominion. This prediction, too, was at least modestly borne out by some of the trends of the 1850s, when the relative size of Virginia's slave population declined.[27] In 1847, Rives even tried to entice some New Yorkers, whose advanced techniques of husbandry he greatly admired, to migrate to Virginia. "A colony of industrious, intelligent & successful farmers, planted among us, from the North," he speculated, could indeed have an "important effect" in a state that so desperately needed their superior example.[28]

Meanwhile, Rives's personal connections were also broadening to encompass more and more of the world north of Virginia. By the outbreak of the Civil War, three of his five children had married northerners and were living much of the time outside their native state — a fact that hardly went unnoticed in the Old Dominion, where the entire Rives family eventually became suspect. Rives himself spent a great deal of time visiting family in New York and New England, where he cemented old friendships from his days in Congress. Back in 1814, when he had made his first trip to the northern states as an arrogant and provincial young man, he had made no effort to disguise his contempt for Madison's alma mater in Princeton. He described it in his travel journal as utterly inferior in every respect to Virginia's great college in Williamsburg.[29] Thirty years later, Rives removed one of his own sons from Mr. Jefferson's riot-plagued university in Charlottesville and sent him north to study law with Supreme Court Justice Joseph Story at Harvard. Writing to that son in 1849, Rives congratulated him for his deci-

27 See, for instance, the statistics analyzed in Alison Goodyear Freehling, *Drift Toward Dissolution: The Virginia Slavery Debate of 1831–1832* (Baton Rouge, La., 1982), 245–246.

28 Rives to John Nicholas, Mar. 4, 1847, in Rives Papers, Library of Congress, box 76. Evidence of Rives's promotion of railroads, as well as of his dedication to agricultural improvement, is scattered throughout his papers for the 1850s. See also Dingledine, "Political Career of William Cabell Rives," chap. 9. For a typical expression of Rives's notion that slavery was destined to disappear from Virginia, see Rives to Robert C. Winthrop, Mar. 5, 1857, in Winthrop Papers, Massachusetts Historical Society.

29 "Fragments of a Journal," New York, June 21, 1814, in Rives Papers, Library of Congress, box 120.

sion to settle down with his new wife, Grace Winthrop Sears, in her native city. After rattling off the names of his many good friends in New England, Rives offered a paean to Boston: "There is no city in the Union which, in my opinion, deserves so much to be admired & studied for its excellent public Institutions of every kind, or is so much embalmed in historical associations connected with our great struggle for liberty."[30] With so many of the Riveses in Boston, he once quipped, the family amply demonstrated its "great partiality for *northern Virginia*."[31]

No wonder Rives incurred the reputation, at least among Virginians of Gilmer's stripe, of having become a traitor to his state. As one of his brothers warned him in early 1851, when Rives was out of the country, "some of your political compatriots are eyeing you askance, and suspecting you of a want of loyalty to Virginia and too great devotion to the Yankees." Indeed, now that "a belief in the virtues of African Slavery, and the absolute inferiority of the Yankee race to southern bloods" had become "so fashionable," poor Rives was apparently doomed, according to his brother, to suffer "under the ban of this suspicion."[32] The ultimate indignity would come ten years later, when, during the first summer of the great war, Rives had to defend his three "northern" offspring from relegation to the status of "alien enemies."[33]

Rives dismissed these persistent charges of disloyalty as unfounded and even contemptible. He considered himself and his family, no matter where individuals might choose to live, utterly

30 Rives to W. C. Rives, Jr., Feb. 2, 1849, *ibid.*, box 29. For a perceptive discussion of the young Rives's education, see Raymond C. Dingledine, "The Education of a Virginia Planter's Son," in John B. Boles, ed., *America: The Middle Period; Essays in Honor of Bernard Mayo* (Charlottesville, Va., 1973), 216–228.

31 Rives to Robert C. Winthrop, Feb. 8, 1846, in Winthrop Papers, Massachusetts Historical Society.

32 Alexander Rives to W. C. Rives, Feb. 6, 1851, in Rives Papers, Library of Congress, box 30.

33 The voluminous correspondence between Rives (and his wife) and the children is generally found in the boxes labelled "Family Correspondence," *ibid.* Biographical details are conveniently provided in Rives's memoranda of 1861, drawn up to refute the "alien enemy" charges; see, for instance, the handwritten biographical sketches in box 36.

faithful to Virginia's finest heritage, especially as the founding pillar of a political Union that joined all Americans in one country and culture. And in politics he hardly took the "Yankee" position on the crucial issues, anyway. His posture was that of a conservative Unionist who defended, from an appropriate historical perspective, the legitimate rights of Virginia and the other southern states. Insisting that the Constitution must mean to the present generation what it had generally meant to its founders, he invoked his mentor as his authority. Appropriately, the second volume of Rives's biography of Madison was as much a general history of the confederation period as it was the life of a single man. And in the preface, especially, Rives preached the inseparability of a sensitive appreciation of the 1780s and a correct understanding of the American regime: "The history of this period, Mr. Madison was accustomed to say, is like the preamble to a statute, – the *key* to a true conception and just interpretation of the Constitution, unlocking and revealing the practical evils it was framed to remedy, and which must ever be kept in mind in seeking its legitimate sense and operation."[34]

This historical approach to interpreting the Constitution generally served Rives – and the interests of the southern states – quite well indeed. Unlike Coles, who was determined to make the Founding Fathers into incipient Republicans, Rives correctly grasped Madison's complex position on the constitutionality of restricting slavery in the territories.[35] And with only a few explicit exceptions, according to Madison's biographer, the founding generation had not conferred upon Congress the power to interfere with the domestic institutions, including slavery, of the individual states. He therefore warned northerners throughout the 1850s that they must respect the spirit of the Constitution, which meant the general sense and under-

34 William C. Rives, *History of the Life and Times of James Madison* (Boston, 1866), II, vi. Although this second volume was not published until just after the Civil War, it had been ready for the press several years earlier.
35 See the intriguing correspondence between Rives and Robert C. Winthrop in 1856, some of which was printed at the time; Rives to Winthrop, June 16, 1856, in Winthrop Papers, Massachusetts Historical Society; Winthrop to Rives, June 24, 1856, in Rives Papers, Library of Congress, box 87; Rives to Winthrop, July 12, 1856, *ibid.*, box 88; and Winthrop to Rives, July 16, 1856, *ibid.*

standing of the people who had ratified it, as well as its explicit provisions, both of which were rooted in the history of the early republic. Southerners had approved the Constitution only with solemn guarantees of their rights and safety, an understanding that northerners at the time had fully accepted; all parties had understood and embraced, in short, the necessary accommodations that made a viable Union possible. Now this "general wisdom" of "our Fathers" had to be honored by the present generation of northerners who, in addition to agitating the slavery issue, recklessly ignored their constitutional obligations regarding fugitive slaves by passing obnoxious "personal liberty" laws. Indeed, Rives warned that if southern Americans were pushed too hard and too long by this "species of political fanaticism" – which had been unknown, of course, "to the better days of the Republic" – they might be driven to take revolutionary action.[36]

Rives pleaded, therefore, for a return to the wholesome spirit of compromise, to that statesmanlike ethos of prudent restraint – to the submergence of all fanaticism, North and South – that had allowed Madison's generation to launch the great experiment. And like Madison in his final years, Rives stoically retained faith that the Union of the Fathers could indeed endure the most explosive trials of a new age; it was only necessary, he said time and again, that their descendants adhere to traditional wisdom and to the example of the past. They must elevate reason over passion, transcend the insistent pressures of party spirit, and sensibly grasp the essential benefits of remaining one people. Indefatigable in his efforts to convey this message to fellow southerners as well as to northerners, Rives even invited southern members of Congress, at one juncture of the sectional crisis, to peruse Madison's papers. Here was a priceless treasure that would reveal, he promised, the origins of the Constitution "in one grand scheme of wise and patriotic compromise." Only this sound grasp of history could expose the consummate folly of all

36 Rives, "Considerations Against a Light Disturbance of the Provisions of the Constitution," n.d., *ibid.*, box 120. For another characteristic statement of these broad themes to a northern audience, see Rives to Edward Everett, Dec. 27, 1859, *ibid.*, box 90. See also, on the fugitive slave issue, Rives to W. C. Rives, Jr., Nov. 29, 1860, *ibid.*, box 35.

reckless attempts, according to Rives, "to alter or displace any part of a structure so painfully, so laboriously, so miraculously raised."[37]

Rives defended this Madisonian position for as long as it could be defended – until, that is, the cause of Union was irretrievably lost. In the fateful election of 1860, he supported the "Constitutional Union" ticket of John Bell of Tennessee, for president, and his old friend Edward Everett, of Massachusetts, for vice-president. Rives even gave the ersatz party its Madisonian name.[38] And after the Republican victory had triggered the first wave of secessions running from South Carolina through the Gulf states, he valiantly assumed the roles of elder statesman and crisis manager. In January 1861 he pushed himself away from the Madison papers and journeyed to Washington, where he buttonholed as many of the political heavyweights, including the Republican leader William Henry Seward, as he could. Rives's wife reported at the time that her husband seemed "to dread the dogmatical rule of the secessionists as much as the pragmatical intermeddling of the abolitionists, and would like to be at the queue of neither."[39] But this precious middle ground was rapidly eroding. On a return trip to Washington as a member of the so-called "Peace Conference," Rives even had an opportunity to meet with president-elect Lincoln. Unfortunately, Lincoln, who knew Rives only by reputation, greeted the proud Virginian by marvelling at how short he was, joking that he had mistakenly imagined the great William Cabell Rives to be "at least six feet high." When the ruffled Rives politely responded that, standing next to Lincoln, he felt like a very small man indeed, the president-elect bellowed back that "you are any how a giant in intellect." The intellectual giant found the western bumpkin "good-natured & well-intentioned, but utterly unimpressed with the gravity of the crisis & the magnitude of his duties."[40]

37 Rives, "Paper Prepared for Meeting of Southern Members of Congress," n.d., *ibid.*, box 120.

38 See Dingledine, "Political Career of William Cabell Rives," 476–478.

39 Judith Rives to W. C. Rives, Jr., Jan. 14, 1861, in Rives Papers, Library of Congress, box 36. See also Judith Rives to Alfred L. Rives, Jan. 21, 1861, in Alfred Landon Rives Papers, Duke University.

40 Rives to W. C. Rives, Jr., Feb. 24, 1861, in Rives Papers, Library of Congress, box 36.

Throughout March and April of 1861 Rives struggled heroically in Richmond to keep Madison's state loyal to the covenant of 1787. Back in January, he had advised leading Republicans in Washington not to try to reinforce Fort Sumter, since the time had long passed when such vigorous action might have stopped the mad course of the deep South extremists. Three months later, the Confederate firing on Sumter and Lincoln's call for troops — the latter of which Rives condemned as "a very silly act, & on its face illegal & void" — mercifully terminated the almost unbearable agony of Virginia's watchful waiting.[41] Even after the ordinance of secession, which he never formally approved, Rives refused to despair. Displaying the kind of optimism characteristic of his old mentor, he expressed confidence that the reign of passion would soon pass, and that reason and Union could promptly be restored. "I have a firm persuasion myself," Rives told his son in Boston, "that a christian people will never permit our present unhappy difficulties to go to the extremity of civil war. Every good & wise man should now exert himself to make the separation, which seems inevitable, a peaceable one." Such restraint would afford, indeed, "the best prospect of an ultimate re-union."[42]

Yet if Rives managed to remain upbeat and even optimistic in letters to his children, he betrayed a more solemn cast of mind when he wrote to another Bostonian, Robert C. Winthrop. Like Rives, Winthrop had been edged out of the limelight of national politics in the 1850s by less moderate elements from his own section. Rives first apologized for not having written to Winthrop for quite some time; he had received a letter from the former Whig senator and speaker of the House of Representatives the previous winter, but had simply been too busy to answer. Now, with Virginia's ordinance of secession before him, Rives had no more time to spare. Both men were conservative Unionists; they had always aired their political differences, privately and publicly, in a mutually respectful and civilized fashion, and Rives knew that Winthrop must mourn Virginia's loss to the Union as deeply as he. He thought it appropriate,

---

41 Rives to W. C. Rives, Jr., April 20, 1861, and Judith Rives to W. C. Rives, Jr., Jan. 14, 1861, *ibid.*
42 Rives to W. C. Rives, Jr., April 22, 1861, *ibid.*

therefore, to convey his enduring respect as well as his fervent hope that their friendship might somehow survive the present troubles.

Rives also presented Winthrop with a more tangible token of his affection and esteem: an inscribed copy of the first volume of his *Life of Madison*. "The political troubles of the country have, of late, a good deal interrupted the prosecution of this work," he confessed to his Massachusetts friend, "but I must now return to it." If their countrymen had gone mad, at least the past was safely removed from the contagion. Now more than ever, Rives could find no better compensation for the "degeneracy of those who have proved themselves unworthy of the precious legacy bequeathed to them" than in doing what he enjoyed most – "contemplating the virtues & wisdom of our ancestors."[43]

II

Wise and virtuous ancestors, degenerate and unworthy sons. Absorbed in his filiopietism, Rives never seriously considered the possibility that the Fathers were part of the problem – or, more precisely, that their legacy might mislead as well as inspire. Blaming the crisis of the Union on the failure of wild-eyed sons in both sections to honor the wisdom of the past, Rives became a prisoner of the conservative tradition he worshipped. Obviously circumstances outran his intellectual and political grasp; but his predicament also arose from the intrinsic weakness – indeed the inherent pitfalls and dangers – of the Madisonian legacy that he strove so faithfully to honor in the quarter-century between Madison's death and the collapse of the Union.

Rives's nearly obsessive concern about the need for responsible leadership in a republic, especially in a newly democratized America, is powerfuly reminiscent of Madison's eighteenth-century vision. The legatee's professed distrust of partisanship was linked to a larger array of concerns about the character of public life amid the modern conditions of unrestricted suffrage and professional party

---

43 Rives to Winthrop, April 19, 1861, in Winthrop Papers, Massachusetts Historical Society.

345

politics. He fretted, too, about the unstable character of a republic in which landed independence was no longer as widespread as it had been in the world of the Fathers. This conservative, elitist strain of republicanism honored values that Rives came to associate more and more not only with Madison, but with a distant, irretrievable past. But it also harbored the ugly potential to degenerate into a contempt for democracy itself. Actually, the elderly Madison had accommodated himself and his vision to these largely unavoidable changes to a greater extent than had his pupil.[44] In the case of the legatee, nostalgia for a better world and frustrated ambition informed a conservative republicanism that ultimately went sour.

Rives's biography of Madison was a protracted lament for a lost republican world in which the worst evils of democracy had been consciously averted. In Madison's time, Rives contended, "the controlling power" in America had been exercised not, as it now was, by "the whole mass of inhabitants without regard to special qualifications of fitness or common interest," but rather solely by those who had "a real stake in the common weal."[45] This was the difference between a democracy, which Rives explicitly condemned, and a republic, which Madison and the Fathers had attempted to build and which Rives now defended. Indeed, Rives elaborated the differences between republicanism and democracy for his youthful, untutored readers who, having grown up in "the latter and degenerate days of the Republic," knew only the latter corrupt form.[46] He itemized "the visible and pernicious manifestations of democratic rule" to include "universal suffrage, frequent and exciting popular elections of every description and grade of public functionaries, an elective and dependent judiciary, [and] the subjection of both private rights and public trusts to the absolute and unchecked control of capricious, interested, or blind as well as irresponsible majorities." The "distinguishing and beneficent characteristics of a republic," on the other hand, restored a proper balance in all of these areas; they included "regulated and qualified suffrage in the election of representatives, the choice of other functionaries by select and intermediate agencies, an independent judiciary, reciprocal checks

44 See the earlier discussion in this volume, especially Chapter 5.
45 Rives, *Life of Madison*, II, 326n–327n.   46 *Ibid.*, III, 36.

and balances between the different departments of delegated power, [and] the living and sole supremacy of the law and the constitution, guarding alike the rights of minorities and majorities."[47]

We might say that Rives had a remarkably sound appreciation of what Madison and the Founders had tried to achieve in the late eighteenth century. But he also overlooked the extent to which an elderly Madison, notwithstanding his continued commitment to conservative values, had accepted as necessary and even just the democratization of that republic. Rives's message as historian was quite simple: the republic had declined because unworthy sons had betrayed the precious legacy of the Founders and resorted to all kinds of reckless innovations. They had turned to universal suffrage, to an indiscriminate admission of foreigners to citizenship (Rives had become a champion of nativism in the 1850s), and to the selection of presidents by illegitimate and irresponsible party conventions, one of which, not incidentally, had denied Rives his due in 1835.[48] The result, of course, was the Civil War — "an awful lesson," Rives told his son, "of what may be affected in a popular government, when the check is lost of a few controlling spirits to whom the people had become accustomed to follow, by the self-seeking & venal agency of low-minded & intriguing politicians."[49] Yes, there had once been giants in the land — natural aristocrats like Madison, statesmen whose philosophical tastes and pursuits were "so much in contrast with the feverish and unremitting excitements, and the all-absorbing professional monomania, of the modern politician's life."[50] Moreover, Americans had once had the restraint and good sense to defer to them. Now they had instead a vicious leveling system that scrambled this republican hierarchy and elevated mediocrity to prominence. According to Rives, they had gotten exactly what they deserved: Abraham Lincoln.

Perhaps Rives never went quite so far as one of his sons, who described Lincoln in early 1861 (apparently after having seen him in

---

47 *Ibid.*, II, 327–328n.
48 *Ibid.*, chap. 36, esp. 619–621.
49 Rives to W. C. Rives, Jr., May 22, 1866, in Rives Papers, Library of Congress, box 37.
50 Rives, *Life of Madison*, II, 3.

William Cabell Rives, Patriarch. Photographer and date unknown. (Courtesy of the Library of Congress, Manuscripts Division)

New York) as "a hideous half-civilized creature, of great length of figure – in color like a rotten pumpkin or Mississippi sediment – & of a certain smartish grotesque obscenity of mind shut off from all light." But he certainly went as far as his wife, who dismissed the westerner in the summer of 1861 as an ignorant rail-splitter who, in Madison's time, might have been considered a useful citizen but nothing more than that – certainly not a man qualified, by background, manner, or education, to be president.[51] Indeed, Rives saw in Lincoln nothing more than republicanism run amok, a fitting example of how a riotous and boorish people, misled by hack politicians and demagogues, could elevate an amiable clown to a position of such momentous responsibility. His contempt for the unrefined Lincoln – a natural aristocrat in the eighteenth-century sense of that concept, if ever there was one – betrays more than the poor judgment that Rives shared with many of his contemporaries who, even if they voted for Lincoln, were generally slow to recognize or appreciate his genius. It reflects as well a conservatism that had become indistinguishable from rank snobbery and a contempt for democracy itself.

Rives's conservative concern for social stability and responsible leadership had the potential to turn sour in yet another way: it inevitably created the temptation to embrace chattel slavery as a solution to so many of the problems that threatened, in his judgment, to corrupt a civilized republic into a barbaric democracy. Rives clearly understood (as Madison evidently had once said at length in his presence) that, in a schematic view of society, the slaves were analogous to the propertyless laboring class in the free states. He also appeared to understand that this enslavement of the working class in the South profoundly affected not only the character of southern society but the political values of its propertied – that is, free – citizens.[52] As we have seen, Madison lived long enough to

---

51 Francis R. Rives to W. C. Rives, Jr., Mar. 13, 1861, in Rives Papers, Library of Congress, box 36; Mrs. William Cabell Rives, autobiography (manuscript prepared in the summer of 1861), *ibid.*, box 103.

52 For evidence of Madison discussing this issue in Rives's presence, see the sketch about a recent visit to Montpelier, reprinted from the Washington, D.C., *National Intelligencer*, in the *Richmond Enquirer*, June 28, 1833.

hear some southern reactionaries suggest that slavery was an indispensable source of public order in the modern age, a solution to the working class problem, indeed the necessary basis for a stable republic. Rives, as his legatee, inherited the burden of refuting this horrendous claim when the few quiet voices of Madison's final years swelled into a deafening, intimidating chorus.

Here Rives fought a noble and courageous battle on behalf of Revolutionary tradition. But there is also evidence of his own struggle to resist an argument that, given his conservative inclinations and concerns, also attracted his sympathy. Only Rives's passionate loyalty to what he correctly understood to be a vital dimension of the Madisonian legacy — its utter repudiation of slavery as violating republican principles and fundamental human rights — prevented him from embracing the position that scholars now refer to as "the pro-slavery argument." And eventually, it seems, the pressure simply became too great: on at least one occasion during the horrible war that he blamed on democracy, Rives publicly suggested that experience had caused him to alter his position on slavery.

Thomas Jefferson's favorite granddaughter, a thoughtful and impressive young woman whose condemnations of slavery did full justice to her inherited idealism, once unwittingly but eloquently voiced the ambivalence that ultimately got the better of Rives. Ellen Randolph Coolidge had married a Boston merchant in 1825, and after ten years of living in New England, which she generally admired, she occasionally felt homesick enough for Virginia society to turn on her adopted home. Writing to her brother-in-law Nicholas Trist less than a month before Madison died, she described Boston as a horrible city, with foul weather, mean-spirited people, and rude servants. With labor so expensive that the "work-people" were "as insolent and reluctant as if they were serving you gratis," an exasperated Ellen Coolidge longed for the Old Dominion: "I am tired," she confessed to Trist, "of cold weather and democracy."[53] In the same month, Rives received a letter from a disillusioned Philadelphian, fearful of the eruption of a "War of Classes" in that city, complaining in a similar vein about the unruliness of urban working people.

53 Ellen R. Coolidge to Trist, June 2, 1836, in Nicholas P. Trist Papers, Southern Historical Collection, University of North Carolina at Chapel Hill.

Rives replied that he was "not unmindful of some of the inconveniences" to which his northern correspondent, who frankly preferred European to American society, was exposed in "domestic & social relations." So he offered some advice: "Come, then, to the 'old dominion,' & take up your domicil among us, where, I assure you, from the peculiar structure of our society, we experience none of the inconveniences you bewail." Rives's correspondent, having chided the prominent Jacksonian leader for his democratic beliefs, had the last and perhaps most penetrating word: "If I had been born in Virginia, I might perhaps have been a democrat – if Mr. Rives had lived in Philadelphia I think he would not be one, and am sure he would at least, scorn the party that bears that name in our City."[54]

If Rives understood, in the mid-1830s, that slavery made possible the kind of stable environment that nourished his liberal views in politics and, in a broader sense, his confidence in republicanism, he refused to acknowledge the connection. Or, more precisely, he refused to elevate it to the level of principle. Obviously too much was at stake. A scant seven months after his letter to his Philadelphia friend (written coincidentally on the day before Madison died), Senator Rives listened as his colleague from South Carolina, John C. Calhoun, citing the sorry evidence of the northern experiment "with almost a pure and unlimited democracy," unabashedly defended slavery as a positive good. An appalled Rives promptly berated Calhoun for applauding slavery "in the abstract" – he adamantly refused to condone this "new school" of southern ideas that praised slavery as "an essential ingredient in republican government." Actually, Rives and Calhoun agreed that the South's peculiar interests must be protected, especially in the face of the avalanche of abolitionist propaganda that now jeopardized the region's security; but Rives also said he relied on the Constitution for that defense, without, like Calhoun, "going back to the exploded dogmas of Sir Robert Filmer." Indeed, Rives honored the Enlightenment as it was embodied in "the example of the greatest men and purest patriots who have illustrated the annals of our country – of the fathers of the

54 J. Francis Fisher to William Cabell Rives, June 8, 1836; Rives to Fisher, June 27, 1836; and Fisher to Judith Rives, Nov. 1, 1836, in Rives Papers, Library of Congress, box 54.

republic itself." Surely Calhoun had not forgotten an important lesson of history, that "it never entered into their minds, while laying the foundation of the great and glorious fabric of free Government, to contend that domestic slavery was a positive good – a great good."[55] Later in the same month, Calhoun and Rives went at each other again, this time, appropriately, over the issue of Congress's proposed purchase of Madison's papers.[56]

It would take the Civil War to convince Rives that Calhoun might have been right. More than twenty-five years later, in the winter of 1863, militant southerners were still taking Rives to task, remarkably, for his old oratorical duels with the South Carolinian. Facing charges that he had been slow to defend the South, and especially that in Congress during the 1830s he had expressed "heterodox sentiments" on the subject of slavery, the embattled Rives both clarified and modified his position. He told readers of the *Richmond Whig* that he had always been loyal to the interests of his state, and that in refusing to allow Calhoun to bully him into declaring slavery an unmixed good, he had merely acted in the great Virginia tradition. Now, however, he was also willing to admit that subsequent experience had rendered dubious the traditional wisdom that he had defended against the likes of Calhoun for so long. "After the exhibition we have seen for the last twenty years, of the operation of what is called free society in the Northern States of America," Rives conceded, "he must be a blind and unreflecting man, indeed, who has not been brought to question the practicability of maintaining Republican Government, with universal suffrage, in any community where the system of domestic servitude does not exist."[57]

Two years earlier, during the crisis winter of 1861, Rives's son in Boston had warned him that if Virginia were ultimately forced to secede, she must join the Confederacy on her own honorable terms. Only by rejecting "the mad and criminal causes of the Cotton States" – which now included a principled defense of slavery in the abstract

55 Rives and Calhoun in United States Senate, Feb. 6, 1837, in *Register of Debates*, 24th Cong., 2d sess., 717–722.
56 See Chapter 4 of this volume, pp. 167–170.
57 Rives, letter in *Richmond Whig*, Jan. 26, 1863, in Rives Papers, Library of Congress, box 105.

– could the Old Dominion unequivocally place herself *"in the right* in the eyes of the civilized world."[58] The elder Rives, of course, had never needed any such reminders; in the exchange with Calhoun in 1837, he had branded the proslavery argument an outrage to "the spirit of the age."[59] But the pressure of an irrational and partisan war engendered such bitter disillusionment – and so fueled his growing contempt for democracy – that even Rives eventually succumbed to this everpresent temptation to condone slavery as an essential pillar of republican stability. He came, apparently, to agree more with another son, living in New York, whose republican faith was shattered by the events of the early 1860s. "I have come to look upon republicanism," wrote Francis R. Rives, "as good in theory, as efficient under exceptional circumstances, but with a dense population tending directly to beastly democracy and a disgusting fickle despotism."[60] (At least Francis Rives, who died in 1891, did not live quite long enough to see his son, George Lockhart Rives, serve as chief attorney for the Rapid Transit Commission during the construction of the New York subway system.)[61]

The tragedy of William Cabell Rives's position on slavery actually ran far deeper. Before the war, his faithful adherence to the traditional wisdom of the Fathers exposed, in a variety of ways, the fundamental dilemma of Madisonian nationalism. By making the preservation of the Union his first priority and by insisting, in effect, that slavery be removed from the agenda of national political debate as a necessary condition of that Union, Rives consigned opponents of slavery outside the South to utter impotence and indeed silence. Rives put the matter quite bluntly to Edward Everett in late 1859: if northerners wished to continue in peaceful union with their southern brethren, they would have to desist immediately from all agitation regarding slavery and "leave the subject to the influence of time, & undisturbed reflection, in the hands of

58 W. C. Rives, Jr., to W. C. Rives, Jan. 21, 1861, *ibid.*, box 36. See also Rives, Jr., to Rives, April 30, 1861, *ibid.*
59 United States Senate, *Register of Debates*, 24th Cong., 2d sess., 722.
60 Francis R. Rives to W. C. Rives, Jr., Feb. 24, 1862, in Rives Papers, Library of Congress, box 36.
61 See entry for George Lockhart Rives, in Dumas Malone, ed., *Dictionary of American Biography* (New York, 1935), VIII, 634.

the communities under whose exclusive cognizance it is placed by the Constitution of the country."[62] Rives even tried to explain to skeptical northerners why his position – which might appear evasive as it pertained to the great moral issue at stake – was in fact an antislavery, rather than a proslavery, position. Indeed, he tried to have it both ways; the necessary means of preserving the Union was, as well, the only effective way of promoting an end to slavery, because northern interference, even when it came from reasonable and well-intentioned opponents of slavery, only compounded the problem and made its solution impossible.

Here Rives embraced a familiar litany of dubious arguments and evasions not unknown to Madison in his later years. Who was chiefly, even solely, responsible for the unfortunate revolution of opinion in the South that saw the emergence and burgeoning popularity of the disreputable proslavery argument? The abolitionists and other northern opponents of slavery, of course. Who made conditions for the poor slaves themselves much worse? As history demonstrated, the northern fanatics were the culprits yet again. According to Rives, in fact, a movement toward emancipation in the South had been gaining considerable momentum in the 1830s until northern fanaticism burst on the scene and destroyed this progress. The lesson was obvious. Agitation of the issue only made matters worse, and if left alone once again, southerners would return to the true faith of their Revolutionary fathers and put slavery on the road to ultimate extinction. Meanwhile, of course, the Union – which experience suggested might exist indefinitely half slave and half free (a point that Madison had confirmed in his parable of "Jonathan and Mary Bull") – would not have to be sacrificed to the devious scheming of ambitious politicians or to the importunate demands of fanatical idealists. Perhaps as a means of reviving confidence in the present generation, Rives even trotted out, in 1859, the venerable Madisonian fiction that slavery had initially been imposed on Virginians without their consent.[63]

Rives was supremely confident that in advancing these familiar views he was projecting both the wisdom and the idealism of his

62 Rives to Everett, Dec. 27, 1859, in Rives Papers, Library of Congress, box 90.
63 *Ibid.*

Revolutionary ancestors into a less enlightened age. Summarizing his position on the slavery question to his friend Robert Winthrop in 1857, he revealingly described it as "altogether *Madisonian*." "With regard to the coloured race," Rives reflected, "the true question, in both a philanthropic & political view, is not pro-slavery or anti-slavery, but the practical well-being of both races in the juxtaposition of which Providence has placed them on our continent." And where was "the only beneficent solution of that question" to be found? "In the free and spontaneous action of the State sovereignties, under the influence of a humane and enlightened public opinion, & the total abstinence of the national sovereignty from all interference." If northerners wondered where that humane and enlightened public opinion was now hiding in Madison's native South, they had merely to be patient and, above all, to realize that they were responsible for its temporary eclipse. The Revolutionary truth about the evil of slavery, Rives was confident, would commend itself "more & more to the moral & christian sentiments of the people of the south" if only they were "left undisturbed by abolitionist agitation." Under these circumstances, time and nature – "far more potent than any political combinations or Legislative solutions," according to Rives – would work their magic. Slavery would gradually disappear, in sum, when (and only if) "the national agitation," in both its free-soil and abolition forms, "could be made to cease."[64]

But with more and more southerners now taking Calhoun's, rather than Rives's, moral position on slavery, Rives could hardly expect to persuade skeptics that his was a formula for anything but the probable continuation of slavery. Nor could he expect a new generation of idealists merely to pledge allegiance to their ancestors' principles and to sustain Jefferson's and Madison's formulaic faith in "the influence of time." Obviously Rives was asking them to accept his – and Madison's – scale of priorities, which just as clearly involved admitting at least the possibility, if not the probability, that the institution of slavery would simply endure. By eloquently exposing the moral bankruptcy of that approach to honoring Madison and the Founding Fathers, Lincoln succeeded in attracting the votes not

64 Rives to Winthrop, Mar. 5, 1857, in Winthrop Papers, Massachusetts Historical Society.

only of Edward Coles and Nicholas Trist, but of a majority of northerners as well. Time proved Rives correct, however, on at least one count: the political triumph of Lincoln's version of an antislavery tradition was inconsistent with the peaceful continuation of a Union that the great Republican, as it turned out, venerated even more than he.

On the matter of race, moreover, Rives's regard for the natural right of all human beings to liberty respected familiar Madisonian limits. In his private affairs, Rives showed extraordinary concern for the well-being of his slaves who, as dependent members of the Castle Hill family, he judged worthy of his most affectionate solicitude. His wife nicely voiced their sense of obligation in 1858, when she opined that "we can only do our best with the poor people by whom we are surrounded, leaving the rest to that Providence which over-rules all."[65] Rives was also an ardent supporter of colonization. Active in the American Colonization Society as early as the 1820s, he consistently touted colonization as an appropriate means of ending slavery in the United States (without, he believed, antagonizing slaveholders) and above all as the best means of doing justice to the poor blacks while resolving the racial dilemma that "Providence" had contrived in North America. In the 1850s, Rives even accomplished something that Madison had not: he arranged for what appears to have been a substantial migration of his own slaves to Africa. To her son Alfred, Judith Rives described December 3, 1856, as the "day of departure of our Liberian colony"; it was also coincidentally the day of interment for a "good and faithful servant" (referred to as "Mammy" – and yes, Rives also owned, literally, an "Uncle Tom"). Both losses, she reported, greatly saddened everyone at Castle Hill.[66] But at least the Liberian pioneers took something of their Virginia heritage with them. Two years later, Judith Rives was amused – and perhaps not a little proud, as well – to read in the newspapers that "the Virginians" in Africa were said to be "too high

---

65 Judith Rives to W. C. Rives, Jr., Feb. 1, 1858, in Rives Papers, Library of Congress, box 35.

66 Judith Rives to Alfred L. Rives, Dec. 5, 1856, in Alfred Landon Rives Papers, Duke University. See also Judith Rives to W. C. Rives, Jr., Nov. 23, 1856, in Rives Papers, Library of Congress, box 34.

headed," always considering themselves "the *quality*" of their new country.[67]

It would be difficult for anyone who has perused the Rives family's papers — except, perhaps, for the most dogmatic of moral absolutists — to deny that they showed an impressive measure of genuine concern for their slaves' well-being. But their support of colonization — which they conceived of as a humanitarian gesture of opposition to slavery and of sympathy for the blacks — also belied a degree of racial contempt of which they were doubtless unaware. A thin veneer of antislavery idealism and principled humanitarianism could not obscure what appears to have been a more powerful desire to get rid not simply of the institution of slavery, but of the blacks themselves, to make Virginia, in short, the white man's republic that Madisonian rhetoric largely pretended it already was. Indeed, Rives sometimes appeared to think that the best way to abolish slavery in Virginia was much less complicated and vexing than going to the trouble of sending the blacks to the other side of the globe, where in theory they might prosper as free and proud citizens. They could always be shipped instead to the cotton states of the Southwest, where their labor was more profitable and therefore in greater demand; perhaps from there they would ultimately find their way out of the United States altogether, into a region where climate and nature generally suggested they belonged. In 1844, for instance, Rives supported the annexation of Texas in part because he thought "old Virginia will be benefitted by it." The addition of this territory to the United States would be a boon to the Old Dominion precisely by "facilitating the gradual transfer of our black population further south, & filling their places with the free white population of the north, who will come among us in ten-fold numbers, as soon as the process commences." Rives even accounted it "among the designs of Providence that slavery in the United States will finally terminate by the progressive flow of our black population into *Mexico*, where they will mix with & be lost in the not dissimilar Indian and Creole races of that border country."[68]

A few years later, during the War with Mexico, which he vig-

67 Judith Rives to W. C. Rives, Jr., Dec. 26, 1858, *ibid.*, box 35.
68 W. C. Rives to Judith Rives, April 3, 1844, *ibid.*, box 26.

357

orously opposed, Rives inadvertently clarified his view of black slaves in the United States when he explained why "the conquest & annexation of all Mexico" – which had plainly become the true object of the war – would create a nightmare for the American people. What would they do, after all, with "the eight millions of the mixed & degenerate castes" of that tropical land? Reduce them to bondage and "make serfs & slaves of them"? Hardly, Rives insisted, because "the spirit of the age, the genius of humanity revolts at it." But it was just as clear to him that these cultural primitives could not be admitted "to an equality of civil & political privileges with American freemen," because this, according to Rives, "would be to degrade the dignity & character of American citizens." In more practical terms, it would "endow an inferior race, incapable of enlightened freedom themselves, with capacities and attributes which would enable them, in the inevitable & constant recurrence of political divisions, to use their weight for the destruction of the common liberty." As free citizens, in other words, Mexicans would become as dangerous as any landless proletariat in Europe or in the northern United States. So if Rives imagined Afro-Americans eventually finding their appropriate homes in the midst of these Mexican mongrels whom they so much resembled, he also wanted to make sure that the happy union of the two peoples occurred outside the boundaries of the United States. The members of both "inferior" races were entitled to enjoy their natural right not to be serfs or slaves; but members of neither group were qualified to become participating citizens in America's great republican revolution.[69]

Rives's scenario of ending slavery by "diffusing" the slaves right out of the country involved, at least initially, selling slaves rather than freeing them – which is exactly what he began to do, on a major scale, during the national crisis of the autumn and winter of 1860–61. An inventory he prepared revealed that he owned 104 slaves – 47 males, and 57 females.[70] In October, Rives reported to his son in Boston: "I have not yet been able to conclude any negotiation for the disposal of our colored people, but am pursuing it

69 Rives, "Draft of an Address for the Whig Convention of Virginia in 1847–1848," *ibid.*, box 120.
70 Rives Papers, Library of Congress, Oct. 1860 file, box 91.

earnestly"; unfortunately, the "political agitation" of the day was creating "great backwardness & timidity with regard to all investments." A few months later, after his father reported considerable success in selling many of the family slaves, young Rives was profoundly relieved. He doubtless spoke for his father, too, when he reported, "I am but too thankful that the Nigs are gone."[71]

III

The ensuing war ultimately secured freedom for the Castle Hill blacks who remained as well as for those who were sold. It also took a dreadful toll on the entire Rives family. It is hardly surprising that when forced to choose in the spring of 1861, even the elder Rives, like other prominent Virginia Unionists, ultimately declared for his state. Nor is it surprising that he found a way of accommodating that capitulation to secession with his commitments to the past and to traditional republican ideals. Yet Rives himself must have been surprised to discover in late April 1861 that he had actually been appointed one of Virginia's delegates to the Congress of the Confederate States.

Accepting the appointment, he attempted to square his past behavior with his new office. As long as there had been "any hope of preserving the ancient union of the states on terms consistent with the rights & honor of the South," he explained, he had adhered to that Union "with the veneration & devotion which, from my earliest youth, I have ever cherished for the work of our fathers." But now Virginia – "the mother to whom I owe everything both of duty & affection" – had spoken, and "as a loyal & faithful son" he accepted the decision with all of its consequences. Indeed, "there is no time for looking back, or for vain regrets." In the short space of several weeks, Lincoln and his Republican cronies had perpetrated "acts of madness & infatuation of which there is no example in the records of official incompetence or delinquincy." Now, "invoking to their aid the blind & exterminating rage of party & sectional passions," the

71 Rives to W. C. Rives, Jr., Oct. 11, 1860, and W. C. Rives, Jr., to Rives, Dec. 1, 1860, *ibid.*, box 35.

new authorities in Washington "leave us no alternative but to stand as one man in defence of our altars & our firesides."[72]

Rives told his son in Boston that he had tried to be excused from serving in the new Congress but that his appeal had been too late. "Providence often casts upon us, in spite of ourselves," he mused, "duties which it is impossible to avoid." He would set out for Montgomery, Alabama, the following day, confident that he and the Confederate regime could now act in the name of honorable principles and a worthy tradition. Since the dubious doctrine of secession was no longer the issue, Rives promised to do all he could to help the southern states make good their independence in the face of Lincoln's outrageous attempt to rule by the sword. As his fore-fathers had in 1776, he would now defend a sacred principle, rule by the consent of the governed, by asserting the revolutionary right of Virginia and her new allies to resist a criminal attempt to impose tyranny by force. Rives's son agreed, although he still appeared nervous about the grounds of his father's new career. "Make the analogy as complete as possible between the attitude of the South to the North," he advised, "and that of the thirteen colonies to England in 1776." And there was something quite explicit to be shunned. Alexander Stephens, vice-president of the Confederacy, had recently condemned the misguided teachings of an earlier generation of southern Americans, including Thomas Jefferson, by publicly insisting that "the cornerstone" of the new southern republic was its formal endorsement of slavery as a just and appropriate condition for an inferior race. The younger Rives emphasized a concern for world opinion that Madison would have appreciated when he reminded his father of Virginia's antislavery heritage: "I trust the dogma of Mr. Stephens in reference to slavery will be discarded, & that the Rebellion will now be put on such grounds by the Southern Congress, as to conciliate the sympathy & win the respect of Europe."[73]

Rives journeyed by train to Montgomery. As he passed through Atlanta, a crowd of citizens, learning that "this eloquent and greatly

72 Rives to John Lanney, president of convention, May 1, 1861, *ibid.*, box 92.
73 Rives to W. C. Rives, Jr., May 6, 1861, and W. C. Rives, Jr., to Rives, May 10, 1861, *ibid.*, box 36.

year, Judith assured him that Virginians were both tired and bitter. She had recently been visited by the county tax collector who, because "he goes every where, and talks about every thing to every body," was regarded as "something of an oracle." She reported her conversation with him about the state of public opinion:

He says "the people, himself included, are sick of this quarrel about *niggers* – that slavery is virtually at an end in Virginia, and that if the war goes on, every body will be killed, so that there ain't much use in fighting on. . . ." Still, when I asked his plan of getting *out* of the scrape, he had no other answer than "we ought never to have gotten *into* it, and if people would have listened to Mr. Rives, they wouldn't have been in such a fix."[80]

In late February of the following year, with the war all but over, Rives's constituents reelected him to the Confederate Congress. Pleading poor health, this time he refused to serve.[81]

Weary of what the crudely plainspoken tax collector had called the interminable "quarrel about niggers," most Virginians after the war seemed relieved to be done with slavery. And when some turned their energy to banishing the blacks, along with the institution, the Riveses were included. In the spring of 1864, after discovering that she had been mistaken in thinking that two of the best young hands at Castle Hill had run away to the Yankees, Judith had proudly observed that "our servants have never been so reasonable and so well behaved as during the war." A year later she could still say that "our people have stuck with us with as much tenacity as the barnacles to an old ship."[82] But if this was, at least in part, testimony to the kindness of the Riveses and to the larger success of the interracial community that they had presided over at Castle Hill, they were in no mood to repay such loyalty or to consider reestablishing that community under the new conditions of freedom. During the Civil War, Rives and his wife had turned bitterly antinorthern; now, in the aftermath of that horrible war – a war that was

80 Judith Rives to Rives, Nov. 25, 1864, *ibid.*
81 Rives to Speaker of the House of Representatives of the Confederate States of America, Mar. 1, 1865, *ibid.*, box 92.
82 Judith Rives to Alfred Rives, April 6, 18, 1864, *ibid.*, box 36; Francis Rives to W. C. Rives, Jr. (quoting letter from his mother), May 19, 1865, *ibid.*, box 37.

all too easy to blame on the slaves, as well as on democracy – their formerly unacknowledged contempt for blacks rose unambiguously to the surface.

The old patriarch seemed especially adamant that the freedmen be treated harshly. Those who wished to leave Castle Hill should be encouraged to do so, he insisted, but only with the stipulation that they never be permitted to return; his goal now was to rid his estate, permanently, of as many of these *"seceding blackies"* as possible.[83] He complained irritably about the trouble and annoyance he experienced "from the *fit-for-nothingness* & total unreliability" of the blacks, whom he proceeded to replace as quickly as he could with white laborers, preferably veterans of the Confederate army. As Rives bluntly told his son in Boston, he was happy "to be rid of slavery, & could wish to be rid of the negroes also."[84] Another son in New York (who still fancied that he lived in Virginia) applauded this campaign "to make ours the white man's neighborhood."[85] And Judith Rives probably summed up all their feelings best when, expressing her disgust with the unworthiness of black servants, the best of whom she proclaimed "indolent and dirty," she became philosophical: "No doubt we must have a certain amount of trouble with servants of any kind, but having tried both, I decidedly prefer white people."[86]

At times Rives showed flashes of his familiar benevolence – in the spring of 1866, he helped arrange for some of the freedmen (who were "crazy to go") to migrate to Liberia, apparently to join their parents – but he consistently made a point of denying that he owed anything to the blacks.[87] He had at least one run-in with the local agent of the Freedmen's Bureau, who tried unsuccessfully to convince Rives that he should fulfill a promise he had allegedly made to

83 Rives to Alfred Rives, Aug. 31 and Sept. 2, 1865, *ibid.*
84 Rives to W. C. Rives, Jr., Sept. 21, 1865, *ibid.* For the reference to Confederate veterans, see George Barclay to Rives, Dec. 20, 1865, *ibid.*, box 93.
85 Francis R. Rives to Rives, Sept. 23, 1865, *ibid.*, box 37.
86 Judith Rives to Alfred L. Rives, April 16, 1866, in Alfred Landon Rives Papers, Duke University.
87 Judith Rives to Mrs. Alfred Rives, Feb. 28, 1866, *ibid.*

"an old colored man" to support him in his dotage.[88] When his son in Boston requested that three particular freedmen, whom he considered part of his Virginia estate, be comfortably housed and cared for, Rives denied the request and gave a stern lecture on the foolishness of such a plan; it would only have encouraged in the three blacks "the laziness of their race" and led to just what the young Rives should strive to avoid, "a free Negro settlement" on his land. Besides, Rives told his softhearted son, these blacks "are already under much greater obligations to you, than you to them." Reluctant to turn these people loose in a hostile America, the younger Rives could only make a pitch to his father to include them in the forthcoming emigration from Castle Hill to Liberia.[89]

Like all southern planters who survived the great war, Rives found the task of reorganizing the system of labor and society at Castle Hill more than a little daunting. Nevertheless, he somehow found or made the time to continue his work on the Madison biography. Rives had never lost faith, of course, in what he referred to in late 1865 as "the true Madisonian theory of the Constitution," which he defended – to anyone who would listen to a former official of the Confederate government – as the only basis on which "the complicated machinery of a federal government can be worked with safety & success, and the essential rights of the states be reconciled with the salutary powers of the Union."[90] Only the first volume of the biography had appeared before the war; the second volume – which Rives admitted to George Bancroft was more accurately "a history of the formation & establishment of the Constitution" – was promptly published in early 1866.[91] Two years later, the next volume, covering Madison's role in the new government through the election of 1796, was also ready for publication. The manuscript contained few surprises, although Rives did have to strain a bit to

88 Major Crandon to W. C. Rives, Mar. 20, 1866, and Rives to Major Crandon, Mar. 22, 1866, in Rives Papers, Library of Congress, box 93.
89 W. C. Rives, Jr., to Rives, Oct. 19, 1865; Rives to W. C. Rives, Jr., Oct. 27, 1865; and W. C. Rives, Jr. to Rives, April 2, 1866, *ibid.*, box 37.
90 Extract, Rives to Beverly Johnson, Dec. 7, 1865, *ibid.*, box 93.
91 Rives to Bancroft, Jan. 1, 1867, in Bancroft Papers, Massachusetts Historical Society.

make an argument for his mentor's continuing "freedom from party excitement"; according to his biographer, whose own animus toward partisan politics had not diminished, Madison – who had been at the center of intense party conflict in the 1790s – had actually remained "extremely averse to the bitterness and violence of party strife."[92]

During the winter of 1867–68, as he completed his work on this third volume and turned his thoughts to the fourth and, he projected, final volume, Rives encountered a disturbing surprise. His publishers – Little, Brown and Company in Boston – tried to delay publication of the forthcoming volume and to discourage him from proceeding. They complained about the length of the work, its lack of commercial success (they had lost $600 on the second volume), and apparently its political slant. Mr. Little nervously inquired of Rives's son, for instance, if the forthcoming volume would contain anything "to conflict with the present times."[93] Like most frustrated authors, of course, Rives blamed the publisher for any commercial disappointment – "the truth is they have no sympathy for the work, & have shown great wont of enterprise in extending its sale" – and insisted that he be permitted to proceed according to the terms of the original contract. Since he did not wish to see all of his "hard toil and anxiety" go for naught, he was even willing "to relinquish any expectation of personal profit from the publication if only they will go on cheerfully & finish the work."[94] His son in Boston resolved the matter only by personally assuming, against his father's wishes, contingent financial liability for insufficient sales. The third volume, which was to be the last, appeared later in the year.[95]

According to his wife, Rives's work on the Madison biography now exhausted and demoralized him. The past had ceased to be the unmitigated source of comfort and reassurance that it had once been; instead, it seemed to intensify the nervous anxiety that afflicted the seventy-four-year-old scholar. As he turned his historical attention

92 Rives, *Life of Madison*, III, 249–250.
93 W. C. Rives, Jr., to Rives, Mar. 11, 25, 1868, in Rives Papers, Library of Congress, box 38.
94 Rives to W. C. Rives, Jr., Mar. 14, 21, 1868, *ibid*.
95 W. C. Rives, Jr., to Rives, Mar. 18, 25, 1868, *ibid*.

to the tumultuous years of bitter party conflict that had followed the adoption of the Constitution, Rives had some reason to feel uneasy.[96] His veneration of George Washington had grown to rival his admiration for Madison, and in the third volume of the biography he confronted the challenging task of explaining how and why the two great Virginians had become political rivals in the mid-1790s. For Rives, of course, Madison had been on the "right" side of the Federalist/Republican schism; but he noted in exoneration of Washington that the president had been misled by the deceit and machinations of his cabinet and that he and Madison had always remained on close personal terms. Despite their differences of opinion about public policy, indeed, the two men had never lost their mutual respect, "for on questions of *principle*" they were no less in agreement. They were both, according to Rives, describing himself as well as his heroes, "republicans of the conservative school."[97]

During the final winter of his life, Rives assumed an even more dignified air. The patriarch's appearance changed dramatically as he began to sport a magnificent silver-gray beard that so impressed his wife and young daughter, who noted an uncanny resemblance to General Robert E. Lee, that they insisted on having him photographed "in this new aspect." Late on the afternoon of Sunday, March 8, 1868, at the height of her husband's dispute with his publisher, Judith Rives finished a letter to their son in Boston by lamplight. Seated around the table with her were the rest of the family. "Papa has been making a regular *speech*," she wrote, "of which Washington has been the hero, and which has lasted for about an hour without intermission. I have tried to warn him when he gets too animated for his strength, but so far without success. I hope he may escape without damage."[98] Six weeks later, Rives was dead.

96 Judith Rives to W. C. Rives, Jr., Oct. 30, Dec. 2, 1867, *ibid.*
97 Rives, *Life of Madison*, III, viii, 554–559. For other evidence of Rives's veneration of Washington, see Rives to George Bancroft, Jan. 1, 1867, in Bancroft Papers, Massachusetts Historical Society.
98 Judith Rives to W. C. Rives, Jr., Dec. 2, 1867, Jan. 5, 1868, and Mar. 8, 1868, in Rives Papers, Library of Congress, box 38.

❈

Edward Coles, though seven years his senior, managed to outlive Rives by several months. Viewed from Philadelphia, the Civil War and early Reconstruction had meant something quite different for Madison's former secretary: he had lived to see the fulfillment of his lifelong dream that slavery might be eliminated from the great republic. Yet the triumph of Coles's version of the Madison legacy contained its own element of bitter personal tragedy, for Coles also lived to mourn the death of his youngest son, Roberts, whom he had once described, as an infant, as "the very best little fellow I ever saw."[99] Just before the war, at the age of twenty-one – the age of his father when he had resolved to free his inherited slaves – Roberts Coles had left his father's adopted home of Philadelphia and returned to Albemarle County. There, amid the congenial company of his Virginia relations, he bought a farm. When the Old Dominion was subsequently "invaded" and its existence "threatened," he rushed to volunteer to defend his ancestral soil. In 1862, as an officer in the Confederate army, Roberts Coles was killed at the battle of Roanoke Island. Shortly before the fatal assault, he had written to his fiancée: "Now I strike for Virginia." It would be another thirty-three years before his remains, initially buried at "Enniscorthy," the Albemarle estate where his father had been born, were placed next to his father's grave in a West Philadelphia cemetery.[100]

Coles's son was only one of more than a half-million young Americans who died in an epic war to save – or to recreate, depending on one's perspective – Madison's union. Contemplating the carnage, Rives and Coles doubtless agreed on at least one point: the war could not be blamed on the Founding Fathers. Those 600,000 men had

99 Coles to Sarah Coles Stevenson, Dec. 30, 1838, in Stevenson Family Papers, Library of Congress, box 10.
100 William Bedford Coles, *The Coles Family of Virginia* (New York, 1931), 699–702. See also the more concise account in John Hammond Moore, *Albemarle: Jefferson's County, 1727–1976* (Charlottesville, Va., 1976), 120–121. Roberts Coles is quoted in Elizabeth Langhorne, K. Edward Lay, and William D. Rieley, *A Virginia Family and Its Plantation Houses* (Charlottesville, Va., 1987), 141.

368

paid with their lives not for the failure of Madison's generation, but for the sins and errors of a degenerate posterity. Many other Americans seemed just as anxious to absolve the Fathers of complicity in the tragedy, including at least one reviewer of the second volume of Rives's *Life of Madison*. Not far into his review, he quoted a particular passage from the book, recounting Madison's public debates with James Monroe in their battle for a seat in the first Congress, in which Rives the biographer had drawn on memories of conversations he had had with his subject: "Mr. Madison," Rives recalled, "often gave a graphic and amusing account of a discussion which took place between him and Mr. Monroe, in the open air, on a cold January day [in 1789], amid the bleak hills of Culpeper." But in "less than one man's lifetime," the reviewer observed, "the great fabric of the Constitution, then the subject of debate, having tumbled into ruin," this same spot witnessed very different scenes, scenes of horror, scenes of "the legions of Grant and Meade, and Lee and Longstreet" tramping over the bleak hills of Culpeper and "around the graves of Madison and Monroe."

Rives would surely have agreed with his reviewer, indeed, that "the figures of the honored dead of the early days of our history look indistinct through the lurid haze which still hangs over the land. We see them through a glass very darkly. They seem to belong to another planet, as well as to another age."[101]

101 "Rives's Madison," in *The Age* (Philadelphia), April 10, 1866 (copy in Rives Papers, Library of Congress).

Madison's tombstone at Montpelier. (Courtesy of the Library of Congress, Prints and Photographs Division)

Epilogue

ON THE DAY after Madison died, his body was interred in the family burial ground at Montpelier, a half-mile south of the house. Paul Jennings and the other slaves joined the solemn procession from the mansion to the cemetery, where the "profound silence" of the occasion, as James Barbour would remember it, was "now and then broken by their sobs." At the moment when the corpse was actually lowered into the ground – and the clergyman uttered "the fearful sentence 'dust unto dust'" – there was an explosion of grief from the bereaved. "How it pierced our souls; how we felt that the separation was now final – that all was gone." Jennings, standing next to Barbour, broke down, and the assembled slaves "gave vent to their lamentations in one violent burst that rent the air."

Six weeks later, Barbour recreated this memorable scene from his friend's private funeral in an oration at an Orange County memorial service. The haunting cry of "the hundred slaves," by his reckoning, was a spontaneous tribute to Madison's extraordinary kindness and indulgence as a master; "scenes like this," he reflected, "give us the true character." And Barbour, the orator, was confident that the collective voice of Madison's human property had scaled even greater heights. "Methought it ascended to Heaven, and was heard with joy by the heavenly host, as a redeeming item in that great account" which Madison, "in common with all the sons of Adam," now had to meet. Barbour said that he had derived consolation at that moment of the funeral, indeed, from his belief "that if, in that great account, slight blemishes here and there, from the inexorable law of our nature, were to be found, this alone would, in the eye of mercy, be sufficient to 'blot out the unfriendly characters that bore record of his infirmity, to be remembered no more.'"[1]

1 James Barbour, *Eulogium upon the Life and Character of James Madison* (Washington, D.C., 1836), 28–29.

Madison's body was buried next to those of his parents. Seventeen years later, Edward Coles was disturbed to learn that no suitable stone or marker of any kind had ever been placed at the site.[2] Efforts to erect a monument eventually produced a plain granite obelisk, bearing the simple inscription:

MADISON

Born March 16, 1751.

Died June 28, 1836.

Writing in the first decade of the twentieth century, a local Orange County historian noted that the monolith "was erected about 1856 by private subscriptions, mostly by admirers of Madison outside the County." W. W. Scott had been born not long after Madison's death, and he reported having been told by witnesses that when the stone was erected, it had been necessary, in order to get a safe foundation, to take up Madison's remains. Apparently those present had known the patriarch and could not resist the opportunity to see him one last time. "The coffin was opened, and, except that one cheek was a little sunken, his appearance was the same as in life." Scott reminded his readers of the remarkable fact that Madison had been buried "about twenty years."[3]

Although Montpelier was no longer in the hands of the family when the monument was erected, subsequent visitors apparently knew where to find the gravesite. In early August 1863, Watkins Kearns, serving in "G" Company of the 27th Virginia Infantry Regiment of the Confederate Army of Northern Virginia, marched with his fellows to within two and a half miles of Orange Court House before camping on what he referred to in his diary as "James Madison's property." It had been a difficult march through excessive heat, with many of the men "giving out," and once in camp, the heat continued. But Kearns found relief in observing – and apparently admiring – his surroundings: "The mansion a fine stuccoed

2 Extract of Coles to Hugh Blair Grigsby, Dec. 23, 1854, in William Cabell Rives Papers, Library of Congress, box 85.
3 W. W. Scott, *A History of Orange County Virginia* (Richmond, 1907), 206.

building in good repair. The grounds around very beautiful. A walnut grove around the house & a little Roman temple over the ice house." On Monday, August 3, two days after the strenuous march, the twenty-six-year-old soldier reported having something to look forward to: "Great party tonight at Madison's old residence. All the ladies in the country round here invited." That same day, Kearns sought out Madison's grave. He went to the trouble of sketching the new obelisk in his diary.[4]

4 Watkins Kearns (1837–1893) diary, May 17, 1863, to Feb. 29, 1864, in Virginia Historical Society, Richmond.

Acknowledgments

ANY KIND PEOPLE have contibuted to the publication of this book, and I wish to acknowledge them here. Without knowing that he had done so, Ralph Ketcham stimulated me to think about Madison's influence on his legatees and thus inspired a vital dimension of the project. My mentor from graduate school, Merrill D. Peterson – also without knowing it – provided the title for the book. Lance Banning and Charles Royster lent welcome moral support and encouragement along the way, and then offered perceptive, immensely helpful comments on preliminary drafts of the manuscript. My students at Harvard University during the past five years have been a remarkably congenial source of stimulation, and two in particular – Gary D. Rowe and Robert Allison – have left some palpable mark on the book. I am particularly indebted to Mr. Allison, now a graduate student in the History of American Civilization program at Harvard, for enriching my thinking about the problem of Madison and slavery. I am grateful, too, to Richard Zinman of James Madison College at Michigan State University for inviting me to present an abbreviated version of Chapter Seven to an exceptionally lively group of his colleagues and students, from whose comments I learned a great deal.

Fellowships from the Charles Warren Center at Harvard University and from the National Endowment for the Humanities provided greatly appreciated support. I also derived considerable benefit from two days of discussion of Madison's political thought with a group of historians and political scientists brought together for that purpose by Liberty Fund, Inc., of Indianapolis, during the summer of 1986; special thanks go to Eugene Miller and William B. Allen, organizers of the colloquium. I wish to thank as well the many archivists who facilitated my research during the past eight years, especially at the Library of Congress, the University of North

Carolina at Chapel Hill, the Historical Society of Pennsylvania, the Virginia Historical Society, and the University of Virginia. The staff at the editorial offices of the *Papers of James Madison* project, located in the Alderman Library of the University of Virginia, extended generous courtesies in allowing me access to material in their files; I am grateful to Robert Rutland, Robert J. Brugger, and especially Thomas Mason for their kindness. Finally, I owe special thanks to Frank S. Smith, my editor at Cambridge University Press, and to Russell Hahn, production editor for this book, for their expert attention at the end.

To my wife, Betsy Friedberg, this book is lovingly dedicated.

Index

abolitionists (of 1830s), xiv, 282, 295, 297, 302, 305, 306, 343, 351, 354, 355
Act for Establishing Religious Freedom (Virginia), 239
Adair, Douglass, 43n
Adams, Charles Francis, 21
Adams, Henry, 9
Adams, John, 16–17, 31, 64, 331
Adams, John Quincy, 32, 105
  as president, 115, 116, 117, 119, 124, 333–4, 336, 337
Africa, 5, 165, 275, 280, 281, 282, 283, 293, 294, 296, 300, 304, 306, 307, 316, 317, 356
  see also Liberia
Agricultural Society of Albermarle, 236
agriculture, 236, 253, 286
  as basis for American economy, 175, 191
  problem of surplus in, 174, 177–82, 188–9, 190, 338
Alabama, 360
Albany, New York, 229, 232
Albemarle County, Virginia, 119, 208, 209, 210, 218, 232, 236, 328, 368
Alexandria, Virginia, 218
Alien and Sedition Acts (1798), 12, 115, 139, 141, 142–3
amalgamation, racial, see miscegenation
amendment (of U.S. Constitution), 69–70, 71–3, 89, 94, 102–3, 116, 128, 132, 136
American Colonization Society, 5–6, 165, 168, 252, 279–82, 283, 297, 299, 301, 303, 304, 307, 316, 356
  see also colonization
American Revolution, xii, xiii, xiv, 18, 39, 52, 65, 66, 67, 69, 87, 102, 193, 197, 224, 226, 229, 230, 233, 262, 263, 264, 269, 278, 285, 303, 304, 320, 360, 361
  effects of, on Virginia, 237–40, 282–3

"American System," 123, 124, 159, 186, 333
Amherst County, Virginia, 333
Andrews, Ethan Allen, 258
Antifederalists (1787–88), 24, 25, 78, 85, 89, 110, 127, 133, 138, 246
antiquity, classical, 234
Appeal From the Judgements of Great Britain . . . , An (1819), 106–7
  see also Walsh, Robert W., Jr.
aristocracy, 234–5, 236, 249
Article V of U.S. Constitution, see amendment
Articles of Confederation, xii, 24, 40, 77, 134, 135, 137, 150, 268
Atlanta, Georgia, 360–1

Bacon, Ezekiel, 32–3
balance of trade, unfavorable, in America, 174, 188
Bancroft, George, 365
Bank of the United States, First, 80–1, 96
Bank of the United States, Second, 81–2, 92, 257
  constitutionality of, 99
Barbour, James, 21–2, 23, 25, 114, 125, 167, 371
Barbour, Philip P., 123
Baton Rouge, Louisiana, 210
Bell, John, 343
"Benevolent Empire," 281
Benton, Thomas Hart, 34
Betty (slave), 255, 259–60
Biddle, Nicholas, 257, 313
bill of rights, federal, 89
Blue Ridge Mountains, xiii, 241, 272
Bonus Bill (1817), 92–9, 101–3, 104, 105, 116, 131, 152
Boorstin, Daniel, 60n
Boston, Massachusetts, 16, 162, 222, 229, 340, 344, 350, 352, 358, 360, 364, 365, 366, 367
Bradford, William, 227–9, 238

377

385